A House Divided

*Slavery and American Politics from the
Constitution to the Civil War*

Ben McNitt

STACKPOLE BOOKS

Guilford, Connecticut

Published by Stackpole Books
An imprint of The Rowman & Littlefield Publishing Group, Inc.
4501 Forbes Blvd., Ste. 200
Lanham, MD 20706
www.rowman.com

Distributed by NATIONAL BOOK NETWORK

British Library Cataloguing in Publication Information available

Library of Congress Cataloging-in-Publication Data available

ISBN 978-0-8117-3977-1 (cloth : alk. paper)
ISBN 978-0-8117-6974-7 (electronic)

∞™ The paper used in this publication meets the minimum requirements of American National Standard for Information Sciences—Permanence of Paper for Printed Library Materials, ANSI/ NISO Z39.48-1992.

For my father, Frank McNitt,
and my teacher, Robert Crow

Contents

PREFACE

THIS BOOK has two goals. The first is to present a narrative overview of slavery's role in American politics from the writing of the Constitution in 1787 to the outbreak of the Civil War in 1861. The second is to demonstrate the continuous pull slavery had on the nation's political life throughout that period. In my effort to meet those objectives, the work draws on a wealth of scholarship over the past several decades that has recast the modern understanding of the role slavery has played in the American experience. It also confronts the doctrine of white supremacy that American slavery was built upon—a straight shot of racism in the white North and the white South's more elaborate cocktail of historical, biblical, and economic justifications for the subjugation by force of one race by another.

Well into the twentieth century American slavery was portrayed as an episodic influence in the nation's life, erupting in events such as the 1820 Missouri Compromise and the Compromise of 1850, until a collision of cultures somehow resulted in the cataclysm of civil war. That version of history is arguably still prevalent among most Americans even today. It is no coincidence that suppressing slavery's place in the creation and formation of the early republic is synonymous with denying the full reality of slavery in our national character. Beginning at essentially the same time as the modern civil rights movement, historians began to reexamine the nation's relationship with slavery. Part of the result, in the words of historian Robert Pierce Forbes, was documenting that the "black hole of slavery drew everything near it within its gravitational field, even when it remained invisible itself."[1] The process included a reevaluation of a less iconic Thomas Jefferson and a new one of a more human Abraham Lincoln. A far clearer view developed of Black resistance to slavery, different dynamics within the abolition movement, political realignments with the collapse of the two-party system, and a complex rather than monolithic white South. These new lines of research brought with them new and continuing debates over the causes of the Civil War.

I approached this work from my background as a reporter, often being guided by existing scholarship but basing the text on primary sources. Although I do not claim to be a curator of decades of recent scholarship on slavery in America, I can confidently assert that this work is informed by that scholarship and gives credit to it in both the text and endnotes. Many are the times I have been humbled by the brilliance of the works I have consulted. A consistent theme of this scholarship, as already noted, is the continuous, rather than intermittent, role slavery played in framing the national narrative. A veritable library of books makes this point as each deals with a specific aspect or era of America's relationship with slavery. However, no single overview narrative has previously been available documenting the ever-present deep current that slavery represents in our political history from the Constitution to the Civil War. *A House Divided* attempts, at least in part, to fill that gap. As such the book is broadly selective rather than comprehensive. I leave it to the reader to decide whether it is justly representative.

Although slavery's continuous pull on the nation's political life up to the Civil War is this book's main through line, two others I had not anticipated came into play as I began the work. They appeared as I wrote the text. The first is the power of Jefferson's assertion in the Declaration of Independence of universal equality encompassing unalienable rights to life, liberty, and the pursuit of happiness. They were the pesky words that would not go away until the house divided decided in war that they did in fact stand as the principle upon which the republic was founded.

Violence, an almost ever-present bloodletting, is this narrative's second unplanned but unmistakable through line. Violence and the threat of it were slavery's foundation. Unleashed Black violence was the white South's deepest dread and its first resort in the threatening rhetoric of disunion. Planned violence in quashed slave revolts and actual murder in uprisings in Virginia and in Haiti seared themselves on the white South's imagination. A history of whites killing enslaved Blacks and Blacks occasionally killing whites evolved into whites killing whites over the status of Blacks in the saga of Bleeding Kansas. Vivid forecasts of civil war played out in violence at Harpers Ferry and on the floor of the U.S. Senate shortly before the conflict erupted in 1861. This legacy of violence has all too often been a case of the past being prologue to the present.

Although this work results from several years of essentially solitary effort, I do wish to thank my journalistic colleague William Barrett for reviewing the manuscript and offering valuable criticisms. This book owes a huge debt to a wealth of original source material available on the Internet. I have drawn extensively from the ongoing American Memory Project established by the Library of Congress, the online resources of the National Archives, and a host of similar sites created at the college and university level. The online resource JSTOR is a massive reservoir of professional journal articles that a glance at my endnotes will show I relied upon extensively. Wikipedia has been a welcome source for reference on numerous occasions. The University of Arizona library made the online newspaper archive Project Muse available to me. A not yet fully recognized revolution is under way in the scope of research materials available to citizens like me.

This text capitalizes the word "Black" in references to persons or communities of African American heritage. It also distinguishes the white South or white southerners rather than simply cite the South or southerners. Blacks constituted up to 57 percent of the whole population in the slave states up to the Civil War. To refer to the South or to southerners in any case not intended to include the whole population is a mental extermination of Black existence.

A few words on my use of quoted material. My text includes perhaps more and longer quotes than other similar works. This is deliberate. I prefer to have the story told in the words of those who created it. Also, not being a professional historian, I believe the work's credibility is enhanced by using quotes rather than my paraphrase of what speakers or writers of the era intended to convey. On a technical note, within quoted material I retain original spellings and capitalizations, although in some instances archaic usages are replaced with modern spellings for ease of reading. I do not note errors in such usages with the insertion of [*sic*] so as not to distract the reader with a purely technical comment. In instances where the original uses contractions such as "wld." or "Sts.," I spell out the full word to read "would" or "States." My object in all cases has been to retain the integrity of the original quote, with minimal alterations.

I cannot end without expressing a word of deep thanks and appreciation to my editor, David Reisch, and Stackpole Books for believing in the project and seeing it through to publication. Whatever errors it contains are mine alone.

This work now belongs to its readers; I hope they will find the effort needed to create it worthwhile.

Ben McNitt
Tucson, Arizona

CHAPTER I

Slavery and the Constitution

IN ALL, seventy-three delegates were chosen by their state legislatures to meet in Philadelphia in May 1787 to frame a new government for the United States. Of those, fifty-five delegates from twelve of the thirteen states attended. Rhode Island, suspicious of tampering with the existing Articles of Confederation, boycotted the gathering. On any given day during deliberations lasting into September, an average of about thirty-five delegates met in the second-story room of Philadelphia's State House where eight of them had signed the Declaration of Independence eleven years earlier. They were men of stature, an elite distilled from service in the Revolutionary War, elected to the Continental and Confederation Congresses, experienced as governors, judges, and state legislators, and in some cases marked by attainment of great wealth in the nation's burgeoning endeavors in finance, land speculation, shipping, and export of profitable crops of tobacco, rice, and indigo to eager European markets.

Another man was also present, although how often is not recorded. He was not a delegate, represented no state, and did not speak. He was Billy Lee, a slave, body servant to the president of the Constitutional Convention, George Washington.[1]

The drafting of the U.S. Constitution was in significant measure an exercise of the end justifying the means. The end was urgent then and honored now: create a nation sufficiently unifying thirteen states and states yet to come so that it could maintain its liberty and independence in a fractious world of competitors. The means were varied. Among them those that helped lead to an irrepressible conflict in a house divided against itself were the accommodations and compromises between the conviction that in civil society all people are created equal and the conviction that some are not, between freedom and slavery.

History is marked by currents, social, political, and economic movements of greater importance at one time, lesser or vanishing at another. Slavery was a deep current, sometimes dominating, sometimes submerged, but abiding and present throughout antebellum American history. The current that perhaps most colors the nation's history from the Declaration of Independence in 1776 to the rise of Jacksonian democracy more than fifty years later is the influence and governance of an elite, the Founders, the men who wrote the nation's title deed to freedom, led the defense of it in the Revolutionary War, drafted its Constitution, and dominated its councils of state from Washington's presidency through that of James Monroe.

A second current, one that brought the Constitutional Convention to the verge of collapse and frustrated the aims of the nationalist elites who had arranged the Philadelphia assembly, was the attitude citizens had to the state that claimed their loyalty.

The thought and phrase "I'm a Virginian," or "a Bay State man," preceded that of "I'm an American" by many decades. The revolutionaries of '76, under a declaration of "free and independent states," had fought a remote central authority they saw as intruding on the prerogatives of those states. When they won, those thirteen independent states loosely aligned under the Articles of Confederation. The government that mattered most to most citizens was the one closest to them in the state where they lived and the county in which they resided. Their state defined their traditions, their livelihoods, virtually the whole of their lives. The bond of state loyalty and identification was not easily or soon expanded to embrace a national sphere of trust and identity.

The delegates assembled in Philadelphia faced stark realities. The Confederation's Congress was essentially powerless, operating on the basis of supermajorities or unanimity. It had no taxing power, only an ability to supplicate the states for requisitions that were more easily ignored than honored. No national executive or judiciary existed. The Revolution's accumulated debt was unpaid, foreign credit nearly unobtainable. In some quarters, inflationary paper money was crowding out specie in gold or silver. With no uniform code of commerce to direct them, states were free to raise revenue by imposing import or harbor tariffs on their neighbors. The Congress commanded no army or navy. A recent rebellion by tax-burdened western Massachusetts farmers was put down by the state militia before a belatedly assembled army temporarily authorized by Congress arrived on the scene. The political and material security of those who had pledged "our lives, our fortunes, and our sacred honor" to the new nation was threatened. The revolutionary experiment was on the verge of failure.

Three choices faced the delegates assembled in Philadelphia. Breaking up into two or more regional confederations was an option, one threatened at several points during the convention. But this was no one's first choice and even if seriously considered would leave unresolved the same issues the delegates had met to resolve: how to form an effective government among the existing states.[2]

The second option, the likely choice and expectation of a majority of citizens who awaited the convention's decisions, was to modify and strengthen the Articles of Confederation enough to keep the enterprise afloat. Revising the Articles was the mandate under which the convention was organized. Some legislatures instructed their delegates not to venture beyond that limited charge.

A third option had gestated for months, out of public view. In private conversations and letters, a vision of the nation's future under a strong national government, with the states subordinate, had taken shape. The object was not to reform the Articles but to scrap and replace them. In setting the terms for his attendance at the upcoming convention, George Washington wrote his Virginia colleague James Madison that the gathering must "adopt no temporizing expedient, but probe the defects of the Constitution to the bottom and provide radical cures, whether they are agreed or not."[3] Men such as Alexander Hamilton in New York and John Rutledge in South Carolina were prepared to bring their views of a strong national government to Philadelphia. To their advantage, some of the most fervent states' rights proponents such as Patrick Henry of Virginia declined delegate appointments to keep their options open should the convention adopt measures they could not support.

The convention opened as a face-off between two factions, the large-state nationalists and the small-state delegations determined not to surrender influence already conferred by the Articles. This standoff was the convention's defining conflict. For months, the large- versus small-state divide was the core of debate, votes, threats, frustration, and near despair in the State House's second-floor meeting room. The central issue was how power should be allocated in the new government's legislature: by population-based proportional representation favoring large states, or by equal state votes favoring small states. The small states held distinct advantages. Precedent was on their side because the Articles gave each state equal voting power. Following that precedent, so did the rules of the Constitutional Convention.

As the issue sharpened, a third faction emerged that proved pivotal to breaking the deadlock, a role that came with a price. The small slave states of South Carolina and Georgia in particular, aligned at crucial moments with slaveholding North Carolina and Maryland, became large-state allies. South Carolina and Georgia, though small in population, were surely destined to soon become large, or so their leaders mistakenly believed. As a South Carolina delegate confidently phrased it, "the people and strength of America are evidently bearing Southwardly and Southwestwardly."[4] In the view of most southern delegates, their state's interest lay in alliance with the large states, with the nationalist, and with power allocated by population.

Accurate population figures for the thirteen states in 1787 do not exist. The closest approximation comes from the census that Congress authorized in 1790.[5] That census reports a total population in the thirteen original states of 3,637,879, almost evenly divided between the eight northern and five southern states. The three largest states that drove the convention's nationalist agenda were Virginia, with 747,610 inhabitants in 1790, Pennsylvania with 434,373, and Massachusetts with 378,787.

These totals, however, mask the deeper reality of slavery. From the first trickle of twenty Africans sold in 1619 from a Dutch merchant vessel at Jamestown, Virginia, by the 1790 census Black slaves numbered 681,834 in the original thirteen states. More than nine in ten of them were held in the southern states of Maryland, Virginia, the Carolinas, and Georgia. In the northern states, 49,241 Blacks were enslaved, less than 3 percent of the population.[6] The South held 632,593 slaves, 35 percent of its population.[7]

By the time of the convention, Massachusetts was the only state to have emancipated its slaves, in a state supreme court case citing the state's constitutional "free and equal" clause. Emancipation had begun in four other northern states and was developing in two more. The various provisions of these actions uniformly required compensation to slaveowners. Statutes provided that freedom could be delayed to compel slaves to pay their way out of bondage with years or even decades of wageless labor. Slavery masquerading as indentured servitude persisted in New Jersey up to the Civil War.[8] Statutes gave permission for owners to bring their slaves into a state pursuing emancipation for an allotted period of time without compromising their bonded status. Freed slaves were denied civil liberties such as the right to vote or to serve on juries. In some cases, owners were granted permission to sell their slaves to out-of-state buyers prior to the deadline set for emancipation. In the end, the eventual decline in the North's slave population may have been due more to slave sales to southern buyers than to emancipation.[9]

In the South, the trend was toward acquiring slaves, not emancipating them. From 1790 to the outbreak of the Civil War, the United States' slave population increased by 580 percent to just under four million enslaved Blacks in a total 1860 population of 31,513,114.[10] Growth in the slave population was fed by both the foreign slave trade, which continued illegally for years after it was officially banned in 1808, and natural increase.

By 1790, the five southern states not only held thirteen times more slaves than the North, but in some sections concentrated them into dawn-to-dusk labor camps on sprawling plantations. One in four North Carolina inhabitants was a slave, but nearly half the population of Brunswick County was in bondage.[11] Two in ten of Virginia's inhabitants were slaves, but 63 percent of King William and Powhatan County inhabitants were in bondage.[12] In the rice-rich coastal plantations of South Carolina's St. Stevens and St. Paul's Parishes, just over 90 percent of those living there were Black slaves.[13]

Although the fifty-five delegates who attended the Constitutional Convention, twenty-five of them slaveowners, initially saw the contest between large and small states as the chief hurdle to their deliberations, slavery's deeper current emerged as the true sectional dividing line between them. Once the Constitution went into effect, there was no significant instance in which votes in Congress split on large- versus small-state lines. The split that did develop was between North and South, eventually including new southern states and those that arose in the Great Lakes region and west of the Mississippi River.[14]

The convention began its deliberations in the last week of May once a quorum of seven state delegations had arrived in Philadelphia. The members were arrayed among thirteen desks—that for Rhode Island remaining vacant throughout—formed in an arc facing the presiding officer. The first order of business was to elect Washington president, his stature like a source of gravity binding the delegates to their task. A secrecy rule was adopted, forbidding any of the deliberations to be disclosed by written or spoken word. A journal was ordered kept, and James Madison wrote extensive daily notes, the chief sources now available of what was said and how votes were cast.* Another rule allowed any vote to be reconsidered, leaving decisions tentative until all were agreed. Sentries were placed at the State House doors.

On Tuesday, May 29, Edmund Randolph, the thirty-three-year-old governor of Virginia and son of one of the state's most eminent families, took the floor. With his speech the large-state strategy began to unfold. The Virginia Plan he presented was a bold outline for an entirely new government. The Articles of Confederation were to be scrapped. In their place a new government was to be erected. The first of three independent branches was to be a legislature divided into two houses, one elected directly by the people, the other elected by the first house based on recommendations from state legislatures. The plan called for separate executive and judicial branches. The states would be subordinate, their actions subject to a national

---

*In his notes, Madison commonly quoted an individual using the pronoun "he," so his texts read "Mr. Smith said, 'He would oppose the measure,'" rather than "Mr. Smith said, 'I will oppose the measure.'"

veto. The plan was largely the work of Randolph's colleague, the bookish James Madison, who had devoted months to study and preparation, steeping himself in Enlightenment thought on creating a government solely on the basis of reason rather than principles of caste or monarchy. He had convinced his fellow Virginians, quite likely some Pennsylvania delegates, and perhaps a few others in discussions held before the convention opened that the necessary strategy was first to determine how power should be allocated in the new government and only afterward decide what powers the new government should exercise.

The plan's first substantive point struck at the heart of the matter: power in the new legislature should be allocated in proportion to taxes paid or based directly on "the number of free inhabitants."[15] This single issue of how power should be allocated consumed the delegates' attention more than any other.

The Delaware delegation protested that they might have to leave the convention as their state mandate for action forbade abandoning equal state voting. New York's Robert Lansing confided in his private notes that the Virginia Plan meant "a strong, *consolidated* union in which the idea of states should be nearly annihilated."[16] Sensing dissatisfaction from small-state delegates, Madison quickly agreed to the vague formulation that "the rights of suffrage in the national legislature ought to be proportioned" without saying how.[17] Instead, the convention decided to postpone the entire matter. But the issue was on the table.

The debate veered to whether one legislative branch should be elected directly by the people. Massachusetts's Elbridge Gerry, crusty, lacking eloquence, but respected as signer of both the Declaration of Independence and Articles of Confederation, did not want popular elections. "The people do not want virtue; but are the dupes of pretended patriots," he said.[18] Roger Sherman of Connecticut, soon to become the small states' chief defender, thought the people "should have as little to do as may be about the government. They want information and are constantly liable to be misled."[19] Enlightenment reasoning was not equally shared by all delegates.

Madison stood his ground. A waif of a man, his voice so faint that delegates often strained to hear him, Madison was a formidable person, commanding respect with his reservoir of knowledge and the logical clarity of his argument. As republican government's foundation was consent of the governed, popular election of at least one legislative branch was a necessity, he argued. He then went further, explaining "The object was to so expand the principle of democracy as to avoid despotism. Having one group oppress another was the account of history. . . . We have seen the mere distinction of color, made in the most enlightened period of time, a ground of the most oppressive domination ever exercised by man over man."[20] This first reference to slavery made at the convention came from a man who owned several slaves and later inherited more than a hundred more. The key to avoiding majority tyranny was, Madison said, "to enlarge the sphere, and thereby divide the community into so great a number of interests and parties" that any majority would be unlikely at the same instant to have "a common interest separate from that of the whole or of the minority.[21]

The first threat of a convention breakup came on Saturday, June 9, when New Jersey delegate William Paterson said his state "will

James Madison. COURTESY OF WIKIMEDIA COMMONS/WHITE HOUSE HISTORICAL ASSOCIATION.

never confederate on the plan before the Convention. She would be swallowed up. He would rather submit to a monarch, to a despot, than to such a fate."[22] "Are not the citizens of Pennsylvania equal to those of New Jersey," countered Pennsylvania's James Wilson, addressing the New Jerseymen seated at the desk immediately to his left. "Does it require 150 of the former to balance 50 of the latter? . . . If the small states will not confederate on this plan, Pennsylvania and he presumed some other states, would not confederate on any other."[23] The split was out in the open. The numbers did not favor the large states. Eleven delegations were present, Rhode Island boycotting and the New Hampshire delegates yet to arrive. If the three large states with more than half the country's population could not gain at least three votes, the fight was lost, assuring a merely federal government in which each state wielded power equal to every other. Wilson, now in charge of strategy, needed allies. He looked south, having just over one day to maneuver before the next session opened on Monday.

He found what he was looking for in the South Carolina delegation. John Rutledge, proud and imperious, master of nearly 250 slaves, was the South's leading strategist. Charles Pinckney was the diplomat, "handsome, vain, eager and slightly rakish," and owner of some 100 slaves.[24] Pierce Butler was the spear point, born of noble Irish ancestry, and master of some 140 slaves. At the time of the convention, Rutledge's finances were shaky. Butler was in debt. Their conviction that population growth would favor the existing southern states was bolstered by the sure prospect of augmented power for the white South from the slaveholding territories of Kentucky and Tennessee that were poised to become the first new states. The South Carolinians were ready to deal for a strong national government and proportional representation.

Their price was to have slaves counted in apportioning representation. Not, of course, so that slaves would be represented, but so that their owners would accrue power in proportion to the number of slaves included. Their position was well grounded in the precepts of the times. Slaves were property, therefore wealth, and wealth deserved some weight in apportioning power. The South's wealth lay disproportionately in slave-labor investments that in turn underpinned the value of the land they worked. Within the country at large, whites North and South widely saw slavery as an evil, but a necessary one. Outright opposition to it was scant. Among the convention's delegates there was no question of any serious challenge to the institution of slavery embedded in the South.

The white South's price for joining the large states, its strategic aim at the convention, was to embed slavery in the Constitution. Even more, the white South was positioning itself to have sufficient voting strength to successfully defend white southern interests against any unified bloc of opposition that might arise in the future.

The vehicle the white South chose to accomplish this was what is now called the Constitution's three-fifths clause, Article I, Section 2, or the federal ratio. This was a device originally written by a committee of the Confederation Congress to count three-fifths of a state's slaves along with free inhabitants to set a basis to apportion tax requisitions. The committee's measure was never adopted, but the federal ratio concept was familiar to the men of the convention. Pinckney had even circulated a plan including the federal ratio among some delegates in late May.[25]

In the discussions over that fateful Sunday, the immediate effect of accepting the federal ratio was the acquisition of votes from slaveholding states, the key to securing proportional representation in at least one house of the legislature. The long-run consequences, however important, were less urgent. The desired end overrode qualms about the means used to achieve it.

Exactly how the deal was struck over Sabbath dining and tavern tables is unrecorded. The gambit began Monday, June 11, with a speech intended to set a tone of accommodation written by eighty-one-year-old Benjamin Franklin and read by Wilson. Franklin had once owned as many as seven slaves but had freed them nearly two decades earlier. At the time of the convention, he was president of the Pennsylvania Abolition Society. Although age had taken its toll, Franklin was widely respected as sage, diplomat, author, and inventor. "I now think the number of representatives should bear some proportion to the number of the represented," Wilson said for him, "and that the decisions should be by the majority of members, not by the majority of states."[26]

A series of votes followed. First, Rutledge proposed that representation in the House* be based on an emphatic proslavery formula. Assuming a middle position, Wilson, with Pinckney's second, then offered a resolution that House representation be "in proportion to the whole number of white and other free citizens and inhabitants of every age, sex and condition, including those bound to servitude for a term of years and three-fifths of all other persons not comprehended in the foregoing description, except Indians, not paying taxes in each state."[27] The "other persons," of course, were slaves.

Elbridge Gerry objected. "Blacks are property, and are used to the southward as horses and cattle to the northward," he said. "Why should their representation be increased to the southward on account of the number of slaves, than horses or oxen to the north?"[28] No delegate joined him. The vote was nine to two, to pass the resolution drawing in New York and Connecticut as well as all the slave and large states.

Attempting to stem the breach, Sherman moved that each state should have one vote in the Senate. "The smaller states would never agree to a plan on any other principle," he said.[29] His motion failed, five to six. Finally, sensing complete victory, Wilson moved and Pinckney again seconded a motion that representation in the Senate be based on the same formula as that for the House. By the slimmest of margins, six to five, it carried, the three large states joined by the three most southern.

The Wilson-Rutledge strategy had prevailed, but the narrow vote was testament to its fragility. Ultimately, Rhode Island and New Hampshire would be called upon to ratify the convention's work. They would surely balk, as would the small northern states that were present, at exclusion of equal small-state votes in both legislative branches. The aim in formulating a constitution was consensus, not simply a majority, particularly one based on a razor-thin margin. At the same time, the slave states' price for union was made clear. An initial draft of how power was to be allocated in the new government had been decided. For the next five weeks the

---

*During most of the convention, delegates spoke of the legislature, the first branch, and the second branch, terms that later became the Congress, the House of Representatives, and the Senate. For readability, the more modern terms are used in this text.

argument continued or shifted to other issues until what is now known as the Great Compromise was struck.

At about this time, John Dickinson of Delaware sought out Madison for a frank private conversation. "You see the consequences of pushing things too far," he told the Virginian. "Some of the members from the small states wish for two branches in the general legislature, and are friends to a good national government; but we would soon submit to a foreign power, than submit to be deprived of an equality of suffrage, in both branches of the legislature, and thereby be thrown under the domination of the large states."[30] Madison was not ready to surrender the victory already won on proportional representation but felt increasing anxiety that the convention might collapse over the issue.

In casting about for a solution, he struck upon a new conception of the convention's basic divide. His insight, perhaps first offered only as a maneuver to recast proportional representation in a new light, foreshadowed a realignment that actually occurred. "Wherever there is danger of attack there ought to be given a constitutional power of defense," he said during the June 20 debate. The states were not really divided on the basis of size, he continued, "but by other circumstances, the most material of which resulted partly from climate, but principally from (the effects of) their having or not having slaves. These two causes concurred in forming the great division of interests in the United States. It did not lie between the large and small states: it lay between Northern and Southern, and if any defensive power were necessary, it ought to be mutually given to these two interests."[31]

His motion that states should be represented in one legislative branch based only on the number of free inhabitants, favoring the North, and in the other based on all inhabitants, free and slave, favoring the South, went nowhere. But a new element had been injected into the debate. Slavery was so sensitive both morally and politically that it had only been brought up obliquely—"three-fifths of all other persons"—or marginally, as in Gerry's lone protest. Slavery now began to seep more deeply into the deliberations.

But first the convention had to run the gauntlet set by earlier votes. A telling blow was struck by Delaware's Gunning Bedford, who made the threat of dissolution chillingly clear in a June 30 speech. To promises of the large states and their southern allies that "they will never hurt or injure the lesser states," Bedford bellowed, "*I do not, gentlemen, trust you. If you possess the power, the abuse of it could not be checked. . . .* Sooner than be ruined, there are *foreign powers who will take us by the hand.*"[32]

The threat that some states might invite foreign protection rather than unite with the rest shook the convention. The question of allocating states equal votes in the Senate was again put forward. Wilson's fragile victory dissolved in a five-to-five deadlock with one state divided.

"We were on the verge of dissolution, scarce held together by the strength of a hair," Delaware's Luther Martin later wrote of this period.[33] "We are now at a full stop," Connecticut's Sherman said in debate, but added, "Nobody he supposed meant that we should break up without doing something."[34]

With the convention in disarray, the obvious expedient was to resort to committees to hammer out differences. Over the next two weeks the convention formed and debated reports from three committees. The issue over how to allocate power that had beset the delegates since late May was back on the table. In early July, Washington wrote Alexander Hamilton, who had left the convention two weeks earlier, that matters were "if possible, in a worse train than ever; you will find but little ground on which the hope of a good establishment can be formed. In a word, I *almost* despair of seeing a favorable issue in the proceedings of the convention."[35]

The debate had recast the issues somewhat. Proportional representation in the House was close to being conceded, the dividing line shifting increasingly to what weight should be given to property, particularly the white South's property in slaves. Stemming directly from this was a struggle over when and by whom the population should be counted in years ahead to reapportion representation as state population totals changed. These two controversies laid bare what Madison had foreseen: a division between the free states of the North and the slave states of the South. Equal state votes in the Senate remained the small states' irreducible demand, without which there would be no concession on representation in the House and likely no constitution.

The first committee's report produced a plan containing the essence of what was ultimately decided. The House would be based on proportional representation, using the federal ratio to count slaves, with one member allocated for every 40,000 inhabitants. Only the House would have power to initiate tax or appropriation bills. States would have equal votes in the Senate. The origination clause was designed as a sop for conceding to equal state Senate votes. It meant little then or later.

Into the fray strode Pennsylvania's Gouverneur Morris, his left leg below the knee replaced by a stout wooden peg following an accident years earlier, his reputation as a tipster and more than a bit of a ladies' man fully intact. He did not like the plan, conceiving "the whole aspect of it to be wrong." He had come to the convention "in some degree as a representative of the whole human race," he said. The delegates needed to take a broad view of their responsibility and not reduce themselves "to truck and bargain" for particular state interests. "This country must be united. If persuasion does not unite it, the sword will," he threatened with exactly the type of subjugation the small states most feared.[36]

The reply was swift. "No man can foresee to what extremities the small states may be driven by oppression," said Delaware's Gunning Bedford, who had earlier warned of some states taking a hand offered by foreign powers. The small states needed security against oppression from the large. To gain it, the small states had "conceded" proportional representation in the House. "If they be not gratified by correspondent concessions as to the second branch," he asked, "is it to be supposed they will ever accede to the plan?"[37]

Another committee came back with a plan to divide fifty-six members among the thirteen states in the first House of Representatives, using the federal ratio and an undescribed accounting of wealth in what was "little more than a guess" meant to provide some starting point for debate.[38] Crucially, the plan gave future Congresses discretion to reapportion representation in the House.

This last provision opened a new vein of debate that pitted the North against the South. The delegates knew that even allowing for the augmented voting power given to the white South under the federal ratio, the eight northern states would hold a majority over the five southern ones in the First Congress. Equally clear was that if a northern majority Congress had discretion on reapportionment, any number of excuses could be found not to exercise it, even as population flowed South and new western states in Kentucky and Tennessee were added to the union. "A pretext would never be wanting to postpone alterations, and keep power in the hands of those who possessed it," Randolph said for Virginia.[39]

New objections to using the federal ratio were voiced by stalwart small-state delegate William Paterson from New Jersey, who said he "could regard negro slaves in no light but as property. They are no free agents, have no personal liberty, no faculty of acquiring property, but on the contrary are themselves property, and like other property entirely at the will of the master. . . . Why then should they be represented?"[40]

The convention referred the matter to a new committee. A standard of allocating one representative for every 30,000 inhabitants was adopted. Their report proposed giving the eight northern states thirty-six seats in the House and the five southern states twenty-nine seats, or a sectional division of 55 to 45 percent, a 10 percent difference. Applying the totals for the free inhabitants in the 1790 census, the North held a population edge of 61 percent to 39 percent over the South, a 21 percent difference. The population figures used at the convention were estimates, apparently those assembled by Charles Pinckney.[41]

They were significantly off in some cases, and the standard of allocating one member for every 30,000 inhabitants being counted was not uniformly applied. Georgia, for example, got an extra member using this scale due to anticipated population growth and Massachusetts got one less. Based on these figures, the South was allocated about eight more members than its free population alone would have entitled it, nearly a third of its total representation. Once representation was allocated on actual census numbers, this original extra allocation would prove close to correct. As historian Leonard L. Richards has noted, "the slave states always had one-third more seats in Congress than their free population warranted—forty-seven seats instead of thirty-three in 1793, seventy-six instead of fifty-nine in 1812, and ninety-eight instead of seventy-three in 1833."[42]

Rufus King of Massachusetts added up the numbers. He saw a stark sectional divide, the four northeastern states having seventeen representatives under the proposed allocation and the four most southern having twenty-three. "He remarked that the four eastern states having 800,000 souls have one-third fewer representatives than the four southern states, having not more than 700,000 souls rating Backs, as five for three. The Eastern people will advert to these circumstances, and be dissatisfied. . . . He was fully convinced that the question concerning a difference of interests did not lie where it had hitherto been discussed, between the great and small states; but between the southern and eastern." Although his desire for union made him ready "to yield something for the security" of the South, "no principle would justify the giving them a majority."[43]

Gouverneur Morris was beginning to see affairs through the same lens. "He thought the southern states have by the report more than their share of representation. . . . Property ought to have its weight; but not all the weight."[44]

Despite these objections and five consecutive votes to alter individual state allocations, the convention approved the apportionment plan for sixty-five representatives, the number that would be allotted to the House in the First Congress.

The federal ratio augmenting white southern power combined with southern insistence on a regular census that southern delegates believed would expand that power conflated into a North-South power struggle. Randolph called for a constitutional mandate that Congress regularly schedule that a census be taken. Gouverneur Morris was blunt in reply. Reapportionment based on a regular census including soon-to-come western states would shift voting power away from the North that, he said, wanted "to keep a majority of votes in their own hands."[45] He was not alone in thinking that power should be securely lodged in the hands of the wealthy and not be diluted among newcomers with less experience from remote sections of the country.[46]

The following day George Mason of Virginia, owner of some 300 slaves, offered an equally blunt reply. "According to the present population of America, the Northern part of it had a right to preponderate, and he could not deny it. But he wished it not to preponderate hereafter when the reason no longer continued." Unless some sure means of adjusting the power balance was inserted into the constitution, he "must declare he could neither vote for the system here nor support it, in his state."[47] He then added the warning that if western states were not folded into the union on equal terms with existing states, they "will either not unite with or will speedily revolt from the union."[48]

Tempers were wearing thin. Some northern delegates began to reassess counting any of the South's slaves in apportioning House representation. Some southern delegates began to dig in to demand that all slaves should be counted.[49] The convention was unraveling again.

Wilson, who had first formulated the federal ratio clause with Rutledge, now said he "did not well see on what principle the admission of blacks in the proportion of three-fifths could be explained. Are they admitted as citizens? Then why are they not admitted on an equality with white citizens? Are they admitted as property? Then why is not other property admitted into the computation?" Including slaves among whites for apportionment, moreover, would "give disgust to the people of Pennsylvania." Yet he remained open to "the necessity of compromise."[50] Gouverneur Morris, less forgiving, "was compelled to declare himself reduced to the dilemma of doing injustice to the southern states or to human nature, and he must therefore do it to the former. For he could never agree to give such encouragement to the slave trade as would be given by allowing them a representation for their negroes, and he did not believe those states would ever confederate on terms that would deprive them of that trade."[51]

A new vote to approve the federal ratio failed, four states in favor and six opposed. Some historians speculate that recriminations flew between northern and southern delegates either outside the meeting room or on the floor but were left unrecorded in Madison's notes.[52] By the following day, July 12, the comments that Madison did record were bitter enough.

North Carolina's William Davie, owner of some thirty-six slaves, took the floor to say "it was high time now to speak out. He saw that it was meant by some gentlemen to deprive the southern states of any share of representation for their blacks. He was sure that North Carolina would never confederate on any terms that did not rate them at least as three-fifths. If the eastern states meant therefore to exclude them altogether the business was at an end."[53]

Gouverneur Morris countered that as Davie had said it was time to speak out, he, as one member "would candidly do so. He came here to form a compact for the good of America. . . . But as the compact was to be voluntary, it is vain for the eastern states to insist on what the southern states will never agree to. It is equally vain for the latter to require what the other states can never admit; and he verily believed the people of Pennsylvania can never agree to a representation of negroes."[54]

Just as adamantly, General Charles Pinckney, owner of some seventy slaves and cousin of fellow South Carolinian Charles Pinckney, replied "that property in slaves should not be exposed to danger under a government instituted for the protection of property."[55] His formulation was noteworthy, not only in that for underscoring the white South's determination to embed protection for slavery in the Constitution, but also for asserting that the purpose of government was to protect property without reference to any protection of liberty, the cause for which the Revolutionary War was fought. Of course, a reference to liberty in defense of slavery would present challenges, a dilemma that southern leaders grappled with for decades to come.

At this juncture, deal maker Wilson offered an olive branch meant to finesse objections to directly linking slavery to congressional representation. He observed that "less umbrage would perhaps be taken against an admission of slaves into the rule of representation, if it should be so expressed as to make them indirectly only an ingredient in the rule."[56] This obfuscation was achieved by providing that representation be based on direct taxation that in turn be apportioned by a regular census and include the federal ratio. Delegates well knew that direct taxes would likely provide scant revenue to the new government. Such income would be difficult if not impossible for a fledging new government in a sprawling country to collect. Import tariffs and sales of the vast tracts of public land in the territories were the readiest means to secure government revenue. But Wilson's olive branch worked, as did the realization that after exhaustive and harsh debate no better way forward appeared open. The motion to adopt Wilson's plan passed six votes to two with two delegations divided. The desired end once again overrode the chosen means.

The convention was staggering to a decision. Gouverneur Morris, outspoken but nearly alone by now, took a final lunge. "A distinction had been set up and urged between the northern and southern states," he said. "He had hitherto considered this doctrine as heretical. He still thought the distinction groundless. He sees however that it is persisted in; and that the southern gentlemen will not be satisfied unless they see the way open to their gaining a majority in the public councils."[57] South Carolina's Pierce Butler spoke truthfully in reply, saying, "The security the southern states want is that their negroes may not be taken from them," but then expressed a fear that haunted the white South for decades to follow by adding, "which some gentlemen within and without doors, have a very good mind to do."[58] Then, to seal the southern strategy, a motion initiated by Randolph that the apportionment rule be applied to new states as they entered the union passed without dissent.

Finally, on Monday, July 16, the convention adopted what has come down in history as the Great Compromise. The House was to be based on proportional representation, a victory for Madison and the nationalists. Apportionment in the House would be based on direct taxation determined by a regular census counting slaves as three-fifths of a free citizen, dual victories for the white South. The House would initiate revenue bills, a nonentity. The Senate would be based on equal state votes, a victory for small states. The compromise was closer to extortion, extracted by the South's threat to bolt the convention if its slave interest was not recognized and small-state threats to bolt if they did not receive equal Senate votes.

Slavery would not simply continue in the South but be embedded in the new Constitution to secure its perpetuation. The government itself would be a hybrid, a federal republic combining the republican principle of popular representation in the House and a federated union among states represented in the Senate.

The arduous decision of how to allocate power in the new government had been made. The delegates next moved to deciding what powers that government should exercise.

In New York City, the Continental Congress reached a quorum with the arrival of Constitutional Convention delegates from North Carolina and Georgia. Action on a proposed Northwest Ordinance was the business before them. What they did is easier to describe than why they did it. On July 11, the Congress took up the ordinance that included land that eventually comprised the states of Ohio, Indiana, Illinois, Michigan, Wisconsin, and a portion of Minnesota. Bringing these 318,167 square miles, an area larger than France, into the union's fold would nearly double the size of the finally determined borders of the thirteen original states. The ordinance provided for including new states from the territory "on an equal footing" with existing states, encouraged education, and included a number of provisions later made part of the Bill of Rights, such as freedom of religion, trial by jury, a habeas corpus clause, and a ban on cruel and unusual punishment. On July 13, they added an amendment prohibiting slavery in the territory. Without further amendment or debate, the ordinance passed unanimously on an eight-to-nothing vote that included the four southernmost states. The amendment also contained a fugitive slave provision calling for the capture and return to owners of slaves who escaped into the territory.

The Northwest Territory covered land west of the Appalachian Mountains and north of the Ohio River ceded by Great Britain to the United States at the end of the Revolutionary War. Land south of the river was not part of the deal. This land included areas claimed by Virginia that became Kentucky, and by North Carolina that became Tennessee, and the sprawling Mississippi Territory. Thomas Jefferson, as a member of Congress in 1784, had proposed slavery prohibition in all the territories.[59] His measure, which failed by a single vote, would have delayed the prohibition until 1800.

The two most prominent explanations for the white southern acquiescence to the prohibition clause center on ongoing treaty negotiations with Spain and the issue pending before the convention of a constitutional provision for the return of fugitive slaves.[60] One inducement to the southern stance was that without slave labor in the Northwest Territory, competition would be unlikely in raising labor-intensive crops such as indigo and tobacco. Negotiations with Spain, being led by John Jay, were of intense interest in Congress. Jay favored gaining shipping access to Spanish colonies, favorable to the North, at the expense of delaying for thirty years free navigation of the Mississippi River through the Spanish-held port of New Orleans, rights for which the white South was prepared to fight. The ultimate rejection of the Jay Treaty, the theory goes, was the white South's price for agreeing to the prohibition of slavery in the Northwest Territory. Another line of argument holds that the white South agreed to the ordinance's slavery ban in exchange for northern assurance that fugitive slave clauses would be included in both the ordinance and the Constitution.

The Northwest Ordinance was ultimately approved by the First Congress under the new Constitution with only one dissenting voice and signed into law by President George Washington. By separating the area north of the Ohio River as free of slavery, it by implication designated territory south of the river as open to slavery. Historian George William Van Cleve concludes that the "bargain permitted southwestern slavery expansion because the desires of northern citizens to pursue western expansion north of the Ohio on their own terms overwhelmed northern concerns about slavery's southwestern expansion."[61] Precedent was also set, which flared into major controversy over Missouri's admission to the Union in 1819–1821, for congressional authority to outlaw slavery as a condition of statehood.

By late July the Constitutional Convention had agreed to nineteen resolutions including not only the crucial allocation of power and suffrage in both legislative branches, but also an executive branch to be headed by a single individual and an independent judiciary. A basic framework had been established. To put the pieces into draft constitutional language the convention appointed a committee of detail that met privately for two weeks before presenting its report on August 6.

As chairman, South Carolina's John Rutledge etched the decisive mark of white southern strategy into the committee's work.[62] A new division of federal and state powers was created. Additional slave-state concessions never considered by the convention were proposed. The decision to grant equal state Senate votes had trimmed Rutledge's enthusiasm for a strong national government. He was now even more keen than before on limiting those powers to bar intrusion into slavery. The convention's decision to grant Congress power to override state legislative decisions was dropped. Drafts of the committee's work show Rutledge's hand in the insertion of seventeen enumerated powers to be delegated to Congress, some drawn from the Articles of Confederation. They ranged from establishing post offices and setting standards for weights and measures, to making war and raising armies and navies.

Into this list committee member James Wilson inserted a final grant of power, broader and more general than any other: "to make all laws that shall be necessary and proper for carrying into execution the foregoing powers, and all other powers vested, by this Constitution, in the government of the United States, or in any department or officer thereof."[63] This language, with slight modification, was included in the Constitution that the convention ultimately proposed for ratification, becoming, along with the interstate commerce clause, the elastic by which the limited enumerated powers could expand, a process that began in the First Congress.

Three additional clauses bearing Rutledge's hallmark were written into the committee's report. None of them were based on convention resolutions. Congress could not impose export taxes, an enormous boon to the southern economy that was based on selling its slave-labor crops abroad. Navigation acts, by which Congress might restrict shipping to favor American-flagged ships that sailed mainly from northern harbors, would require two-thirds votes in both houses of Congress to be approved, giving the white South a veto over ocean-borne commercial regulation it did not approve. Finally, the new government would have no power to abolish or tax the foreign slave trade or the movement of slaves between the states.

The committee report's new slave-state concessions provoked outrage. Rufus King said he had consented to the federal ratio with the expectation that it was a necessary concession to forming confidence in a strong national government. But the report, he said, "put an end to all

John Rutledge. COURTESY OF THE SUPREME COURT OF THE UNITED STATES.

these hopes. In two great points the hands of the legislature were absolutely tied. The importation of slaves could not be prohibited—exports could not be taxed. . . . Shall one part of the U.S. be bound to defend another part, and that other part be at liberty not only to increase its own danger, but to withhold the compensation for the burden? . . . There was so much inequity and unreasonableness in all this, that the people of the northern states could never be reconciled to it."[64]

Gouverneur Morris soon took the floor to deliver what became the only frank avowal for abolition spoken at the convention. "He never would concur in upholding domestic slavery," Madison recorded him as saying. "It was the curse of heaven on the states where it prevailed. . . . The admission of slaves into the Representation when fairly explained comes to this: that the inhabitant of Georgia and South Carolina who goes to the coast of Africa, and in defiance of the most sacred laws of humanity tears away his fellow creatures from their dearest connections and damns them to the most cruel bondages, shall have more votes in a government instituted for protection of the rights of mankind, than the citizen of Pennsylvania or New Jersey who views with a laudable horror, so nefarious a practice." The North would be bound to defend the South against slave insurrection or foreign attack, he argued, while the white South was to be encouraged to increase the danger by not being "restrained from importing fresh supplies of wretched Africans . . . and are at the same time to have their exports and their slaves exempt from all contributions for the public service. . . . He would sooner submit himself to a tax for paying for all the negroes in the United States than saddle posterity with such a Constitution."[65]

Morris's call echoed through the decades, even to the Lincoln administration that fruitlessly argued during the Civil War that a tax to purchase freedom for slaves would be less costly than prolonging the conflict.

By the third week of August, threats to reject the emerging constitution again divided the convention as slavery again illuminated the sectional split underlying the deliberations. In a debate over the Rutledge committee's southern concessions, including the slave trade, Maryland's Luther Martin, said "it was inconsistent with the principles of the revolution and dishonorable to the American character to have such a feature in the Constitution."[66] That prompted Rutledge's blunt reply: "Religion and humanity have nothing to do with this question. Interest alone is the governing principle with nations. The true question at present is whether the southern states shall or shall not be parties to the union."[67] Charles Pinckney repeated the threat. The southern delegates were in no mood to endure decisions regarding their property based on appeals to liberty and freedom.

The following day, August 22, produced one of the convention's most divisive debates. In addressing the slave trade, the sectional split was compounded by a split among the southern states. In March 1787, South Carolina had enacted a temporary three-year ban on slave imports, leaving North Carolina and Georgia as the only states then pursuing the African slave trade.[68] The Border South states of Maryland and Virginia were dispersal states, their economies tied to selling excess slave labor into the Deep South. Prohibiting a ban on the slave trade would depress the price of their own exports. From a Deep South perspective, slaves purchased from Africa were cheaper than those bought in Virginia or Maryland.

With haunting foreshadowing, Virginian George Mason denounced the "infernal traffic" that brings "the judgment of heaven on a country. As nations can not be rewarded or punished in the next world they must be in this. By an inevitable chain of causes and effects providence punishes national sins, by national calamities. . . . He held it essential in every point of view, that the general government should have power to prevent the increase of slavery."[69] Eighty-seven years later, in his second inaugural, Lincoln invoked a divine retribution by which "every drop of blood drawn with the lash, shall be paid by another drawn with the sword."[70]

The South Carolinians and Georgians were having none of it. "If slavery be wrong, it is justified by the example of the world," said Charles Pinckney. "In all ages one half of mankind have been slaves."[71] His cousin General Pinckney put it frankly: "South Carolina and Georgia cannot do without slaves." He would consider a ban on the foreign slave trade "as an exclusion of South Carolina from the union."[72] Georgia's Abraham Baldwin, a former divinity teacher, noted simply that the slave trade was one of his state's "favorite prerogatives" that was of local, not national concern.[73] Elbridge Gerry interjected that the convention "had nothing to do with the conduct of the States as to Slaves, but ought to be careful not to give any sanction to it."[74] As the members circled the foreign slave trade issue, some recognized that they ran the risk of giving sanction to the very thing they wanted curtailed.

If the South was just left to its own devices, Baldwin and General Pinckney speculated, the slave trade might be abolished at some indeterminate time in the future. Adding his own speculation in seeking a tone of moderation, Connecticut's Oliver Ellsworth said "Slavery in time will not be a speck in our country."[75] His colleague Roger Sherman took a similar tack, observing that "the abolition of slavery seemed to be going on in the United States and that the good sense of the several states would probably complete it."[76] Wishful thinking was applied as a balm to sooth discord.

Once again, Rutledge played the South's hole-card threat. "If the Convention thinks North Carolina, South Carolina and Georgia will

Gouverneur Morris. COURTESY OF WIKIMEDIA COMMONS/NEW YORK PUBLIC LIBRARY.

ever agree to the plan, unless their right to import slaves be untouched, the expectation is vain."[77] Let the southern states import slaves if that was their price for union, Roger Sherman argued, but do not tax such human cargo because doing so "implied they were *property*."[78] Again, a warning was sounded to keep explicit recognition slavery's basic premise of a right to property in man out of the emerging constitution.

The threats of deadlock made the prospect of failure palpable enough to prompt Ellsworth to warn that without finding some "middle and moderate ground," several states might "fly into a variety of shapes and directions, and most probably into several confederations and not without bloodshed."[79] Facing impasse, the delegates formed another committee to report on the matter. That report produced a series of compromises, agreed to in a series of votes during late August. Congress would be prohibited from banning the slave trade until 1800, a date General Pinckney succeeded in moving back to 1808. A tax could be placed on the importation of slaves, later set at $10 per slave. A two-thirds vote to pass navigation acts was reduced to a majority vote in both houses of Congress, a clause that was fought over but eventually approved.

The convention's deliberations on the slave trade were crucial to how the document ultimately dealt with slavery. Unlike the attempt to conceal slavery behind taxation in the federal ratio, this compromise could not hide slavery's place in the Constitution. The importation of taxable property in the form of human beings could only mean slaves. The committee report's wording of this provision treated slave imports as merchandise. Roger Sherman, who three days earlier had warned against constitutionally conflating persons with property, again objected, pointing out that the report's language acknowledged "men to be property, by taxing them as such under the character of slaves."[80]

Madison then stepped in. The slave trade had already shown itself to be one of the issues on which the convention could flounder. Northern delegates had thus far reluctantly gone along with the federal ratio, but Gerry and Sherman had made clear that they were unwilling to countenance raising slavery, whose legal status rested entirely on state laws, to a nationally recognized property right. Madison told the convention that he "thought it wrong to admit in the Constitution the idea that there could be property in men."[81]

The convention finally resolved the matter by changing the report language to the wording that became Article I, Section 9, permitting the importation "of such persons" as any state might think proper, subject to a tax "not exceeding ten dollars for each Person." Slavery was to be recognized in the Constitution, but the document itself defined slaves as persons, not merchandise. Historian Sean Wilentz has termed this episode the convention's "most dramatic contest over slavery" ending in an affirmation "that the convention was intent . . . on excluding from the Constitution the very idea that there could be property in man."[82]

Although slaves were defined as persons, the document sanctioned the continuation of the foreign slave trade for at least another two decades, with no assurance that it would stop then. "Twenty years," Madison said, "will produce all the mischief that can be apprehended from the liberty to import slaves. So long a term will be more dishonorable to the national character than to say nothing about it in the Constitution."[83] In practice, the compromise protected the legal importation of some 170,000 to 200,000 slaves up to 1808, with many thousands more illegally smuggled into the country thereafter.[84] For the North, the compromise meant no insuperable congressional hurdles to the regulation of Atlantic shipping crucial to Massachusetts, Pennsylvania, and New York.

The final slavery concession was the least controversial: inclusion of a fugitive slave clause for the return of runaway slaves. The Northwest Ordinance's fugitive slave clause was the basis for the measure introduced by Pierce Butler on August 29, which failed to elicit any debate and immediately passed on a unanimous vote.[85] Its final form as Article IV, Section 2, of the Constitution reads: "No person held to Service or Labour in one State, under the Laws thereof, escaping into another, shall, in Consequence of any Law or Regulation therein, be discharged from such Service or Labour, but shall be delivered up on Claim of the Party to whom such Service or Labour may be due." The ease with which the fugitive slave clause was adopted may have been due to a bargain struck off the convention floor. The vote confirming that only majority congressional votes be needed to regulate navigation, of particular value to the North, passed unanimously immediately before the fugitive slave clause was approved without dissent. Although the subject matter was undoubtedly distressing to some delegates, the content was not. Few Northerners had any desire to have their states become havens for slaves who fled the South.

A pair of seemingly small but important changes were made in arriving at the fugitive slave clause's final wording. As introduced by Butler, the provision referred to persons "legally held to service in one state" who were to be returned to the person "justly claiming their service." The words "legally" and "justly" were deleted at two separate stages in the drafting process, so the Constitution neither affirmed nor denied the legality of state slavery laws nor the justice of a slaveowner's claim for the return of an escaped slave.

The final result was that slaveholding states won their substantive goal of embedding slavery into the Constitution under the federal ratio, putting off a decision on the foreign slave trade for at least two decades, and securing a provision for the return of fugitive slaves. In realizing those gains, southern delegates tried to insert wording to legitimize property in man but raised no great objections when they won the practical advantage without gaining the definitional one. In the decades ahead, slaveowners argued there was no meaningful difference between a constitutional recognition of slavery and explicit constitutional language sanctioning it. They claimed, too, that the Constitution did authorize, not just recognize slavery. Northern disagreement on that point became an enduring source of sectional division, one the Supreme Court attempted to resolve in its 1857 *Dred Scott* decision.

After the August fights over slavery and shipping laws, in the first two weeks of September a protracted debate followed over the executive branch, the convention's most contentious issue after allocation of power in Congress. That contest produced an additional slave-state gain. Differing groups favored selecting the president by popular vote, or a vote in the Senate, or votes in the state legislatures. The committee formed to resolve the issue produced a complicated Electoral College formula calling for the state legislatures to decide on the means to choose presidential electors. The choice could be made by legislative, popular statewide, or district votes. Then, electors would cast ballots for two candidates, one of them at least from another state. The person receiving a majority of votes would be declared the winner. If a tie ensued with two candidates having a majority, the House would choose between them, and if unable to do so would then vote from among the top-five vote getters. A state's allocation of electors would be based on the size of each state's congressional delegation, a decided advantage to small states given their equal votes in the Senate and to the slave states given the federal ratio's augmentation of their votes in the House. Within a few years of ratification, the system's defects became apparent, and it remains a target of criticism now with its ability to select a president by winning the electoral vote with a minority of the popular vote.

With its work near an end, the convention appointed a committee on style to put its resolutions into a proposed final form. As a member of that committee, Gouverneur Morris secured his place among the nation's Founders as the principal drafter of the document presented to the convention. On September 17, delegates Mason and Randolph of Virginia and Gerry of Massachusetts refused to sign, but George Washington and thirty-eight others from twelve states did. The Constitution of the United States was ready to be sent to the Confederation Congress, to the state legislatures for their information, and to the people represented in state conventions for ratification.

——

Accounts to their legislatures by two convention delegates provide fitting bookends to how slavery was addressed in Philadelphia. One comes from Luther Martin of Maryland, who walked out of the convention before it completed its work. He was described by a fellow delegate as "so extremely prolix, that he never speaks without tiring the patience of all who hear him."[86] No doubt that judgment carried some truth, but Martin, who opposed ratification, also held deep convictions. To have in "a government formed pretendedly on the *principles* of *liberty* and for *its preservation*," he wrote in his legislative report, "a provision not only putting it out of *its* power to *restrain* and *prevent* the *slave-trade*, but *even encouraging that most infamous traffic*, by giving the *States power* and *influence* in the *Union, in proportion* as they *cruelly and wantonly sport with the rights of their fellow creatures, ought to* be considered as *a solemn mockery of, and insult to that God* whose protection we had then implored, and could not fail to hold us up in *detestation*, and render us *contemptible* to every *true friend* of liberty in the world."[87]

Charles Cotesworth Pinckney saw it in an entirely different light, telling the South Carolina legislature that "we have secured an unlimited importation of negroes for twenty years. Nor is it declared that the importation shall be then stopped; it may be continued. We have a security that the general government can never emancipate them, for no such authority is granted; and it is admitted, on all hands, that the general government has no powers but what are expressly granted by the Constitution. . . . We have obtained a right to recover our slaves in whatever part of America they may take refuge, which is a right we had not before. In short, considering all circumstances, we have made the best terms for the security of this species of property it was in our power to make."[88]

Both men were wrong. The account of history has not excoriated the Constitution—quite the opposite. As to Pinckney's assertion, emancipation, when it first came, was invoked as a war power inherent in the Constitution.

The convention delegates as a whole also got some things wrong. They failed to foresee the rise of political parties organized around ideological principles expressing economic interests, a political reality that set in as soon as the new government started to function. Instead, the delegates saw the most challenging barrier facing them as a clash of interests between large and small states. That was true within the confines of allocating power within Congress, but not true beyond that struggle. Only as the debate progressed did the larger sectional divide between North and South, free and slave, gain clarity.

Some delegates left the convention believing that slavery had been set on a course of ultimate extinction, a belief reinforced when the slave trade was legally abolished in 1808. In a December report to the Pennsylvania ratifying convention, James Wilson wrote that he considered the constitutional provision authorizing a ban on the foreign slave trade "as laying the foundation for banishing slavery out of this country."[89] That belief was a self-induced delusion.

Other delegates left Philadelphia believing that slavery was secure where it then existed. It was, even up to the outbreak of the Civil War. No Congress or president up to that time attempted to abolish or intervene in slavery in any state where it already existed. In the speech that propelled him into prominence as a leading Republican candidate for president, Abraham Lincoln's 1860 Cooper Union address included the assertion aimed directly at the white South that "Republican doctrines and declarations are accompanied with a continual protest against any interference whatever with your slaves, or with you about your slaves."[90] As Madison put it to Virginia's ratifying convention, "No power is given to the general government to interpose with respect to the property in slaves now held by the states."[91]

The crucial issue on which the delegates held conflicting views was whether the Constitution gave the government power to restrict or prohibit slavery in territory that then did or in the future would belong to the United States. The slavery prohibition in the Northwest Ordinance and Article IV's wording that "Congress shall have Power to . . . make all needed Rules and Regulations respecting the Territory or other Property belonging to the United States" gave strength to a northern conviction that slavery could be confined. The white South saw the issue in an exactly opposite light. By restricting slavery prohibition to territory north of the Ohio River, the ordinance implicitly sanctioned its existence south of it. Further, a Congress limited to only those powers explicitly enumerated could not control slavery in territories outside those in the Northwest Ordinance, as no such specific power was granted.

In confronting their convention differences, the delegates faced a choice between the imminent catastrophe of a breakup into sectional confederacies or, in terms of slavery, possible longer-term conflicts over an institution that many depended upon, even more profited from directly or indirectly, and none could then and there fundamentally alter.

The delegates also fully grasped the positive inducements to working through sectional differences for the sake of union. The Constitution gave assurance that all regions could flourish economically in a union strong enough to stand as an independent nation. The right to property was secure, for whoever owned it and of whatever kind. Historian Richard Beeman insightfully summarized the convention's treatment of slavery, writing, "If there is a villain in this story it is the collective *indifference* of the Founding Fathers to the inhumanity of the institution to which they gave sanction. It was an indifference born both of their sense of innate superiority over African Americans and of their preoccupation with protecting *property rights*, even if that meant accommodating themselves to a 'necessary evil.'"[92]

The document the Framers produced recognized slavery's existence but did not give it formal sanction, leaving it as a state institution, not a national one. The words "slave" and "slavery" did not appear in the document so that those odious terms were not subject to direct attack in northern states during ratification. Southern conventions accepted assurances that slavery was secure. Objections to slavery or clauses recognizing it in the Constitution played a minor role in northern ratification conventions.[93]

The white southern strategy to embed slavery in the founding document was successful, even though an explicit recognition of the right of property in man was excluded. The concessions granted to secure southern compliance were hardly compromises. The only real concession the South granted was acceptance of majority congressional votes to regulate navigation, a trade-off paid for twice, once certainly at the price of delaying consideration of banning the slave trade and again probably at the price of adopting a fugitive slave clause. The Deep South states did not give up anything in return for securing the federal ratio because they wanted proportional representation in the first place, only on their own terms. The prospective ban on the foreign slave trade coincided with the interest of Virginia and Maryland slaveowners to sell their excess human property to states in the Deep South.

What the sum of the accommodations did realize was a new government, part republic and part federal. It had three distinct branches and limited enumerated powers containing a pair of elastic clauses that were understood differently by different delegates and different leaders who came after them.

They also produced a chance for the nation to survive. Survive, grow, and prosper it did, until the internal contradiction between freedom and slavery challenged its survival at the cost of hundreds of thousands of lives in civil war.

CHAPTER 2

The Federalist Era

A RAINBOW OF trends formed the arc of definition during the republic's first decade. Revolution and war in Europe divided politics in the New World along a fracture line roughly equivalent to that in the Old World. Tumult in France and Great Britain's will to impose order were reflected in America by those inspired by the French revolution's call to liberty and equality and those drawn to Britain's conservative standard of continuity and security. Domestic politics split along a line of those dedicated to consolidating the Revolution by the triumph of republican principles and those seeking to consolidate the federal government's ability to function effectively. Over time the divisions evolved into separate political movements that later became political parties.

A primary distinction between these trends was sectional, most markedly between the Deep South and New England, more generally between those states south of the Mason-Dixon line and those north of it. Beneath it all lay the tectonic rift between slave and free. During the decade slavery only occasionally became the open flash point of public conflict, as controversy over foreign and domestic policy was fought out between Federalist proponents of the first two administrations and the standard of republicanism that Thomas Jefferson articulated.

In early 1789 as the new government assembled in New York City, it had the unique job of inventing itself based on the 4,400 words in the Constitution. Ratification had been a close-run thing, but once accomplished the venture's precariousness persuaded many who doubted it to rally to it as the only choice at hand. The government had an unfaltering asset in George Washington, elected president by a unanimous Electoral College vote. Massachusetts's John Adams was elected vice president. Washington drew Alexander Hamilton to his side as treasury secretary.

He recalled Jefferson from a diplomatic post in France to become secretary of state. James Madison was the president's close adviser and chief lieutenant on the floor of the House of Representatives. The Revolution's trusted elite were in charge.

The First Congress consisted of the original eleven ratifying states, but it was soon expanded once North Carolina and Rhode Island adopted the Constitution. Political parties did not then exist, but those broadly in support of Washington's administration became known as Federalists, taking the name from the pro-Constitution newspaper articles largely written by Hamilton and Madison during the ratification struggle. The opposition, also only loosely affiliated, became by default the Antifederalists, a moniker that evolved into Republicans or Democratic Republicans. Although members of neither group initially saw themselves nor voted as a bloc, in general terms Washington could count on majorities in both houses. The Senate was composed of eighteen Federalists and eight Antifederalists, five of those from the six southern states. Membership in the House included thirty-six Federalists and twenty-eight Antifederalists, twenty-one of those from the South.[1] A foreshadowing of a later more explicit sectionalism was apparent at the outset.

The first session of the First Congress was devoted to fashioning and fitting the mortises and tenons of a new government structure. A judiciary act was passed creating the Supreme Court. Washington deftly asserted the presidency's independence from Senate encroachment. Revenue was raised, a census ordered. Responding to the widespread complaint during the ratification process that the proposed constitution did not include a bill of individual rights, Madison drafted twelve amendments that Congress submitted to the states in September 1789. Ten of them, now known as the Bill of Rights, were ratified in December 1791.

The First Amendment's affirmation of freedom of religion, the press, and the right to peacefully assemble includes the provision that Congress shall make no law abridging the right of the people to petition the government for a redress of grievances. In modern America the right to petition has largely been taken over by lobbyists and interest groups.

But in the republic's early decades, citizen petitions to state legislatures and to Congress were a treasured means for the practical realization of republican governance. The normal procedure was for the body to receive the petition, refer it to the appropriate committee, and await a report of what, if anything, should be done.

In 1790, a pair of petitions revealed the first congressional rift between free and slave states. A petition from Philadelphia Quakers urged Congress to act "to the full extent of your power, to remove every obstruction to . . . the abolition of the slave trade."[2] The second petition, which Benjamin Franklin signed as president of the Pennsylvania Society for the Abolition of Slavery, called on Congress to "step to the very verge of the power vested in you for discouraging every species of traffic in the persons of our fellow-men."[3]

The Senate, after Vice President Adams produced the petitions with "rather a sneer," one member wrote, deferred action to the House and never acted upon them.[4]

In the House, the petitions produced starkly different and telling results. Debate and votes extended from February through March 1790. Northern members had the chance to describe what powers they believed the Constitution granted Congress over slavery. They had the chance, too, to demonstrate their resolve to stand by those presumed powers. They succeeded to a degree on the first opportunity and collapsed on the second. The petitions provoked the first full-throated defense of slavery as an institution heard on the House floor, presaging themes that rumbled like drums of war for decades to follow. With Madison's abetment the episode also locked down what historian George William Van Cleve has termed the Constitution's "iron cage" of limited political or legal means to contest slavery's expansion.[5]

"Do these men expect a general emancipation of slaves by law," asked South Carolina Congressman Thomas Tudor Tucker in the first remarks made on the floor after both petitions were presented together to the House for the first time on February 12. His words were eerily prophetic. Barely had the new government begun functioning than the threat was hurled: "This would never be submitted to by the Southern states without a civil war."[6] Tucker's outburst provides insights into the Deep

South's prevailing attitude on slavery decades before it rose to preeminent national concern. Although neither petition argued that Congress had power to emancipate slaves, and both focused on the slave trade, Tucker instantly transformed the question onto the plane of freeing all slaves, escalating the stakes to the threat of civil war. A similar pattern of threatening disunion as an automatic rhetorical reflex became the white South's hallmark to congressional discussion of slavery for decades to come.

In response to Tucker's threat, Madison noted that the debate "has taken a serious turn." He urged the calming expedient of committing the petitions to committee "in the usual way," especially because they asked Congress to act only "so far as they were constitutionally authorized." With a prescience beyond that of Congressman Tucker, Madison then added, in a marker he later picked up, that "regulations might be made in relation to the introduction of [slaves] into the new states to be formed out of the Western Territory."[7]

Madison prevailed. A committee of seven members, six of them from northern states, was appointed to report on the petitions. As W. E. B. Du Bois pointed out, the predominance of northerners on the committee "compelled it to make this report a sort of official manifesto on the aims of Northern antislavery politics."[8]

The House undertook a section-by-section review of the committee report in March, but not without first hearing the Deep South's own manifesto on slavery. That salvo was delivered by South Carolina's William Loughton Smith. In a lengthy address, Smith laid out what historian Donald L. Robinson termed "the most thorough defense of slavery heard by Congress during the first twenty years of its existence under the Constitution."[9] Smith began with the charge that stung generations of white southerners most deeply, impugning their honor and affixing the stigma of tyranny upon them because their fortunes were based on slavery. The charge bred hatred, a marrow-deep contempt for what white southerners—both slave owning and non-slave owning—experienced as the North's self-righteous sense of moral superiority. The prospect of northern-imposed abolition was never real. The white South's hatred of northern disparagement was. The reproach hurled at the South for the "blood guiltiness" of the African slave trade, Smith said, was intended by the accusers "to fix a stigma of the blackest nature" on the people of South Carolina. Smith discounted the charge as the "officiousness" of those acting in "an intolerant spirit of persecution."[10]

The House journal account of Smith's constitutional argument is likely abbreviated. His essential contention was that "the state governments clearly retained all the rights of sovereignty which they had before the establishment of the Constitution, unless they were exclusively delegated to the United States," and no such delegation of authority over slavery existed.[11] He then took aim at the "fanciful schemes" of those who advocated emancipating slaves on the condition that they be colonized in some foreign region. Such plans admitted the danger of keeping free Blacks within the country, he said, and by expelling ex-slaves from the land of their natural attachments they were "repugnant to the principles of freedom." In a question that was also posed by generations of free Blacks who opposed colonization, Smith asked, "How could they be called freemen, if they were, against their consent, to be expelled [from] the country?" Reasoning that it was well known that Black slaves "were an indolent people, improvident, averse to labor," Smith argued that freeing them without removal would result in either race mixing to "degenerate the whites" or "the massacre and extirpation of one or the other." To liberate newborn slaves after a certain date would only debase them, he said, because they would remain living with their enslaved parents. Slavery's gradual extinction through a ban on the foreign slave trade was impossible unless the government also banned sex among slaves or, "like Herod," ordered "all their children to be put to death as soon as born."[12]

Having reviewed the alternatives, Smith concluded that there was no practical way out of slavery. He then embarked on an examination of slavery itself, portraying the institution as a positive good for Blacks held in bondage and for the nation. Slaves, he said, were "a happier people" than "the lower order of whites in many countries." The institution provided the South wealth that was a treasury of strength in case of war and profited northern merchants who shipped southern crops abroad. Slavery was sanctioned by the example of history dating back to ancient Greece and Rome, he said, and was not "disapproved of by the Apostles." Southern society produced by slavery was marked by "industry crowned with affluence," its children given "the highest polish of education," its women renowned for "an engaging softness and delicacy of manners," its men imbued with zealous ardor for liberty, "nor is there any trace of the influence of slavery on the character of her citizens." To banish slavery from this idyllic scene would convert South Carolina into a deserted wasteland because its plantations "can only be cultivated by slaves; the climate, the nature of the soil, ancient habits, forbid the whites from performing the labor."[13]

Smith had had enough of northern "squeamishness." He came to the point face on.

"The Northern States knew that the Southern states had slaves before they confederated with them," he said. "If they had such an abhorrence for slavery, why . . . did they not cast us off and reject our alliance? The truth was, that the best informed part of the citizens of the Northern states knew that slavery was so ingrafted into the policy of the Southern states, that it could not be eradicated without tearing up by the roots their happiness, tranquility, and prosperity; that if it were an evil, it was one for which there was no remedy, and, therefore, like wise men, they acquiesced in it." The South was just as aware of Quaker abhorrence of slavery as the North was of slavery's place in the South. "We therefore made a compromise on both sides," Smith said. "We took each other with our mutual bad habits and respective evils, for better or worse, the Northern states adopted us with our slaves, and we adopted them with their Quakers."[14] The implied contract required that the North take no step to injure the white South's property or tranquility.

Smith's address, all but forgotten in history, created the framework from which white southerners stood to slavery's defensive ramparts for decades to come. His portrayal of slavery as a positive good, although hedged by references to it as an evil, was made forty years before that doctrine met with wide acceptance in the white South. The mainstream southern argument in Smith's time, and for many years to follow, was that slavery was a necessary evil entailed on the South against its will during the colonial era by the British who were aided by the greed of high seas slave merchants operating from ports in the North. Smith's address is also notable as one of the first expressions in Congress of the doctrine upon which slavery was based: the assertion of white supremacy. The concept is infused in references he made to white "superiority over the blacks" and to blacks being "an inferior race even to the Indians."[15]

To counter, northern members would have had to match Smith's rhetorical fervor. None did. The House soon turned to eviscerating the committee report.

A preamble noting that the committee was "induced to examine the powers vested in Congress . . . relating to the abolition of slavery" was deleted altogether before the House moved on to examine the report's operative clauses.[16] Using language drawn directly from Article I, Section 9, of the Constitution, the report's first clause acknowledged that Congress was restrained from prohibiting slave imports into "any of the states now existing" until 1808.

The next clause, however, cracked open a new door. It provided that Congress was equally restrained from interfering in emancipation in "any of the said states"—that is, the states then existing when the Constitution was adopted, the original thirteen. The phrasing left the clear implication that bans on the slave trade and slavery itself might apply to new states and that emancipation might even be countenanced in the original thirteen states after 1808. The wedge was inferential, not declaratory, but a crack appeared in the white South's armor shielding slavery.

The report's third clause acknowledged that Congress had no power to regulate the treatment of slaves within the states, but it admonished them to enforce humane requirements for such things as marital rights, food, housing, and clothing.

The House modified the first clause only by making it adhere more closely to the Constitution's language. But the report's inference of latent powers over slavery remained. At this point, Madison stepped in, picking up his marker from the earlier debate, by sponsoring changes that dropped the report's third clause and rewrote the second to read unambiguously "that Congress have no authority to interfere in the emancipation of slaves, or in the treatment of them within any of the states."[17] In terms of the final House report, the door was slammed shut to any inference of power to emancipate slaves in new states. Finally, the Virginian then secured modifications acceptable to the North and Border

South that recognized congressional authority to restrain U.S. citizens from carrying out the slave trade with foreigners and to provide for the humane treatment of slaves aboard the ships importing them into the United States.

In these maneuvers, Madison was in part placating the North with restraints on slave trading with foreign nations or persons and acquiescing in humane regulation of slave imports to the United States. At the same time, he protected the white South against attempts to emancipate slaves in new states. Because Virginia was a dispersal state selling slaves southward, Madison was on safe ground with his constituents in the modest concessions to the North. The 1794 Slave Trade Act was passed with little controversy along lines presaged by Madison's stance in the petitions' report debates. Equally, his stance to cut short any implication of congressional authority over emancipation in new states suited Virginia.

Madison's actions during these debates cast light on the inconsistencies of a man who owned slaves but deprecated the institution. He implicitly acknowledged them when, in a letter to a colleague about emancipation in the following year, he wrote, "Those from whom I derive my public station are known by me to be greatly interested in that species of property, and to view the matter in that light. It would seem that I might be chargeable at least with want of candor, if not of fidelity, were I to make a situation in which their confidence has placed me to become a volunteer in giving a public wound, as they would deem it, to an interest on which they set so great a value."[18] The Father of the Constitution was merely acknowledging that on the issue of protecting slavery he was the servant of his constituency rather than a proponent of his principles.

The final report passed the House on a twenty-nine to twenty-five vote on March 23. It had no standing in law, being a mere expression of the body's views on the matter at the time of the vote. But given the initial foray in the committee report to stake out new ground on restraining slavery and the slave trade, and the crushing defeat of those efforts by inflamed southerners, it set a precedent. Slavery's expansion on a states' rights reading of the Constitution was to be the model as new states entered the union.

A reason for the North's lack of resolve in the face of southern vehemence during the debate is referred to in a letter Smith wrote to a South Carolina friend. Some members, he noted, were merely playing to the throngs of Quakers who packed the House gallery. As the southerners stretched out the debate, he wrote, northerners became "sick" of what they had provoked and "declared to us that we were unnecessarily alarmed, that they had not the most distant idea of interfering, and they only wished to commit the petitions out of compliment to the Quakers."[19] The North had no desire to disrupt the union that provided for their security and prosperity at its very inaugural. They took comfort that New York had just passed a gradual emancipation law; that similar measures were on the books in Pennsylvania, New Hampshire, Connecticut, and Rhode Island; and that Massachusetts had abolished slavery outright. Given that the slave trade was likely to be banned in 1808, from their vantage point, slavery was on a path to gradual extinction, or at least so they could convince themselves.

"Our early and violent opposition had this good effect," Smith's letter said, "it convinced the House that South Carolina and Georgia look with jealous eye on any measure in which the negroes are at all concerned. . . . We assured them that whenever Congress should directly or indirectly attempt any measure leveled at our particular rights in this respect, they must expect a revolt in those States."[20]

—

In May 1788, three men kidnapped John Davis from his home in Pennsylvania and forcibly took him to Virginia, where he was enslaved. Several years earlier John had been taken from Maryland, where he was enslaved, to Pennsylvania. His freedom was triggered by Pennsylvania law requiring that slaves be registered, a procedure John's owner failed to follow. Despite the change in his legal status, John was next taken to Virginia and rented out to a man named Miller. Some of John's former neighbors, later identified as members of the Pennsylvania Abolition Society, found him and brought him back to Pennsylvania. Miller, fearing that he would be held liable by John's owner for the loss, hired three men to find and return him. Their action prompted a court in Washington County, Pennsylvania, to indict for kidnapping the men Miller had hired. Thus began a sequence of events resulting in the 1793 passage of the Fugitive Slave Act providing enforcement provisions for the Constitution's fugitive slave and fugitive from justice clauses, a law that remained in effect until the upheaval of the Compromise of 1850.[21]

President Washington received the case when Pennsylvania's governor informed him that his Virginia counterpart had refused to extradite the three men on kidnapping charges. After a fruitless attempt to get the two governors to resolve the issue between themselves, in October 1791 Washington referred the case to Congress.

Because John Davis was enslaved in Virginia, and his abductors were charged with a crime in Pennsylvania, the case involved the issues of both fugitive slaves and fugitives from justice. The Constitution's Article IV, Section 2, secured a slaveowner's right to the return of a slave who fled to another state, but it provided no guidance about how to do it, or under what, if any, restraints.

In a lengthy process, the Senate considered three versions of legislation before passing a final bill.

One early provision presumed that although a person might be alleged to be a slave, as a person he or she nonetheless had rights. The provision required that before a certificate of removal could be issued, a hearing must be held for alleged fugitive slaves who had either been born in the state or had lived there for a number of years that was left to be later determined. At such a hearing both the alleged fugitive slave and the claimant would argue their case under the laws of the state where the case was being heard. This provision was dropped.

The final bill provided for a three-step process favorable to slaveowners that scrapped any notion of slaves as persons in favor of treating them solely as property. The owner or agent could seize an alleged fugitive slave without a warrant or notice to or assistance from local authorities. The claimant next brought the alleged slave before any federal or state judge, local magistrate, justice of the peace, or alderman. Upon presentation of "proof to the satisfaction" of the judge or magistrate, a certificate of removal was to be issued authorizing the return of the fugitive slave to the state or territory he or she had fled. The proof might consist of oral testimony from the slaveholder or his agent or an affidavit by a judge or magistrate in the state from which the fugitive came, certifying that such a person had escaped. Hindering arrest or harboring a fugitive was punishable by a stiff fine, $500. Washington signed into law the final bill that included minor House amendments in February 1793. John Davis remained enslaved for the rest of his life. His kidnappers remained free.

Years later a lawyer arguing for the return of a fugitive slave in Pittsburgh told the local official hearing the case, "This is a question with regard to *personal property*," like that for recovery of "a horse, a cow or any other species of personal property."[22] He captured the essence of the matter. To recover property an owner had no more obligation than to identify it and offer some credible basis of ownership. The property, including the human property of a slave or a person alleged to be a slave, was the object of the proceeding, not an agent in it.

Reliable figures are not available on the number of runaway slaves or of fugitive slaves who escaped to freedom. Runaways were common at plantations throughout the South, many of them fleeing for short periods of time into forests or swamps before being tracked down by dogs and search parties, or returning out of exhaustion and hunger. In the three decades before the Civil War, runaways may have numbered in the range of 50,000 each year.[23] Slaves who reached freedom may have numbered between 1,000 and 5,000 each year during the same period.[24]

In 1851, a New Orleans physician determined that a slave's impulse to seek freedom was actually a mental disease to which he ascribed the name "drapetomania" from a combination of Greek words for "runaway slave" and "madness." Dr. Samuel Cartwright, its author, prescribed a regime of sufficient food, housing, and food as a cure, but if that did not work, owners should whip their runaways "into that submissive state which it was intended for them to occupy in all after-time."[25]

Friction over fugitive slaves ran most prominently along the line separating southern border states and their northern neighbors, particularly between Maryland and Pennsylvania and between Kentucky and both Indiana and Ohio. The Appalachian region of what was then northern Virginia and is now West Virginia contained few slaves. But a slave in

Kentucky, or one who got that far after escaping from farther south, had but to look across the Ohio River to see a land of freedom.

During the first decade or two following passage of the Fugitive Slave Act, a kind of rough comity existed between slaveowners who sought return of their property and the citizens and officials in free states. The constitutional requirement to return escaped slaves was generally accepted, but kidnapping or attempts at it created conflict. A 1799 congressional committee report, never acted upon, found that "There is reason to believe that many blacks and people of color entitled to their freedom . . . are under color of the Fugitive Law entrapped, kidnapped and carried off."[26] The incentive to kidnap free Blacks was the price that could be fetched for selling them into slavery. In the early years of its application, the Fugitive Slave Act "was liable to great abuse," a Pennsylvania trier of such cases recalled. "It constituted a sort of secret tribunal that cut the fugitive off from all chance of having his case examined. He might be a freeman, and yet the judge or magistrate might be induced . . . to believe he was a slave, and he was forthwith remanded to the land of bondage, without the privilege of a public hearing."[27] One recourse, frequently used by lawyers that abolition societies recruited, was to file a writ of habeas corpus, prompting a hearing at which the alleged fugitive slave's status could be determined.

In 1810, the Indiana territorial legislature enacted an anti-kidnapping law providing that a person attempting to remove an alleged fugitive slave from the territory must first prove to a judge or justice of the peace that the person was, in fact, a slave. Failure to comply carried a $1,000 fine. The obvious lesson was that the Fugitive Slave Act did nothing to prevent states or territories from enacting their own laws respecting arrest and rendition of alleged fugitive slaves.

In his first message to the newly formed Indiana state legislature, Governor Jonathan Jennings called for further protections. The legislative response was the 1816 Act to Prevent Mansteling.[28] Any claimant under the Indiana law was first required to obtain an arrest warrant from a justice of the peace or state supreme circuit court judge. A sheriff or constable had to make the arrest. Both the alleged fugitive slave and claimant then had to appear in court, where testimony could be taken from both sides. If the justice of the peace or judge found that the claimant had a good case, the matter was set for jury trial.

In 1826, Pennsylvania went Indiana one step better in a law requiring not only that a warrant be issued by a judge before an alleged fugitive slave could be arrested, but also that a judge had to rule on the merits of the case in a hearing where "the oath of the owner or owners or other persons interested shall in no case be received in evidence."[29] A claimant winning a case had to pay court costs. By the late 1820s and early 1830s, other northern states passed similar personal liberty laws, inserting themselves between slaveowners and the Fugitive Slave Act with requirements for the issuance of arrest warrants and jury trials as protections against kidnapping free-born Blacks or slaves who had won their freedom. Laws passed in New York and Vermont in 1840 required that in jury trials, lawyers be provided to alleged slaves.

To avoid state-imposed restraints, slaveowners could pursue the Fugitive Slave Act's streamlined procedures under the federal court system, but that was an option largely in theory only, because most states had only one federal judge, or at most two. In practice, slaveowners found it difficult to pursue escaped slaves in northern states increasingly hostile to the institution of slavery.

In 1842, the Supreme Court stepped in. In overturning Pennsylvania's antikidnapping law, the ruling in *Prigg v. Pennsylvania* struck down state personal liberty laws. The Constitution gave the federal government exclusive jurisdiction over the return of fugitive slaves, the court found, and enforcement of that authority was embodied in the Fugitive Slave Act of 1793.[30] Southern states' rights advocates were pleased with the outcome even though it was based on a nationalist reading of federal powers.

The ruling, however, was a double-edged sword. States were prohibited from interfering with the Fugitive Slave Act, but the federal government had no power to coerce states to cooperate in the enforcement of that law. Massachusetts was the first to act, prohibiting its judges and justices of the peace from recognizing or granting certificates of removal. New types of personal liberty laws soon arose forbidding state officials from performing duties under the Fugitive Slave Act or using state jails to hold suspected fugitives. Vermont, Connecticut, New Hampshire, Pennsylvania, and Rhode Island enacted such statutes.[31] With federal judges left as essentially the only authorities available in northern states to enforce the law, and there being so few of them, the Fugitive Slave Act became a dead letter. As the number of fugitive slaves fleeing north rose, so did the anger of white southerners over the denial of a property right that the Constitution assured to them. For practical purposes, the Fugitive Slave Act was nullified.[32]

As the conflict was being woven into the Compromise of 1850, Virginia senator James M. Murray commented, "You may as well go down into the sea, and endeavor to recover from his native element a fish which had escaped from you as to expect to recover [a] fugitive."[33] A decade later South Carolina cited northern refusal to enforce its "constitutional obligations" to return fugitive slaves among the immediate causes justifying its secession from the union.[34]

*   *

"You call this the land of liberty," a high-ranking foreign official once remarked to Congressman John Randolph of Virginia during a walk in the recently formed national capital of the District of Columbia. "Every day that passes things are done in it at which the despotisms of Europe would be horrorstruck and disgusted."[35] He was referring to the spectacle of slaves being led in the street, men in shackles and chains, women and children following behind in horse-drawn wagons, to an auction site for sale to the South.

The Constitution provided that the nation's capital city be created on land to be ceded by one or more states but did not designate the location. The Pennsylvania and New York delegations in the First Congress competed fiercely to win the site, but a deadlock ensued partly because white southerners wanted a location somewhere along the Potomac River. When Treasury Secretary Hamilton's bill to have the federal government assume all state and national debts came up a second time in the House, after first failing for the lack of a few southern votes, the makings of a compromise were in place.

Slave coffles were a common sight in the nation's capital, like those depicted in this 1819 drawing showing the Capitol building before work began on the dome. SOURCE: *SLAVERY IMAGES.*

The deal struck gave Hamilton his assumption legislation, Philadelphia the honor of being the temporary capital until 1800, and President Washington authority to designate a permanent site along the Potomac. He chose an area just below the vantage point of his home at Mount Vernon. Maryland and Virginia ceded the land with the provision that state laws continue in force until the government was ready to move to its new capital. When that time came, the existing state laws were grandfathered in as part of the District of Columbia's legal structure. Maryland and Virginia were slave states, so their laws governing slavery were legacy grants to the capital of a government dedicated to liberty. The Constitution, however, also granted Congress authority "to exercise exclusive legislation in all cases whatsoever" over the District.

Local government was divided among three towns: the central District of Columbia, where government buildings were being constructed; adjacent Georgetown; and Alexandria, across the Potomac on the Virginia side of the river. Congress set up committees to exercise its governing functions, with the president having power to appoint judges, magistrates, a U.S. attorney, and marshals.

Work began on the Capitol building and president's house soon after the authorizing legislation passed, supervised by three commissioners chosen by Washington. Whites, free Blacks, and slaves hired out by their owners were employed in the work. By 1794, the commissioners agreed to hire up to 100 slaves for the following year at $60 each per year, a sum later increased to $70.[36] They cut stone at nearby quarries, sawed planks from trees cut down along street alignments, made bricks, and in some cases acquired new trades as carpenters, masons, roofers, and plasterers. When the government moved to the District in 1801, the White House was still under construction, and the roof leaked. Enough of the Capitol was complete for Congress to meet in the north wing. Within two years, the government's payroll for employees working in the capital included 291 persons, from clerks to the president.[37]

The District's 1800 population of some 14,000 souls included approximately 3,200 slaves, most of them household servants.[38] The law presumed that all Blacks were slaves. A free Black suspected of being a runaway and unable to immediately produce proof of his or her freedom could be jailed, and if later able to show such proof, would be let go after paying jail fees. If unable to prove free status, a free Black suspected of being a runaway could be sold into slavery.[39] Cases of such abuse, including the kidnapping of free Blacks, were alleged, but the nature of such cases left few records confirming it. Blacks could not give court testimony against any "Christian white person."[40]

Whipping was the common punishment for pilfering or stealing, but a slave's right ear could be cropped off if he struck a white man. Runaways who resisted arrest could be shot and killed. The death penalty was reserved for conspiracy to insurrection, murder, rape of a white woman, or house arson, but only a single case of a slave execution—for attempted rape in 1813—was ever recorded.[41] "Where any slave shall be guilty of rambling, riding or going abroad in the night, or riding horses in the day time without leave," a punishment of "whipping, cropping or branding in the cheek with the letter R" was prescribed.[42] Possession of newspapers "calculated to excite insurrection or insubordination" was punishable by fines for free Blacks and whipping for slaves.[43]

Private meetings or religious assemblies of free Blacks or slaves were prohibited after ten o'clock at night. Any free Black or slave at large in the District after that hour without a signed pass was to be fined, if free, or given up to thirty-nine lashes if enslaved. Up to ten lashes were meted out to a slave who abusively lashed a horse. Slaves could not keep horses, cattle, or hogs, but free Blacks could keep a dog. Masters who excessively beat their slaves, or deprived them of sufficient food, shelter, or clothing, could be fined up to 1,000 pounds of tobacco.

As the city grew, so did its reputation as a slave depot. Robey's was a prominent private slave pen, located about a half mile from the Capitol on the east side of Seventh Street, S.W., south of B Street.[44] Slaves were confined there and at other holding pens until an auction date was set. "Scarcely a week passes," a local newspaper noted, "without some of these wretched creatures being driven through our streets."[45] Many of the slaves thus herded were taken to the auction house of Franklin and Armfield in Alexandria that reported a profit of $33,000 on sales in 1833, about $1 million in modern currency.[46] This firm alone sold between 1,000 and 1,300 slaves a year during this period. Most were loaded aboard schooners tied up at the Alexandria pier for shipment south. District newspapers ran frequent ads for the purchase or sale of slaves, a typical one reading: "TWO HUNDRED SLAVES WANTED! The subscriber will give higher prices in cash for likely young slaves of both sexes than any other person in this market or who may come."[47]

The slave traffic elicited scores of petitions to Congress, many from religious societies of free Blacks in the District, to halt the trade or to abolish slavery there outright. They were typically referred to committee, where nothing further was heard of them. By 1836, southerners in Congress had had their fill of it.[48]

In January of that year, Thomas Morris, who had bootstrapped himself from store clerk to senator from Ohio, introduced a pair of petitions calling for the abolition of slavery in the District of Columbia. His action provoked a constitutional debate and the full-blown fury of the one man living who then spoke more than any other for the white South and its peculiar institution, the stern-faced senator from South Carolina, John C. Calhoun.

The petitions, he said, "contained a gross, false, and malicious slander on eleven states represented on this floor." Brushing aside the constitutional authority to legislate on all matters relating to the capital city, he propounded, "The question of emancipation exclusively belonged to the several states. Congress had no jurisdiction on the subject, no more in this district than the state of South Carolina: it was a question for the individual state to determine, and not to be touched by Congress."[49] A body of northerners was prepared, he continued, to support "any insurrectionary movement of the blacks," and such petitions only agitated the matter to the danger of holding the union together. Instead of accepting and referring the petitions to oblivion, Calhoun called for rejecting them at the outset.

Morris agreed that emancipation in the states was beyond congressional reach, but that because "Congress has primary and exclusive legislation over this district," the petitioners had a right to be heard. The Constitution, he said, secured a "fundamental right, belonging to the people, to petition Congress for the redress of their grievances." To prescribe how, or when, or on what subject that right might be exercised would be to make the right a "mockery."[50]

Lengthy addresses followed from two other southern senators. One decried the charge, inherent in the petitions, that slaveholders were "tyrants, oppressors, and murderers."[51] The other denounced "the blood-thirsty fanatics" behind the "wanton and malicious" abolition movement.[52] Then, tellingly, a northern senator and future president of the United States, James Buchanan of Pennsylvania, arose. He cited the 1790 House report that Congress had no right to act on emancipation in any state. The report, he said, "is clear, precise, and definite. It leaves the question where the Constitution left it, and where, so far as I am concerned, it ever shall remain."[53] To grant the petitions' prayer, he continued, would be to "erect a citadel in the very heart of [the South] . . . from which abolitionists and incendiaries could securely attack the peace and safety of their citizens."[54]

Soon another future president of the United States rose. John Tyler of Virginia was chair of the Senate District of Columbia committee. Let the petitions be admitted, he said: "Let them go to the lion's den, and there will be no footprints to show their return. The committee will meet them with a declaration that there is no power in Congress to do what the petitioners ask."[55] An avalanche of criticism descended on North Carolina Senator Bedford Brown when he recommended that the petitions simply be laid upon the table, to reside and die there quietly. "All men of all parties are shaken and excited," Calhoun's South Carolina colleague William Preston responded, "and lo! The Senator from North Carolina exhorts us to be quiet. An enemy, savage, remorseless, and indignant, is thundering at our gates, and the gentleman tells us to fold our arms. . . . The storm is bursting upon us that is to sweep away the bulwarks of our freedom and union, and fill the land with convulsion and anarchy; but sit still, says the honorable Senator."[56] Chastened, Bedford assured the chamber he was "ready to go with Southern gentlemen in any measure" to repress discussion of the petitions. He would, in fact, "go further." At any northern attempt to interfere with slavery, "let us," he said, "depart from them—depart peaceably."[57]

The debate continued intermittently for the next eight weeks. Before it was over, thirty-three of the forty-nine members took the floor. Their speeches circulated throughout the country, reprinted from dispatches first published in one of the District's three newspapers. The remarks fell into a distinct pattern. Northern senators defended the right to petition, granted the claim that Congress had no power to interfere with slavery in the states, decried abolitionists' fanaticism, and offered assurances that they opposed emancipation in the District. No plausible grounds ever existed that the Senate might vote to end slavery in the capital.

For white southerners, however, that was not really the point. The petitions represented to the white South an intolerably grating agitation of the issue. "I warn you," Mississippi's John Black said, that the consequences of such agitation raised "the spectacle of slaves cutting the throats of their masters, mistresses, and their children" and a retaliation of Black extermination by whites.[58] Calhoun saw the imperative of not accepting the petitions as "our Thermopylae."[59] Northern abolitionists, he said, were conducting "a war of religious and political fanaticism" aiming "to humble and debase us in our own estimation, and that of the world in general; to blast our reputation, while they overthrow our domestic institutions."[60]

Buchanan offered the temporizing balm that if excitement over the issue was avoided, abolitionists' agitation "will pass away in a short period, like the other excitements which have disturbed the public mind, and are now almost forgotten."[61] Calhoun's analysis was far more accurate than Buchanan's. The irony was, of course, that Calhoun's rush to block the pass exposed the abolitionists' ability to goad the white South. To have accepted the petitions and referred them to committee for burial would have passed in silence. As the exhaustive debate drew to a close, Morris withdrew the Ohio petitions so attention was drawn exclusively to a set of petitions offered by Buchanan, which he had assured the Senate he could not support.

The result was compromise. The petitions were received, upholding the principle that citizens had the right to petition. Calhoun won on the substance. In a final vote, the Senate split thirty-six to six to reject the petitions' prayer, thus declaring that the question of abolishing slavery in the District of Columbia did not merit even the sham process of being referred to committee.[62] The lopsided vote was mere gauze, however, over the bitterness the debate had invoked. Two days later the Senate voted to lay all such future petitions on the table, a sentence of legislative oblivion.[63]

Decades later, first-term Illinois congressman Abraham Lincoln introduced a bill for the gradual abolition of slavery in the capital, subject to approval by District voters and compensation to slaveowners if the measure passed. It vanished from sight thereafter. Slavery in the nation's capital, like the Fugitive Slave Act passed by the First Congress, remained an open national sore until both became central to the attempt to save the union in the Compromise of 1850.

In 1793 Eli Whitney, a Massachusetts native who had just graduated from Yale, stopped off at the Mulberry Grove plantation of a friend in Savannah, Georgia, on a trip south to begin a job. In conversation with planters, he learned of the need to find a way to efficiently remove the small seeds from cotton. Within ten days he had an answer. He invented the cotton gin. One man operating a prototype of his device, he wrote to an inquiring Thomas Jefferson, cleaned sixty to eighty pounds of cotton per day "and left work every day before sunset."[64]

Whitney's invention, along with others such as the power loom and carding machines, had cascading effects. In upland areas of South Carolina and Georgia, crops of flax and barley largely produced without slave labor had begun to take hold. In the year Whitney wrote to Jefferson, South Carolina exported nearly 100,000 bushels of Indian corn.[65]

But Whitney's gin, and variants of it that soon became available, increased the efficiency of cleaning cotton fiftyfold. Switching to cotton, one South Carolina historian wrote, "has trebled the price of land suitable to its growth, and when the crop succeeds and the market is favorable, the annual income of those who plant it is double to what it was before the introduction of cotton."[66] The nascent trend toward growing grain crops was swept aside in the rush to convert to cotton. The surge in cotton production brought a corresponding surge in the demand for slave labor. Unlike grain crops, cotton required attention during nine months of the ear, a regime well suited to slave labor that could be used in clearing new land, repairing roads and canals, and other tasks during the remainder of the year.

In 1790, the United States produced 3,000 bales of cotton, each weighing 500 pounds. In ten years, cotton production was up to 73,000 bales, growing by ten times that amount by 1830, and reaching nearly 4.7 million bales by 1860.[67] As demand grew for more land to produce cotton, the demand for more slaves grew accordingly. On average, the country's slave population grew by 28 percent each decade from 1790 to 1860.[68] As demand for slave labor grew, Virginia became a continuing source for the sale of slaves into the Deep South, and slavery underwent a conversion into an industrial system.

The South's ability to supply cotton was matched by Great Britain's corresponding demand for it as feed stock to textile mills that sparked its own industrial revolution.[69] By 1805 half of the cotton used in British textile mills came from the United States, with demand reaching more than a half million bales by 1820.[70] On the eve of the Civil War, Britain imported 88 percent of its cotton from the American South, a trade that netted nearly 60 percent of the dollar value of all U.S. exports.[71] The profit loop encompassed New England shipping merchants who transported the crop across the Atlantic. Massachusetts's earliest stirrings of industrial development occurred as southern-supplied textile mills opened there, often employing young women.

More slaves to grow more cotton required more land. As historian D. A. Tompkins phrased it, "Side by side slavery and cotton pushed westward into the 'back country' of the Carolinas, across the pine hills and prairies of Georgia and Alabama, took complete possession of the alluvial lands along the Mississippi and Red rivers, and by 1860 were laying claim to the great central region of Texas."[72] On reaching the lower Mississippi, the push ran into an already well-established slave labor plantation culture, fed by refugees from Caribbean revolts during the 1790s and Spanish imperial support to link the region with the wider world of Atlantic commerce.[73] A few regions of the South proved inhospitable to slave-dependent cotton plantations. For reasons of soils and topography, eastern Tennessee, the northern Georgia piedmont, northern Alabama's sandhill region, and central Mississippi's oak lands remained largely free of slavery.[74] Free labor yeoman farmers dominated those regions that became pockets of opposition to succession and, in some instances, loyalty to the Union when the Civil War came.

⌁

The political struggle during the First Congress over Treasury Secretary Alexander Hamilton's economic plans initiated a series of regional divides that significantly contributed to the ultimate demise of Federalism as a national force and the triumphant rise of Jeffersonian Republicanism. Nationalists, who read the Constitution liberally, as well as the nation's commercial interests, divided from states' rights advocates of strict constitutional construction representing agrarian interests. The rift between North and South became more prominent. Slavery did not play an overt role in the conflicts; its influence remaining submerged in the open debates over the direction of the nation's development.

History has bestowed a mantle of brilliance on Hamilton's financial reforms that set the wobbly nation on its feet economically by offering its citizens wealthy enough to do so the chance to buy a stake in its future. To borrow, the nation needed credit. To get credit, the nation needed to pay its bills. Those bills amounted to $79 million by Hamilton's estimate, foreign and domestic debt and interest currently due against projected revenue of $2.8 million. Instead of attempting the impossible—repaying the debt with higher taxes—Hamilton urged that the new government assume all of it, both state and national, and then refinance it by issuing bonds, making an individual's investment in them an investment in making the enterprise of nationhood work. A national bank was the capstone of his plan, an independent corporation created by government charter with power to both borrow and lend.

The bank bill came before Congress in December 1790, the last of Hamilton's reform measures but the one that set off the most intense debate in the House after passing the Senate, ten to six, in January. Madison led the opposition, a stance that sealed his estrangement from Washington and his administration and marked the beginning of his switch in emphasis from the Constitutional Convention's chief nationalist to the nation's most prominent voice, after Jefferson, for states' rights.[75]

Madison's attack centered on the core issue of whether Congress could exercise any power not specifically enumerated in the Constitution. South Carolina's John Rutledge had drafted the initial list of enumerated powers during the Constitutional Convention to assure that state prerogatives would remain secure from national encroachment. Colleagues of his such as Charles Pinckney had pointed to those restraints during the ratification debates as proof that a shield existed protecting the white South and its institutions including slavery.

During a February 2 floor debate, Madison meticulously examined the bank bill and found no constitutional support for it. The Constitution granted no authority to form corporations, he said, nor was a bank necessary for the enumerated powers of collecting taxes or borrowing money. In the minds of many members, the issue turned on the elastic clause James Wilson had originally inserted at the end of Rutledge's list of specific powers. That clause gave Congress the undefined power to make laws "necessary and proper" to carry out the enumerated powers. To discover authority to create a bank from the powers granted in the Constitution, Madison said, "would give to Congress an unlimited power; would render nugatory the enumeration of particular powers; would supersede all the powers reserved to the state governments."[76]

Fellow southerners bolstered Madison's argument. If the principles upon which the bank was being promoted were right, then where was the Constitution to be found, asked Maryland's Michael Stone. "Is it written? No. Is it among the archives? No. Where is it? ... It is registered in the brains of the majority!"[77] Georgia's James Jackson alluded to a division between the North and South, saying, "This plan of a national bank ... is calculated to benefit a small part of the United States, the mercantile interest only; the farmers, the yeomanry, will derive no advantage from it."[78] "A radical difference of opinion between ... the Eastern and Southern states" was evident in the debate, Virginian William Branch Giles said, from which an "unlimited ocean of despotism" could arise.[79]

Massachusetts's Fischer Ames led the debate in favor of the bank. His argument set a template that numerous Congresses later followed. "To declare, in detail, everything that government may do," he said, "could not be performed, and has never been attempted. It would be endless, useless, and dangerous. . . . Congress may do what is necessary to the end for which the Constitution was adopted, provided it is not repugnant to the natural rights of man, or to those which they have expressly reserved to themselves, or to the powers which are assigned to the states."[80]

The House passed the bank bill, with all but five of the thirty-nine votes in favor coming from the North and all but one of the twenty votes opposed coming from the South. After the Senate approved the bill on a voice vote, President Washington signed the bank bill into law.

The measure was not simply a legislative defeat for men such as Madison. It signaled for them an essential breach in the underlying compact of union. Spearheaded by Hamilton and pushed through by pro-administration majorities in Congress, the bank in their eyes was a dangerous consolidation of power. The principles upon which it was passed constituted a violation of the Constitution. The depth of this feeling can be read in a letter Jefferson wrote to Madison the following year in reference to a plan to set up a state bank in Virginia that would recognize and work with the Bank of the United States.

The Virginia Assembly, Jefferson wrote, should reason that "the power of erecting banks and corporations was not given to the general government. It remains with the state itself. For any person to recognize a foreign legislature [Congress] in a case belonging to the state itself, is an act of *treason* against the state, and whosoever shall do any act under colour of the authority of a foreign legislature whether by signing notes, issuing or passing them, acting as director, cashier or in any other office relating to it shall be adjudged guilty of high treason and suffer death accordingly, by the judgement of the state courts."[81] These are not the words of a man disappointed with a legislative outcome. They express the secretary of state's belief that the administration, and more particularly Alexander Hamilton himself, had provoked a crisis in governance. By decade's end, it was a crisis that would lead both men to contemplate the use of force and possible disunion to right the situation.

From passage of the bank bill to 1800, Jefferson struggled to vindicate his concepts of liberty and republican government in the face of what he saw as concerted efforts to destroy them. His stance and Federalist opposition to it eventually coalesced into the model of competing political parties familiar in modern times. But in Jefferson's time that competition was a desperate affair. Jefferson led a sectional struggle in which he believed the stakes were no less than freedom or tyranny. The struggle verged on a violent national rupture ultimately producing the predicates for states' rights justifications of nullification and secession that ended in the Civil War.

Events in Europe framed the political context in America. In 1793, France declared war on Britain. Washington declared American neutrality, infuriating those who believed the country should side openly with France. British warships began seizing American merchant vessels and impressing American sailors. War fever arose in the country just as France dispatched Edmond-Charles Genêt as its ambassador to the United States. Citizen Genêt was received on a wave of pro-French sentiment in the nation it had helped to win the Revolutionary War. To forestall war with Britain, Washington sent his own negotiator to London. The resulting treaty achieved its purpose but only after laying bare a sectional rift between pro- and antiadministration factions. The split can be seen in the House vote over funding the treaty where 80 percent of northern members approved it and 74 percent of those from the South were opposed.[82]

During this period of polarization over foreign affairs, Jefferson sharpened a scathing attack on the direction of domestic policy embodied in Alexander Hamilton's economic program. Hamilton's system "was calculated to undermine and demolish the republic," Jefferson wrote privately to Washington. The wealth that members of Congress accumulated from it was corrupting that institution and made it impossible to view legislative decisions "as measures of a fair majority."[83]

The Constitution, he wrote, was undermined by a Hamiltonian interpretation giving the government power to do whatever it decided advanced the general welfare that Jefferson saw as a grant of unlimited power. From these beliefs emerged Jefferson's conviction that "monocrats" were in league at the pinnacle of power to impose a monarchical regime overthrowing American liberty while corrupting representative government in Congress. "An Anglican, monarchial and aristocratical party has sprung up," wrote Jefferson in another letter during this period to a friend in Italy, "whose avowed object is to draw over us . . . the forms of the British government. . . . It would give you a fever were I to name to you the apostates who have gone over to these heresies, men who were Samsons in the field and Solomons in the council, but who have had their heads shorn by the harlot England."[84] Even Washington was complicit.

No attempt or plan ever existed to overthrow the government with monarchy.[85] No serious corruption of Congress by bribery for votes infected that institution. Jefferson's repetition of these charges appears to the modern eye as hyperbole stretched into fantasy. As such, many have interpreted Jefferson's words as an anomaly, a rhetorical excess of verbal exuberance from the republic's most eloquent spokesman. Following on from this judgment is the easy dismissal that there was any real foundation to Jefferson's belief that he was engaged in a life-or-death struggle to redeem the great prize won by revolution, the liberty of the American people. The entire affair, for many historians, has been reduced to an excessive display of partisanship that nonetheless forged a dominant two-party system in America.

This reading is wrong on the first count and misleading on the second. Jefferson had ample reason to believe a monarchical plot to corrupt the government was fully alive at the seat of power. The cure he fought for was not a political party to compete in opposition to a legitimate rival, but an overwhelming political movement to wipe out the evil perceived. His opponents saw the struggle in much the same light, a fight in which one side must crush the other.[86]

The Revolutionary War was the crucible that forged Jefferson's political beliefs. In the Declaration of Independence, he articulated the great cause that had emerged to liberate humanity. Against a free peoples' unalienable rights to life, liberty, and the pursuit of happiness was arrayed a British king ruling over a monarchical consolidation of power, backed by a standing army and secured by a Parliament corrupted by the influence of money and the placement of royal sycophants among its members. Jefferson's frame of reference was his own experience and the example set by the Whig opposition to King George III.

In that context, monarchy was not limited to the literal image of a king with scepter and crown. The word connoted a pervasive consolidation of power into a centralized system run by ministers ruling over distant domains. A standing army was not so much a prudent precaution for defense readiness as the monarch's coercive presence among the people. Corruption was more insidious. It might be exercised, in the case of Britain, by the influence of the Bank of England over the personal or commercial affairs of members of Parliament. Court money might be used to purchase parliamentary elections. Corruption was compounded by the placement of officers loyal to the crown, or owing other favors to the king, in the halls of Parliament intended as the people's check on abusive monarchical power.[87]

The Constitution contains a clause, little noted today, illustrating the framers' awareness of the corrupting power of what were then commonly called "placemen." Article I, Section 6, provides that no senator or representative shall be appointed to any civil office while serving and that no one holding any office under the United States shall be a member of Congress during the term of office. This provision was adopted as a roadblock to the corruption of Congress by the means that the crown had used to infiltrate Parliament.

From Jefferson's perspective, the forces that had compelled the colonies to rebellion were rampant in America's new government. His

Alexander Hamilton.
COURTESY OF THE LIBRARY
OF CONGRESS.

opposition to them was not a flight of exuberance but a rallying cry to patriots to defend the principles of the Revolution. A manifesto laying out the nascent terms of Jeffersonian republicanism was published in 1794 by Jefferson's close friend and fellow Virginian John Taylor. Taylor, known as John Taylor of Caroline to denote the county of his residence, was one of the most influential political thinkers of his time. Though largely overlooked today, his writings became guidebooks for generations of proponents of a states' rights, limited government view of governance. He wrote a draft of *An Enquiry into the Principles and Tendency of Certain Public Measures* in the spring of 1793. Madison received the draft and shared it with Jefferson who, Madison wrote, "is in rapture with the performance of our friend in C-l-n-e."[88] Jefferson arranged for its publication shortly before the opening of the next Congress to produce "the greatest possible" effect.[89]

"The bank of the United States, is the master key of the system which governs the administration," Taylor wrote at the opening of his ninety-two-page pamphlet. The system's purpose was to erect "aristocracy and monarchy" through which "a *money impulse*, and not the *public good*, is operating in Congress."[90] So far as members of Congress were bank stockholders "an illegitimate interest is operating in the national legislature," and insofar as foreigners could buy bank stock, "The English who could not conquer us, may buy us."[91]

As was well known at the time, one-third of the members of Congress subscribed to the Bank of the United States' initial public offering.[92] The bank, Taylor wrote, created a division not just between monocrats and republicans, but had a sectional reality as well, dividing "the great mass of the people by geographical line."[93] As was also well known at the time, the twenty-five-member bank board of directors included only three southerners, an indication that commercial northern interests rather than southern agrarian ones derived the greatest benefits from it.[94]

Washington himself was implicated, as those who were betraying the Constitution were "getting possession of the fortress, while the commandant is unsuspicious of the fraud. . . . They style themselves 'federalists,' though it is obvious that they disregard the constitution, in its principles, as well as letter."[95]

Taylor singled out Hamilton, writing, "A minister intoxicated with influence, will exclaim, 'Public debt is a public blessing.' . . . Where does the constitution contemplate an influential character in the person of the Secretary of the Treasury, entitling him to prescribe to Congress political dogmas? Or where arises the right of the federal government, to apply stimulants to industry?"[96] The bank, he concluded, "is unconstitutional . . . and that with other measures of administration, it proceeds unerringly and infallibly to autocracy and monarchy."[97] Those who opposed Hamilton's system deserved "the appellation of 'a band of patriots,' [rather] than the epithet of 'a party,' as they are not contending for the benefits of a part, but for the whole community."[98]

Jefferson could hardly have said it better. He much preferred, in fact, that other men assume the public face of opposition, even though he had resigned as secretary of state in early 1794 and returned to his plantation, Monticello. The need to maintain a discreet secrecy was reinforced in 1797 when Jefferson became vice president, losing the presidential election to John Adams by three Electoral College votes. As Adams's

John Taylor of Caroline. SOURCE: WIKIMEDIA COMMONS/ THE ABBEVILLE INSTITUTE.

principal opponent in the election, Jefferson obviously led the emerging Republican faction. As vice president, however, he felt constrained not to break openly with an administration he ostensibly served. For the next four years an extensive part of his communications was conducted in secrecy through private conversations and letters often entrusted to couriers to avoid prying by Federalist postal officials.

As the nation's first peaceful transition of power was made from one administration to another, Washington fulfilled what he saw as his last great public obligation. His farewell address is often remembered today for its admonition to avoid foreign entanglements. The main body of it, however, and its opening warning was for the citizenry to hew closely to union. "Your union," Washington wrote, "ought to be considered as a main prop of your liberty." In surveying "causes which may disturb our Union," he first warned against parties competing "by geographical discriminations, Northern and Southern, Atlantic and Western. . . . The common and continual mischiefs of the spirit of party are sufficient to make it the interest and duty of a wise people to discourage and restrain it."[99]

The just decided election, however, was a clear marker of both emerging party and regional division. Jefferson's Democratic-Republican slate had not received a single Electoral College vote north of Pennsylvania. That section of the country gave Adams' Federalist electors two-thirds of his winning margin. The coming political battles would be fought along that fault line, a commercially centered North, supportive of strong government, and the more agrarian white South prepared to assert the priority of states' rights.[100]

—◦—

The pendulum of political sentiment in America was shifting as Adams took office. The treaty with Britain calmed war fever. A treaty with Spain assuring free navigation of the Mississippi won the administration wide support among westerners. France's Citizen Genêt had long since squandered the rousing support of his initial reception into widespread contempt for, among other things, purchasing and fitting out French privateers in American ports. His conduct, Madison wrote to James Monroe, "has been that of a madman."[101] French ire at the British treaty prompted the ruling Directory in Paris to authorize seizures of American shipping in retaliation. A new war fever directed at France began to seize the country. Envoys sent to Paris were refused an audience with Foreign Minister Talleyrand unless they first paid a bribe, touching off the XYZ affair, an anonymous reference to the French officials who demanded the bribe, which did not become public knowledge until the following year. Once the bribe demand was disclosed, Adams' resistance to declaring war against France left him isolated in his own administration. The Federalists split between the president and his scattered and poorly organized supporters and a High Federalist faction Hamilton led that wanted war with France and a British alliance that would likely open lucrative shipping rights in the French West Indies.

Adams agreed to legislation levying new taxes to outfit the navy and conceded to raising an army of twelve infantry regiments of 700 men each. The new warships were authorized to seize French vessels preying on American merchant carriers off the eastern seaboard. The new army was nominally to be led by Washington, but ground command was allotted to Alexander Hamilton, who had long harbored dreams of military glory. A quasi war with France was under way.

The vice president viewed the scene with dismay. In June 1798, he wrote John Taylor of Caroline, who had forwarded information about consideration being given to have Virginia and North Carolina break from the union. Jefferson urged patience. A "reign of witches" led by Massachusetts and Connecticut "ride us very hard, cruelly insulting our feelings as well as exhausting our strength," he wrote, but the distress would pass. His letter notes that "there must from the nature of man be opposite parties . . . and one of these for the most part must prevail over the other for a longer or shorter time." These words are often pointed to as proof that Jefferson accepted the framework of rival political parties legitimately vying for power. But his letter also states that "our present situation is not a natural one."

The populace of New England "will ever be the minority," his message read, that must eventually be overtaken by the far broader majority of "our countrymen [who are] substantially republican through every part of the union."[102] The natural state of affairs Jefferson envisioned was one in which republicanism ruled the country and pushed its Federalist opponents into a pocket of northeastern irrelevance.[103] The challenge was for the "band of patriots" to rekindle the revolutionary Spirit of '76, sweep aside the monocrats infecting government, and restore liberty on republican principles. Jefferson's object was not to compete for power with the Federalists, but to lead a Republican restoration of true principles.

By mid-summer 1798, Congress had passed legislation that struck Jefferson as an acute attack on the foundation of American liberty. A pair of Alien Acts gave the president sole discretionary power to designate any foreign national as an undesirable alien and order his or her deportation. Any male citizen of a hostile nation was subject to imprisonment or deportation. To avoid arrest, many French ex-patriots soon began booking passage home. The Sedition Act essentially made criticizing the government a crime. More than twenty newspaper publishers supportive of the Democratic-Republican movement were jailed for writing "false, scandalous and malicious" reports about the government.

In the early republic, freedom of speech and the press were not viewed as rights that the First Amendment granted to the people. They were rights that the people possessed irrespective of government, unalienable rights, birthrights of freedom that must be shielded from government intrusion. The idea that a citizen could be jailed for criticizing a government official was anathema to the concept of liberty and a profound blunder by the Federalists who espoused it. The recourse of dictators was to shut off dissent. The offensiveness of the Alien Acts was ameliorated because they applied to foreigners, not citizens, but coming in tandem with the Sedition Act they raised the specter of violating a citizen's fundamental rights to due process of law and trial by jury that early critics of the Constitution had insisted be incorporated in the Bill of Rights.

The Federalists dug in their heels, fighting criticism of the government's military preparations and new taxes to pay for them as slander punishable by the Sedition Act. They wanted war with France, and to get it, they wanted Republicans opposed to war intimidated, thrown on the defensive, and silenced. In reaction, protests against the Alien and Sedition Acts arose in many sections of the country, North as well as

South. A gathering in Lexington, Kentucky, drew more than 4,000 people who passed resolutions condemning the measures and vowing to arm themselves should violent resistance become necessary.[104] Petitioners in Mifflin County, Pennsylvania, declared "all laws restraining the freedom of speech and of the press, are nugatory and void."[105]

To Jefferson, the acts' violations of constitutional freedoms were obvious. The Sedition Act could hardly stand against a plain reading of the First Amendment's requirement that "Congress shall make no law . . . abridging the freedom of speech, or of the press. . . ." In addition, he saw the acts accurately as deliberate measures to silence and intimidate his supporters in the upcoming 1800 presidential election. His own views, if publicly expressed, could result in his arrest. His situation, both politically and personally, was desperate. Acting behind a cloak of secrecy, Jefferson decided on a radical strategy. In defense of liberty, he set out to articulate the rationale for states to declare federal law null and void, propositions that ultimately encompassed possible secession and disunion.[106] Jefferson's militant states' rights stance would be recrafted and repeated by white southern leaders up to the Civil War and used after it to obscure the primary role slavery played in the union's breakup.

In August, Jefferson began writing a set of resolutions, intended for state legislative action, framing his strategy to confront the Federalists. The Constitution, he reasoned, was a compact among states that had delegated "certain definite powers" to the federal government, reserving all others to themselves. The Tenth Amendment made that limited grant of power explicit. From this premise it followed that "whensoever the general government assumes undelegated powers, its acts are unauthoritative, void, and of no force." It was further within the purview of each individual state to determine when the federal government had assumed undelegated power, or abused delegated power. In the latter case, voters could alter the composition of Congress to redress the grievance. But if undelegated power was assumed by the federal government, "a nullification of the act is the rightful remedy," and each state has the right "to nullify of their own authority."[107]

Having set the premise, Jefferson's resolutions then declared the Alien and Sedition Acts unconstitutional, having no basis in delegated authority and being outside the Constitution's requirements for due process, in terms of the Alien Acts, and violative of the First Amendment's protection of freedom of the press, in terms of the Sedition Act. Next, Jefferson launched into a rhetorical fury at the consequences should legislation such as the Alien and Sedition Acts be allowed to stand. Congress, he wrote, could declare any act a crime and delegate to the president, or to anyone else, the authority of being "accuser, counsel, judge and jury" so that citizens would be reduced "as outlaws, to the absolute dominion of one man." Unless checked, such acts would "drive these States into revolution and blood" as new pretexts were found "for those who wish it to be believed that man cannot be governed but by a rod of iron." These words reflect how desperate the situation had become, at least so far as Jefferson saw it. Despotism or a new revolution were impending.

Finally, the resolutions called for the formation of a committee of correspondence among the states, inviting them to "concur in declaring these acts void, and of no force." In sum, the vice president was advocating a state's right to nullify federal law, and, as a remedy of last resort, secession.[108]

In October, Jefferson's close friend Wilson Cary Nicholas gave the draft resolutions, under a strict vow of secrecy as to their author, to John Breckinridge, a Kentucky planter and horse breeder, who was then a member of the state House of Representatives. Struck by some of the draft's more extreme language, Breckinridge modified it before introducing it in the legislature. The entire section describing the terrible consequences of blood, despotism, and revolution was stricken, and along with it the assertion that each state had a right to nullify federal law found to be based on undelegated powers.[109] Jefferson's intent remained intact, however. The Kentucky Resolutions passed by both legislative houses in November called on other states to concur in declaring the Alien and Sedition Acts "void and of no force." But it ended paradoxically with a more moderate plea, not included in Jefferson's original draft, that the states join Kentucky "in requesting their repeal at the next session of Congress."[110]

The ambiguity suited Jefferson. In a letter to Madison a few days after the Kentucky Resolutions passed, he wrote, "I think we should . . .

leave the matter in such a train as that we may not be committed absolutely to push the matter to extremities, and yet may be free to push as far as events will render prudent."[111]

Madison took the next step, drafting resolutions designed for the Virginia legislature. John Taylor of Caroline introduced them in December. Opening with professions of loyalty to the Constitution and union, they declared that the federal government resulted from a compact, to which the states were parties, granting limited, enumerated powers. When the federal government exercised "deliberate, palpable, and dangerous" powers not granted by the Constitution, the resolutions asserted, the states had the right and duty "to interpose for arresting the progress of the evil." The resolutions called on the states to join Virginia in declaring the Alien and Sedition Acts unconstitutional. Just before the final vote, Taylor deleted wording that Jefferson had first proposed declaring the acts "null, void and of no force, or effect."[112] The final result was that the General Assembly concluded the Alien and Sedition Acts were unconstitutional, asked other states to join them in that view, and instructed the governor to send the resolutions to other states and to Virginia's congressional delegation.[113]

Even before he learned that the Virginia Resolutions had been approved, Madison cautioned Jefferson about a crucial point concerning the compact among states theory of the Constitution. "Have you ever considered thoroughly the distinction between the power of the state, and that of *the legislature*, on questions of the federal pact," he asked.[114] The state legislatures had neither written nor adopted the Constitution. The charter's opening phrase, "We the people of the United States," was a deliberate formulation acknowledging that only the citizenry had the sovereign power to delegate its authority to a government of its own choosing. The conventions held in each state to ratify the Constitution were elected by the voters in those states, not by the legislatures. This distinction would later underlie the position that no state had unilateral authority to dissolve a constitution created by the consent of the people of all of the states that had ratified it, that secession was unconstitutional.

The anonymous author of a pamphlet titled *Plain Truth*, issued in response to the Virginia Resolutions, caught the distinction, writing that the assertion that the Constitution was a compact among the states was "untrue . . . and dangerous in principle." *Plain Truth* asserted, "In point of right, no state can withdraw itself from the Union. In point of policy, no state ought to be permitted to do so." The Constitution, the article stated, "was in truth what it professes to be—entirely the act of the people themselves. It derives no portion of its obligation from the state governments. It was sanctioned by the people themselves."[115] Virginian Henry Lee, father of Robert E. Lee, wrote *Plain Truth*.

The *Richmond Observatory* saw the matter differently. "Is not the Constitution a contract between the different states?" the paper asked. "Are not they to judge whether this contract be broken or violated? If congress can annual a contract with a foreign nation because of its violation will not the same justice operate to modifying or annulling a contract between states?"[116] The Virginia Resolutions nowhere argued for succession, but the *Observatory* read them as a possible justification for just that.

The resolutions received no endorsements from southern legislatures. In the North, they were uniformly condemned. The Pennsylvania legislature declared the Kentucky Resolutions a "revolutionary measure" and condemned the Virginia Resolutions as "calculated . . . to destroy the very existence of government."[117] The legislatures in Delaware, New York, Connecticut, Rhode Island, Massachusetts, New Hampshire, and Vermont answered Virginia with varying levels of disapproval.

The controversy produced consideration on both sides, at least, of going beyond mere petitions, resolutions, and debates. In February 1799 Alexander Hamilton wrote to Massachusetts Senator Theodore Sedgwick urging that a report be quickly prepared defending the Alien and Sedition Acts. Even slight concessions might be recommended. Nothing, however, that might "court a shock" should be adopted. Then, more menacingly, Hamilton wrote, "In the meantime the measures for raising the military force should proceed with activity. . . . When a clever force has been collected let them be drawn towards Virginia . . . and then let measures be taken to . . . put Virginia to the test of resistance."[118]

Rumors spread in Congress of preparations for armed resistance in Virginia. The governor and legislature there took action on plans that had long been in the making to purchase 5,000 rifles and build an armory. Tensions were verging toward violence.[119]

Jefferson was dismayed at the cool reception the Kentucky and Virginia Resolutions had received in the white South and the vehement opposition to them in the North. A defense of the resolutions was needed. Critics must not be allowed the last word. He was convinced that public opinion not only in the white South, but in large sections of the North as well, saw the Alien and Sedition Acts as dangerously overstepping legitimate constitutional authority. But he urged caution. At the same time Hamilton called for raising an army, Jefferson wrote a colleague that "the only thing we have to fear [is] the appearance of an attack of force against the government."[120] In a second letter the following day, he wrote, "we fear that the ill-designed may produce insurrection, nothing could be so fatal. Anything like force would check the progress of the public opinion and rally them round the errors of the government."[121]

Conferring with Madison, who had left Congress for a seat in the Virginia House of Delegates, Jefferson urged his friend to draw up a report for the General Assembly to answer the critics of the states' resolutions. The message should firmly defend the principles declared in the resolutions but "express in affectionate and conciliatory language our warm attachment to union with our sister-states." Not all errors or wrongs committed by the government should be considered as "cause of scission." The people's patience and indulgence would ultimately produce a return to true principles, but, he wrote, if that did not happen, the report should express a determination "to sever ourselves" from the union.[122] This advice was given in private. The depth of Jefferson's resolve to take the matter even to consideration of dissolution of the union was not revealed until decades later when his correspondence was made public. His authorship of the Kentucky Resolutions was not widely known until 1821.

Madison was more reserved. He drafted what became known as the Report of 1800, a document that proponents of nullification later used to justify their stance. It opened with "a firm resolution to maintain and defend the Constitution," declaring "a warm attachment to the union of the states." No threat of secession was made. In tightly reasoned legal arguments, the report justified each of the resolutions as fully consistent with constitutional principles. "The right of freely examining public characters and measures," the report asserted, "is the only effectual guardian of every other right." On the crucial issue of legislative declarations that acts of Congress are unconstitutional, the report concluded that they "are expressions of opinion, unaccompanied with any other effect, than what they may produce on opinion."[123]

The Report of 1800 roused little notice as the nation moved toward an election to decide whether Federalists or Republicans would lead the country into the new century. But the concepts of interposition, nullification, and, by extension, secession articulated by Jefferson and Madison persisted. At its core, Jefferson postulated that republican government, limited in authority to block a consolidation of power by a strict interpretation of the Constitution, resting securely on states' rights, was not an option or a choice, but was *necessary* for liberty to thrive. By extension, to preserve liberty it became *necessary* to break with a government that no longer upheld those values.

The genie was out of the bottle.

CHAPTER 3

Thomas Jefferson and the Empire of Liberty

THOMAS JEFFERSON has had more influence than any other figure in American history as the source of political lineages that have governed and defined the nation, and continue to do so to this day. His ideas were not complex or even original. Jefferson readily acknowledged that the Declaration of Independence's founding principles were drawn from the common sentiments and writings of the day.[1] His gift was to give them eloquence. The core of his political philosophy can be set down in a few lines of text. Their strength is their origin and simplicity. They come from the common people who had won their freedom and intended to keep it. They are expressed, with the added forcefulness of Jefferson's wording, in the language that they themselves used and understood. Thomas Jefferson did not so much establish a political party, as a great mass of the people created one around a definition of America he articulated. Every major political party since then has crafted itself, at least in some measure, around that definition, tracing itself back to the validating source of Jefferson.

And no American more embodied the contradiction between liberty and slavery that tortured much of the white South during the nation's early years as did Thomas Jefferson.

———

The 1800 presidential election that was to see the first transfer of power from one partisan faction to another was fraught and closely run.[2] When the Electoral College ballots were counted, Jefferson tallied eight more votes than John Adams, seventy-three to sixty-five. But in an Electoral College quirk it would take a constitutional amendment to fix, Jefferson's vice-presidential running mate Aaron Burr also received seventy-three ballots. The tie shifted the decision of who would be the next president of the United States into the House of Representatives, where each of the sixteen state delegations was accorded one vote. Jefferson's partisans had won a nearly two-to-one majority in the 1800 House elections. But the House that would select the next president was made up of the Federalist-controlled rump session of that body elected two years previously. The Senate, which might conceivably choose a new president if the House deadlocked and the office remained vacant past the mandated March 4 inauguration, was also Federalist controlled.

Chances for intrigue were rife. One line of speculation had the Federalists pulling off a coup, bypassing both Jefferson and Burr via a series of maneuvers and installing one of their own in a White House still under construction. A second line held that Burr might betray his mentor, strike a deal with the Federalists, and win the prize. As inconclusive ballot followed inconclusive ballot in the House, Pennsylvania's governor made plans to call out the militia if the Federalists attempted to steal the presidency.[3] As it turned out, the Federalists received indirect assurances that Jefferson would neither shrink the navy nor sweep Federalist appointees from office. These proved sufficient so that on the seventh day of voting, and the thirty-sixth ballot, Thomas Jefferson was declared the victor.

Although he captured the presidency, Jefferson's victory was marred, notably in the eyes of many northern voters. At least twelve of his electoral votes came from the inflated Electoral College representation given to southern states by the Constitution's federal ratio, counting three-fifths of all slaves in determining population figures to apportion seats in the House of Representatives. Without those votes, derived from the nation's nearly 900,000 slaves, John Adams would have won reelection.[4] Despite protests, particularly from New England, that the new administration was riding into the temple of liberty on the backs of slaves, the constitutional process had worked its will.

For Jefferson, nothing about the victory was marred or marginal. The triumph was far greater than an affirmation of his candidacy. What occurred was "the revolution of 1800, for that was as real a revolution in the principles of our government as that of 76 was in its form," he declared upon reflection some years later.[5] The Federalists, and with them the dangers of consolidated government and a corrupted Congress, had been reduced to a mere enclave in New England and a few scattered members elsewhere. The election confirmed in Jefferson's mind that "the republicans are the *nation*"; the victory was not the temporary ascendancy of a political party but a popular validation of values that made America exceptional among the nations of the world.[6] Jefferson had no doubt that "the last hope of human liberty in this world rests on us."[7] To realize that hope, Jefferson had long envisioned an "empire of liberty," of as yet unbounded extent but one such as "has never been surveyed since the creation."[8]

Taken as a whole, Jefferson's vision is breathtaking. He spoke in terms of the politics of destiny that would unite generations in a common cause. To a remarkable degree, arguably greater than any other figure in American political life, his vision has endured the test of time. Liberty remains a standard that inspires the men and women of this country, and of others across the globe. America has served as a beacon to the world, a status now under severe test. The continental empire of republican governance he envisioned came to pass. Not until Abraham Lincoln did an American leader express such a compelling cause as did Jefferson.

And Lincoln's call for a rebirth of freedom was based on the premise that all men are created equal as expressed in the Declaration largely written by Jefferson. No single strand of Jeffersonian tradition predominated in American life. Shortly after assuming power, Jeffersonian Republicans began diverging. Old Republicans of strict constructionist, states' rights views flowed into a path that created Andrew Jackson's Democratic Party, which held almost uninterrupted sway in American politics up to the outbreak of the Civil War. A more moderate Jeffersonian wing pursued an expanding empire of republican governance fostered by the national government's incentives for internal improvements and tariff protections of domestic manufactures that evolved into the Whig Party. Democratic icon Andrew Jackson and Whig leader Henry Clay both claimed fealty to the true principles of Jeffersonian democracy.

Jefferson's grand vision was as grand a presumption set against the realities facing the country as the nineteenth century opened. Fewer than 300 elected officials and bureaucrats set about running the national government from the isolated town called Washington, D.C. Their task was to set national policy for a new country that had recently doubled in size and would double again with the soon-to-be-realized Louisiana Purchase. That great expanse of territory added to the nation's present dangers at least as much as it augured well for its future.

The country with a tiny navy and skeletal army had recently barely escaped two wars, one with the British who still dominated the Atlantic and glowered from the north in Canada, and another with France, now entering the Napoleonic Era, that harbored renewed ambitions in the West Indies, America's second-largest trading partner. Looking south, a weaker empire, the Spanish, occupied the Florida territories and the lower Mississippi Valley, America's vital outlet to the sea. Cherokee, Chickasaw, Choctaw, Creek, Shawnee, and other native tribes stood hostile to white migration across the Appalachians toward the Mississippi.

At home, a disgruntled group of New England Federalists briefly conspired in a plot of disunion that collapsed as Jeffersonian Republicans continued to win elections.[9] That Jefferson and his new government could, under such conditions, effectively direct the destinies of his nation and its 5.3 million inhabitants has the aspect of absurdity.

But Jefferson's genius was that he had no intention of directing America's destiny. He was fully content to have the people direct it themselves. So long as the nation was united under a written constitution, strictly construed to protect states' rights by thwarting any concentration of power and governed by republican principles of representative government, the president was confident that the people could find their own way forward. And therein lay a national tragedy. For not only did the people—the white male governing class—have a passion for their own liberty, but many of them also had a passion that became an insatiable appetite to own other human beings as well.

Thomas Jefferson was fifty-seven years old when he entered the presidency. Tall, lanky, with rusty colored hair and a refreshing absence of pretense, he was nervous in front of large audiences but sparkling in private conversation, often given added fluency from his large store of imported wines. His array of attributes beyond political leadership is legendary: master of the violin and cello, architect, inventor, naturalist, one of the most progressive agriculturalists of his time, president of the American Philosophical Society, prolific letter writer and avid reader and collector of books (his 6,500 volumes became the seed stock of the Library of Congress), polyglot who was fluent or had a working knowledge of several languages including Greek and Latin and to a lesser degree French, and advocate for education and reason. The Age of Enlightenment reached self-realization in the person of Thomas Jefferson. He was, too, a remarkably self-contained man. Accounts from his letters and private conversations contain little if any hint of the self-questioning inner life that is part of normal human experience.

What Jefferson did reveal was a self-confident optimism in his country, its free people, and its future. The optimism that defined him was shared by and became a defining characteristic of free Americans. "A rising nation," Jefferson said in his first inaugural, "spread over a wide and fruitful land . . . advancing rapidly to destinies beyond the reach of mortal eye—when I contemplate these transcendent objects, . . . I . . . humble myself before the magnitude of the undertaking."[10]

The foundation of that abiding confidence, for Jefferson, rested on a few essential pillars based on the intellectual uprising of the Radical Enlightenment. Liberty was the first. He wrote that "rightful liberty is unobstructed action according to our will, within limits drawn around us by the equal rights of others."[11] For the first time in human history (for white male Americans), "the world's best hope . . . a chosen country" of free people was liberated from being shackled to having their station in life predetermined by birth and class or their government imposed upon them from above.[12] The foundation of liberty was, in turn, a written constitution of enumerated powers subject to strict construction balancing federal and state responsibilities under a republican system of representative government. To this edifice it was necessary to add reason, education, and a free press because, as Jefferson wrote, "If a nation expects to be ignorant and free . . . it expects what never was and never will be."[13] In this formulation no heed need be given that slaves remained shackled to their station predetermined by birth.

To thrive and to advance this enterprise, Jefferson looked to "the most valuable citizens, . . . the most vigorous, the most independent, the most virtuous," to the yeoman farmer.[14] "Those who labor in the earth," he believed, "are the chosen people of God . . . whose breasts he has made his peculiar deposit for substantial and genuine virtue."[15] Because this excerpt comes from his *Notes on the State of Virginia*, Jefferson presumably was referring to people he thought of as farmers who lived there. Although he called himself one, Jefferson never was a farmer. He never plowed, sowed, and harvested a single acre of land in his life. He had slaves do that for him on the plantations he owned. He had little understanding of the yeoman farmer's hardscrabble life without lines of credit available to the plantation owner, or the ability that he once exercised to sell more than fifty slaves to cover debt.[16] His own leisure to practice and contemplate the virtues of republican governance contrasted sharply with the constant labor and parochialism common to small-farm life.

The yeoman farmers of his time were not his Virginia neighbors but Dutch and German immigrants of the Hudson River Valley and

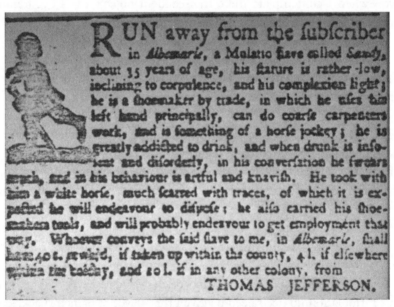

Thomas Jefferson placed this ad offering a reward for the return of his runaway slave Sandy in the *Virginia Gazette* in September 1769. SOURCE: *SLAVERY IMAGES*.

Pennsylvania, New Englanders, and upcountry Carolinians of mixed English and Scottish ancestry. For Jefferson, it was as if in expressing his vision he made slavery vanish from his mind, leaving only the image of the independent white farmer, hardworking and honest, prospering by the fruits of his labor, and ready to contribute to the public weal and defense of liberty. The image lives on in a thoroughly interdependent and largely urban nation where tradition still holds that the "heartland of America" is a special depository of virtue and democratic wisdom.

Jefferson paired his enshrinement of the yeoman farmer with contempt for wage-labor centers of manufacturing. "The mobs of great cities add just so much to the support of pure government," he wrote, "as sores do to the strength of the human body."[17] Artificers who made things with their hands were dependent on the caprice of their customers, Jefferson believed, and "dependence begets subservience and venality, suffocates the germ of virtue, and prepares fit tools for the designs of ambition."[18] His distrust of wage labor went so far, in one instance at least, as to override liberty's tenet of the individual's right to chart one's own future. In an extraordinary outburst when he was in his seventies, Jefferson wrote:

> *The agricultural capacities of our country constitute its distinguishing feature: and the adapting of our policy and pursuits to that, is more likely to make us a numerous and happy people than the mimicry of an Amsterdam, a Hamburg, or a city of London. Every society has a right to fix the fundamental principles of its association, and to say to all individuals that, if they contemplate pursuits beyond the limits of these principles, and involving dangers which the society choses to avoid, they must go somewhere else for their exercise, that we want no citizens . . . on such terms. We may exclude them from our territory, as we do persons infected with disease.*[19]

Jefferson had a penchant for the bold statement. On this issue, in the same year, he also wrote, "Experience has taught me that manufactures are now as necessary to our independence as to our comfort. . . . No one axiom can be laid down as wise and expedient for all times and circumstances."[20] But his heart surely sided with his own mythized vision of the yeoman farmer. The white yeoman farmer.

Jefferson's vision of the empire of liberty, where every free person held an equal rank of citizenship, so defined him and his country that over time the two became as one. What defined Jefferson defined America. The nation's sense of itself and of its aspirations were those embodied and expressed by Jefferson. This is the Jefferson who still lives in public imagination and whose image as sage and founder is etched in marble and cast in bronze.

The irony is that the fuller, more complete Jefferson, the one who abhorred slavery and at the same time helped lay the path for its expansion, was just as well the embodiment of the true America of his time, or at least of the Border South. His own internal contradictions played out in the contradictory roles his beliefs had in pre-Civil War America. To the South he was quoted as the author of states' rights theory underpinning slavery. To the North he was quoted as the author of the Declaration's assertion of the unalienable rights to life, liberty, and the

Thomas Jefferson from painting by Thomas Sully.
SOURCE: LIBRARY OF CONGRESS.

pursuit of happiness. In attempting to understand Jefferson's relationship to slavery, one begins to unlock an understanding of the white South's relationship to itself.

～

Jefferson's abhorrence of slavery is evident in his writings, particularly his private letters, throughout his life. "The whole commerce between master and slave is a perpetual exercise of the most boisterous passions, the most unremitting despotism on the one part, and degrading submissions on the other," he wrote in the early 1780s in *Notes on the State of Virginia*, a volume intended for private circulation but which became public.[21] Nearly thirty-five years later, well after he had left the White House, in a letter to a friend seeking advice on whether he should free his own slaves, he wrote, "The love of justice and the love of country plead equally the cause of these people, and it is a mortal reproach to us that they should have pleaded it so long in vain."[22]

A second strand in his convictions about slavery and Blacks in general is equally consistent. He wanted white America to be free of them. "Nothing is more certainly written in the book of fate than that these people are to be free," he wrote in his 1821 *Autobiography*. "Nor is it less certain that the two races, equally free, cannot live in the same government."[23] For Jefferson, two equally bleak prospects faced the nation if enslaved Blacks won their freedom. One was "amalgamation" producing "a degradation" to which no white person who loved his country could "innocently consent."[24] The other, and by far the more likely prospect in his mind, was "the extermination of one or the other race" in a bloody convulsion precipitated by "deep rooted prejudices entertained by the whites [and] ten thousand recollections, by the blacks, of the injuries they have sustained."[25]

The solution for the country and for the slave, Jefferson believed, was that "when freed, he is to be removed beyond the reach of mixture."[26] The removal Jefferson most favored was colonialization, perhaps to Africa, but certainly to some location beyond American borders. Soon after entering the presidency, Jefferson contemplated an empire of liberty that would expand across the continent, noting that "nor can we contemplate, with satisfaction, either blot or mixture on that surface."[27] Nearly two decades later, with slavery expanding to a flash point in Missouri and colonialization a discredited refuge of supposed reform, Jefferson confessed to the enormity of the danger that slavery posed, writing, "We have the wolf by the ear, and we can neither hold him, nor safely let him go."[28]

To the two major strands of Jefferson's beliefs about slavery can be added two major strands of what he did about it in his public life. With few exceptions, and those largely early in his political career, Jefferson preferred to remain a behind-the-scenes influence on the issue of slavery. The second strand, and most prominent as the years passed, was Jefferson's deference to what he saw as a public mind not yet ready to grapple with the issue. The private Jefferson recognized slavery as a moral evil and mortal threat to the country. Yet the most unmistakable aspect of his public stand on slavery, particularly after his return from France to join Washington's administration, is his silence on it. The dissonance between these two realities defines the contradiction within the man himself.

By his own account, Jefferson took political action on slavery seven times before becoming president. From a legislative perspective, all those efforts failed. The lessons he took away from the experience were not only that opposition to reform prevailed, but that too vocal a stand could harm him politically. In 1769, as a twenty-six-year-old freshman member of the Virginia legislature, Jefferson made his first foray. By his own account, written many years later, he enlisted the support of the more senior Richard Bland on a measure to permit masters to manumit their slaves. "I seconded his motion," Jefferson recalled, "and, as a younger member, was more spared in the debate; but he was denounced as an enemy to his country, and treated with the grossest indecorum."[29]

Five years later, as arguments mounted to justify a break from Great Britain, Jefferson wrote a document to help instruct Virginia's delegates to the first Continental Congress. "The abolition of domestic slavery is the great desire," he wrote, of Britain's American colonies. The British had "unhappily introduced" it, and the king had thwarted colonial efforts to end the African slave trade.[30] These sentiments were tucked into a lengthy exhortation of the crown's wrongs against the colonies. They became fodder two years later for the Declaration of Independence.

In his original draft of that instrument, Jefferson elaborated on Great Britain's and its king's guilt for waging "cruel war against nature itself" by violating the "most sacred rights of life and liberty in the persons of a distant people." It was they, not the colonists, who had introduced slavery to America, and George III who had refused petitions to end the slave trade.[31] Jefferson's peers deleted this clause, no doubt thinking it best not to disparage an institution vital to northern shipping interests and the southern economy as a whole. His 1776 draft for a Virginia constitution arrived in Richmond too late to be considered. It contained a clause freeing any slave brought into the state, effectively banning all forms of the slave trade in Virginia.[32]

In 1778 Jefferson chaired a committee charged with revising the state's laws. He proposed a measure to bar free Blacks, with an exception for seamen, from entering the state. Under a second measure, any slave freed by his or her master in Virginia would have to leave the state within one year, or be subject to reenslavement. A white woman bearing a Black man's child would also have a year to leave, or else be banished and her children bound to service. The legislature rejected these proposals. It never heard what he later described as a plan for gradual emancipation in the state prepared while he chaired the committee.

His *Notes on the State of Virginia* recount the plan, for which no other record exists. Under it, upon reaching adulthood, the children of slaves would be colonized to some "place as the circumstances of the time should render most proper." They were to be provided with supplies sufficient to start life. Once gone from Virginia, they would be declared "a free and independent people."[33]

Implementing such a plan would have entailed the wholesale and likely permanent separation of children from their parents and the deportation of those children to locations entirely foreign to them. The object of the measure Jefferson described was not so much to free Blacks from slavery as to free Virginia from the presence of Blacks. The aim was to forestall "amalgamation," to erase "any blot," to prevent racial war. Whether such a plan was ever rendered into legislative language is unknown. Jefferson certainly never introduced it. He later wrote that the plan died without being debated because "the public mind would not yet bear the proposition."[34]

When he first privately circulated copies of his *Notes on the State of Virginia* in 1785, Jefferson made clear that the sections concerning slavery "are the parts which I do not wish to have made public" lest they produce an "irritation" that would cause more harm than good.[35] He was, in fact, already resigned to the belief that major slavery reforms in the South could not be achieved by his own generation. "It is to . . . the rising generation" that he looked "and not to the one now in power for these great reformations."[36] Jefferson was then forty-one years old, and the Constitution had not yet even been written.

Jefferson's most ambitious proposal for emancipation in Virginia came in 1783. Consideration was then being given to revising the state's constitution. The idea did not then come to fruition, but it did prompt Jefferson to draft his own version. His provision on slavery read, "The General Assembly shall not . . . permit the introduction of any more slaves to reside in this state, or the continuance of slavery beyond the generation which shall be living on the 31st day of December 1800; all persons born after that day being hereby declared free."[37] Jefferson sent the draft to James Madison, asking him not to disclose his authorship. He also noted that his ideas may "serve as a basis for your amendment," indicating he realized that his sketch needed further work.[38] The slavery provision certainly would have provided a major incentive for Virginia slaveowners to sell their property southward before the emancipation deadline, an outcome he might have favored. The provision also allowed ample time for the state to develop an expatriation plan well in advance of emancipation. Either way, with no convention called, Jefferson's draft received no public attention.

As a member of the Continental Congress in 1784, Jefferson addressed slavery one more time, shortly before being sent to Paris on a diplomatic mission. As noted earlier in this work, his proposal to ban slavery in all the territories ceded by Britain in the treaty ending the Revolutionary War failed by a single vote. His plan included a sixteen-year grace period during which slavery could legally expand into all the territory north of the Ohio River where the Northwest Ordinance eventually prohibited it outright. Had his proposal been enacted, the ban most likely would have fallen to the force of events, and slavery become more entrenched north of the Ohio than it ever became.

Such then is a summary of Jefferson's record as a political leader on slavery before he became president. None of his legislative plans were enacted, only two bear some record of being openly discussed, and in nearly all his role was deliberately shielded from public attention. Of his two rhetorical forays on the subject, his peers suppressed that intended for the Declaration of Independence. His 1774 assertion that America's colonies wanted emancipation is contradicted by his later admission that "the public mind would not bear the proposition." The record is clear that Jefferson recognized slavery as a moral evil. Equally clear is that his preferred solution was a permanent separation of the races, by expatriating Blacks beyond American borders. The sum of it all reveals a political leader fully aware of a threat he felt paralyzed to confront effectively.

Jefferson expressed this duality throughout his life. In 1785 he wrote that the duty of those holding public office is "to conform themselves to the decided choice of their constituents."[39] Three years later, in relation to curtailing the slave trade and slavery itself, he vowed that "certainly nobody will be more willing to encounter every sacrifice for that object" than himself.[40] During his presidency he repeated that vow, writing in 1805, "Should an occasion ever occur in which I can interpose with decisive effect, I shall certainly know and do my duty with promptitude and zeal."[41] Yet only four months earlier he had confided to a friend "I have long since given up the expectation of any early provision for the extinguishment of slavery among us."[42]

Later in life his tone became even more resigned. "I wish to avoid all collisions of opinion with all mankind," he wrote in 1816.[43] A decade later, within weeks of his death, Jefferson wrote, "A good cause is often injured more by ill-timed efforts of its friends than by the arguments of its enemies. . . . The revolution in public opinion which this case requires is not to be expected in a day, or perhaps in an age, but time, which outlives all things, will outlive this evil also."[44] For Jefferson, time never presented the right opportunity to expend his enormous political capital in a cause he knew to be both morally compelling and necessary to his nation's safety.

During his presidency, with his ability to influence events at its height, Jefferson dealt with slavery on three separate occasions, each to be narrated later in this chapter. The pattern did not change, with the exception being Jefferson's call on Congress to abolish the foreign slave trade. That call was made in his sixth annual message to Congress. About midway through, the message includes two sentences dealing, not with the institution of slavery, but with ending the foreign slave trade that was almost universally deprecated throughout the country. Beyond making the call, Jefferson kept his role in enacting it shrouded from public view.

In 1773, within a year of his only marriage, Thomas Jefferson owned some 200 slaves and 10,000 acres of land dispersed among his Virginia plantations, Monticello, Poplar Forest, Shadwell, Lego, Milton, and Tufton.[45] He had married well, inheriting a considerable portion of his land and bondsmen from his father-in-law, John Wayles.

By the standards of his day, Jefferson was a fair master. The guide he recommended for the treatment of slaves was "to feed and clothe them well, protect them from ill usage, [and] require such reasonable labor only as is performed voluntarily by freemen."[46] He also, on occasion, exercised a master's harsher prerogatives. He had a slave named Jame Hubbard, who had twice run away, "flogged in the presence of his old companions."[47] In another case, he wanted a slave named Cary, who had badly injured another slave in a fight, sold south to Georgia, or to "any other quarter so distant as never more to be heard of among us . . . as if he were put out of the way by death."[48]

He was loath to sell any of his landholdings to pay debt, but on several occasions used proceeds from slave sales to do so. He could view his human property coolly in terms of their relative economic value. In a letter planning for the sale of twenty slaves to defer debt, Jefferson wrote, "I consider a woman who brings a child every two years as more profitable than the best man of the farm. What she produces is an addition to the capital."[49]

Thomas Jefferson expressed his beliefs about Blacks most fully in *Notes on the State of Virginia* and in a few private letters. In the *Notes* he wrote that he suspected that Blacks "are inferior to the whites in the endowments both of body and mind."[50] Some years later he acknowledged that "no person living wishes more sincerely than I do, to see a complete refutation of the doubts I have myself entertained and expressed on the grade of understanding allotted to them by nature, and to find in this respect they are on a par with ourselves."[51] No basic change of Jefferson's mind ever occurred.

He did concede as to Blacks that "whatever be their degree of talent it is no measure of their rights."[52] By implication this indicates that he thought Blacks were embraced within the Declaration's premise that "all men are created equal" and are endowed with "unalienable rights" to life, liberty, and the pursuit of happiness. As a slaveowner, he denied those rights while deploring the practice as an evil to both owner and slave. His practice contradicted his beliefs. His actions never forcefully or effectively attempted to resolve the conflict.

Jefferson's *Notes on Virginia* present a generalized sketch of Blacks that likely would have been readily subscribed to by his peers among the planter elite. Their color alone, he wrote, rendered Blacks less attractive than whites, whose skin could reflect the blush of emotions unseen in the "eternal monotony" of those with Black skin. He observed that because Blacks urinated less, and sweated more than whites, they had "a very strong and disagreeable odour." Although Blacks were at least as brave as whites, and more adventuresome, the slightest amusement would keep them up to midnight even though they knew work would begin at dawn. Black men were, he wrote, more ardent in love, than white, their griefs more transient and their afflictions less felt and sooner forgotten. "In general, their existence appears to participate more of sensation than reflection," while "in memory they are equal to the whites; in reason, much inferior." As to characteristics that defined Jefferson's own refinement, he observed that Blacks were incapable of thought more elevated than plain narration, their imaginations "dull, tasteless, and anomalous," and without any trait for painting or sculpture. He granted that Blacks were "generally more gifted than whites" in music but showed no talent in complex melody or complicated harmonies. To this litany may be added Jefferson's view of Blacks that "we find among them numerous instances of the most rigid integrity, and as many as among their better instructed masters, of benevolence, gratitude, and unshakable fidelity."[53]

A girl named Sarah "Sally" Hemings was one of the slaves Jefferson inherited.[54] She was his wife Martha's half sister. Both women were daughters of Jefferson's father-in-law, John Wayles, whose slave Elizabeth Hemings gave birth to Sally sometime in 1773. During her marriage to Jefferson, Martha gave birth to six children. Only two of them, Martha "Patsy" and Mary "Polly," survived to adulthood. Never in robust health, and with complications following the birth of her sixth child, who would die within two years, Martha was on her deathbed. Sally was likely one of those who attended her there. Martha's death in 1782 devastated Jefferson. When a little more than a year later he was called upon to become his country's minister to France, he readily accepted. With his daughter Patsy and Sally's older brother James, Jefferson departed Boston harbor in July 1784 to begin his service abroad. Three years later he arranged for Polly, accompanied by Sally, to sail for France, where she was to join her sister in a convent school at Panthemont outside Paris. The daughters visited their father at his Hôtel de Langeac residence where James Hemings became chef de cuisine. Sally, then fourteen years old, remained at the residence, too.

Sally Hemings was an attractive young woman with a pleasing disposition. No portraits exist of her, but a bondsman who knew her later during her life at Monticello described Sally as very handsome, "might near white," and with "long straight hair down her back."[55] In Paris, Jefferson purchased clothes for her and gave her a wage. She learned French and became familiar with the city. In 1789 Sally became pregnant with a child by Jefferson. At some point during that year, both she and her brother James also realized that under French law they were free. When Jefferson began preparations to return to America, Sally told him she would not go with him. She relented, according to the later account by her son Madison, when Jefferson promised her "extraordinary privileges, and made solemn pledge that her children should be freed at the age of twenty-one years."[56] Put differently, Jefferson promised to keep his own children with Sally enslaved only until they reached their majority. When she left Paris in September 1789, Sally Hemings was a sixteen-year-old slave girl who would give birth to the first of her six children with Jefferson the following spring.

In a work marked by both grace and candor, historian Annette Gordon-Reed writes of the Jefferson-Hemings relationship, "For some, the reality that Jefferson 'could have' raped Hemings is the only reality that counts. For it is here that we find, in concentrated form, the evil of slavery, the enormous power that one group had to control and wreak havoc in the lives of another. The problem with making what Jefferson 'could have' done the sole question is that it suggests that the actual details of Hemings's life are meaningless."[57]

Those details have never become known. What the record does reveal is that Jefferson's Monticello household, especially after his presidency, was largely kept in order by members of the Hemings family, including Elizabeth Hemings's siblings, their children, and her own children including Sally. In a role not unlike that of wife, Sally took care of Jefferson's rooms, clothing, and sewing, and remained with him until his death in 1826.

During his lifetime, Jefferson probably owned more than 400 slaves. He freed three of them while he was alive and five by his will when he died. All were his children by Sally or members of her family.[58] After his death Sally moved with her sons to a rented home in Charlottesville, where she lived until her death in about 1835.

In his ownership, treatment, and "boisterous passions" involving his bonded property, Jefferson fit well within the broad pattern of Virginia's elite slaveholding class, and of much of the slaveholding South generally. His belief that Blacks were an inferior race, however waveringly held, reflected a deep strand of racism that pervaded virtually all of white America during his lifetime. White America's unreflective conviction in its own superiority was not a sectional distinction, the Quaker and a few other exceptions notwithstanding. Jefferson's clinging to slavery, even after death, flatly contradicts his conviction of slavery's evil.

George Washington's will provided that his slaves be freed upon the death of his wife. As historian Paul Finkelman has pointed out, Jefferson's fellow Virginian John Pleasants freed all of his slaves during his lifetime; Powhatan county's Joseph Mayo freed his 150 slaves, and kinsman John Randolph granted freedom to 400 slaves in his will that also provided funds to purchase land for them.[59] Edward Coles, who had rejected Jefferson's 1814 advice not to free his slaves, took them instead to Illinois five years later, where he gave 160 acres of land to each family along with their freedom.

Jefferson's contradiction was in large measure the white South's contradiction. A great number of white southerners believed, as did Jefferson, that slavery was a mortal threat to the nation. Like him, they either could not summon the will to confront it or believed that the fight would be fruitless. Over time, a great number of white southerners resolved the conflict by adopting the view that slavery was a positive good and should be recognized as such, perpetuated and expanded. Those convictions helped transform the threat of civil war into reality.

Slavery was a stronger, more expansive institution when Jefferson left public life than when he began it. His share in the responsibility for that outcome makes up part of the narrative of the remainder of this chapter. Judgments of him on slavery, as might be expected, are divided. Looking to the causes of the Civil War, historian Robert Shalhope concludes "The Virginian helped to create the ideological underpinnings of the southern proslavery stance that made that war inevitable."[60] Keeping in mind the power of the principles expressed in the Declaration of Independence and Jefferson's lifelong descriptions of slavery's evils, scholar David Brion Davis writes "No one can deny that Jefferson's democratic ideals were of monumental importance for the later antislavery cause."[61] As his life was contradictory, so, too, are judgments of that life. It was as if Thomas Jefferson endured a civil war over slavery within himself.

In the spring of 1800, Gabriel Prosser began organizing an uprising among his fellow slaves aimed at seizing Richmond by force and negotiating their freedom. Gabriel was unusual among slaves in that he could not only read and write but was also a skilled laborer whose owner hired him out as a blacksmith in the Richmond environs. Gabriel was an imposing figure: about six feet two inches tall, muscular, quick of wit, and persuasive in speech. He was missing two front teeth and had some scars on his head and a brand on the palm of his hand put there as punishment for stealing a hog and striking a white man. He was twenty-four years old when his plan to seize freedom germinated in a political atmosphere in which Republican messages of liberty and equality were inspiring confidence among white Virginians that the coming elections would see the overthrow of the old regime and a new dawn under Jefferson.

Gabriel harbored the hope that a place might be found in the coming transformation for slaves like himself, if first they seized the initiative to declare their freedom. He recruited among the wide gamut of those he encountered along the James River wharfs of Richmond and its back-streets—fellow slaves with trades from plantations in the region, free Blacks and seamen, and other slaves moving goods for export down the river and imports up the river for delivery to the network of surrounding plantations where thousands of other slaves worked. Gabriel's relative freedom of movement gave him perfect opportunity to use Richmond as the hub from which to string out lines for coordinated rebellion. As summer approached, several hundred slaves from nearby Petersburg, Norfolk, and several surrounding counties were loosely tied into his plans.

With his forces marching under the flag of death or liberty, and using scythes fashioned into swords and other makeshift weapons, Gabriel laid out plans for a three-pronged attack on Richmond starting near his owner's plantation a few miles north of the city. Two of the armed bands were to create a diversionary fire in the warehouse district and seize a key bridge, while the third overran the armory and seized Governor James Monroe at his home near the statehouse. Those who resisted would be met with force, but Gabriel wanted no Quakers, Methodists, or French citizens killed. Once in control of the city, and with Monroe as hostage, reinforcements would come in from the surrounding area, and Gabriel believed he would be in a strong position from which to negotiate.

The uprising was set to begin Saturday night, August 30. Instead of clear, moonlit roads into the city, Gabriel and his immediate band of followers were met with a powerful thunderstorm that rendered the operation impossible. By late the next morning it had entirely collapsed. A recent slave recruit informed his master of Gabriel's plans; he warned Monroe, and the militia began its roundup. Trials for those charged

James Monroe. COURTESY
OF THE LIBRARY OF CONGRESS.

with seditious rebellion began by early September. Historian Douglas Egerton painstakingly reviewed the records of those proceedings, and subsequent political actions, to produce the fullest account yet written of Gabriel's rebellion.[62]

In all, twenty-six slaves were hanged following conviction for the roles they played in the aborted rebellion, including Gabriel who went to his death with no record left of any last words. One particularly disturbing aspect of the hangings struck Monroe, others in Virginia, and beyond. The crime for which these men were being killed was rebellion from despotism to seize their freedom.

By mid-September with verdicts mounting, Monroe wrote for advice to Jefferson, who was still carrying out his role as vice president pending the election. "Where to arrest the hand of the Executioner, is a question of great importance," he told his friend and mentor.[63] Jefferson responded quickly, noting that while "I should be unwilling to be quoted in the case," he believed that, "there is strong sentiment that there has been hanging enough." He then added, "Surely the legislature would pass a law for their exportation?"[64] Thus began a process in which Jefferson, as president, came to be asked by two Virginia governors and its legislature to assist in a plan for slave emancipation and removal to some location outside the state, a framework like that which he claimed to favor and for which he said he was prepared to act forcefully.

By year's end the Virginia legislature passed measures to strengthen the militia and the patrols of armed citizens who searched the roadways at night on horseback looking for runaways or worse. Arrangements were made to have eight slaves who had been sentenced to death be sold instead in the port of New Orleans, then under Spanish authority. Perhaps responding to Jefferson's initial suggestion, an additional resolution called on Monroe to correspond with Jefferson about purchasing land outside Virginia "whither persons obnoxious to the laws, or dangerous to the peace of society may be removed."[65]

In forwarding the resolution, Monroe urged now-President Jefferson to take the most expansive view possible of its potential. Whether or not the legislature intended it, he confided, a major distinction could be drawn between mere criminals and those society considered to be dangerous. Acknowledging that he was writing on "a subject of great delicacy," Monroe urged Jefferson's attention to a "more enlarged construction of the resolution," meaning that emancipated slaves might be included among those considered dangerous. "As soon as the mind emerges, in contemplating the subject, beyond the contractual scale of providing a mode of punishment for offenders, vast and interesting objects present themselves to view," Monroe wrote.[66] His plea to engage Jefferson in a plan for emancipation could not have been clearer. Governor Monroe's suggestion, based on his legislature's pleading, was the most significant opportunity to strike a blow against slavery since Washington signed the Northwest Ordinance. It is all but forgotten in history due to its barren outcome.

Jefferson was in no hurry. Five months later, and only after a second letter from Monroe seeking a reply, Jefferson drafted his response. His letter deserves close examination. He opened by making clear that he did not want his message to become public, lest it "have an ill effect in more than one quarter." He granted that the issues raised could involve "a much larger scope" than resettlement of Blacks convicted of crimes.

He next reviewed, and provided reasons to oppose, resettlement land purchases or arrangements across the northern border, or within the Northwest Territory, or to the south, or to the west in territory then held by Spain. Neither Britain nor the Indian nations of Canada would likely look favorably, he noted, at the colonization of the Black population under consideration. Jefferson acknowledged that there was nothing to stop the state of Virginia from purchasing land north of the Ohio River in the Northwest Territory, but he doubted that Congress would be amenable to such an expensive acquisition. Additional questions would arise, he warned, asking "whether the establishment of such a colony, within our limits, and to become part of our Union, would be desirable to the state of Virginia itself, or to the other states, especially those who would be in its vicinity?" Casting his eye to the south or to the west to lands then occupied by Spain, the president took the longer view of their likely future incorporation into the United States. On that land, as has been cited earlier in this chapter, Jefferson could contemplate "no blot or mixture" of Blacks with whites. As Jefferson saw it, all the options to the south, west, and north were unpromising.

Looking to the West Indies, "the island of St. Domingo" might "offer a more probable and practicable retreat." Although his letter did not mention the fact, only a few months earlier, a new constitution had been proclaimed there, abolishing slavery and permitting the importation of Blacks to rebuild a population decimated by a decade of fighting, as will soon be narrated. "I should conjecture," he wrote, "that their present ruler might be willing . . . to receive even that description which would be exiled for acts deemed criminal by us, but meritorious perhaps by him." His reference was to Toussaint Louverture, the Black leader of the slave revolt that was soon to see Haiti declared an independent nation. Looking farther across the Atlantic, Jefferson wrote that Africa "would offer a last and undoubted resort." He concluded the letter by asking that the legislature refine its request, but he warned that any arrangements made with foreign nations or sovereigns during the current period of "vast revolutions and changes of circumstances" may "be totally deranged" in short order.

In sum, Jefferson ruled out consideration by him of land purchases or settlement rights within or adjacent to U.S. territory. In looking abroad, he foresaw possible upheavals that might readily overturn any initial progress. Jefferson's letter can hardly be read as a response from a political leader anxious to pursue the possibilities of an opening made to him by the governor and legislature of the nation's largest slave state on an issue of paramount importance. His reference to Virginia being unrestrained in pursuing land purchases in the Northwest Territory was a gratuitous aside. The entire tenor of Monroe's initial query was to seek leadership from the president and national government on the prospect of emancipation, not to advise Jefferson of plans the state might pursue on its own. Jefferson's words were an expression of refusal to assist in resettlement of Blacks within the nation's current or future borders and grudging willingness to make enquiries elsewhere if pressed on the matter.[67]

Monroe and the legislature pressed.

Events in Richmond were given added urgency when yet another slave conspiracy was uncovered. The plan was for a general uprising to be launched on either Good Friday or Easter Sunday. After a citizens' patrol broke up a meeting of Blacks during the night of January 1, one of the slaves there revealed the plot. Twenty-five Blacks would eventually be hanged for their roles in the affair.[68]

On January 16 Monroe made an initial report about the plot to the legislature. He had earlier given them his correspondence with Jefferson. On learning of a new conspiracy, the Virginia House of Delegates went into secret session. Before the day was over, they had passed two resolutions, soon endorsed by the Virginia Senate, to clarify Virginia's position in response to the president's letter to Monroe. The first resolution asked Monroe to appeal to the federal government for the purchase of land where Blacks convicted of rebellion could be colonized. A location in Africa or within existing Spanish or Portuguese settlements in South America was preferred. The second resolution was the only one of its kind ever passed by a southern state legislature. Governor Monroe was requested, the resolution stated, "to correspond with the president of the United States for the purpose of obtaining a place without the limits of [Virginia], to which free negroes or mulattoes, and such negroes or mulattoes as may be emancipated may be sent or chose to remove as a place of asylum."[69] In forwarding the resolutions to Jefferson, Monroe emphasized that for the second one concerning emancipated slaves, "a preference is not expressed in favor of any particular region or Country. . . . In removing these people without our limits no restraint is imposed to preclude the attainment of an asylum any where . . . [including] an alternative of places."

Monroe's letter not only included Jefferson's long-favored emancipation and colonization formulation but was open to dispersal of free Blacks to various "places," including within the United States or its territories.

Three-and-a-half months later in his reply to Monroe, Jefferson ignored consideration of any asylum other than one in Africa, which was his preference, or in the West Indies or South America. He ignored, too, any discussion of using funds from the national government to achieve the Virginia legislature's aims. He informed Monroe that he had spoken with a British diplomat about sending slaves convicted of rebellion to the African colony for free Blacks recently established in Sierra Leone. Jefferson was advised to expect no objections from the private British company that had set up the colony to sending American Blacks there, so long as they were sent as free persons. Only later, at Monroe's prompting, did it occur to Jefferson that meeting this condition would require emancipating slaves convicted of rebellion before dispatching them abroad, a measure that would make rebellion a pathway to freedom. In his letter, Jefferson speculated that if emancipated slaves referred to by the legislature could be sent aboard ships free to buy and sell within the colony, the venture might prove to be financially viable. Otherwise, he wrote, "so distant a colonization of them would perhaps be thought too expensive."[70]

Jefferson next wrote to the United States' ambassador in London, asking him to sound out officials and company agents there about sending to Sierra Leone both slaves convicted of rebellion and others freed by emancipation. His letter ignored recently received advice from Monroe concerning freeing convicted slaves before deporting them.[71] The reply he received was negative. The Sierra Leone colony was in financial straits. Internal turmoil might soon require assistance by British troops. There was little "reason to hope," Jefferson was told, "that an incorporation of the blacks of the United States with those at Sierra Leone can be reconciled."[72] At this point, whatever interest Jefferson had in the plan essentially vanished.

That did not stop the Virginia legislature from continuing to press the point. In February 1804 it requested then-Governor John Page "to continue a correspondence" with Jefferson on the subject. Jefferson's reply was brief. Conditions on "the island of St. Domingo" were too unsettled to contemplate any "permanent arrangements," the president wrote. In fact, Haitian independence had been declared nearly a year earlier, and the island nation's leader had written Jefferson seeking closer commercial and political ties. Jefferson had not responded.[73]

Turning to the recently concluded Louisiana Purchase, the president wrote Governor Page, "Whether the inhabitants of our late acquisition beyond the Mississippi, or the national legislature, would consent that a portion of that country should be set apart for the persons contemplated is not within my competence to say." The language is little short of contemptuous in that, had he been interested, Jefferson surely could have broached the idea with members of Congress. But the land involved was part of the empire of liberty where Jefferson wanted "no blot" of Blacks to exist. He closed his letter by assuring the governor that he had the legislature's object "sincerely at heart. I will keep in under my constant attention, and omit no occasion which may occur of giving it effect." With that, Jefferson's involvement with the issue ended.

Whether any significant progress toward emancipation could have been made had Jefferson demonstrated more leadership on the Virginia proposal is unknowable. Certainly, the obstacles were great, including that of Jefferson's unwillingness to contemplate seeing free Blacks become any significant part of America's population. What clearly comes through from Jefferson's involvement, however, is his timidity in grasping the proposal's potential, readiness to credit difficulties to it, and unwillingness to risk his own political standing to pursue it. The record of the affair, including Jefferson's correspondence about it, remained secret until details began to emerge in 1816.

Years later during the Missouri crisis of 1820, when he no longer exercised any direct authority, Jefferson offered his own solution to the slavery problem in a letter fraught with irony. After a certain date, past, present, or to be designated in the future, owners should give up all slaves, who would then be placed under state guardianship until, Jefferson wrote, they are "sent at a proper age to St. Domingo. There they are willing to receive them."[74]

In the wake of Gabriel's rebellion, however, the legislature did pass a law that had been proposed by Jefferson years earlier but rejected. Slaves emancipated by their owners in the state had one year to leave Virginia or be subject to reenslavement. In addition, four of the slaves sentenced to death for involvement in Gabriel's plot and thirteen others convicted of capital crimes were sold to a slave trader and, after apparently being marched to the mouth of the St. Mary's River in Spanish Florida, were never heard of again.[75]

A white child impaled at the point of a stake held aloft by a rampaging Black man was among the first traumatizing images to reach America of the slave revolt that broke out on the Caribbean island of St. Domingue in August 1791. A white man employed as a plantation carpenter "is seized by the negroes, who bind him between two planks, and saw him deliberately in two," according to a widely read account. In another reported incident, a plantation owner's two daughters were savagely raped as their father was forced to watch before marauding Blacks slaughtered all three. Referring to those slaves who were best treated by their owners, a witness recalled, "It was *they* who betrayed and delivered those humane masters to the assassin's sword."[76]

The slaveowners' nightmare had come true. During a decade in which British, French, and Spanish troops died by the tens of thousands, it became worse. Blacks, the supposedly inferior race fit only for bondage to whites, not only defeated their enemies and abolished slavery, but also declared their independence as the nation of Haiti and set up their own government to defend it. The Haitian Revolution produced "the only successful large-scale and generalized slave revolt known in history," according to historian Robin Blackburn.[77] The images and symbols arising from the revolt seared themselves on the American memory—in vastly different ways among the white and Black populations—for decades to come. The revolt also proved to be pivotal to Thomas Jefferson's signal accomplishment as president, the Louisiana Purchase.

An image of Haitian soldiers taking revenge for cruelties inflicted upon them by the army of France. SOURCE: *SLAVERY IMAGES*.

In sailing west across the Atlantic in 1492, Christopher Columbus named one of the islands where he made landfall Hispaniola. By the time George Washington became president, the western third of the island was a French colony called St. Domingue; the remaining Santo Domingo portion was held by the Spanish. St. Domingue was at that time an enormously profitable plantation colony where 480,000 slaves made it the world's leading producer of sugar and coffee.[78] A white, largely French population of 32,000 administered the colony and owned the plantations. A third segment of 24,000 freemen, mostly mulattoes, was wedged in as a small merchant and trades class. With the land devoted to commodity crops, the ruling class turned to American shipping merchants, several hundred miles to the northwest, to provide staples. Flour, livestock, processed beef, and dried and pickled fish flowed from the United States to St. Domingue, making it the nation's second-largest trading partner after Great Britain.[79]

The revolt erupted in August 1791 when some 20,000 slaves laid waste to plantations in the northeast plain and murdered whites by the hundreds. Within a month, American newspapers were flooded with lurid accounts of "murder and devastation."[80] Soon refugees from the island began pouring into American ports at Charleston, Norfolk, Philadelphia, and New York, an initial tide that numbered at least 10,000 exiles.[81] They brought with them eyewitness accounts of the rebellion that had swelled to include some 100,000 Blacks. Washington, acting in accord with his secretary of state Jefferson, advanced France $400,000 and provided another $320,000 to white planters on the island to assist efforts to suppress the rebellion.[82]

When America's quasi war with France broke out, President John Adams reversed policy to support the revolt. Toussaint Louverture, leader of the rebellion, purchased arms and provisions from the United States.[83] Louverture was a former slave of possible royal African ancestry who proved to be a skilled military strategist and deft at diplomatic maneuver. American warships transported his troops and shelled French positions during the fighting of 1799.[84] A year later those warships gave Louverture's troops close support during further action against the French.[85]

By the time Jefferson became president, the revolt was nearing its climax. By then some 15,000 refugees had fled to America.[86] The British had invaded the island, backed by Spain, aiming to protect their interests in Jamaica and elsewhere in the Caribbean from the spread of rebellion. They never accurately reported their losses, but something like 10,000 troops died fighting the Black insurgents and another

Toussaint Louverture. SOURCE: *SLAVERY IMAGES.*

12,000 to 18,000 were lost to yellow fever.[87] The British withdrew in 1798. Before it was over, the rebellion killed or drove off nearly the entire white and mulatto population, and nearly a third of the island's total population died in the conflict.[88]

As president, Jefferson moved quickly to realign American policy to support French plans to regain control. He had received reports of a secret treaty by which Spain had ceded to France its territories in Florida and a vast tract of land west of the Mississippi River. The president's eyes were set on Florida. By supporting France in the Caribbean, he thought, Napoleon Bonaparte, the new first consul of France, might be more easily persuaded to relinquish Florida. In July 1801, the French envoy reported on a meeting with the president in which Jefferson reportedly said that so long as France made peace with England "then nothing would be easier than to furnish your army and fleet with everything, and to reduce Toussaint to starvation."[89]

The peace with Britain was secured, but Napoleon had a deeper motive than Jefferson realized. A large French invasion force was assembled for dispatch to St. Domingue under the leadership of Napoleon's brother-in-law, General Charles Leclerc. In his orders to Leclerc, Napoleon laid out a plan to first quickly subdue Louverture, reestablish slavery on the island, and then move his army to the lower Mississippi Valley. Once there, he was to convert the area into a French colony to provision a St. Domingue restored to be among the world's most profitable sugar and coffee producers.[90] The worst of the surviving Black rebels would be sent to a penal colony near New Orleans.[91] Over time, the new colony could become the breadbasket for a new French empire. Jefferson's support would unwittingly help create a thriving French presence at the mouth of the Mississippi, replete with jails filled with Black insurrectionaries.

The president again reversed policy when word reached him of Napoleon's broader designs. Instead of providing active French support, America would be neutral in the conflict. With the French navy too small to enforce a blockade, the policy meant American merchants could supply Louverture but deny provisions to Leclerc's army. That force, an initial 12,000 strong, sailed straight into disaster. Although Leclerc did secure Louverture's surrender, his forces were decimated by dual attacks from fighting and yellow fever. As Louverture was sent to a French prison, where he later died, Leclerc succumbed to disease, as did thousands of those he commanded. A total of some 40,000 French troops died in the campaign.[92]

With his Caribbean venture in shambles and a new war with Britain impending, Napoleon made a stunning proposal to America's envoys to Paris: Was the United States prepared to purchase all of the Louisiana Territory?[93]

Jefferson would reverse policy again with an 1805 arms embargo on the island and an 1806 complete trade embargo against Haiti. The United States did not recognize the country until 1862.

The name of Toussaint Louverture and the slave rebellion in Haiti remained vivid in American memory for decades. To the white South, both were symbols of the deepest dread of slaveholders' fears. To free Blacks, slaves, and a later generation of northern abolitionists, Louverture and the revolution became a different type of symbol. Gabriel was said to have been inspired in his plans for revolt, at least in part, by the example Louverture set.

Missouri Senator Thomas Hart Benton captured the white southern attitude toward Haiti in an 1825 speech responding to the suggestion that President John Quincy Adams might recognize the island nation. "We receive no mulatto consuls, or black ambassadors from [Haiti]," he intoned. "Because the peace of eleven [slaveholding] states will not permit the fruits of a successful negro insurrection to be exhibited among them. . . . It will not permit the fact to be seen and told, that for the murder of their masters and mistresses, they are to find friends among the white people of these United States."[94]

The Louisiana Purchase thrust America past the eastern boundary of the Mississippi River, beginning a westward expansion to the Pacific Ocean later proclaimed as Manifest Destiny. With that expansion came the spread of slavery to the south and clashes, not over questions of morality, but hard realities of political and economic power with the North. The country's western reaches were to become the testing ground for the long-term viability of the accommodations struck in the Constitutional Convention.

Jefferson had sent Robert Livingston to Paris as his ambassador with instructions to negotiate for the purchase of New Orleans, the cork at the mouth of the Mississippi River that controlled the eastern half of the continent.[95] If he could make headway in acquiring the Florida territories, so much the better. On the day James Monroe arrived in France, sent to assist Livingston, Napoleon had his treasury minister offer the United States the entire Louisiana Territory for $15 million. The American envoys were stunned. Their instructions allowed them to commit no more than $10 million for the purchase of New Orleans. Realizing the magnitude of the opportunity, they ventured on their own to agree to the deal. On July 4, 1803, Jefferson received the Louisiana Purchase Treaty that included the proviso that it must be ratified no later than October 30.

The strict constructionist Jefferson at first wrestled with the problem that the Constitution enumerated no power to purchase foreign territory and incorporate it into the union. To solve the problem, he drafted a constitutional amendment, one that granted all the territory's "white inhabitants" U.S. citizenship. But when he received word from Monroe that Bonaparte was looking for a way out of the sale, Jefferson bypassed his constitutional scruples and asked his friend Senator John Breckinridge of Kentucky to move the treaty speedily to ratification. Although the Constitution had no provision authorizing the purchase, Jefferson wrote the senator, Congress "must ratify, and pay for it and throw themselves on their country for doing for them unauthorized what we know they would have done for themselves."[96] The Senate acted with alacrity, ratifying the treaty by a large majority on October 19, two days after convening. The nation, with few exceptions, rejoiced at Jefferson's singular triumph. The vexing problem of control over New Orleans was solved. The empire of liberty was taking shape before their eyes.

In a real sense, no one was quite sure what the money had purchased. A report to Congress began by noting that "no general map, sufficiently correct to be depended upon, has been published."[97] When its boundaries were finally determined, the purchase nearly doubled the county's size by 868,000 square miles, at a cost of just under three cents an acre.[98] All or portions of thirteen new states would eventually be carved from the purchase lands stretching west from the Mississippi River to the Rocky Mountains and north like a funnel from New Orleans on the Gulf of Mexico to the Canadian border.

Only about 8,000 Native Americans were thought to live in the purchase territory of Missouri, approximately a quarter of them slaves.[99] To the south, however, about 42,000 people were believed to live in the region stretching from New Orleans to about Natchez, 21,000 of them whites, nearly 2,000 free Blacks and mulattoes, and the remainder slaves.[100] Since the early 1790s the region had seen a large influx of planter refugees from St. Domingue and other Caribbean islands.[101] Many brought their slaves with them, creating a thriving plantation economy that produced some 21,000 bales of cotton and 45,000 casks of sugar in 1803.[102]

Future prospects appeared even brighter. "It may be said, with truth, that for fertility of soil no part of the world exceeds the borders of the Mississippi: the land yields an abundance of all the necessities of life, and almost spontaneously," Congress was informed.[103] But profit from cotton and sugar, not necessities, excited the imaginations of those who now contemplated seeking their fortunes in the lower Mississippi Valley. Within a few years, a North Carolinian was writing that in Louisiana "one good Negro can make five bales of cotton" worth $500. At that rate a planter need work a field hand little more than a year to recoup his purchase price.[104] From there on out, a bonanza of profit awaited those ready to invest in slavery along the Mississippi.

South Carolina's legislature was not blind to the opportunity. Before the ink on the ratification document was hardly dry, the Palmetto State lifted its ban on the foreign slave trade. Over the next four years, before the national prohibition of the African slave trade went into effect, South Carolina imported 39,000 slaves by official estimate, and perhaps more than 50,000 according to recent scholarship.[105] That surge equaled better than 10 percent of all the slaves brought into British North America in the previous 200 years.[106] Many of those slaves worked out their lives on what became a seemingly endless and isolated expanse of plantations that flanked the riverbank along the lower Mississippi.

With the title deeds in hand, Congress had next to decide how to govern the new territory. The union had already admitted three new states, the free state of Vermont, followed by the slave states of Kentucky and Tennessee. Its precedent for new territories, however, was the Northwest Ordinance outlawing slavery, and the Mississippi Territory Ordinance of 1798 that permitted slavery but not slave imports from outside the United States. Jefferson advanced his own governance plan to Breckinridge with the admonition that to avoid "the bloody teeth and fangs" of Federalist attacks, "I must do it in confidence that you will never let any person know that I have put pen to paper on the subject."[107]

He started by dividing the region into two sections, a formulation adopted by Congress: the more populous but smaller District of Orleans south of the thirty-third parallel and the less populous but far larger District of Louisiana north of it. The only restriction on slavery he recommended was to permit imports only from states not participating in the African slave trade. He envisioned that Orleans should be annexed to the Mississippi Territory. To the north, he thought the vast landscape "will probably be locked up from American settlement" to become a "tempting" location for "all our Indians on the east side of the Mississippi to remove to the west."[108] That vision was overwhelmed by white westward migration within Jefferson's lifetime.

What happened next was extraordinary in the annals of Congress and never to be repeated. Led by the Senate, the body passed the tightest restrictions on slavery enacted by Congress since the Northwest Ordinance. They survived less than a year. The initial restrictions on slavery passed the Senate without a tirade of dissolution threats from the South or monologues on morality from the North. In fact, at least seven of the sixteen senators representing the eight largest slaveholding states spoke openly of slavery's evil or their desire to see the institution restrained.[109] That such deprecation of slavery by southerners occurred is due, in large measure, to the fact that only the Senate's votes, not its debates, were officially recorded. New Hampshire Senator William Plumer, however, kept his own account of the debates in his private journal that provides a reasonably accurate, if not precisely literal, record of the proceedings.[110]

As revealed in that journal, the efforts by northern senators to secure the greatest possible restrictions on slavery are not surprising. Unprecedented is the near anguish with which several southern senators spoke of slavery. In the end, the most prescient voice was that of Georgia Senator James Jackson, who believed that Congress had no effective power to overcome the demand for slaves by the people within the purchase territories.

By late January 1804, the Senate began consideration of how slavery would be treated in the purchase lands. The purchase treaty had provided that inhabitants should be "maintained and protected in the free enjoyment of their property," thus giving some security for slavery as it then stood. Senator Breckinridge of Kentucky, who had assisted Jefferson years earlier with the Kentucky Resolutions, was the bill's sponsor. Close to 20 percent of his state's population was Black, the vast majority of them slaves.[111] He opened the discussion by declaring "I am against slavery. I hope the time is not far distant when not a slave will exist in the Union. I fear our slaves in the south will produce another St. Domingo."[112]

His words reveal a conflict over slavery not unlike Jefferson's. Breckinridge was one of Kentucky's largest slaveholders, owning at his death just three years later nearly seventy bonded servants.[113] Shortly after Breckinridge's statement, North Carolina's Jesse Franklin struck a similar tone, saying "Slavery is in every respect an evil to the states in the south and in the west. It will, I fear, soon become a dreadful one. Negro insurrections have already been frequent."[114] Nearly a third of the population in his state was enslaved.[115] The most anguished voice on slavery was that of Maryland Senator Robert Wright, who said "It is wrong to reproach us with the *immorality* of *slavery*. That is a crime we must answer for at the bar of God. We ought not therefore to answer it here."[116] These sentiments, and other like ones from southern senators, are little short of astonishing, revealing that at that moment in time many of the South's principal leaders were not just wary of slavery but despairing of it.

The South also had a leader who argued with hard-eyed pragmatism. Senator Jackson of Georgia held no brief for slavery as a moral construct, but he did see it as a practical necessity. "I think it would be for the real interest of the United States to have an end to slavery in this country," he said. "But we cannot get rid of them. . . . I dislike the traffic in human flesh. But we must decide not on the morality but the policy of the case."[117] The point he repeatedly drove home was, "You cannot prevent slavery. Neither laws moral or human can do it. Men will be governed by their interest, not the law."[118] It would be as impossible to prevent the importation of slaves into the purchase territory, he said, "as to move the sun into the moon."[119]

The majority only partially agreed with him. They did turn back a northern attempt at gradual emancipation of any slaves brought into the purchase territory.[120] But they approved a ban on the importation of slaves from outside the United States decisively, twenty-one to seven.[121] The prohibition included slaves who had been imported since 1798, when Georgia's ban on the international slave trade went into effect, thus shutting off an importation route from South Carolina's recently reopened African slave market.

The legislation also aimed to stop the decade-long flow of immigrants and their slaves from the turmoil in the Caribbean. Many French planters who first fled St. Domingue with their slaves initially found refuge in Cuba, hardly 100 miles away. Only later did they embark with their human property to the lower Mississippi Valley. The bill banned foreign immigrants from bringing their slaves into the purchase territory. Plumer noted in his journal that the "zeal" southerners displayed to prohibit foreign imports was motivated by the desire "to raise the price of their own slaves in the market" for sale in the Deep South and to reduce their slave populations by dispersion into the new territories.[122] The dual argument to restrict imports and diffuse existing slave populations was most prominent in the Border South. Senator Breckinridge argued that dispersal would "free the southern states from a part of its black population, and of its danger."[123]

The Senate, however, went beyond blocking imports and fostering diffusion. It did so with crucial southern support. In what was potentially its most decisive provision, the legislation provided that no slave could be brought into the territory except by a citizen of the United States moving into the territory with the intention of settling there with his slaves. Violation of the statute would result in freedom for the slaves.[124] Senator Jackson predicted that the provision would "render a standing army necessary" to enforce it.[125] The enforcement of this and the bill's other slavery provisions would have effectively shut down any legal slave trade into the purchase lands, severely limiting the ability of planters already in the territory from purchasing more slaves. Slavery could only be augmented by planters willing to pull up stakes in one state and set themselves down with their slaves in the newly acquired territory. As it turned out, few American slaveholders were willing to do that until nearly ten years later.[126] The measure was decidedly not one giving greatest range to the diffusion of slavery by giving free rein to the domestic slave trade. Yet the unprecedented restriction was approved by both senators from Kentucky, Maryland, and Delaware, Senator Franklin from North Carolina, and Senator Cocke from Tennessee. Without those votes the measures would have failed.[127]

The legislation Congress passed in March 1804, however, contained an escape clause. The law would expire if not reenacted within a year of its enforcement date.[128]

The reaction was as Senator Jackson had predicted. Even before the legislation passed, William C. C. Claiborne, soon to be governor in the territory, wrote from New Orleans to James Madison that a report of Senate action to ban the foreign slave trade "has occasioned great agitation in this city. . . . The prohibiting the importation of Negroes . . . is viewed as a serious blow at the commercial and agricultural interest of the Province."[129] He later warned Jefferson, "The people here have United as one Man! . . . *They must import more Slaves, or the Country was ruined forever.*"[130]

Formal "remonstrances" from leading citizens in the New Orleans region and from St. Louis soon reached Congress. The document from Missouri was polite but made clear that "the right of importing slaves" was crucial to the citizens there.[131] That from New Orleans' worthies was blunt. They wanted to be free to decide for themselves on matters of slavery. Unless the "necessity of employing African laborers" was permitted, "cultivation must cease, and the improvements of a century be destroyed, and the great river resume its empire over our ruined fields and demolished habitations."[132] The law threatened to replace an empire of liberty with an empire of ruin.

Jefferson stood aside, but the Washington lawmakers took note. The people they were attempting to govern were not American patriots of proven loyalty. They were instead, as John Craig Hammond has described them, "a threatening amalgamation of land speculators, merchants, and slaveholders; ancient and 'new' French planters, Old Regime Conservatives, Bonapartist imperialists, Saint Domingue refugees, British loyalists,

Spanish officials, and expatriated Americans."[133] He might also have added pirates and smugglers.

Congress quickly backed off its willingness to test slavery restrictions. Revised governing legislation was passed in 1805 annexing the northern Louisiana District to the existing Indiana Territory, without the Northwest Ordinance prohibition against slavery. In the Orleans District only the foreign slave trade was banned. That lone remaining prohibition was essentially meaningless due in part to smuggling, as will next be discussed, and because landing newly arrived African slaves in the Palmetto State disguised their transport from South Carolina to the new territory as part of the domestic slave trade. Charleston soon became a funnel moving enslaved Blacks from Africa to Louisiana and the west bank of the Mississippi.

Some historians have blamed Jefferson for failing to curtail slavery in the purchase territory, or at least in the Missouri portion of it. A strong argument can also be made that Congress avoided provoking a civil war in the newly purchased western lands where the truculent white population already had slavery and demanded more of it.[134] In any event, with slavery now a matter for local decision, a core tenet of Jeffersonian democracy, the floodgates were open for it to expand as the empire of liberty grew. Eventually slave labor and the power of slave states spreading from the southwest collided with free labor and the power of free states expanding from the northwest when Missouri sought to enter the union in 1819, touching off the first great crisis leading to civil war.

The country welcomed Jefferson's December 1806 call on Congress to pass legislation ending the African slave trade by the earliest constitutionally allowed date of January 1, 1808. Only South Carolina then permitted it. The slave trade prohibition was needed, the president said, to end "those violations of human rights which have been so long continued on the unoffending inhabitants of Africa, and which the morality, and reputation, and the best interests of our country, have long been eager to proscribe."[135]

Congress, taking up the challenge before the month was out, ran headlong into a pair of stumbling blocks. What was to be done with shiploads of kidnapped Africans aboard vessels seized for attempting to violate the ban? The ships carrying them were likely to be seized in or near southern ports where white residents were unwilling to countenance having destitute Blacks who spoke no English and were thoroughly unfamiliar with American culture set free. The same could be said for northern white citizens. Returning them to their homes would involve knowing where those homes were and the expense of getting them there. Congress also struggled with what penalties should be meted out to the kidnappers themselves, the ship captains, and other principals who were caught breaking the law.

The first dilemma arose immediately upon the House receiving proposed legislation for the ban. The bill prescribed that both seized slave ships and their cargo, including kidnapped Blacks, be "forfeit"—that is, sold at auction as property. Quaker Congressman James Sloan of New Jersey spoke first, moving that the bill be amended so that human cargoes be entitled to freedom.[136] As "melancholy" as forfeiture might be, replied Georgia's Peter Early, "we who live in that part of the United States where the evil referred to principally exists, know from experience that this is the only effectual plan that can be pursued."[137] As the debate heated, so did Early. Free Blacks, he said, "are instruments of murder, theft, and conflagration." Although it was admittedly "cruel and disgraceful" to hold them in slavery, if they were allowed to go free, "we must either get rid of them, or they of us. There is no alternative. . . . No one of them would be left alive in a year."[138]

The House journal summary of the lengthy debate read, in part, "By the same law we condemn the man-stealer and become the receiver of his stolen goods. . . . We assume to ourselves, as a government, the exclusive right of selling slaves imported into the United States."[139] Early provided the white South's reply. "We want no civil wars," ran his disguised threat, "no rebellions, no insurrections, no resistance to the authority of the government. Give effect then to this wish" for forfeiture and slavery, not freedom for kidnapped Blacks.[140] A crucial moment arrived when the House voted on a motion that "no person shall be sold as a slave by virtue of this act." The tie, sixty votes in favor from New England and four middle states and sixty votes opposed from a solid bloc of all the southern states, was broken by the negative vote of the Speaker of the House, from North Carolina.[141] In the end, northerners salvaged a fig leaf to protect the nation's honor from becoming a slave trader in the name of ending the slave trade. Kidnapped Blacks taken into custody from seized slave ships would be turned over to state authorities, not to officials of the national government. Only then would they be sold into slavery.

When a Senate version of the bill reached the House, containing a death penalty provision for those convicted of violating a slave importation ban, Early again spoke for the white South. Not a single southerner, he said, would ever dare inform on a violator if death was the punishment. "A large majority of the people of the southern states do not consider slavery a crime," he said, speaking obviously only for the white population. "They do not believe it immoral to hold human flesh in bondage." He began describing how many southerners considered slavery a political evil, but then corrected himself. "I will tell the truth," Early said. "A large majority of the people in the southern states do not consider slavery as even an evil."[142]

In contradicting his own earlier reference to slavery as an evil, Early may not have realized it, but he was giving voice to a newly developing attitude in parts of the white South. Decades passed before slavery as a positive good became the dominant belief among white southerners. But to get there, southerners had to move away from thinking of slavery as an evil, as Jefferson did. Early's words show that the process was under way. Early was thirty-three years old; Jefferson, sixty-three. The debates and votes also demonstrated a hardening of differences between the North and South. As historian Donald Robinson has described it, the discussions "marked a turning point," showing a "growing southern unity, and . . . a marked sectional cleavage. As the object of legislation moved closer to the institution of slavery itself, the resistance of the South stiffened and became increasingly monolithic."[143]

The foreign slave trade prohibition that Congress passed provided for a maximum term of ten years imprisonment for violations and left the work of enslaving kidnapped Blacks up to the states. In one of the first official acts under the new law, Jefferson pardoned Phillip M. Topham on March 1, 1808, for "carrying on an illegal slave-trade."[144]

Lax enforcement, official corruption, and a brisk trade in slave smuggling marked the law's opening years up to about 1820. Recent scholarship estimates that 54,000 Blacks were brought into the country illegally after the ban became law, swelling the total number of slave imports to approximately 427,000 from the beginning to the end of the trade.[145]

Two years after the act was passed, Congress approved the immigration to Louisiana of exiles from Haiti who had become refugees in Cuba. In the process, some 3,000 slaves belonging to the immigrants and another 3,000 free Blacks entered the country.[146]

As evidence of lax enforcement, historian W. E. B. Du Bois cited an 1819 report from the Register of the Treasury to Congress noting that after scouring the accounts of the collectors of customs and U.S. marshals, "it doth not appear . . . that any forfeitures had been incurred" as a result of enforcing the foreign slave trade ban.[147] A tax collector at the port of Mobile wrote his superiors that "we have only a small boat, with four men and an inspector, to oppose the whole confederacy of smugglers and pirates."[148] A former Georgia governor was convicted of assisting in the illegal smuggling of some 100 slaves.[149]

Historian David Head recounts the story of Jim Bowie, of later fame at the Alamo, during his slave-smuggling days between Galveston, Texas, and the Louisiana bayous. By his account, while in Galveston Bowie and his brothers bought imported slaves from the pirate Jean Laffite and his companions. Bowie then transported his cargo to Louisiana, where he declared to local officials that he had unwittingly discovered the human contraband while about his normal business in the swamps. The slaves were then sold at auction to Bowie, who received a 50 percent discount for having turned them in in the first place. By process of the official auction, Bowie also received official papers allowing him to resell his slaves legally. By Head's account, "the Bowies tried the ruse at least four times between 1819 and 1820, smuggling some 180 slaves and making an estimated $65,000, or approximately $1,400,000 in current dollars."[150]

The law's forfeiture provisions were revised in 1819 so that kidnapped Blacks taken from slave ships would be relocated outside the United States, Liberia being the African destination Congress likely intended. After 1820 the illegal slave trade declined considerably. In that year Congress revised the law to define slave trading as piracy punishable by death, a penalty not imposed until the Lincoln administration.[151]

The ban on the foreign slave trade, however imperfectly enforced, eventually choked off the flow of slaves into the United States. It likely led to Kentucky and Tennessee having far fewer slaves by 1861, by sales to the south, than would otherwise have been the case, and in turn contributed to Kentucky's decision to remain in the union and the continuation of strong union sentiment in eastern Tennessee.

The ban on the foreign slave trade coming at about the same time Thomas Jefferson left office marks what may be considered the first phase of slavery's impact on American politics. Northern thrusts against the institution had been consistently repulsed, with the exception of that allowed by the Constitution's provision to end the slave trade to which the white South widely agreed. White southern concerns about the future that slavery had entailed upon them did nothing to stop its spread. Lines of demarcation, not rigid but nonetheless clear, emerged between an agrarian South, dependent on slavery, and the North, where free labor supported a far more diverse economy. White southern disunion threats prompted by the slightest perceived encroachment on their rights to slave property were, and were understood to be, more posturing than programs of intent. But they also consistently produced northern accommodation and compromise.

The disputes over slavery were, after all, more about abstraction and morality than of immediate impact for most white northerners, and exactly the opposite for white southerners. The bond of union that protected both sections allowing them to prosper had opened seemingly endless new vistas to the west that far overshadowed sectional differences. But as the empire of liberty spread beyond the Mississippi River into the West, slave to the south and free to the north, the sections were destined to collide.

CHAPTER 4

The Missouri Crisis

THE CRISIS STRUCK as the westward expansion of slave labor from the South and the corresponding free labor expansion from the North collided upon reaching Missouri. A collision somewhere in the new territories west of the Mississippi was inevitable. That it should occur in Missouri was predictable. The actual impact, however, came as an unexpected shock in the nation's capital, first consuming Congress for two years beginning in 1819 and later spreading across the country in America's first full-blown debate over slavery and, with it, the fate of the republic.

The narrow decision over whether to admit Missouri as a state with or without slavery framed far broader and more fundamental issues. Up to the Missouri crisis, sectionalism had been something of an abstraction without enduring lines of separation. It had arisen in the Constitutional Convention. Washington had warned against it. The few sharp clashes between slave and free states in Congress had been brief and were settled by compromise that normally translated as northern concessions. The most widely acknowledged sectional difference was between New England and the white South.

The most obvious political dynamic observed by nearly all was that under the Constitution, with all its compromises, a republic of enormous promise had been created that had shown itself fully able to take its place among the nations of the world. The country had fought Great Britain to a standstill in the War of 1812, which many saw as a second war of independence. That conflict had ended, even after a treaty of peace had been agreed in Europe, with the British suffering a humiliating defeat in the battle of New Orleans at the hands of General Andrew Jackson, a new star in the political firmament. As the Missouri issue began to unfold, the nation was slammed with recession in the Panic of 1819. Despite its severity, the downturn did not shake the conviction that the union was the best safeguard for each region's security and prosperity.

The existence of slavery in Virginia or Georgia did not affect the lives or prospects of free citizens in Pennsylvania or Ohio. Missouri changed that. The nation was suddenly confronted with the prospect of setting a precedent in Missouri that would determine whether the title deeds to the vast lands west of the Mississippi were to be in free labor or slave labor hands. Tracking parallel to that decision was power in Congress, whether or not the Constitution's three-fifths clause was to augment the slave states' votes in the House of Representatives and add two senators beholden to free labor or to slave labor constituents.

Up to this time a vague northern belief that slavery was on a path to extinction was set alongside southern hand-wringing about the evils of an institution entailed upon them against their will. For both the North and the white South, Missouri galvanized long-standing arguments about morality into urgently present decisions about economic and political power. The personal interests of white people, both North and South, were at stake. The question of one race keeping another in bondage was closely examined in the Missouri debates. But the debates' intensity and Missouri's ability to rivet the nation's attention rested on a decision not about the morality of enslaving Blacks but the future economic prospects and political influence of whites. In making the decision, an enduringly stark sectional line was drawn dividing the free labor North from the slave labor South.

The Missouri debate exposing the depth of the country's sectional rift came at a moment of exceptional political tranquility. For the first time since its founding, the nation's domestic affairs were not entangled by the cleavages of European wars.

The Era of Good Feeling pervaded the nation as James Monroe, the last president drawn from the Revolutionary era elite, entered the White House. Jefferson's vision of a broad political consensus overtaking deep factional divisions had prevailed. Monroe would be reelected in 1820 virtually without opposition. The Congress elected in that year was flush with 156 Republicans in the House confronting a paltry opposition of forty-two Federalists and a Senate dominated by thirty-five Republicans against seven Federalists.[1] The Republicans had their differences between supporters of the national bank and internal improvements and old-school strict constructionists, but these remained different wings within a single party.

The Federalists were finished as a national electoral force. They had one crucial power center in the person of John Marshall, chief justice of the Supreme Court, whose rulings consistently strengthened the national over the state governments. The Federalists' chief spokesman was Rufus King. Formerly a Massachusetts delegate to the Constitutional Convention, King had relocated to New York, where he had been elected to the Senate beginning in the First Congress, served as minister to Great Britain, and then returned to the Senate. He is perhaps best remembered from the convention for noting the divergence of interests between the eastern and southern states that could only be deepened by accepting the three-fifths clause to augment slave-state representation in the House.

The Federalists had permanently damaged their reputation when New England members had contemplated disunion at the Hartford Convention near the end of the War of 1812. Their principal complaint, like that of King in Philadelphia, was the disproportionate power the three-fifths clause granted to slave states. What most of the country remembered from the episode was that a group of New England dissidents had come close to treason. A longstanding white southern concern was resolved just as the Missouri debates opened when Monroe secured the cession of Florida from Spain, assuring the eventual addition of a new slave state there. That agreement contained a provision satisfying to northerners, however, keeping Texas in Spanish hands by setting its border with the United States at the Sabine River to the east rather than incorporating it, as southerners desired, all the way to the Rio Grande to the west, thus potentially opening even more land to slavery. The white South won its point a quarter century later in war with Mexico that set the stage for the next great reckoning with slavery in the Compromise of 1850.

The first great reckoning began on February 13, 1819, when James Tallmadge, a one-term Republican congressman from New York, introduced a pair of amendments to the Missouri statehood bill. Missourians

James Tallmadge. SOURCE:
WIKIMEDIA COMMONS/
NEW YORK PUBLIC
LIBRARY.

had drafted a constitution expressly sanctioning slavery. They expected quick action on admission, especially because the Louisiana Purchase Treaty included a clause providing that statehood would be granted "as soon as possible."

At the time Missouri held only about 10,000 slaves, roughly the same number as did New York, among its nearly 67,000 inhabitants. The Tallmadge amendments provided "that the further introduction of slavery or involuntary servitude be prohibited . . . ; and that all children of slaves, born within the said state, after the admission thereof into the Union, shall be free at the age of twenty-five years."[2] Tallmadge's motives have been long debated, but the most plausible explanation is that although he was credited with both ambition and a desire for fame, he was also sincerely opposed to slavery. Two years earlier he had fought to pass New York's gradual emancipation bill to free all slaves by 1827.

Tallmadge's New York colleague John W. Taylor helped frame the debate on broad lines when he argued in the House, shortly after the amendments were introduced, that "those whom shall authorize to set in motion the machine of free government beyond Mississippi, will, in many respects, decide the destiny of millions."[3] He was looking to successive generations that would settle the West and whether freedom or slavery would "inherit the land." The real shock came a few days later when, with separate votes, the House approved the ban on bringing slaves into Missouri and freedom for the children of slaves at age twenty-five.[4]

Emboldened, Taylor and his northern allies next targeted the Arkansas Territory bill. Their measure to restrict slavery there ended in a tie vote broken when Henry Clay, Speaker of the House, came down on the side of slavery. The southern rampart protecting slavery had nearly been breached in Arkansas and had thoroughly given way in Missouri. The scattering of House votes, which the white South previously had been able to count on from Pennsylvania and New York to reach a majority on slavery-related issues, had vanished. For the first time, at least as concerned Missouri, a northern majority determined to prevent the expansion of slavery held sway in the House of Representatives.

The Senate was a different story. Large majorities there turned back both clauses of the Tallmadge amendment. The Fifteenth Congress ended in a stalemate on the issue. Missouri statehood and the fate of slavery there would be for the next Congress to decide.

— ❦ —

In the end, the Sixteenth Congress reached a Missouri compromise advanced by white southerners and acquiesced to by just enough northerners to pass both houses. Missouri was admitted as a slave state. Maine's admission as a free state was tied to passing the deal as a whole. Slavery was prohibited in all Louisiana Purchase territory lying north of a line running westward from Missouri's southern border, but not including the state, along the latitude of thirty-six degrees, thirty minutes.

Reaching that compromise was an arduous process.[5] A great deal of the months-long debate in each house centered on exhaustive examinations of legal principles. Did the Constitution's guarantee of republican government for new states prohibit the existence of slavery in those states? Southerners argued that declaring existing slaves free at age twenty-five violated property rights protected by the Constitution. "You cannot force a portion of the people to emancipate their slaves," Congressman Alexander Smyth of Virginia argued.[6] The Northwest Ordinance ban on slavery in states formed from that territory either did (to the North) or did not (to the South) set a precedent for congressional authority to do the same in Missouri. Congressional authority under the Constitution to "make all needed rules and regulations as to the territories" was sufficient to justify slavery restrictions from the northern viewpoint, but from the white southern viewpoint it did not amount to an enumerated power needed to do that.

The meaning of the word "may" received hours of attention. The constitutional clause stating Congress "may" admit new states clearly did not include authority to supersede Missouri's proslavery constitution, as southerners read it, and certainly did imply authority to do exactly that, as northerners read it. The white South certainly had its advocates from northern states, particularly both senators from recently admitted Illinois, and Congressman John Holmes of Massachusetts, who was principally occupied in securing statehood for Maine. The Massachusetts legislature had agreed to relinquish its claim to Maine if Congress granted that territory statehood before a March deadline. Once Maine's admission was tied to accepting Missouri as a slave state, Holmes was a compromise advocate. When the deadline for securing Maine's statehood was met, Holmes was elected to the Senate from that new state. During the debates, he avowed his opposition to slavery while voting to allow it in Missouri. Northern votes, in fact, were decisive in passing the compromise that secured slavery in Missouri.

Beyond the legal disputes lay a larger and more illuminating aspect of the Missouri debates. The members called it "the expediency" of the issue, what was advisable for the country beyond the technical points of legal and constitutional interpretation. Perhaps growing weary of all the legal wrangling during the debate, Congressman William Darlington of Pennsylvania blurted out "Sir, we have the right of self-preservation" to protect the union from slavery's expansion.[7]

Any southern member of Congress could have used identical words defending the opposite position. An old saying goes that if you want to know the future, closely examine the present. The future is embedded in it. Nowhere was that truer than in what was said in the House and the Senate during the Missouri crisis. Most of the main currents that ultimately joined to form the principal causes of the Civil War were given voice and early definition there. Slavery was common to all of them. From it stemmed separate streams of economic imperatives, moral and cultural convictions, and political motives that divided the country between its free and its slave states. Hindsight gives a clearer relief to the articulation of the causes of the Civil War than those who spoke could possibly have understood. But the participants knew full well that the stakes in the debate could result in disunion and bloodshed.

Tallmadge posed the essential question for which Missouri was a symbol. "See your empire," he said, "occupying all the valuable part of our continent." See it "inhabited by the hardy sons of American freemen . . . owners of the soil on which they live." Or reverse that scene and see the empire become the domain of plantation slavery, he continued, and "you put poison in your bosom, you place a vulture on your heart."[8] The less florid Senator Prentiss Mellen of Massachusetts made the same point. "It should be remembered that we are not legislating for a year," he said, "but for centuries to come—not in respect to Missouri, merely, but to that almost boundless region beyond the Mississippi, over which our dominion now extends. We are, then, by our decision, preparing evils or blessings for an extensive country and for posterity."[9]

Although slavery and freedom might be able to live side by side, they could not occupy the same ground. Unless slavery was stopped in Missouri, argued Pennsylvania's Congressman Darlington, Congress will "permit the temporary interest of a few individuals . . . to entail this same transcendent curse upon the unborn myriads of our posterity, who will in future times, inhabit the fertile regions of the West."[10] Pennsylvania Senator Jonathan Roberts reflected that view, saying, "There is no ground on which slavery can be extended in Missouri that will not apply to the whole region west of the Mississippi."[11]

The debate asked which of the two economic systems carried with it the nation's destiny. By the second decade of the nineteenth century, the North was on a path to a preindustrial society. Yeoman farming was being augmented by commercial enterprise that depended on financial credit, all of it tied together by government-supported roads and canals to transport produce, livestock, products, and people. A rail network would come soon. A system of free labor, small proprietorships, and the beginnings of wage labor had traction not only in the North but across the recently added western states of Ohio, Indiana, and Illinois as well. The white South, on the other hand, was principally occupied with growing more cotton with more slave labor.

The dichotomy between an evolving preindustrial free labor society and a relatively static agrarian slave labor society was already apparent. The 1820 census showed that the North produced 60 percent of the nation's jobs in commerce and 70 percent of those in manufacturing. Nearly a quarter of the North's population was engaged in those industries, compared to only 10 percent in the South.[12] Even more telling was that the South's white population was shrinking in proportion to that in the North. From 1790 to 1820 the number of white inhabitants in the South grew by 118 percent, but in the North that growth rate was 168 percent. Over the next two decades, the South's white population increased by just over half, but that in the North nearly doubled so that by 1840, 4.3 million whites lived in the South and 10.1 million lived in the North.[13] As waves of immigrants arrived, the poor but stout newcomers were far more likely to seek a freehold of their own on free-labor ground than to compete with slave labor in the white South's plantation economy. At the same time, the already established citizenry of the North depended on having territory available to the west to absorb the immigrants and expand the free labor economy.

The two systems were not necessarily antagonistic. Southern cotton supplied New England textile mills, the seedbed of the region's manufacturing industry. Using industrial techniques stolen from Great Britain, the Boston Associates, representing the leading Lowell, Cabot, Russell, and Lawrence families, created the Boston Manufacturing Company, employing young women in wage labor and generating enormous profits. By 1860, northern textile mills were using nearly 500 million pounds of southern cotton annually.[14]

Although textiles provided a synergy between New England and the South, the two economic systems had conflicting political goals. The free labor states of the North shared political priorities for internal improvements to transport products more quickly at lower cost, tariffs to protect manufactures from foreign competition, and a banking system that provided paper currency and ready credit. The white South saw internal improvements financed by the national government as an expense they shouldered for a benefit they did not share, opposed tariffs that made the foreign goods they bought more expensive, and distrusted banks that fostered speculation.

As seen during the debates, one of the divergent economic systems would drive out the other in Missouri. "All our South Carolina friends may have to desert us, if they are not permitted to bring their slaves," a Virginian who had recently moved to Missouri wrote in a December 1819 letter to the *Richmond Enquirer*. The trend the writer observed, however, was that "scarcely one Yankee has moved into the country this year. At the same time Virginia, the Carolinas, Tennessee and Kentucky are moving [here] in great force."[15] In Baltimore, *Niles' Weekly Register* observed "As to Missouri, the moment that the right to hold slaves is acknowledged in her constitution . . . the laboring white man, the bone and sinew of every society, will avoid it, to be spared the humiliation which common prejudice tells him must be his lot, if subjected to associate with and to labor by the side of a slave."[16] Congressman Taylor said "If slavery shall be tolerated, the country will be settled by rich planters, with their slaves; if it shall be rejected, the emigrants will chiefly consist of the poorer and more laborious classes of society. . . . Do you believe that these people will settle in a country where they must take rank with negro slavery?"[17]

At the same time that the Missouri crisis placed the North's pre-industrial free labor economy in competition with the white South's commodity crop slave economy, those economic differences carved a deep sectional line across the country, distinguishing the free from the slave states. "Mason-Dixon" line was the shorthand term that gained prominence during the Missouri debates used to describe the nation's sectional divide. The Mason-Dixon line was a pre-Revolutionary War survey line originally drawn to set the borders between Pennsylvania and its southern neighbors. After 1820 it described the border between free and slave states.

Although the distinction between free and slave was clearly marked, loyalties between the sections were fluid and would not be finally cast, in some cases, until after secession was well under way in 1861. The free states touching along the Great Lakes region sold produce and livestock both down the Mississippi to the cotton South and across the lakes and canals to the East. But the sectional divide was already prominent enough to lead Virginia's Congressman Philip P. Barbour to lament during the Missouri debates, "Already is the northern part of our country, together with that northwest of the river Ohio, divided from us by those distinguishing names of slaveholding and non-slaveholding." As a westerner, Congressman Daniel P. Cook of Illinois noted that as to slavery "from a similarity of interests, of institutions, and of feelings, the North and the West" were united.[18] The border states would split their loyalties between the North and South when war came.

Missouri provided the first deep chop at where the cleavage ultimately fell. In the eyes of some, the demarcation between the sections was visible in the landscape. Early in the Missouri debates, Congressman Taylor commented that anyone who had traveled along the line dividing Pennsylvania and Maryland must have "observed that no monuments are necessary to mark the boundary; that it is easily traced by following the dividing lines between farms highly cultivated and plantations laying open to the common and overrun by weeds; between stone barns and stone bridges on the one side, and stalk cribs and no bridges on the other; between a neat, blooming, animated, rosy-cheeked peasantry on the one side, and a squalid, slow-motioned, black population on the other."[19]

Contrasts similar to this would be invoked repeatedly in the years to come. As seen by a British traveler in 1857, "on the one hand you have the industrial energy and political independence of a self-governing yeomanry; on the other, the stagnation of a people, where the rich are too proud to work, and the poor are too subservient to be free; while one-third of the whole population is practically reduced to the status of beasts of burden."[20] For decades, the common white southern rejoinder was some version of harmony and prosperity centered about a gracious plantation big house compared to wage slavery in squalid northern cities.

Each retelling of either portrait sketched the nation's sectional divide ever deeper into the public mind.

The economic divide defined by sectional borders produced a political clash. Missouri, Kentucky Congressman Benjamin Hardin said, is "a contest for political power."

The white South had three principal objectives at the Constitutional Convention. The first two were to embed slavery in the governing document and to limit the national government's authority to enumerated powers. The goal to embed slavery had been accomplished, but for the white South the Missouri crisis raised the prospect that its expansion would be halted by Congress exceeding its authority. The third objective was to assure an eventual white southern majority in the House of Representatives by allowing three-fifths of their slave population to be counted in apportioning membership. That strategy, based on the flawed belief that population trends would favor the South, had proven to be an utter failure.

In the First Congress, the South held twenty-nine seats in the House compared to thirty-six allotted to the North. By 1820 the North held a dominating 107 seats in the House over the South's seventy-nine. The white South had been accustomed to drawing support from the farming regions of the North, particularly Pennsylvania and New York. But when Missouri required a direct vote to approve or reject slavery's extension, the South found that it had run out of sufficient northern allies to carry the day in the House. The white South's essential priority became securing at least parity in the Senate. During the crux of the Missouri debates, the slave and free states were equally divided at eleven each. The white South could count on up to five Senate votes from the North, but that was a temporary advantage unsecured by sectional loyalty. The white South's desperate need was for equal standing in the Senate.

To the north, Missouri was seen no less as a struggle for political power but for widely divergent reasons. The Federalists had not forgotten losing the presidency to Thomas Jefferson due to the augmented Electoral College votes the three-fifths clause gave him in the 1800 election. The same clause had made possible the two congressional actions most despised by Federalists: Jefferson's embargo legislation that had damaged New England's economy and Madison's declaration of war against Great Britain in 1812. Missouri widened the clash over political power by drawing in northern Republicans. By the time the Missouri Compromise was reached, two themes that resonated up to the Civil War had received their first full-blown dress rehearsal: a northern conception of an insidious slave power that wielded disproportionate influence over national affairs and a white southern conviction that it was beleaguered by attacks and threatened by domination from the North.

Rufus King, in a Senate speech widely reprinted in newspapers and distributed as a pamphlet, said adoption of the three-fifths clause was the greatest concession made to draw the South into the union. Looking to Virginia, he calculated that seven of the state's twenty-three House members held their seats by virtue of slavery and the three-fifths clause. Extending the concession, he said, "of this disproportionate power to the new states would be unjust and odious."[21] In the House, Congressman Taylor struck the same theme, saying that although the South's gain through the three-fifths clause should be honored as to the existing states, "we are not willing to aggravate the inequality."[22] The clause "unquestionably is a hard bargain," Congressman Joseph Hemphill of Pennsylvania remarked, "but it is one that has not been made with the inhabitants of Missouri."[23]

South Carolina Congressman Charles Pinckney, who like King had been a convention delegate and was an architect of the three-fifths clause, took up the challenge. The only concession made, he said, was by the South, which gave up representation of two-fifths of its slave population. Those slaves, he argued, were more productive than any northern counterparts, producing nearly twice the dollar value of annual exports as those from the North. "The true motive for all this dreadful clamor throughout the Union," he said, "is to gain a fixed ascendency in the representation in Congress" by using the excuse of the three-fifths clause to accomplish it.[24]

That is very much as Edwin Holland, editor of the influential *Charleston Times*, saw it, writing in an anonymous pamphlet that the conflict's real cause was a desire in the North and East "to wrest from the Southern and Western states ascendancy that their wealth and talents have given them in the councils of the nation, and, by diminishing their representation, to secure to themselves the whole management of the affairs of government."[25]

In Boston, the view of the *Daily Advertiser* was that unless slavery's extension was stopped, "the future weight and influence of the free states" would be "lost forever."[26]

Kentucky's Congressman Hardin asked if the time had not come "to haul down the colors on which are engraven humanity, morality, and religion, and in lieu thereof unfurl the genuine banner, on which is written a contest for political consequences and mastery?" He then added, with stark candor, "On our side of the House, Mr. Chairman, we are contending not for victory, but struggling for our political existence."[27]

The white South felt besieged. The speeches, pamphlets, and newspaper commentaries about the evils of slavery and the prospect of freeing slave children in Missouri, many in the white South believed, were kindling that could ignite a new St. Domingue. Some thought they were deliberately designed to do so. When under attack the white South reverted to the last redoubt of slavery, the states' rights doctrine. That concept had been written into the Constitution by Pinckney's colleague at the convention, John Rutledge. It was constructed as a final barrier to intrusions by the general government into states' affairs by granting only enumerated powers to the general government, leaving all others to the states or to the people. The doctrine had been shoved aside for a broader view of constitutional authority almost as soon as the government first formed with the enactment of Hamilton's bank bill and national financial agenda. Jefferson had raised it as a bastion against the Alien and Sedition Acts, adding to it the corollary of nullification in the face of grave national offense. John Marshall's Supreme Court had spread the counter doctrine of broad constitutional interpretation as recently as the decision in *McCulloch v. Maryland*, blessing the use of the "necessary and proper" clause to validate actions not specifically enumerated in the Constitution. That March 1819 decision also forbade state actions designed to impede the legitimate exercise of congressional power.

The Missouri debates provided yet another platform to extend the controversy, in this case the white South deploying states' rights as a defense for slavery while the North drew on what was proper for the nation's well-being to justify restricting it. "It is a question calculated to test the powers of the Federal government; to determine how much sovereignty or power is left to the states and to the people," Virginia's James Johnson told the House.[28] From the North, Illinois Congressman Daniel Cook saw the issue as a matter of logic rather than power, asking, "is it more reasonable that the sixty thousand" white citizens of Missouri "should settle this great question than the ten millions by their representatives, who compose the nation, and who have all an equal interest in it?"[29]

Newspaper editorialists from the two sections struck similarly divergent positions. One could hear Jefferson's voice when the *Kentucky Reporter* asked, "Are not the powers thus attempted to be assumed by implication, symptoms of a dangerous system of consolidation—a merging of states' rights into the powers of the general government?"[30] From the Yankee heartland, the *Concord Observer* replied, "Slavery in the old states was an evil which the constitution could not remedy; but when new states are formed, the same evil does not exist, and may be forever excluded. Congress is therefore bound . . . to interpose for the perpetuation of a free and truly republican government, in all the new states."[31] The debate was over not just what the Constitution meant, but what kind of nation it had created. A government exercising power to do what a majority determined was necessary and proper was dynamic by definition. A majority that could define its own power was a threat to minorities.

No one outdid Maryland Senator William Pinkney in his rhetorical portrait of the wretchedness to which Missouri would be reduced if Congress overturned its sanction for slavery. Stripping Missouri of slavery, he said, would be "a humiliating badge of remediless inferiority patched upon her garments . . . a brand upon her forehead . . . [and] feeble Missouri is to be repelled with harshness, and forbidden to come at all, unless with the iron collar of servitude about her neck." Mandating freedom was the imposition of servitude, he reasoned, because if Congress had such power, "you may squeeze down a new-born sovereign state to the size of a pigmy."[32]

Perhaps the most articulate rendering of the opposing view came in a House floor debate pitting Virginia's Alexander Smyth arguing the states' rights position against Pennsylvania Federalist John Sergeant, who upheld the broad view of constitutional interpretation. Smyth led off speaking with the certainty of unclouded conviction. "Has the power to legislate over slavery been delegated to the United States?" he asked. "It has not. Has it been prohibited to the states? It has not. Then it is reserved to the states, respectively, or to the people. Consequently, it is reserved to the state of Missouri, or to the people of that state. And any attempt by Congress to deprive them of this reserved power, will be unjust, tyrannical, unconstitutional, and void."[33] No more succinct statement of the case could have been made.

A few days later Sergeant replied. "All powers are implied that are necessary for the execution of the enumerated powers," he said, "and the necessity need not be absolute. . . . Whence the authority to incorporate a bank? Whence the authority to apply the public treasure to the improvement of the country by roads and canals? . . . They all rest upon this single position, that an original power having been granted, every other power is implied which is necessary or useful for carrying that power into execution." He then went a step farther, asking, "Is it essential to the character of a free republican state that it should have the power of originating, establishing, or perpetuating a system of slavery—so essential that it is not a free republican state without the power?"[34]

The reply came from Philip Barbour of Virginia, who would later be appointed to the Supreme Court by Andrew Jackson. "It is asked," he said, "whether it is essential to sovereignty that a state should have slavery in its bosom? I answer no, sir, but it is of the very essence of sovereignty that a state should have the power of deciding for itself whether it will or will not tolerate slavery."[35]

The Virginian John Tyler, who would later rise to the presidency, attempted to place the issue beyond considerations of freedom and slavery. "It is the principle alone for which we contend," he said, "and for it we shall persist in contending 'to the last syllable of recorded time.'"[36] Viewed through the lens of self-interest, the white South used states' rights as a cloak to disguise slavery, then defended the garment rather than the thing hidden under it. Generations of Lost Cause apologists would continue that defense for more than 100 years after the cause was lost, and a few still do so to this day. Tyler's contention that the white South was fighting for principle alone—when the morality of its economic system was under attack, its balance of power with the North in Congress was at stake, and the expansion of slavery was in question—is absurd.

Another theme that emerged during the Missouri debates can be traced directly to the union's breakup: the profession on one side that slavery must be perpetuated and extended and, on the other, that it must be contained. Vague white southern references were made to emancipation, but by the time the debate ended, it was clear that for both political and economic reasons, the white South required slavery's expansion. The North sought to halt that expansion at Missouri. This struggle between the demand that slavery extend its domain and the adamant conviction that its growth must be halted continued up to the war's outbreak and contributed significantly to it.

During the summer and fall of 1819, in a welter of town meetings, rallies, petitions, and state legislative resolutions, northern opinion was forged into a demand that Congress forbid the admission of any new slave states. Initially motivated by Federalist efforts, the call to end slavery's expansion swept the North until the legislatures of New Hampshire, Vermont, Massachusetts, New York, Pennsylvania, Ohio, and Indiana had all adopted resolutions opposing Missouri's admission with slavery.[37]

One Kentucky newspaper was led to sniff that the people of Philadelphia, New York, and Boston "have about as much right to interfere with the constitution of Missouri as the people of China."[38] Such criticism did not deter the *New Hampshire Patriot*, whose editor wrote, "Whatever may be the public feeling *south* of the Potomac, there is but one sentiment *north* of the Chesapeake on this subject—and that is, if the evil which already exists cannot be prevented, at least that slavery shall not be permitted to spread beyond its present confines."[39] The *Patriot's* conclusion was essentially identical to the main platform plank Abraham Lincoln won the presidency on forty years later.

The white South met the North's containment doctrine with the diffusion theory, a plan that had a history of its own and survived into the 1840s as a rationale for slavery's expansion.

In 1798, a Virginia congressman had argued that diffusing slavery into the Mississippi Territory would "spread the blacks over a larger space, so that in time it might be safe to carry into effect the plan [for emancipation] which certain philanthropists have so much at heart."[40] The idea had a certain theoretical cohesion in that it was widely understood that emancipation laws in many northern states had been made possible, in part, because of the relatively low proportion of Blacks to whites in the population. In practice, the diffusion argument was a wedge used to justify slavery's expansion. By the time it spread into the new state of Texas in the late 1840s, enlarging slavery's reach required no pretense that doing so made eventual emancipation more attainable.

John Tyler, who as president was instrumental in making Texas a new state, declared in the Missouri debates that by pursuing a diffusion policy on the problem of slavery, "you may reduce it to a summer's cloud."[41] The rhetorical flirtation with fantasy was not limited to Tyler. Ninian Edwards had been born in Maryland and, after moving to Kentucky, had risen to be the state's chief justice. He was appointed governor of the Illinois Territory in 1809. By the time of the Missouri debates, Edwards was an Illinois senator and a solidly reliable vote for the white South. He argued that because diffusion was the heart of the white South's policy in Missouri, the principles for which it was contending "are calculated not only to diminish the power of their respective states, but to promote the abolition of slavery itself."[42] Kentucky Senator Richard Johnson polished that picture's rosy complexion with his contribution: "I advocate the best interests of the sons of bondage when I entreat you to give them room to be happy, and so disperse them as that, under the auspices of Providence, they may one day enjoy the rights of man, without convulsing the empire or endangering society."[43] Some years later Johnson served as vice president under Martin Van Buren.

None of the slaveholders planning to move to Missouri or to sell their slaves there if its constitution were upheld were doing so in anxious anticipation of bringing forward the day of emancipation. Their motive was profit. Opening new lands to slavery brought greater demand and higher prices for slaves. "If Congress provide that men may permanently be held in slavery in the vast regions of the West," the *New Hampshire Sentinel* commented, "the value of this species of property must necessarily rise."[44] New markets for dispersal were particularly important to Virginia and

Maryland, which held slaves in excess as tobacco fields became unproductive due to soil depletion. Although the nation's slave population grew by an average of 28 percent each decade up to 1860, that in Missouri after the compromise was struck increased by two-and-a-half times by 1830 and doubled again to reach 58,000 by 1840.[45]

Virginia's Congressman Smyth derided northern members who "proposed to hem in the blacks in a sterile country, where they are hard worked and ill fed, that they may be rendered unproductive, and their race prevented from increasing."[46] Instead, he urged, "If you are truly desirous that the slaves shall be treated with humanity, let them be as much as possible dispersed. The smaller their number in any district, the better will be their situation." Smyth's Virginia colleague Philip Barbour saw an additional advantage to diffusion in that "by diminishing the proportion which the slaves bear in point of numbers to the whites, you diminish their motives to insurrection."[47] Failure to diffuse slaves excited Kentucky's Congressman Hardin to envision Black revolts that would be marked "first by murders, assassination, massacres, and conflagrations; and when this spirit of insurrection is quelled, numbers will be punished with exemplary vengeance, and the situation of the rest rendered more miserable."[48] Misery, war, death, and bloodshed might all be avoided by spreading slavery westward.

Further, at least according to the *National Intelligencer*, the expansion of slavery was not even under consideration. In the tone of a frustrated teacher trying to get the obvious through to dull pupils, the paper insisted, "Once and for all, no such question [as the extension of slavery] is presented to the consideration of Congress, or of the nation. The question concerns only the *diffusion* or the *concentration* of slaves now in the country."[49] From Monticello the aging Thomas Jefferson saw the issue in a similar light, writing, "Removal of slaves from one state to another . . . would never make a slave of one human being who would not be so without it."[50]

Georgia's Senator Freeman Walker put the case frankly without attempting to shift the moral burden to the North. "The evil, if it be one, already exists," he said. "It has taken deep root in our soil, and I know of no means of extirpating it. As the poison cannot be entirely destroyed, then, the political physician would recommend that it should be scattered and disseminated through the system, so as to lose its effect."[51] Beneath his vivid analogy lay the more central message that not only did slavery exist, but that it must be perpetuated and expanded.

Congressman William Darlington reached a different conclusion when comparing slavery to illness. "Would you disseminate small-pox, with a view to dilute its malignity, or to mitigate its effects," he asked. "No, sir, that would be quackery."[52] Southerners' references to some vague prospect of future emancipation were palliatives. Their need to maintain at least parity in Senate voting power was real. Beyond these, however, the pressure of confining a rapidly growing servile population within its existing boundaries evoked admissions of fear from slaveholders. The white South was in a situation regarding slavery, Congressman George Tucker of Virginia said, "in which we can neither safely set them free, nor hold them in subjection." If the restrictions proposed for Missouri were enforced, he said, the choices left to the South would be eventual abandonment of the land by white owners, or a struggle between the two races that "would end in a war of extermination."[53] At nearly the same time, Jefferson was writing of the South having the wolf by the ears "and we can neither hold, nor safely let him go." The Missouri crisis had awakened him "like a fire bell in the night . . . and filled me with terror."[54] Both North and South had high economic and political stakes at play in the Missouri debates. Only in the white South did the intangibles of guilt and fear also thrive.

The northern majority in the House remained unpersuaded by the array of diffusion arguments. By enlarging the limits of slavery, Congressman Sergeant said, the South "was preparing the means for its indefinite increase and extension" and enabling the present slaveholding states "to throw off the surplus, with all its productive power, on the West."[55] Diffusion was an illusion, Congressman William Hendricks of Indiana said, because "no matter how extensive the region over which you scatter your slaves, the day will come when all that region will be in the same situation in which the Southern states now are."[56] Illinois Congressman Cook broached what was later to become a mainstay of northern belief, that containing slavery was the first step to ending it. A leading consideration to him was "to limit the sphere of this dangerous population, with an eye to its ultimate eradication."[57]

The argument the white South most feared, the one that questioned a constitutional sanction for slavery, came from Vermont's Charles Rich, who believed that "a *right* to hold a fellow-being in slavery, under any form of government, does not exist." He qualified his assertion by saying he spoke of natural rights and that necessity might convey its own set of rights. But, he continued, "I utterly and absolutely deny that because the necessity still exists in some sections of the Union, and with it the right, that hence the right is coextensive with the limits of our country, and with *any* limits, which, at all future periods, may be given to it; and that we are bound to pursue a policy which will perpetuate the necessity, and with it the existence of slavery."[58]

White southerners responded to challenges to slavery's legitimacy with a battery of argument. The Constitution "recognized," "intended," "acknowledged," "sanctioned," "guaranteed," and "encouraged" the right to property in man, southern representatives assured Congress and the public throughout the debates.[59] Future president Tyler made northerners complicit in slavery by pointing to the fugitive slave clause and declaring that "you have not only acknowledged our right to this species of property, but that you have gone much further, and have bound yourselves to rivet the chains of the slave."[60]

Tellingly, none of the southern arguments pointed to specific constitutional language granting a right to property in man, a reference that would have been easily made if the case was of citing state laws that did so. That could not be done because the Constitution contained no such language to cite. Instead, the references were to the Constitution's three clauses that dealt with slavery, but in the deliberately crafted terms of "such persons" in the three-fifths and fugitive slave clauses or without using the originally proposed words "justly" and "lawfully" in the foreign slave trade clause.[61] Noting that "the word 'slave' is nowhere to be found in the Constitution," Congressman Rich argued that although the framers "were obliged indirectly to admit the fact of its existence, they purposely, and very carefully, avoided the use of any expressions from which . . . an argument could be derived in favor of its legitimacy."[62] Slavery was sufficiently embedded in the Constitution that the North conceded it could not be interfered with in states where it already existed, a concession the white South did not trust that the North would honor. The two sections continued to fight over whether the document conceded a right to property in man.[63]

The fault lines of sectional economic and political differences exposed in the Missouri debates also produced threats to make the fracture permanent by disunion. Given the length and intensity of the debates, however, invocations of the disunion threat were less frequent and vehement than might have been expected. It was as if in coming close to the cauldron, many of those engaged backed away from its intense heat.

Henry Meigs, a New York member of the House, expressed this more cautious tone as well as any. "Our free Constitution was made by men who were wise enough to know the danger of sectional divisions," he noted. "This Constitution is no more than a profoundly wise agreement to differ." Meigs was touching a cord central to the young country's brief existence. Larger than all Europe, the nation was a sprawling enterprise ranging from flinty-eyed Yankee traders to raw-boned Alabama frontiersmen and Indian fighters speaking dialects almost unintelligible to one another. The history books decreed that such republics were surely destined for tyranny or dismemberment. To have any hope of realizing the benefits of union, the disparate parts must bind themselves together by compromise. "If we, sir, shall be unhappily so unwise as to forget this," Meigs continued, "nothing will be left for us and our posterity but awful combats at parallels of latitude, or physical lines of demarcation."[64]

A veiled disunion threat from Virginia's General Assembly was met by sniping from a New York newspaper. The assembly passed a resolution vowing resistance "with manly fortitude" to any congressional attempt to impose restrictions on Missouri's entrance into the union. The *New York Daily Advertiser* shot back at the "haughty dictatrix of public opinion" for encouraging "a standard of rebellion."[65] Anonymity gave room for venting in a letter reportedly written by a member of Virginia's House delegation to the *Petersburg Intelligencer*. Unless the Constitution was amended to "arrest this mad career of aggression and outrage upon property and state rights," the unnamed author wrote, "I would abandon [the union] with as much indifference as I would turn from an association of swindlers, pick-pockets and cut-throats."[66]

At times the threats were direct. Early in the debates, a Georgia representative rebuked Tallmadge for kindling "a fire which all the waters of the ocean cannot put out, which seas of blood can only extinguish." The Missouri amendments' author staunchly replied that "if a dissolution of the Union must take place, let it be so! If civil war, which gentlemen so much threaten, must come, I can only say, let it come!"[67] Georgia's Senator Walker chose lurid for his frame. "I behold the father armed against the son," he intoned, "and the son against the father. I perceive a brother's sword crimsoned with a brother's blood. I perceive our houses wrapt in flames, and our wives and infant children driven from their homes."[68] Four decades later when war did come, it more than matched Walker's imagery.

Some historians have dismissed the threats of disunion and civil war as posturing without intent to carry through on the measure.[69] The prospect of breakup seemed real enough to many of those engaged at the time. At the end of the debate, when a vote on the major compromise was at hand and fear of disunion abated, one member cast his eyes forward and beheld the danger still to come. "A precipice lies before us," said Connecticut Congressman James Stevens, "at which perdition is inevitable."[70]

The rancor the Missouri debates unleashed also led to the first steps in a reversal in the white South's attitude toward two issues central to the causes of the war to come. The debates forecast a white southern switch in opinion on emancipation from good to bad and on slavery from bad to good. Throughout the debates, emancipation was almost universally hailed North and South as at least a desirable goal and slavery deprecated as an evil, unfairly entailed upon slaveholders. But in the debates, a few southern voices reversed both these positions. Only over time did the reversals take hold. The white southern transformations in thought about emancipation and slavery did not occur in their entirety during the debates. Virginia would be wrestling with emancipation a dozen years later. Proslavery doctrine did not gain prominence in the white South until the late 1830s. A few isolated voices calling emancipation futile and slavery both natural and good had been raised in the past. From a broad perspective, however, the white southern abandonment of emancipation as a goal and the embrace of slavery as a good to be indefinitely expanded may fairly be said to have been introduced on the national stage during the Missouri crisis.

Virginia's James Barbour delivered a Senate oration of biblical prophecy to thrust emancipation into a future so distant as to be ethereal while forecasting the day of its arrival. If it be consistent with God's will, Barbour said, "in the fullness of time, to break the fetter of the slave, he will raise up some Moses to be their deliverer. To him commission will be given to lead them up out of the land of bondage."[71] He went on at considerable length to describe seas subsiding, mountains disappearing, and dungeons surrendering their victims. For all its trappings of revelation, Barbour's message was clear—although slaves might be freed, it would be by divine inspiration, not by human hand, and certainly not by white southern agency.

In the House, Barbour's Virginia colleague Alexander Smyth picked through the issue more carefully from the perspective of present-day reality. He began by noting that the flaw undermining the American Colonization Society's program was that freed Blacks did not want to be deported to Africa. They wanted to remain in America. To examine the state of free Blacks in the country, he turned to the South's leading political intellectual, John Taylor of Caroline. His recent work, *Arator*, had concluded that free Blacks are "destined to a life of idleness, anxiety, and guilt." This being the case, Smyth said, "the situation of blacks would not be improved" by emancipation, and that of society "would be greatly injured" should emancipation occur. "But perhaps it will be said that a partial and gradual emancipation is what is sought for," he continued. "If a total emancipation would be a great evil, a partial emancipation would be a lesser evil." The reversal was complete. It was not slavery but emancipation that was evil. He concluded by waving St. Dominque's bloody shirt of slave rebellion and attributing its outbreak to a small cadre of freed Blacks. In sum, Smyth said, "emancipation of the present race of blacks in this country cannot be effected."[72]

The corollary to rejecting emancipation was to declare slavery perpetual. Permanent slavery, with the servile population increasing even with the closure of the foreign slave trade, also meant slavery must expand.

Abandoning emancipation was far less difficult than reaching the conviction that slavery was a positive good, a conviction that some white southerners never reached, particularly among the majority who did not own slaves. Emancipation was, after all, an idea in the South, not a program with all the apparatus of policy as it developed in the North. Slavery, on the other hand, was the South's central reality, the basis of its economy, and a legacy from its earliest days of colonization. The necessary evil argument had served as the white South's main defense of slavery since before the republic's founding. The defense absolved current slaveholders and their ancestors of guilt by attributing the original sin of introducing and promoting slavery to the British. In this formulation the slaveholder was the true victim, entailed with a burden not of his making. Any complicating discussion of the slaveholders or their ancestors having been willing or even eager buyers of the evil aboard British slavers was conveniently excluded from the necessary evil argument.

The argument's flaw was that it still left white southerners defending evil. For a Christian people proud of their honor, that was a most difficult position to sustain. In scholar William Freehling's words, "the 'necessary evil' argument rested on the premise that utility was the appropriate standard for political decision and expediency the proper criterion for government action."[73] Tyrants could be satisfied with utility and expediency. Citizens of the world's only free republic, and inheritors of an Age of Enlightenment, required more worthy motives. The Missouri crisis, in a day-after-day, leading to month-after-month assault on slavery, left the white South's necessary evil shield badly battered. In a basic sense, many white southerners were also fed up with hearing themselves described as evil's defenders. They needed a new shield. The positive good argument provided it. Converting evil into good proved to be a difficult mental exercise.

In an extraordinarily revealing address, Georgia Congressman Robert Reid can be heard struggling with the conversion even as he spoke. "The slaveholding states have not brought this calamity upon themselves," he began. "They have not voluntarily assumed this burden. It was fastened upon them by the mother country." From this classic necessary evil premise, he then ameliorated the evil itself. "Sir, the slaves of the South are held to a service which ... is certain and moderate. They are well supplied with food and raiment. They are 'content and careless of tomorrow's fare.'" Reid continued with assurances that the South's slaves received the blessings of religion and the protection of the laws. Switching again, he went on, "It is true, they are often made subject to wanton acts of tyranny," but then so were many whites. "Believe me," he said, "I am not the panegyrist of slavery. It is an unnatural state; a dark cloud which obscures half the lustre of our free institutions!" Veering yet again, he continued, "But it is a fixed evil, which we can only alleviate."

After analogizing the South to a man who has cancer but refuses surgery because it might kill him, Reid completed his confusion by adopting both sides of the emancipation question. "I would hail that day as the most glorious in its dawning, which should behold, with safety to themselves and our citizens, the black population of the United States placed upon the high eminence of equal rights, and clothed in the privileges and immunities of American citizens! But this is a dream of philanthropy, which can never be fulfilled; and whoever shall act in the country upon such wild theories, shall cease to be a benefactor, and become a destroyer of the human family."[74]

In the years ahead, white southerners in their tens of thousands either struggled privately or had a eureka moment in which they sloughed off the necessary evil and adopted the positive good version of slavery—at least as the public face of their belief. The deeper one went in the South, and the higher the proportion of Blacks to whites in the population, the more likely the conversion was to have occurred.

South Carolina Senator William Smith cleared a path for them in what may have been the most important speech of the Missouri crisis for initiating a long-term change in the white South's attitude toward slavery. He observed that slaves "are so domesticated, or so kindly treated by their masters, and their situations so improved ... their comforts are as great, and their labor not more arduous than any other class of laboring people." Denying the most pervasive fear among the South's white population, Smith asserted that slaves "are the shield of their masters instead of their deadly enemy." He then drove home the positive good argument for slavery. "There is no class of laboring people in any country upon the globe, except in the United States," he said, "that are better clothed, better fed, or more cheerful, or labor less, or who are more happy, or, indeed, who have more liberty and indulgence, than the slaves of the South-ern and Western states." The root of all this benevolence, Smith said, was that "the whole commerce between master and slave is patriarchal . . . . The black children are constant associates of the white children; they eat together, they play together, and their affections are often times so strongly formed in early life as never to be forgotten; so much so that in thousands of instances there is nothing but the shadow of slavery left."[75] He finished with standard references to biblical sanctions for slavery, but his image of Black slaves living in virtual freedom under the affectionate care of fatherly masters was a revelatory conception.

Senator Benjamin Ruggles of Ohio expressed his "astonishment" at what Smith had said. "That gentleman justified slavery on the broadest principles, without qualification or reserve. This was taking entirely new ground. It was going farther than he had ever heard any gentleman go before."[76]

An irony of Smith's version of slavery is that the patriarchal model upon which it was based was at that time being replaced by the indus-trial model of what it became.[77] Smith's dollhouse vision of slavery with Massa in the big house and happy darkies dancing and playing banjos under the magnolias on the surrounding grounds took deep hold in southern whites' imagination. It was what they wanted slavery to be. But as Smith spoke the lower Mississippi Valley was being transformed, as tidewater South Carolina had long been transformed, into vast tracts of commodity agriculture where gangs of slaves lived and died under the eyes of overseers on plantations that might only rarely or never be visited by their owners.

The closest northern equivalent of Smith's speech was delivered by New York Federalist Rufus King. He did not so much mold public opinion, however, as give expression to a fiery conviction at the heart of the absolute abolitionist creed that never captured more than a minority of northern adherents. King's remarks made slaveholders grit their teeth and clench their fists as he spoke, according to observer John Quincy Adams. "I have yet to learn that one man can make a slave of another,"

Rufus King. COURTESY OF
THE LIBRARY OF CONGRESS.

King said. In an avowal that denied any legitimacy to slavery, as a necessary evil or otherwise, King continued, "If one man cannot do so, no number of individuals can have any better right to do it. And I hold that all laws or compacts imposing any such a condition upon any human being are absolutely void, because contrary to the law of nature, which is the law of God, by which he makes his ways known to man, and is paramount to all human controls."[78]

King's assertion of a higher law of divinely inspired rights broke with a virtual political pact that northern members of Congress would not contest the constitutional legitimacy of slavery in those states where it already existed. King himself quickly backed away from his stance. But the conviction that a higher law ruled the destiny of nations blazed white hot in the hearts of abolitionist leaders such as William Lloyd Garrison, who would soon declare that he was in earnest and that he would be heard.

The natural law doctrine had no greater expression than the Declaration of Independence's transcendent sentence avowing that all men are created equal. Those pesky few words simply would not go away. During the debates, southerners tried to dismantle them. Tyler said they were "lovely and beautiful" but still only a "fallacy."[79] Hardin of Kentucky insisted they did not mean what they said but were intended by the Founders to apply only to free white men.[80] Yet the words themselves would not change. They were a lodestar for leaders such as Lincoln. They were a nagging conscience to plain northern whites and to more than a few in the South, particularly yeoman farmers who did not own slaves. For slaves who heard or were able to read the words, they stood as prophecy yet to be fulfilled.

In terms of causes leading to civil war, mention should also be made of factors that arose during the Missouri crisis that are more psychological than empirical. The most obvious was that slavery was a positive good, positing a superior white race benignly tending to its slaves in a mutually affectionate relationship. Over time in large portions of the white South this belief became a full-blown societal delusion.

The white South's delusion of racial superiority, largely shared by northern whites, became elaborated over time into a narrative of a uniquely southern chivalric society that ballooned in some quarters into the conviction that southern elites descended from the eleventh-century Norman bloodline in England, creating not just a separate section of the country, but a separate and superior race of Americans.[81]

The opposite side of slavery as a positive good belief was the higher law premise of the abolitionists' unceasing shouts that slaveholders were a vile species of humanity. William Freehling, one of the preeminent scholars of antebellum America, has cited his own belief that the focus of discussion of the causes of the Civil War belongs "on the psychological torment which led southerners to rage at the slavery issue" so as to precipitate nearly every prewar sectional crisis.[82] In this light, the 1836 observation that abolitionists "madden" southerners warrants being taken literally. The comment was made by William Drayton, a leading writer espousing slavery as a positive good.[83] The most maddening of all consequences that abolitionists were said to be deliberately pursuing was the bloodbath that must inevitably follow immediate emancipation. This, too, became a mass white southern delusion. As Drayton put it, in language that suffused southern writing on the subject, "the madness which a sudden freedom from restraint begets—the overpowering burst of long-buried passion—the wild frenzy of revenge, and the savage lust for blood, all unite to give to the warfare of liberated slaves, traits of cruelty and crime which nothing earthly can equal."[84]

It is difficult to overemphasize the white southern conviction that abolitionists were plotting the vicious violations and murders of southern children, women, and men by freed Blacks. What the white South feared most did happen. Sudden and complete emancipation did come. What followed was not as white southerners long dreaded, the massacre of whites by Blacks, evoking the worst scenes from the St. Domingue rebellion. It was the lynching of Blacks by whites to keep the ex-slaves in their place. The terrifying delusion of race war being a consequence of full emancipation can be traced back to Jefferson and others before him. But by giving impetus to both the proslavery and higher law doctrines, the Missouri debates also gave impetus to delusions in the minds of large swaths of the white southern population that significantly contributed to the Civil War.

Although other trends arose in the years ahead, contributing to the causes of eventual war, those outlined above constituted the panoply of divisions exposed during the Missouri crisis that led to the Civil War. Political leaders would attempt to dampen these divisions. Other issues intruded, demanding public attention. But Missouri set the template for why the war came.

The main compromise was reached, and the issue seemingly resolved, in early March 1820. The compromise was a package deal that House Speaker Clay pushed through in three separate votes after the Senate had already acted.

The admission of Maine came first, promising voting parity in the Senate, once Missouri came in, of twelve free and twelve slave states.

Next, the crucial provision admitting Missouri without any restriction on slavery was approved on a narrow ninety to eighty-seven vote margin with just enough northern supporters joining a solid South to secure passage.

The final clause, splitting the remaining territories west of the Mississippi between slave and free along the thirty-six-degree, thirty-minute line of parallel passed overwhelmingly.

Congress had hardly acted before the conflict flared up anew. Missourians opted for another constitutional convention during the summer. The delegates inserted language requiring the legislature to enact prohibitions on free Blacks from entering the new state. Congress began a new round of Missouri debates, this time over the question of whether Missouri had violated the federal Constitution's guarantee of equal rights and immunities for all citizens.

In this fight, northerners no longer held the high ground of defending freedom and attacking slavery. The question was narrowed to the constitutional issue of whether free Blacks, as citizens, had the right to enter any state as did any other citizen. White Southerners found a weak point, arguing not only that free Blacks were not considered citizens in their section of the country, but that their disenfranchisement in several northern states proved that they were not considered citizens there as well. At the time, free Blacks could vote without restriction in only five northeastern states, and New York imposed an onerous property qualification.[85] New Jersey had stripped free Blacks of the right to vote in 1807. Connecticut did so in 1814. Rhode Island would follow in 1822, as would Pennsylvania by 1837. Within two decades, only about 7 percent of northern free Blacks had a right to vote.[86]

The broader pattern was clear. Although northerners might disparage slavery, they opposed any sort of equal footing with Blacks on political, economic, or social grounds.[87] Rhode Island Senator James Burrill spoke for many north of the Mason-Dixon line when he said early in the debates "I am not only averse to a slave population, but also to any population composed of blacks, and of the infinite and motley confusion of colors between the black and the white."[88] Not too many years later famed French observer Alexis de Tocqueville noted, "The prejudice of race appears to be stronger in the states that have abolished slavery than in those where it still exists; and nowhere is it so intolerant as in those states where servitude has never been known."[89] Racism, in short, was an American value widely shared by whites in all sections of the country. The

North tended to dispense its version of racism as a straight shot of whites neither liking nor wanting to compete with Blacks. The white South developed an elaborate cocktail of white supremacy including religious, cultural, and legal justifications.

In Congress, Henry Clay, no longer speaker, fashioned a compromise in the House with the contorted language that the Missouri constitution "shall never be construed to authorize the passage of any law" denying any citizen's privileges and immunities under the federal Constitution.[90] The short version of the compromise is that it amounted to a congressional declaration that Missouri's constitution did not say what it plainly did say. By 1825, state law in Missouri provided that no free Black or mulatto could "come into the state under any pretext whatever."[91] The irony was unintended at the time, but the only way to square Clay's compromise provision and the Constitution is to decide, as did the Supreme Court in the *Dred Scott* case on the eve of the Civil War, that free Blacks are not citizens.

On this note the Missouri debates finally came to a close.

In the immediate aftermath of the Missouri crisis, an assessment came of winners and losers. "I consider myself and associates as conquered," wrote Rufus King, expressing the view not only of Federalists like himself but of the northern Republican majority who voted against the compromise.[92] Charles Pinckney was anxious to inform the citizens of Charleston of a decided victory as soon as the deal was struck. The compromise paved the way for the inclusion of not just Missouri, but of Arkansas and Florida as slave states that will, he wrote, "give the south ... in a short time an addition of six, and perhaps eight members in the senate of the United States. It is considered here by the slave holding states as a great triumph."[93]

The outcome, however considered, was closely run in the House. To see how close, one needs to look at the sectional voting on the two central compromise measures. A strong majority of eighty-seven northerners voted to retain the Tallmadge amendments' slavery restrictions. A crucial fourteen votes to strike the restrictions were cast by northerners, just enough—with a single vote to spare, along with all the votes from southern members—to pass the measure. The absence on the floor of an additional four northern representatives helped to seal the decision.

The crucial southern vote came on the provision creating the thirty-six thirty line, dividing future slave and free states. This was the white southern part of the compromise, restricting slavery's future growth north of that line. On that measure southerners cast a bare majority of thirty-nine votes in favor against thirty-seven opposed.[94] With these two issues settled, the third piece of the package, actual admission of Missouri, passed with slight opposition. The core of the compromise, however, rested on the votes of a decided minority of northern members combined with a bare majority of southerners. The House compromise coalition was exceedingly fragile.

The decision's narrowness belied the status it achieved. Hezekiah Niles, editor of *Niles' Weekly Register*, spoke for many when he wrote that "the circumstances of this case give to this law a *moral force* equal to that of a positive provision in the constitution."[95] Slavery's containment came to be seen in the North as a solemn pact by which Congress had taken a decisive step toward the ultimate eradication of the South's peculiar institution. What first seemed like a defeat came to be viewed as a stride toward victory.

The opposite occurred in the South. Initially, as Pinckney proclaimed, the white South stood to gain Senate votes, as three new slaves states seemed sure to soon enter the Union, and a fourth might not be far off. A doctrine of local control had won out in Missouri upholding the states' rights view of the Constitution. The vast tracts of western lands north of the compromise dividing line were hardly to be expected to grow and organize themselves into candidates for statehood anytime soon. But things did not work out that way. Arkansas's entry into the union as a slave state was stalled for fifteen years until it could be paired with Michigan as a free state. By the time Florida was approved for entry in 1845, with Texas soon to follow, a host of prospective free states was waiting in line ready to tilt the Senate to northern control with votes from Iowa, Wisconsin, California, Minnesota, Oregon, and Kansas. The South was cooped up and would come to look for new territory for expansion.

The Missouri ordeal may also be seen, as was the Seven Days battle before Richmond in the Civil War, as marking the end of a kind of national innocence and the beginning of a sense of hard reckoning across the country. The battle in which General McClellan lost his advantage before the southern capital to General Lee ended the Civil War's first phase. In that early period both sides thought the war would be short, the white South sure its sons would be easy masters in battle, the North confident its overwhelming power would quickly subdue the rebellion. After Richmond, the grim part of the conflict set in: total war, endless attrition, battlefield butcher lists. After the Missouri crisis a certain grimness, a hardening of attitudes both North and South, set in. The sectional estrangement deepened, the contest for political power was grueling, the view on one side or the other shifted gradually from that of fellow countryman to that of enemy, potential or real.

The Missouri crisis demonstrated that the Constitution and the political system it created had no solution to the problem of slavery. Instead, slavery was so intractable and explosive that mere discussion of it threatened disunion. Some political leaders concluded that if the issue was too hot to handle, the best thing to do was not to handle it. The strategy of withdrawing slavery from the national agenda, of deciding not to talk about it, was pursued with varying degrees of success until the outbreak of the Civil War.

Except for the abolitionists, Rufus King's brief foray in advancing a higher law theory against slavery was but a mild gust of wind compared to the torrent of outrage they soon launched.

In March 1819, just before the Missouri crisis began, Elihu Embree drew the first sheet of his new weekly newspaper, the *Manumission Intelligencer*, off his press in Jonesborough (now Jonesboro), Tennessee.[96] Embree, a thirty-five-year-old Quaker, was on a crusade. The *Intelligencer*, of which only a few copies still exist, is credited with being the country's first known newspaper devoted entirely to the antislavery cause. Embree had owned slaves but sold them as a young man, reportedly at considerable personal financial cost. He had settled with his second wife in the hilly east Tennessee town among neighbors belonging to the Society of Friends. Several years later, findings based on the 1827 convention of

American abolition societies would show that twenty-five of the 130 antislavery groups were based in Tennessee, where the eastern part of the state maintained an antislavery tradition up to and through the Civil War.[97] In April 1820, Embree began printing a new monthly newspaper, *The Emancipator*, with the avowed aim "to advocate the abolition of slavery." Within the year the paper had 2,000 subscribers, ranking among the largest in Tennessee.[98] "Compromise" and "accommodation" were not part of his vocabulary. He saw slavery as "this horrid wickedness, sin of oppression, so incompatible with the law of nature, and the whole tenor of the gospel." His voice was cut short in December 1820 when he died after suffering a physical and nervous collapse.

His banner was quickly taken up by Benjamin Lundy, son of a Quaker, who determined to begin publishing a paper of his own when he heard of Embree's death. Lundy's paper, *Genius of Universal Emancipation*, began appearing in January 1821. Within a few years, abolitionist papers sprang up in Philadelphia, New York City, Boston, Providence, Bennington (Vermont), and New Orleans.[99] The movement hit its stride with the arrival of William Lloyd Garrison. As publisher of *The Liberator* and rhetorical leader of the American Anti-Slavery Society beginning in 1831, Garrison dealt out unremitting blasts of abolitionism that infuriated slaveholders while provoking their deepest fears.

Finally, and most important, the Missouri crisis was what historian Richard H. Brown called the "wellspring" for the political coalition that began with Andrew Jackson and created the Jacksonian Era in American politics.[100] The new Democratic Party that formed around Jackson was built on an agrarian and frontier coalition that consciously suppressed agitation of slavery as a legitimate part of the national agenda. The creation of the Democratic Party was left to the deft hands of its chief architect, Martin Van Buren. Virginian Thomas Ritchie may be seen as a proxy for the Southern white voters who constituted its base.

As noted, a substantial southern minority opposed the compromise's ban on slavery above the thirty-six thirty line. Ritchie was one of them. Assessing the deal that ended the crisis, Ritchie wrote as editor of the *Richmond Enquirer*, "Instead of joy, we scarcely ever recollected to have tasted a bitterer cup." His advice to those living below the Mason-

Martin Van Buren. COURTESY
OF THE LIBRARY OF CONGRESS.

Dixon line was that they "owe it to themselves to keep their eye firmly fixed on Texas. If we are cooped up to the North, we must have elbow room on the west."[101]

Ritchie was spokesman for the Old Republicans, those who stood firm with Jefferson for states' rights and limited government. That faction of the Republican Party held it as doctrine, as the debates made resoundingly clear, that Congress had no authority to overrule the decision of any territory or incoming state to sanction slavery. To determine otherwise was a violation of states' rights that threatened slavery and the southern way of life wherever it existed. Ritchie was a member of the Richmond Junto, a secretive group of about twenty Virginians who dominated the state's politics in the early 1800s. Spencer Roane, Virginia's leading jurist and friend to Jefferson, led the group. He had started the *Enquirer* and chose Ritchie, his cousin, to edit it.[102] The Junto was disenchanted with a Republican Party that had become so broad in amalgamating all viewpoints that many of its members could support the old Federalist agenda of a national bank and more recent demands for tariff protection and internal improvements funded by the national government. By the time of the Missouri crisis the party that Jefferson had seen as a national consensus around republican principles of limited government had been stretched to include those from the North who white southerners believed threatened their very existence by employing an expansive view of constitutional interpretation.

Martin Van Buren was an American original. Many have since imitated him but none ever matched his ability to harness political power into a dominant political party. Born in upstate New York, Van Buren earned his sobriquet the Little Magician as leader of the Bucktail faction of Old Republicans. He was a man of caution, reason, and self-discipline who calculated the mechanics of building an enduring political apparatus. He was not one to be caught up in ideological fervor. He had supported the concept of internal improvements with the caveat that they receive state legislative sanction. He had approved continuing to allow free Blacks to vote in New York but backed the restriction that they have a $250 property hold to be eligible.

In the fall of 1821, Van Buren stepped onto the national stage as a senator from New York just after the Missouri crisis had ended. He saw President Monroe's amalgamated Republican Party as internally weak and potentially disastrous to the union. He believed political parties and partisan conflict were healthy and necessary adjuncts to government. Directed from the top down, as was the Richmond Junto and Van Buren's own Albany Regency, they could impose discipline, set priorities, and smooth over divisions. Without party influence, he believed, sectional antagonism, like that inflamed during the Missouri debates, was inevitable. His special genius was to dispense with ideological imperatives in looking at the whole American political landscape and to extract from it a formula for self-perpetuating majority rule. He did not have far to look.

His own natural constituency of small farmers in upstate New York had been among Jefferson's original majority party strung together from agrarian communities running down the Hudson River Valley, through Pennsylvania, and along the eastern side of the Appalachians from Virginia south to Georgia. New York and Pennsylvania electoral votes were crucial to Jefferson's 1800 run for the presidency. The steadfast belief that the government that governs least governs best held together Jefferson's far-flung coalition. This was the alliance Van Buren set out to re-create. Under it not only could a southern man who could draw northern agrarian votes win the presidency, but so could a northern man with southern sympathies.

Soon after arriving in the nation's capital, Van Buren cast a line to the South by influencing New York's congressional delegation to support Virginia's Philip Barbour in his successful bid to become Speaker of the House. Soon afterward the Little Magician paid a visit to Spencer Roane in Virginia. He also developed a personal friendship with Thomas Ritchie. For Van Buren, the presidential election of 1824 was essentially a test run for his ideal of a candidate with a strong southern base but enough northern support to gain a majority.

As it turned out, four Republicans ran against each other with John Quincy Adams, who began his political career as a Federalist, capturing the presidency. His victory came not at the polls, where no candidate received a majority of Electoral College votes, but in the House of Representatives. In that body, although candidate Andrew Jackson captured a plurality of popular and electoral votes, Adams won when Henry Clay swung his support in the House behind the son of a former president. The deal was forever after dubbed the Corrupt Bargain when Adams, as president, named Clay his secretary of state, a position then seen as heir apparent. The Republican Party that had tried to be all things to all voters was wrecked.

In January 1827, Van Buren laid out his vision for a new political party, built on the old Jeffersonian model, in a letter to Ritchie.[103] Promoting the candidacy of Andrew Jackson, Van Buren wrote that it would be one thing for the general to win the White House solely on the basis of his military career. It would be "a far different thing," he continued, if a Jackson victory came "as the result of a combined and concerted effort of a political party, holding in the main, to certain tenets & opposed to certain prevailing principles." The "substantial reorganization of the Old Republican Party," he wrote, "would be highly salutary in your section of the union." The "most natural & beneficial" basis for such a national party would be a coalition "between the planters of the South and the plain Republicans of the north." In the past under this type of coalition, he wrote, "attacks upon Southern Republicans were regarded by those of the north as assaults upon their political brethren & resented accordingly."

The absence of the sympathies inherent in such a coalition, he continued, produced "the clamor against Southern Influence and African Slavery."

Taken as a whole, Van Buren's proposal was both simple and brilliant. He advocated a new national party combining southern planters with northern plain Republicans in common sympathy to suppress sectional conflicts, particularly over slavery, that could become the vehicle not just for a Jackson victory, but for a new majority party. To this broad outline Van Buren ultimately added a procedural requirement to assure the intersectional bond. To win the Democratic Party nomination for president, a candidate had to garner at least two-thirds of the delegate votes, guaranteeing a candidate's ability to draw support from both the South and the North.

Van Buren's vision soon prevailed. Jackson swept the South and West, captured all of Pennsylvania's electoral votes and more than half of New York's in defeating John Quincy Adams for the presidency in 1828. Within four years, a complete party apparatus was in place. With it the Democratic Party became the vehicle by which the white South dominated national politics up to 1860 with a succession of slave state or proslavery presidents, Supreme Court and cabinet appointments, and congressional appointments of committee chairs and Speakers of the House.

One man who evidently read Rufus King's Senate speech about a higher law forbidding slavery was Denmark Vesey. Vesey lived in Charleston, South Carolina, where he made a comfortable living as a carpenter. He was an imposing figure, physically strong, gruff, and driven by the conviction that God condemned slavery and southern slaveholders. Vesey had been born a slave in the West Indies, probably in the late 1760s, but exactly where or when is unknown. No portrait or likeness of him exists. His owner settled with him in Charleston, where Vesey purchased his freedom for $600 in 1800 from the winnings of a $1,500 lottery ticket.[104] Little is known of him except that he was executed by hanging as the mastermind of a planned Black insurrection that transfixed Charleston in the summer of 1822.

Records from the period indicate that Vesey began planning for a Black uprising in late 1820 during the height of the Missouri debates over slavery. Men convicted with him said that Vesey read everything he could find about the controversy shaking Congress, especially King's pivotal speech about "the law of nature, which is the law of God" that forbids one man to enslave another. That reference struck at the core of Vesey's beliefs. His was the Old Testament God of vengeance, one of sure judgment and strict reckoning. The *Exodus* drama of Moses leading his people out of slavery had the ring of prophecy to his ears. The biblical verses he most often cited, though, were those of Zechariah and the coming sack of Jerusalem and the line describing the fall of Jericho: "Then they utterly destroyed all in the city, both men and women, young and old . . . with the edge of the sword" from Joshua 6:21.[105] In them he saw a righteous prophecy for Charleston.

A large pool of potential recruits was all around him in the port city, where close to half the population was enslaved. As a free Black tradesman, Vesey moved easily along the city's wharf, streets, alleys, shops, and warehouses. There he was in contact with free and enslaved Blacks who labored as draymen, smiths, assistants in all manner of trade, house servants, and plantation slaves in town on their masters' business or with a written pass on their own account. He was a member of the recently formed African Methodist Episcopal Church. At his home he was a church class leader, conducting weekday evening sessions with fellow congregants. Some of them were slaves owned by Governor Thomas Bennett Jr., whose home was less than two blocks away from Vesey's on Bull Street.

As a trial court report later described it, Vesey and a core group of lieutenants planned to launch their insurrection at midnight July 13, 1822.[106] Many whites were away from the city during the summer, and the 14th was a Sunday when it was not unusual for plantation Blacks to be in Charleston. The plan designated six separate attack forces, two of them to be made up of plantation slaves initially armed with little more than axes, hatchets, hoes, and shovels.

Gullah Jack was to lead many of the plantation slaves. He was an African-born slave with small hands and feet, and huge whiskers. Gullah Jack was also a sorcerer who handed out crab claws and other charms to render those possessing them invulnerable. He could be neither captured nor killed, the belief ran, and held great sway especially among plantation Blacks, making him reputedly second only to Vesey among the insurrection leaders.

The slave Rolla Bennett's group was assigned to murder his master, Governor Thomas Bennett Jr., then move quickly to the nearby home of Mayor James Hamilton and murder him, too. Ned Bennett, another slave belonging to the governor, was to capture an arsenal outside the main city, where up to 300 muskets and bayonets belonging to a militia company were stored. At least two stores where more muskets could be found were also targeted.

Vesey, disguised in a wig and makeup to pass for white at midnight, was to kill the sentry at the guard house near the city's center, then with others take the arsenal across the street, where more firearms and ammunition could be seized. Within short order the insurrectionists would be well armed. Fires were to be set at various points in the city to create diversions.[107] No mercy was to be shown to women or children. The slaughter was to be like that in Jericho. The way Charleston's white citizens later heard of it, at least some of the slaves (as many as 9,000) in and surrounding the city at least had heard of "the business" Vesey was planning—to cut their masters' throats as they lay asleep in bed, "prostitute the partner of his bosom, violate the child of his affections, and dash out the brains of his innocent and unoffending infant."[108] As for himself, once in control, Vesey may have intended to seize ships in the harbor and set sail for Haiti and freedom.

But none of that was to be. To this day disagreement exists among historians if any of it was more than talk and ferment among deeply disgruntled men, although the account of historian Douglas Egerton perhaps best describes what happened.[109] What is sure is that on two occasions, several days apart, two household slaves who had heard the talk of rebellion revealed it to their masters. Although initially dubious, city officials were eventually convinced. Five military companies under the command of Colonel Robert Y. Hayne spread an overwhelming armed presence onto Charleston's streets by the evening of June 16. The hour to begin the uprising had been rescheduled for midnight that night. Instead, arrests began immediately.

Over the next several weeks, 131 suspects were arrested. Thirty of them were released without trial. Of the remainder, thirty-five including Vesey were hanged, thirty-seven were deported outside the United States, twenty-three were acquitted, and two died in custody.[110] The bodies of those hanged were dissected by medical students and disposed of as waste.

A special court of magistrates and freeholders authorized by the city council expended considerable effort to present a defensible facade of fair trials for the accused. According to court records, accused slaves had assistance from counsel and their masters present when on trial. Other evidence indicates that the court simply collected damaging evidence from compliant witnesses who were themselves under threat of execution and then pieced together those accounts against various defendants before passing sentence. It is not possible to know exactly how the court operated because the proceedings were held in secret behind closed doors with no members of the public allowed entrance.

The process was sufficiently flawed that Governor Bennett complained it was a "usurpation of authority, and a violation of the Law." Three of his slaves, including Rolla and Ned Bennett, were among those executed. Soon after those sentences were carried out, Bennett sought an opinion from the attorney general, the same Robert Hayne who led the June 16 military deployment and would remain prominent in South Carolina politics for years to come. Hayne gave an acerbic reply, writing, "If I had been asked whether a *free white man* could be lawfully tried by a Court sitting with closed doors and without being confronted with his witnesses I should have had little difficulty in giving the answer. . . . But nothing can be clearer than that *slaves* are not entitled to *these rights*. Magna Charta & Habeas Corpus and indeed all the provisions of our Constitution in favour of Liberty, are intended for *freeman* only."[111]

At his execution, Vesey is reported not to have spoken a word. One slave who did speak was John Horry, a coachman owned by Elias Horry. His master, not believing his servant could have had any murderous intent, asked him to his face if he was guilty. The trusted slave answered that what he had planned to do was "to kill you, rip open your belly and throw your guts in your face."[112]

CHAPTER 5

Slavery—The Thing Itself

In 1482 the Portuguese built Elmina castle, the first slave trading post along Africa's Gold Coast serving as a holding, sale, and transfer point for Blacks made captive farther inland to be shipped later west across the Atlantic to the Americas. The voyage, forever after infamously known as the Middle Passage, might take a few months in the trade's early decades but was winnowed to about six weeks with good weather for slaves bound to the United States in the early 1800s.

Enslavement began with intertribal wars and raids in the African interior. Captive men, women, and children were marched to fortified compounds such as Elmina on the coast to await the arrival of slave ships seeking new cargoes for Brazil, the West Indies, or Charleston. For every Black set aboard ship, another one, by historical estimates, died in fighting, marching, or waiting.[1]

Once the sale was complete, boarding began. As told to a narrator by a slave who made the journey, "each party, as they were brought upon deck, were made secure, and then each person was thrown into such a position as was best suited to the purpose, and *branded* . . . on some part of the person, by having a red-hot iron in the form of certain letters or signs dipped into an oily preparation, and then pressed against the naked body till it burnt a deep and ineffaceable scar, to show who was the owner. . . . They were then chained two and two, the right arm and leg of one to the left arm and leg of another and crowded into the slave rooms between decks. The women were stowed in without being shackled."[2]

Clearance to the ceiling above the slave deck was typically about three feet. As one ship's surgeon observed, captives "had not so much room as a man in his coffin, neither in length or breadth, and it was impossible for them to turn or shift with any degree or ease."[3] Profit dictated that the ship be packed as tightly as possible. For the same motive, slaves were often left naked, although in some cases a yard or more of rough cotton cloth was provided for them to clothe themselves.

"On each fair day," one narrative recounts, "between eight and nine o'clock in the morning, they were all permitted to come on deck, which was surrounded with high nettings to prevent them from jumping overboard. For their additional security a ring was attached to the shackles of each pair, through which a large chain was reeved, which locked them all in a body to ring-bolts in the deck. About three or four in the afternoon they were again put below, to remain till morning. In the interval, while on deck, they were fed twice with rice, yams, horse-beans, and occasionally a little beef and bread, and allowed a pint of water each during the day."[4]

Aboard one ship an observer recalled "instances of a dead and living slave found in the morning shackled together."[5] Sometimes a desperate captive got through the netting to drown in the ocean rather than remain enslaved. Instances of slaves attempting to starve themselves to death were so common that ships were supplied with mouth-opening devices derived from medieval design that broke teeth and cut lips in forcing slaves to eat. Slaves were tortured with thumb screws to induce them to eat. "I have seen coals of fire, glowing hot, put on a shovel and placed so near their lips as to scorch and burn them," a doctor aboard the slave ship *Tartar* recalled.[6]

Disease was by far the leading cause of death aboard slave ships. Scurvy was common on the long voyages. The greatest scourge was what was then called the flux, described as bloody, obstinate, or violent; all were a form of what today is known as dysentery. Smallpox, pneumonia, and consumption also took their toll.[7] The dead were unceremoniously dumped overboard. In one case that was certainly an example of others, a ship's captain ordered those still living but already ill with disease to be heaved into the sea.[8]

At night, an observer reported, a sound often arose from those crowded, chained, and naked below decks of a collective "howling, melancholy noise, expressive of extreme anguish."[9]

An estimated 12.5 million slaves were embarked from Africa during the course of the slave trade. Nearly two million of them died during the

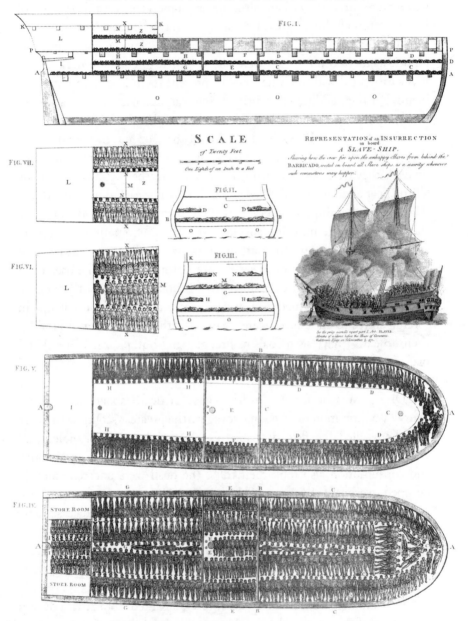

Section plan of the slave ship *Brookes*. SOURCE: *SLAVERY IMAGES*.

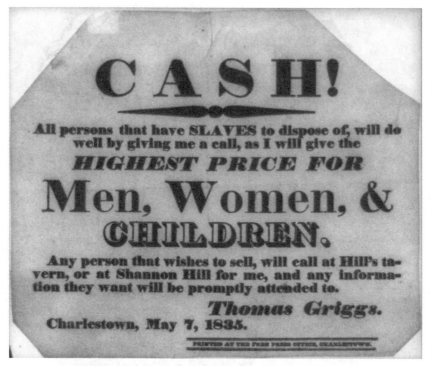

SOURCE: *SLAVERY IMAGES.*

Middle Passage. Of those who lived to step ashore somewhere in the Americas, about a half million landed in the colonies, or what became the United States, before the foreign slave trade was banned in 1808.[10]

Slaves put on the auction block "had to be in trim for showing themselves to the public for sale," recalled ex-slave Henry Bibb in his narrative of servitude. The auction might be held on the steps of the county courthouse as part of a deceased owner's estate sale. Some sales were arranged for private bidders. The most common practice was a public auction advertised in newspapers and by handbills. Bibb recounted that every slave's "head had to be combed, and their faces washed, and those who were inclined to look dark and rough, were compelled to wash in greasy dish water, in order to make them look slick and lively."[11] A vivid account of a typical slave auction was written during an 1852 visit to Richmond by Charles C. Rawn of Pennsylvania, who witnessed:

Henry Bibb. SOURCE:
SLAVERY IMAGES.

the inspection & sale of 5 or 6 females ranging from 17 to 26 or 30 yrs old, 3 of them with infant children, one perfectly white & the mother quite black another stout strong looking man 40 to 44 yrs old all put up "warranted sound" and title perfect.... The man was taken behind a screen, his [trousers] stripped down to his feet, and his shirt pushed up on his waist as though his private parts, *behind & spine and thighs and legs were the parts most desirable to be perfect. I saw the fellows laugh as they looked at his privates. He was put on the "block" as they call it, being something like a large table or platform ... where the slave stands while the auctioneer sells him. ...*

They are carefully examined by the hardened looking dealers who appeared to be there in numbers from 50 to 100. Their arms and legs are felt, and looked at up towards the knees, I mean the women while selling. The feet and ankles especially looked at frequently by raising the petticoats, &c, teeth examined by requiring them often to open wide their mouths. Throats, heads & necks felt &c, one female was taken behind the screen for more special examination—several men going and any one that chose to, to look at her. They undid some part of her dress about the shoulders & chest. I understand since that this is frequently for the purpose of examining their backs, shoulders &c to see if they have been much injured *by whipping. I saw them undo her dress and look at her about the back & shoulders.*[12]

Slave prices varied over time depending on economic conditions, reaching their peak in 1860 when both the price and demand for cotton were high. A prime field hand in his early twenties could fetch up to $2,000, as might a slave skilled in carpentry or blacksmithing.[13] That sum is equivalent to approximately $58,800 in today's dollars.[14] A trained

Depiction of an 1853 slave auction in Charleston, South Carolina. SOURCE: *SLAVERY IMAGES*.

house servant could bring nearly as much. Older slaves, young children, and those with excessive scarring, marks of a runaway or troublemaker, might sell for a few hundred dollars. These prices compare with about $40 per acre for the best farmland and about $200 to $250 as the yearly cost to hire free labor.

Ownership of human property brought with it the right to name it. "There were two reasons given by the slave holders why they did not allow a slave to use his own name, but rather that of the master," Jacob Stroyer explained in his narrative of being a slave on a South Carolina plantation. "The first was that if he ran away, he would not be so easily detected by using his own name, as if he used that of his master instead. The second was, that to allow him to use his own name would be sharing an honor which was due only to his master, and that would be too much for a negro, said they, who was nothing more than a servant."[15] Popular imagination in white America has been coaxed into seeing the slave's destination after sale as some variant between *Uncle Tom's Cabin* and Tara, the mythical plantation in *Gone with the Wind*. The problem with this stereotype of the typical slave is that it thoroughly distorts the realities of slavery. Trying to posit a typical slave is akin to positing a typical person between the ages of nine and sixty-nine. No such person exists. Some understanding of slavery begins with recognizing the diversity of slave experiences.

Starting with antebellum southern society as a whole, a substantial majority of whites, well over 60 percent by current historical reckoning, neither owned slaves nor belonged to families that did. The share of white ownership of slaves was greater in the Deep South, less in the Middle South and Border States. The largest single proportion of non-slave-owning white southerners were farmers and their immediate families who worked their own land without bondsmen, largely for subsistence crops.[16] Although many of these yeoman farmers bore resemblance to Jefferson's proud bearers of true republicanism, isolated provincialism was also a defining characteristic.

Of those who were slaveowners, about half owned fewer than five slaves and nearly 90 percent owned fewer than twenty. These nine-out-of-ten slaveowners owned approximately 45 percent of all slaves. The

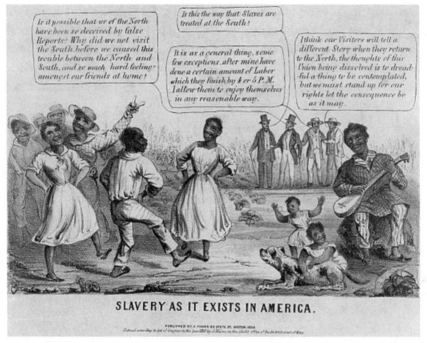

Patriarchal slavery—the white southern image of its peculiar institution. COURTESY OF THE LIBRARY OF CONGRESS.

southern planter aristocracy of legend and mythology—"oligarchy" is a more apt term—was confined to roughly 10,000 families who owned more than fifty slaves each. The elite of that aristocracy, those who lived in the grandest of the big houses, constituted a sliver of white southern society comprising fewer than 3,000 families that owned more than 100 slaves each. Although small in numbers, the self-styled aristocrats of the South owned well over half of the South's slaves. The distribution of the South's most valuable capital investment by far, its slave population, was concentrated in an upper echelon of privilege wielding power vastly disproportionate to its numbers.[17]

The concentration of slave ownership among the elite did not obscure its ubiquity in southern society as a whole. A brilliant study of three North Carolina counties by historian Daniel L. Fountain provides a plausible portrait of how pervasively slavery was spread across southern society even as it was concentrated among relatively few. In 1860 Alamance, Orange, and Wade Counties, he writes, slaveowners "included the governor of North Carolina, the secretary of state, the state treasurer of North Carolina, two state supreme court justices, the president of the University of North Carolina, the superintendent of the Raleigh and Gaston Railroad, the treasurer of the North Carolina Railroad, the mayor of Raleigh, twelve University of North Carolina professors, two bank officers, two county officers, a sheriff and deputy sheriff, as well as the constable of Raleigh. There was also a total of 205 slave owners who identified themselves as either merchants, doctors, ministers, lawyers, dentists, engineers, editors, or publishers, which would place them among the region's most important and influential professionals and cultural leaders."[18] Slaves serving these masters fulfilled any number of functions from cook or house servant to clerks, draymen, and gardeners. Not only the planter class, but the core of the town and city power structure, were integral to slaveowning society and the lives of those in bondage.

A netherworld between freedom and slavery existed for a relatively small number of slaves who hired out, paying their master a set sum by the week or month, then living and working on their own to earn as much as they could to get by. Although proscribed by law in many jurisdictions, the practice was widely tolerated in southern cities and towns. Slaves working in this way pursued such trades as carpentry, barrel making, and blacksmithing. Frederick Douglass recalled of his days hiring out in Baltimore before he escaped to freedom: "I was to be allowed all my time; to make all bargains for work; to find my own employment, and to collect my own wages, and, in return for this liberty, I was required, or obliged, to pay . . . three dollars at the end of each week, and to board and clothe myself, and buy my own calking tools."[19] Some slaves purchased their freedom in this way, and in a few cases freedom for members of their families. Another stratum of slaves worked in industry, frequently boarded in company barracks.

At Richmond's famed Tredegar Iron Company, supplier of Confederate ammunition and cannons during the war, about half of its 900 workers in 1860 were slaves.[20] Enterprises to mill rice, refine sugar, roll tobacco, and manufacture hemp used slave labor in the South. Other slaves mined gold, coal, salt, iron, and lead; built railroads; labored in rock quarries and sawmills; and made bricks to build and sustain southern society. The prewar southern economy and its accoutrements of fine homes, public buildings, schools, roads, harbors, and such were built with the proceeds of or directly by slave labor.

Much of the northern economy also owed its achievements to slave labor. Tariffs on imported goods purchased by white southerners from the profits of slavery helped finance government-sponsored improvements in the North. Northern shipping merchants transported southern cotton. Northern banks handled vast numbers of southern plantation and cotton accounts. Northern farmers used the Mississippi River to send their products south for sale. As noted earlier, southern cotton was the staple that first got northern mill towns running. Profits from slavery and slave labor underpinned a considerable portion of the American economy as long as slavery existed.

Black masters owned some slaves. The richest was John Stanly, slave son of a white merchant and African Ebo mother, who was emancipated by his owner in 1795. By 1830 Stanly owned more than 150 slaves working 2,600 acres on two North Carolina plantations.[21] In that year free Blacks held just under 4,000 slaves in the South. Most of them, just under 3,000, were owned by masters holding four or fewer slaves, indicating that many of them were family members.[22]

More than a half million lighter-skinned mulattoes made up nearly 12 percent of the South's enslaved population, according to the 1860 census, a figure that is unquestionably low because census takers made the designation only upon appearance.[23] Female slaves of mixed white and Black parentage, especially younger and more attractive mulattoes, quadroons, and octoroons—southern whites were careful to mark such distinctions—often fared as did Sally Hemings, used for sex by their masters.

On a train trip from Washington to Richmond, a correspondent for the *Wheeling Intelligencer* noted in 1860, "I was particularly struck by the beauty of a white girl, about seventeen years old, with white, rosy,

Handbill announcing the pending sale of slaves, mules, hogs, and other property in Columbia County, Georgia. SOURCE: *SLAVERY IMAGES.*

transparent complexion, finely chiseled features, and auburn tresses. I concluded she must be the young and handsome daughter of the [slave] trader [aboard the train]; but he told me he had paid $1200 for her up in Maryland, to a man whose wife had become jealous of her. This story fully explained the mystery of the gold rings that hung from her ears and encircled her fingers."[24] As told to Frederick Law Olmsted by a southern planter, "there is not an old plantation in which the grand-children of the owner are not whipped in the field by his overseer."[25] In her study of sexual contact between whites and slave women and girls in the antebellum South, historian Brenda E. Stevenson concluded, "It was a common occurrence by any measure, widespread and obvious."[26] The former slave Jacob Manson recalled, "At dat time it wus a hard job to find a marster dat didn't have women 'mong his slaves. Dat wus a ginerel thing 'mong de slave owners."[27]

The liaisons Stevenson and Manson describe might or might not have involved women of mixed race, but the lighter skinned among them were clearly the most prized. Louisa Picquet was one. Born in the late 1820s as a slave near Columbia, South Carolina, Louisa was "of fair complexion and rosy cheeks, with . . . every appearance, at first view, of an accomplished white lady."[28] Her mother, Elizabeth, was her mistress's seamstress and the quadroon concubine of James Hunter Randolph. At his wife's insistence, Randolph sold them off. Louisa, separated from her mother, eventually wound up the property John Williams, a gray-haired father of three in New Orleans. "Mr. Williams told me what he bought me for, soon as we started for New Orleans," Louisa recalled. "He said he was getting old, and when he saw me he thought he'd buy me, and end his days with me. He said if I behave myself he'd treat me well: but, if not, he'd whip me almost to death."[29] Louisa had four children by Williams before he died, and she made her way to Cincinnati and freedom.

John Maddox, a judge and plantation owner in Marion County, Georgia, bought himself a "pretty mulatto . . . seamstress," and accord-ing to a bondman's account, Ethel Mae, the "yaller gal, told me 'bout Marsa bringing his son Levey . . . down to the cabin. They both took her—the father showing the son what it was all about—and she couldn't do nothing 'bout it."[30]

In the rural South, farmers owning from a few to up to a score of slaves most closely fit one element of the proslavery paradigm of an aristocracy in a direct, mutually reciprocal relationship with its bondsmen. On these holdings of up to a few hundred cultivated acres, owners and their younger sons often worked alongside their slaves. The closeness of the relationship may well have fostered less frequent use of the whip and other harsh disciplines. For the slave, living on a smaller farm with fewer slaves may have been more desirable than the anonymous isolation and the threat and use of coercive force common on large plantations.

Whatever the treatment of slaves, and there is no common denominator to describe it, these farms were hardly fabled estates of aristocratic elegance. The homes of middle-class and small slaveowning farmers were, at best, "large, airy, comfortable, with glass windows and ample verandas. . . . At worst, the house was an enlarged log cabin, dirty and full of flies and mosquitoes; the food a dreary monotony of bacon, 'corn-pone,' hominy and coffee."[31] Frederick Law Olmsted, commissioned by the *New York Times*, drew penetrating portraits of life in the slaveholding states during his travels there in the 1850s. The Tennessee home of a farmer who owned six slaves "was in great need of repair," he observed, "and was much disordered. . . . He and his wife made the signs of pious people, but were very morose or sadly silent, when not scolding and re-ordering their servants."[32]

A telling contrast to the dual stereotypes of cruel master and indolent slave is contained in Olmsted's account of his visit with a northern Mississippi farmer who owned twenty slaves. "The negro cabins were small, dilapidated, and dingy," he wrote. "The walls were not chinked, and there were no windows. . . . The furniture in the cabins was of the simplest and rudest imaginable kind, two or three beds with dirty clothing upon them, a chest, a wooden stool or two made with an axe, and some earthenware and cooking apparatus." By the master's account, his slaves "never want no lookin' arter; they jus tek ker o' themselves. Fact, they do tek a greater interest in the crops than I do myself. Theres another thing—I 'spose 'twill surprise you—there ent one of my niggers but what can read; read good, too—better'n I can, at any rate."

He told Olmsted that they read religious books, that they were Baptists and kept the Sabbath, attending the church of a Black minister. Olmstead describes this slave owner as "a man of the fat, slow-and-easy style," who spent most of his own time hunting and fishing, left the crops to his servants, said he had not raised a whip against any of them for the past five years, and began his day with a strong draught of rye whiskey. In his own home, also built of logs but boarded over and painted on the outside, his wife made the clothing for servants and family alike, and all ate of the same fare prepared by a Black cook, only the slaves "ate in the kitchen, and he ate in the room we were in, with the door open between them." In summary, Olmstead wrote, "religious, instructed, and seeking further enlightenment; industrious, energetic, and self directing; well fed, respected, and trusted by their master, and this master an illiterate, indolent, and careless man!"[33]

———

"I would as soon stand fifty feet from the best Kentucky rifleman and be shot at by the hour, as to spend a night on my plantation in summer," an antebellum rice and cotton planter living in Charleston once remarked.[34] His reason was the notorious "sickly season" that descended in summer on the vast rice plantations most prominent along South Carolina's barrier islands and Georgia's Savannah River. Heat, humidity, and mosquito-borne malaria from May through September were added to an already prevalent mix of yellow fever, dysentery, pneumonia, and cholera. "During the summer, for from four to six months, at least, not one rice-planter in a hundred resides on his plantation, but leaves it, with all his slaves, in charge of an overseer," an 1850s visitor noted.[35] Slaves had no such choice. On being sold off to a rice planter, Charles Ball recalled in his narrative of slavery, "It is the common opinion, that no stranger can work in a rice swamp, at this season of the year, without becoming sick; and all the new hands, three in number, besides myself, were taken ill within the first five days, after we had entered this field."[36]

Rice farming was labor intensive, with a hundred slaves and often several times that number working the fields of a single owner. The dense concentration of the slave labor force promoted the easy transmission of communicable disease. Summer work in the rice paddies' knee-deep water exposed slaves to any number of waterborne infections. A study of Gowrie, a Savannah River rice plantation, details the toll that the "sickly season" and conditions there took on its slaves. The mortality rate drawn from the plantation's day journals was three times that of North America as a whole.

When an 1834 cholera outbreak killed four of every ten Gowrie slaves, the plantation's mortality rate "approached the level experienced in Europe during the Black Death." One of the plantation reports received by the owner who lived in Charleston informed him that "the woman Jane is yet sick. I fear she will never get well. Hector turned in[to] the Sick House. . . . I have never had such a desperate case of Diarrhea. . . . Cudjue died very suddenly on Tuesday. . . . He lay up one day & died that night." Charles Manigault, Gowrie's owner, ranked himself among the benevolent class of slave masters. He once wrote his overseer to "be Kind in word & deed to all the Negroes for they have always been accustomed to it."[37] He must have been surprised, then, on being informed in 1852 of the fate of his slave London. Hoping to avoid a flogging, a note informed Manigault, London fled to the river, where pleas were made for him to return. But the slave answered that "he would drown himself before he would [return] and he sank soon after." London's body was left in the water "to let the negroes see when a negro takes his own life they will be treated in this manner."[38]

By 1850, an estimated 125,000 slaves worked on rice plantations, a slightly larger number on lower Mississippi River sugar plantations. But the largest proportion of slaves, 1.8 million, raised and harvested cotton on farms as small as a few dozen acres to sprawling plantations owned by a single individual that might encompass thousands of acres divided into many tracts, possibly located in two or more states.[39] The cycle of work in raising cotton spanned the entire year, much of it in stoop labor.

In March the sowing of furrows of cotton seed began, along with planting corn to feed both hogs and humans during the year. From May through August, the growing plants were tended, boll worms plucked from stalks and leaves, weeds hoed, and watering canals and ditches kept in good repair. The picking season could begin in late summer and last as late as Christmas as the plants produced a series of blooms.

Plucking the cotton bolls soon after they opened was crucial as they could fall to the ground within a day. Women often made the best pickers, their slender fingers nimbler for the work. A good picker could bring in 250 pounds of cotton each day, and slaves were typically given quotas to meet depending on their age and skill, as determined by their white overseer. Failure to meet the quota could result in a whipping. The most productive land could yield a harvest of up to about eight 400-pound bales of cotton per acre, the poorest perhaps two bales.[40] Simultaneously with the picking, the cotton needed to be ginned to remove seeds, pressed into bales, and shipped by steamboat, rail, barge, or wagon to transfer points for mills in the North or those across the Atlantic in Great Britain. By the time this process was complete, the cycle renewed itself as the season to plant a new crop began again.

Additional chores arose such as hog killing and dressing early in the year, repair of fences and roads, clearing new fields, chopping wood, and all descriptions of work needed to keep the operation going.

Somewhere along the continuum from small farms with few slaves to large plantations with many, a transition took place in the lives of whites and Blacks alike. The white working-class farmer gave way to those finding their way into the southern aristocracy. For the planter class, the pattern was almost universal: profits were poured back into buying more slaves, to work more land and raise more cotton. Because cotton crops depleted the soil, demand for new land was incessant. For the slaves, the process from small farm to plantation meant an increasing distance between the men and women who worked as field hands and the men, and sometimes women, who owned them. Along this continuum as the plantations grew larger, the concentration of slaves grew denser, with the majority of slaves, as already noted, living on plantations of fifty or more slaves and the greatest concentration being among the smallest number of owners who held a hundred or more slaves. The elite master class fostered the understanding of slavery as a face-to-face patriarchal system of mutual responsibilities, of proper care and fair treatment by the owners of their property, and of reasonable work and proper submission by the slaves in return for that care and treatment.

For the elite, the system thus defined had a nearly perfect internal harmony of prosperity, and the freedom to fully engage in life's higher callings for the owner, a lifetime of security and a share of actual happiness for the slave. In the eyes of many elite owners, this system had an actual reality. The slaves they knew best, those working in and around the big house or at their spacious retreats in town, were, after all, well trained in discretion and manners as house and body servants, coachmen, and stable boys. Many were mulattoes, the caste frequently called to the big house, and more frequently than any of the elite cared to acknowledged were the sons and daughters of the owner, his father, or his sons.

The field hands the owners observed when riding on horseback about their estates could be counted on to give a deferential bow from afar. The unpleasant application of force, the use of the whip, was often the work of the overseer. And the higher up the aristocratic ladder one climbed, the less the owner actually saw his slaves at all. Absentee ownership might be driven by such things as the "sickly season" in tidewater South Carolina and far more often by the sheer size and diverse locations of land devoted to cotton plantations. A newspaper account of the region near Jackson, Mississippi, in the early 1830s describes

> *immense bodies of rich land . . . converted into cotton fields, and negro quarters—leaving so sparse a white population, as to preclude the possibility of building up anything like an interesting state of society. Many of the owners of those large plantations reside in the older settled parts of the State, and not a few of them in other States—leaving on a plantation containing, perhaps, several sections of land, no white person except the overseer.*[41]

Nearly three-quarters of the wealthy planters who lived in Natchez by 1860 owned slaves living on plantations along the Yazoo Delta or northeast Louisiana. Levin R. Marshall who owned three plantations in

Mississippi also owned more than 600 slaves on plantations in Louisiana. The Virginia planter Philip St. George Cocke owned 375 slaves in Mississippi.[42] Frederick Law Olmsted describes riding mile after mile past vast plantations along the Mississippi River interspersed occasionally by a frame house occupied by an overseer and a few "show houses," awaiting the owner's arrival. These owners "must have ice for their wine, you see," he was told, "or they'd die; and so they have to live in Natchez or New Orleans; a good many of them live in New Orleans."[43]

Although absentee ownership was relatively infrequent among most planters, it was most common among those holding the largest estates with the most slaves. In this situation the reality the enslaved field hand saw and experienced was exactly opposite of that which convinced owners that slavery was benignly patriarchal. On the largest plantations with the greatest number of slaves the white person the field hand knew best and encountered most was the overseer. No relationship of paternalism existed between the two. The one was charged with extracting the greatest amount of labor possible short of impairing the viability of the capital investment, the other with surviving under a system of coercive submission.

In short, the proslavery paradigm of seigneurial paternalism by which the southern master class justified itself was a myth. "Plantation paternalism," in the words of Kenneth Stampp, one of America's leading historians in exposing the realities of slavery, "was in most cases merely a kind of leisure-class family indulgence of its domestics."[44]

—⁓—

The big house and its surroundings were the embodiment of the southern aristocracy's achievements, its refinement of manners, learning, and chivalric values, its graciousness and hospitality. The Berry Hill plantation near Halifax, Virginia, was one such spacious home. Built in the Greek revival style, fronted by eight Doric columns supporting the pediment of the porch, the main house was flanked by a pair of smaller detached structures resembling Doric temples. Within, a grand staircase to the private rooms on the upper floor greeted a visitor to the main hall. Ancestral portraits adorned the walls, crystal chandeliers flickered with light, solid silver washbasins provided water to cleanse one's hands.[45] Frederick Douglass provided a sumptuous description of the environs of the big house along Maryland's eastern shore that he remembered as a boy in service to Colonel Edward Lloyd.

Fish, flesh and fowls, are here in profusion. Chickens, of all breeds; ducks of all kinds, wild and tame, the common and the huge Muscovite; Guinea fowls, turkeys, geese, and pea fowls are in their several pens, fat and fattening. . . . The graceful swan, the mongrels, the black-necked wild goose; partridges, quails, pheasants and pigeons; choice water fowl, with all their strange varieties, are caught in this huge family net. Beef, veal, mutton and venison, of the most select kinds and quality, roll bounteously to this grand consumer. The teeming riches of the Chesapeake Bay, its rock, perch, drums, crocus, trout, oysters, crabs, and terrapin, are drawn hither to adorn the glittering table of the great house. . . . The tender asparagus, the succulent celery, and the delicate cauliflower; egg plants, beets, lettuce, parsnips, peas

Frederick Douglass.
SOURCE: WIKIMEDIA COMMONS/
FRONT PIECE *MY BONDAGE, MY
FREEDOM*, 1855.

and French beans, early and late; radishes, cantelopes, melons of all kinds; the fruits and flowers of all climes and of all descriptions, from the hardy apple, to the lemon and orange of the south, culminated at this point. Baltimore gathered figs, raisins, almonds and juicy grapes from Spain. Wines and brandies from France; teas of various flavor, from China; and rich, aromatic coffee from Java, all conspired to swell the tide of high life. . . .

Behind the tall-backed and elaborately wrought chairs, stand the servants, men and maidens—fifteen in number—discriminately selected, but with special regard to their personal appearance, their graceful agility and captivating address. . . .

These servants constituted a sort of black aristocracy. . . . They resembled the field hands in nothing, except in color, and in this they held the advantage of a velvet-like glossiness, rich and beautiful. . . . The delicate colored maid rustled in the scarcely worn silk of her young mistress, while the servant men were equally well attired from the over-flowing wardrobe of their young masters. . . .

Viewed from his own table, and not *from the field, the colonel was a model of generous hospitality. His house was, literally, a hotel, for weeks during the summer months. At these times, especially, the air was freighted with the rich fumes of baking, boiling, roasting and broiling. The odors I shared with the winds; but the meats were under a more stringent monopoly—except that, occasionally, I got a cake from Mas' Daniel.*[46]

Behind this image of splendid liberality lurked a more than occasional anomaly noted by a British traveler: "The planter lays himself to bed with pistols under his pillow, never knowing when the wild whoop of insurrection may awaken him to a bloody fight."[47]

~⌣~

As Douglass noted, a hierarchy existed among slaves on large plantations. At the pinnacle were the house servants, who paid for their privilege by being under the most minute and constant scrutiny of those to whom they owed service. They had the least opportunity to let down the facade of willing submission and simply be human. Within this caste were the plantation's body servants, cooks, lady's maids, chambermaids, nurses, wet nurses, laundresses, and seamstresses. They largely lived apart, and were highly restricted from any interaction with common field hands.

A second tier within this hierarchy were the slaves with skills who worked within the big house orbit. These included blacksmiths, carpenters, coopers, wagoners, wheelwrights, livestock and dog handlers, coachmen, stable men, and gardeners. Many wealthier plantations included slaves trained at maintaining and running cotton gins, mills for grinding wheat and corn, and steam-powered threshing machines. In addition to being the most scrutinized, slaves who worked in and about the big house were the least likely to be whipped, but a slave proverb warned, "Temorrow may be de carridge-driver's day for ploughing."[48]

A unique and isolated position was held by Black slave drivers. These were men, working under an overseer's supervision, who drove gangs of slaves to their tasks in the field. Olmstead described one encounter with a large gang of field hands who were

constantly and steadily driven up to their work, and the stupid, plodding, machine-like manner in which they labor, is painful to witness. This was especially so with the hoe-gang. One of them numbered nearly two hundred hands ... moving across the field in parallel lines, with a considerable degree of precision. ... A very tall and powerful negro walked to and fro in the rear of the line, frequently cracking his whip, and calling out, in the surliest manner, to one and another, "Shove your hoe, there! Shove your hoe!" But I never saw him strike any one with the whip.[49]

Drivers lived somewhat apart from the field hands, usually in better cabins and with more food. Size and strength were the job's prerequisites. Mulattoes and occasionally those with claim to a royal ancestry in Africa were often chosen for the job.

The overseer was the enslaved field hand's most immediate frame of reference to the white world. A bad overseer brought misery with him. In the eyes of most whites, overseers were only a slightly less degraded class of beings than slave traders. Overseers, according to an article in the *Southern Agriculturist* magazine, "are taken from the lowest grade of society, and seldom have had the privilege of a religious education, and have no fear of offending God, and consequently no check on their natural propensities; they give way to passion, intemperance, and every sin, and become savages in their conduct."[50] Whether savage or not, it was a hard business and one that forced overseers on cotton plantations to navigate two powerful interests that operated in direct conflict with one another. The tension often made their tenure brief. One or two years was an overseer's typical stay at any given plantation.

Rice plantations ran on the task system. Each slave was given a set task to perform each day, the task derived from well-established tradition depending on the slave's age and general abilities. A different system applied in the cotton fields. Overseers were hired for a set wage in a given year. Their contracts also often included bonus payments for each bale of cotton produced above a given quota. The overseer's incentive was to drive field hands to the extreme in order to maximize his bonus. Two brakes operated on abuse. One was that an exhausted field hand was less productive than one not pushed to that extreme. The other was the owner's reaction if his capital investment turned up dead, crippled, or broken down. No sympathy existed in the equation. Overseers did not get bonuses for tolerance.

A gauge into how grueling the system was can be sought in the death rates of enslaved Blacks. The general historical consensus, in this controversial field, is that once an enslaved Black reached age twenty, life expectancy was less than his or her white counterpart by roughly four to five years.[51] Field labor began at about age twelve, and field hands were generally considered to be fully productive up to age fifty-five, which also happened to be the average life expectancy of a male slave purchased at age twenty.[52] The economic incentive to extend the productive life of invested capital in enslaved labor seems in large measure to have prevailed over other factors. As an essayist for the Southern Central Agricultural Society put it, "every attempt to force the slave beyond the limits of reasonable service, by cruelty or hard treatment, so far from extorting more work, only tends to make him unprofitable, unmanageable; a vexation and a curse."[53]

A dramatically different consensus has been reached about enslaved Blacks who had no immediate productive value. The death rate for enslaved Black children up to the age of fourteen was close to or double that for the population as a whole and concentrated especially among those less than five years old, where the death rate exceeded 200 percent that of the general population.[54] On some plantations, suckling children were left in the care of nannies past the age for field work. A common practice, as described by Henry Bibb of his life as a slave, was for mothers to take their infants into the fields with them. "The cotton planters," his narrative recounts, "generally never allow a slave mother time to go to the house, or quarter during the day to nurse her child; hence they have to carry them to the cotton fields and tie them in the shade of a tree, or in clusters of high weeds about in the fields, where they can go to them at noon, when they are allowed to stop work for one half hour . . . and they are often found dead in the field . . . for want of the care of their mothers."[55] Whatever the specifics of a given case, infant children, enslaved at birth, died at an appalling rate.

For the overseer, violence was part of the job description and death an occasional necessity. Asked if he found using a whip disagreeable, an overseer once replied, "Yes, it would be to those who are not used to it—but it's my business, and I think nothing of it. Why, sir, I wouldn't mind killing a nigger more than I would a dog." And if he had killed a slave? "Not quite," came the reply, explaining that some Blacks were determined never to let a white man whip them "and will resist you when you attempt it; of course you must kill them in that case."[56]

Whipping could be a routinely mechanical, emotionally barren exercise, as conveyed in an incident witnessed by Olmstead while on a lower Mississippi River valley plantation. A Black girl, about eighteen years old who identified herself as Sam's Sal, was found hiding in a ditch by the overseer. Not satisfied with her excuse for not being at work, he ordered her to her knees and "struck her thirty or forty blows across the shoulders with his tough, flexible 'raw-hide' whip. They were well laid on." Not satisfied when he told her to explain herself a second time, he ordered her to strip naked. She did, lying on her back on the ground naked, her face toward the overseer who whipped her again about her legs and loins. The girl "shrunk away from him, not rising, but writhing, groveling, and screaming, 'Oh, don't, sir! oh, please stop, master! please, sir! please, sir!' . . . It was the first time I had ever seen a woman flogged. . . . I glanced . . . at the perfectly passionless but rather grim business-like face of the overseer. . . . Only my horse chafed with excitement." When asked if so severe a beating was necessary, the overseer answered, "Oh yes, sir! If I hadn't punished her so hard she would have done the same thing again tomorrow, and half the people on the plantation would have followed her example. Oh, you've no idea how lazy these niggers are. . . . They'd never do any work at all if they were not afraid of being whipped."[57]

To curb abuse many masters, in accordance with advice published by leading magazines such as *De Bow's Review*, gave their overseers written instructions on the treatment of their slaves. James Henry Hammond, governor of South Carolina, senator, and leading proslavery advocate, was one. His lengthy list of orders to his overseer includes one reading,

> *The negroes must be made to obey & to work, which may be done by the Overseer, who attends regularly to his business, with very little whipping. Much whipping indicates a bad tempered, or inattentive manager, & will not be allowed. The Overseer must never on any occasion—unless in self-defense—kick a negro, or strike with his hand, or a stick, or the butt-end of his whip. No unusual punishment must be resorted to without the Employer's consent.*[58]

As for Hammond himself, after a lengthy sexual relationship he had with a slave mistress and her daughter, possibly fathering children with each, he ultimately handed over both women to a son who reputedly had a child with the daughter.[59]

⸺ ⸺

"I grew up like a neglected weed," Harriet Tubman wrote in a poignant metaphor for slavery, "ignorant of liberty, having no experience of it. . . . I think slavery is the next thing to hell."[60] In Frederick Douglass' description of slavery "I was broken in body, soul and spirit. My natural elasticity was crushed; my intellect languished; the disposition to read departed; the cheerful spark that lingered about my eye died; the dark night of slavery closed in upon me; and behold a man transformed into a brute."[61]

Charles Ball spent a half century in slavery. His narrative of working as a field hand on a South Carolina cotton plantation recounts the monotonous repetition of a typical workday similar to narratives in scores of other accounts. Shortly before dawn the blowing of a horn signaled the slaves out of their cabins and into the fields. Once there, Ball wrote,

> *I saw a cart drawn up by a yoke of oxen, driven by an old black man, nearly blind. The cart contained three barrels, filled with water, and several large baskets full of corn bread that had been baked in the ashes. The water was for us to drink, and the bread was for our breakfast. The little son of the overseer was also in the cart, and had brought with him the breakfast of his father, in a small wooden bucket.*
>
> *The overseer had bread, butter, cold ham, and coffee for his breakfast. Ours was composed of a corn cake, weighing about three-quarters of a pound, to each person, with as much water as was desired. . . . We worked in this field all day; and at the end of every hour, or hour and a quarter, we had permission to go to the cart, which was moved about the field, so as to be near us, and get water.*
>
> *Our dinner was the same, in all respects, as our breakfast, except that, in addition to the bread, we had a little salt, and a radish for each person. We were not allowed to rest at either breakfast or dinner, longer than while we were eating; and we worked in the evening as long as we could distinguish the weeds from the cotton plants.*

And at the end of this particular day, Ball recounted, three women were given twelve lashes each for performing their work poorly.[62]

The workweek typically ran through Saturday, or in crucial harvest times during the year, especially on sugar plantations, straight through the week until the needed job was done. The evening meal was typically more corn cake—a mixture of cornmeal, water, and a bit of salt baked in ashes or wrapped in cabbage leaves—with, perhaps, some bacon or pork and yams or sweet potatoes. The normal fare for adult slaves throughout the South was a peck of cornmeal—two gallons by dry weight—and three to four pounds of salt pork or bacon per week, handed out on Sundays. With hogs and corn raised on the plantation, basic provisions were covered at essentially no cost. The annual cost of maintaining a slave—food, clothing, and medicine—ran to about $20 between 1840 and 1860.[63]

Slaves supplemented their diet with a variety of produce grown in small plots about their cabins, hunted or trapped game, fish from rivers or the sea, augmented by an occasional hog, or even a steer filched from the plantation stock. A visitor to a Savannah River plantation in Georgia recalled an overseer who bought his slaves "every week, or twice a week, a beef's head from market. With this, they made a soup in a large iron kettle, around which the hands came at meal time, and dipping out the soup, would mix it with their hommony, and eat it as though it were a feast."[64]

In the spring and early summer, Charles Ball recalled, "the rains are frequently so violent, and the ground becomes so wet, that it is injurious to the cotton to work it," and slaves remained indoors. "At such time they made baskets, brooms, horse collars" and other items that they sold. Some earned a penny a pound for cotton picked above their quota. The money was spent, Ball wrote, "for sugar, molasses, and sometimes a few pounds of coffee . . . and a no inconsiderable portion . . . is squandered . . . for tobacco, and an occasional bottle of rum."[65]

"A negro house should never be crowded," *De Bow's Review* advised its readers in an 1847 article, defining not crowded as a space of "sixteen or eighteen feet square [as] not too large for a man and woman and three or four small children." Those dimensions fit the typical slave cabin, in that a pair were often built together for two families with a common fireplace in between. "The great object," the article continued, "is to prevent disease and prolong the useful laboring period of the negro's life. Thus does interest point out the humane course. . . . A peck of meal, four pounds of good meat, with such vegetables, potatoes, peas, etc., as can be provided without any expense, is a good week's allowance."[66]

The slave's allowance also included handouts of winter and summer clothes. Each man, in Olmstead's recounting, received "a coat and trousers, of course woolen or woolen and cotton stuff . . . for Winter, trousers of cotton osnaburghs for Summer, sometimes with a jacket also of the same; two pairs of strong shoes, or one pair of strong boots and one of lighter shoes for harvest; three shirts, one blanket, and one felt hat. The women have two dresses of striped cotton, three shifts, two pairs of shoes, etc."[67] Osnaburg is today's equivalent of sackcloth. Young children often ran naked or were dressed in a simple "tow shirt" reaching to the calves or ankles. "I went as naked as your hand," recalled Mattie Curtis of her girlhood in slavery, "till I was fourteen years old. I was naked like that when my nature come to me. Marse Whitfield ain't carin' but after that mammy told him that I had to have clothes."[68]

The ceremony of slave marriages took different forms, but perhaps the most common was called "jumping the broom." As described by former slave Joe Rawls, "dey jis' lay de broom down, 'n' dem what's gwine ter git marry' walks out 'n' steps ober dat broom bofe tegedder, 'n' de ole massa, he say, 'I now pronounce you man 'n' wife,' 'n' den dey was marry.' Dat was all dey was t' it—no ce'mony, no license, no nothin', jis' marryin."[69] At times the master or overseer would perform the ceremony, or a Black or even a white minister would be called in to do so. The slaves, and on occasion even a master, would lay on a marriage dinner. About three in four slave marriages were between men and women living on the same plantation.[70]

Incentives beyond affection existed for men to marry "abroad," to a woman on a nearby plantation. In that way, a man would not risk having to see his wife whipped and be helpless to stop it, and he would not risk his children seeing him whipped. An escaped ex-slave explained: "No colored man wishes to live at the house where his wife lives, for he has to endure the continual misery of seeing her flogged and abused, without daring to say a word in her defense."[71] Either way, slave marriages were not legally recognized in the South on the ground that property was unable to enter into a contract. As explained by a North Carolina judge, slave marriages "may be dissolved at the pleasure of either party, or by the sale of one or both, depending on the caprice or necessity of the owners."[72]

The master class's veneer of benevolent paternalism wore thin in the face of their fear of slaves being able to read or write, or to conduct religious services on their own. Fear of slave literacy among those who

Jumping the broom—a slave marriage. SOURCE: *SLAVERY IMAGES*.

extolled their own educational attainments ran particularly deep. Benev-olence was best protected by ignorance. "Slaves were not allowed books, pen, ink, nor paper, to improve their minds," recalled ex-slave Henry Bibb.[73] A literate slave might get ahold of copies of the abolitionist press such as William Lloyd Garrison's *The Liberator*, pamphlets from the American Anti-Slavery Society, or find passages in the Bible contrary to their master's assumption of rights to property in human beings.

"In our State," an article in the *St. Louis Observer* noted, "many Christians no more think of instructing their slaves, than they do their horses. This may seem a strong expression, and it is; but it just contains the simple truth, and nothing more."[74] Frederick Douglass quoted what he termed the "oracular exposition" on slave literacy of his master, Hugh

Ault, as "he should know nothing but the will of his master, and learn to obey it," "Learning would spoil the best nigger in the world," "if you teach that nigger . . . how to read the bible, there will be no keeping him . . . ," and "If you learn him how to read, he'll want to know how to write; and, this accomplished, he'll be running away with himself."[75]

Teaching slaves to read and write was banned by Georgia in 1755, Virginia in 1831 and again in 1847, South Carolina in 1834, Alabama in 1832, and Louisiana in 1830.[76] Despite these bans, some whites taught their slaves to read, often as part of religious education. Illiteracy, however, was the norm. Nearly every southern state restricted religious assemblies by slaves, unless whites were present or a white minister presided. An 1830s Virginia law declared it illegal for slaves or free Blacks "to preach, exhort, or conduct, or hold any assembly or meeting, for religious or other purposes, either in the day time or at night."[77]

Former slave Lunsford Lane well recalled the texts of Sabbath sermons that white preachers delivered. "'Servants be obedient to your masters,'—'He that knoweth his master's will and doeth it not, shall be beaten with many stripes,' and others of this class: for they formed the basis of most of these public instructions to us. The first commandment impressed upon our minds was to obey our masters, and the second was like unto it, namely, to do as much work when they or their overseers were not watching us as when they were."[78] Harriet Jacobs's recollection of the Reverend Pike's exhortations during her slave days was similar. "Hearken, ye servants," he called out. "Give strict heed unto my words. You are rebellious sinners. Your hearts are filled with all manner of evil. 'Tis the devil who temp[t]s you. God is angry with you, and will surely punish you, if you don't forsake your wicked ways. . . . Instead of serving your masters faithfully, which is pleasing in the sight of your heavenly Master, you are idle, and shirk your work. God sees you. You tell lies. God hears you."[79]

Peter Randolph, who himself became a reverend after securing his freedom, explained that slaves had their own way around their masters' version of spiritual enlightenment. "Not being allowed to hold meetings on the plantation," he wrote, "the slaves assemble in the swamps, out of reach of the patrols. They have an understanding among themselves as to the time and place of getting together. This is often done by the first one arriving breaking boughs from the trees, and bending them in the direction of the selected spot. Arrangements are then made for conducting the exercises. . . . Preaching in order, by the brethren; then praying and singing all round, until they generally feel quite happy."[80]

The Virginia slave Moses Grandy remembered well a particular Friday morning a few months after he was first married. As he was working among canal boats, he heard some noise coming from the road behind him. "I turned to look," he wrote, "and saw a gang of slaves coming. When they came up to me, one of them cried out, 'Moses, my dear!' I wondered who among them should know me, and found it was my wife. She cried out to me, 'I am gone!' I was struck with consternation. Mr. Roger's son was with them, on his horse, armed with pistols. I said to him, 'For God's sake, have you bought my wife?' He said he had; when I asked him what she had done, he said she had done nothing, but that her master wanted money. He drew out his pistol, and said that, if I went near the wagon on which she was, he would shoot me. I asked for leave to shake hands with her, which he refused, but said I might stand at a distance and talk with her. My heart was so full that I could say very little. I asked leave to give her a dram. He told Mr. Burgess, the man who was with him, to get down and carry it to her. I gave her the little money I had in my pocket, and bade her farewell. I have never seen or heard of her from that day to this. I loved her as I loved my life."[81]

Separating husbands and wives and breaking up families was remarkably common, particularly in the Border South slave-selling states of Virginia, Maryland, and Kentucky, as well as in Tennessee and North Carolina. It certainly was not new to Moses Grandy. He remembered when his brother was sold. "My mother," Grandy wrote, "frantic with grief, resisted their taking her child away. She was beaten, and held down; she fainted; and, when she came to herself, her boy was gone. She made much outcry, for which the master tied her up to a peach-tree in the yard, and flogged her."[82]

The planter elite never did find a way to reconcile their self-image as benign patriarchs with the practice of destroying families and marriages for money. Slave sales between planters were generally considered honorable. Sales to speculators nearly always carried a tinge of disrepute. Owners might try to conceal their role in such transactions. The sales might be caused by the necessity of easing debt, as had been the case with Thomas Jefferson, or as part of liquidating an estate after death. Either way, the prospects of disrupting the closest of family ties and the knowledge of where sold slaves were headed made the practice odious. Being "sold South" into Louisiana swamplands or the Mississippi River cotton plantations was tantamount to being sentenced into oblivion.

On average, an estimated 200,000 slaves were sold in the interstate slave trade every decade between 1820 and 1860. The wreckage of these forced migrations meant that about one-third of all slave children living in the Border South during this era were "sold South." A nearly equal proportion of the region's first marriages were destroyed by one form or another of forced separation.[83] The master class did find a way to make these circumstances work to their advantage. The threat to sell a slave South added a weapon of terror to the arsenal of coercion available to bring an unruly slave into line.

Once sold, Border South slaves destined for New Orleans, the largest slave-trading market in the country, often made the journey by ship. Most, however, in coffles ranging from a couple of dozen to more than 100, made the journey by foot. Charles Ball was one of them. He recalled: "The women were merely tied together with a rope, about the size of a bed-cord, which was tied like a halter round the neck of each; but the men . . . were very differently caparisoned. A strong iron collar was closely fitted by means of a padlock round each of our necks. A chain of iron, about a hundred feet in length, was passed through the hasp of each padlock, except at the two ends, where hasps of the padlock passed through a link of the chain. In addition to this, we were handcuffed in pairs, with iron staples and bolts, with a short chain, about a foot long, uniting the handcuffs and their wearers in pairs. In this manner we were chained alternately by the right and left hand; and the poor man to whom I was thus ironed, wept like an infant when the blacksmith, with his heavy hammer, fastened the ends of the bolts that kept the staples from slipping from our arms."[84]

A few refused to make the journey. A slave in Baltimore slit his throat in public view as he was about to be boarded on a ship set to sail to New Orleans.[85] An article that made the rounds of southern newspapers in 1853 reported, "A negro woman, belonging to George M. Garrison, of Polk Co., killed four of her children, by cutting their throats while they were asleep. Her master knows of no cause for the horrid act, unless it be that she heard him speaking of selling her and two children, and keeping the others."[86]

Bloodhounds! I would respectfully inform the citizens of Missouri that I still have my Nigger Dogs, and they are in prime training, and ready to attend to all calls of Hunting and Catching—runaway Niggers . . . if the Nigger has weapons, the charge will be made according to the difficulty had in taking him . . . I venture to suggest to any person having a Nigger runaway, that the better plan is to send for the Dogs forthwith when the Nigger goes off. (Lexington Democratic Advocate, *February 14, 1855)*[87]

Disobedience was the slave's most common form of resistance to the master. Means of resistance were limited, chances of gaining freedom scant, and consequences of retribution near certain. But slaves did resist. Among the most overt acts of resistance was to deny labor to the master by running away. Some slaves made their way to freedom in the North or in Canada. Far more common was for a slave to run off and hide out for several days or even a few months and then to voluntarily return or be hunted down and captured, often by a pack of dogs.

The case of a slave named Harry is typical. He lived on a North Carolina plantation. In the narrative of a white man who was also there at the time, Harry ran away into the woods during the absence of his master. "This the slaves sometimes do," the narrative recounts, "when the master is absent for several weeks, to escape the cruel treatment of

SOURCE: *SLAVERY IMAGES.*

the overseer. It is common for them to make preparations by secreting a mortar, a hatchet, some cooking utensils, and whatever things they can get that will enable them to live while they are in the woods or swamps. Harry staid about three months, and lived robbing the rice grounds, and by such other means as came his way. The slaves generally know where the runaway is secreted, and visit him at night and on Sundays. On the return of his master, some of the slaves were sent for Harry. When he came home he was seized and confined in the stocks."[88]

The returned runaway might not be the only one punished. The former slave Christopher Nichols recalled, "If a man ran away after he had been whipped, the rest of us were put on half allowance till he came back, and the runaway must make up his lost time by working Sundays."[89]

Masters who did not want to count on a runaway's voluntary return could hire or call out their own dogs. Frederick Law Olmsted discussed this business with an Alabama farmer who had his own pack of thirteen mixed-breed bloodhounds. When hard pushed by pursuing dogs, Olmstead recounted, "a negro always took to a tree; sometimes however, they would catch him in an open field. When this was the case the hunter called off the dogs as soon as he could, unless the negro fought—'that generally makes 'em mad (the hunters), and they'll let 'em tear him a spell. The owners don't mind having them kind o' niggers tore a good deal; runaways ain't much account no how, and it makes the rest more afraid to run away, when they see how they are [scarred].'"[90] A Louisiana slave hunter provided a similar account: "If I can catch a cuss'd runaway Nigger without killing him, very good; though I generally let the hounds punish him a little, and sometimes give him a load of squirrel-shot. If mild measures, like these, do not suffice, I use harsher punishment."[91]

Harsher punishment could devolve into the outright sadistic, as Olmstead documented from a conversation with six Texas planters and herdsmen. "I can tell you how you can break a nigger of running away, certain," one of the men said. "There was an old fellow I used to know in Georgia, that always cured his so. If a nigger ran away, when he caught him, he would bind his knee over a log, and fasten him so he couldn't stir; then he'd take a pair of pincers and pull one of his toe-nails out by the roots; and tell him that if he ever ran away again, he would pull out two of them, and if he run away again after that, he told them he'd pull out four of them, and so on, doubling each time. He never had to do it more than twice—it always cured them."[92]

The same torture, according to a contemporary account, involved a slaveholder who "had a slave who had often run away, and often been severely whipped. After one of his floggings, he burnt his master's barn: this so enraged the man that when he caught him he took a pair of pincers and pulled his toe nails out. The negro then murdered two of his master's children. He was taken after a desperate pursuit, (having been shot through the shoulder) and hung."[93]

An account of a runaway slave who refused to be retaken was published in the *Feliciana Whig*, a Louisiana newspaper. The slave had made his way onto a driftwood raft, armed with a club and pistol, when confronted by his pursuers and their dogs. "In this position," the report ran, "he bade defiance to men and dogs—knocking the latter into the water with his club, and resolutely threatening death to any man who approached him. Finding him obstinately determined not to surrender, one of his pursuers shot him. He fell at the third fire, and so determined was he not to be captured, that when an effort was made to rescue him from drowning he made battle with his club, and sunk waving his weapon in angry defiance at his pursuers."[94]

Having to use dogs to capture runaway slaves was one indicator the master class's portrayal of their slaves' contentment was not air-tight. Another was the presence of armed patrols, on foot or mounted, throughout the slave South keeping an eye out for discontented or errant bondsmen during the hours of darkness. Slave patrols were ubiquitous. They usually ran in two four-hour shifts, one beginning about nine at night, an hour before the typical curfew for Blacks to be out, the second taking over from one in the morning to daylight. In towns and cities patrols might go about on foot. Rural areas were divided into districts patrolled by men on horseback. Patrols could comprise just a few men or more than a dozen, appointed as a civic responsibility or paid. The patrols drew men from militia units, including officers, and the poorer ranks of non-slave-holding whites who thereby had the chance to act out the coercive arm of white supremacy.

As recalled by former slave W. L. Bost, "the paddyrollers they keep close watch on the pore niggers so they have no chance to do anything or go anywhere. They jes' like policemen, only worser. 'Cause they never let the niggers go anywhere without a pass from his masters. If you wasn't in your proper place when the paddyrollers come they lash you til' you was black and blue."[95] Patrols operated with varying levels of discretion, from inflicting punishment on the spot, to jailing their captives or returning them to their owners as they thought any given incident might warrant. Their efforts also rounded up not a few whites suspected of or engaged in some form of outlawry. A continuous cat and mouse game played out in the dark as slaves hid or waited out the patrols and the patrollers varied their routes and timing to catch errant Blacks.

Resistance to their condition among slaves took many forms, a flicker of attitude being the most subtle and by far the most common. Frederick Douglass described the offense that led to a slave named Nancy being whipped as "one of the commonest and most indefinite in the whole catalogue of offenses usually laid to the charge of slaves, viz: 'impudence.' This may mean almost anything, or nothing at all, just according to the caprice of the master or overseer, at the moment. But, whatever it is, or is not, if it gets the name of 'impudence,' the party charged with it is sure of a flogging. This offense may be committed in various ways; in the tone of an answer; in answering at all; in not answering; in the expression of countenance; in the motion of the head; in the gait, manner and bearing of the slave."[96]

Offenses that could not sustain the charge of outright defiance accumulated in the everyday interaction between slave and master. They underlay the common complaint that slaves could not grasp the most basic instruction without constant supervision. They included foot dragging or feigning illness, leaving a livestock gate open or forgetting where some needed tool was last placed. Broken hoes, dull cutting tools, slack straps, something left in the rain that should have been brought in, an impenetrable indifference to the routine and the urgent, all were acts of incomplete submission, grudging subordination. The lazy slave is a stereotype of white southern frustration rarely understood as the recourse to resistance that might yet avoid recrimination.

Slavery, whatever its date or location, is a system based on the threat or use of violence, the threat more effective the more sure and severe the violence. As described by South Carolina's James Henry Hammond, "remember, that on our estates we dispense with the whole machinery of public police and public courts of justice. Thus we try, decide, and execute the sentences, in thousands of cases, which in other countries would go into the courts."[97] He could as easily have said that slave plantations dispensed with the entire structure of normal justice, substituting for it the given will of a given master or overseer at any given time or place, usually at an isolated location where no word of the type of justice applied ever leaked out.

Accounts by former slaves of good treatment by masters are certainly part of the antebellum record. Giles Smith provided one, saying in an oral history, "Yas sar, de marster an' de missy am de best folks dat de Lawd could make. Dey am good wid de wuk, de feed, de clothes, an' de play. Deer am no whupping', an' sich. . . . We-uns all lak de marster 'cause of him's way. Yas sar, 'twas mo' dan lak him; we-uns think mo' ob him dan anyone in de world, an' de missy, too. . . . [S]he told me dat de marster always says, 'If de nigger won't follow de o'dahs by de kind treatment, den sich nigger am wrong in de head an' am not worth keepin.'"[98]

Accounts such as Smith's can be stacked up against those about men like Essex Henry: "Mr. Henry wus little wid a short leg an' a long one, an' he had de wust temper dat eber wus in de worl'. He loved ter see slaves suffer, near 'bout as much as he loved his brandy. We knowed when we seed him comin' dat dar wus gwine ter be a 'whuppin' frolic,' fore de day wus gone."[99] To place the feathers of benign treatment on the scales against incidents of harshness or cruelty to try to find where the balance of slavery lay is a pointless exercise. One does not cancel the other. For more than two decades prior to 1860, the master class was intent on promoting a positive facade for a system founded on violence. "A great deal of whipping is not necessary," one Virginian remarked during that period. "*Some* is."[100] To avert attention from what that "*some*" was is to add a coat of gloss to the master class's veneer of benevolent suzerainty.

Masters living in towns or cities had the option of sending a slave they wished disciplined to the local jail, or in Charleston what was called the workhouse, to have the whipping done. "It saved them trouble . . . and possibly a slight wear and tear of feeling," recalled Louis Hughes, who spent thirty years in bondage until freed during the Civil War.[101] Another former slave provided a more descriptive account, writing, "The people in town, for decency's sake, and perhaps, too, because they are more polished in their manners altogether, keep these things as quiet as possible. When they wish to chastise a slave, they send him to the workhouse, . . . and there the poor wretch received a regular lashing, according to law: that is to say, not more than thirty-nine strokes can be inflicted in one day; and for this accommodation the owner must pay half a dollar."[102] Instruction on how many lashes might rightfully be applied was drawn from Deuteronomy 25:3, which set the maximum for any given day at forty.

For the less genteel, the task was more routine, as reflected in September through December 1837 entries for the 200-slave Louisiana Barrow cotton plantation diary that noted, "Had a general Whiping frollick. . . . More Whiping to do this Fall than altogether in three years. . . . [Tom ran off again, so] will whip him more than I ever Whip one. . . . Whipped about half to day. . . . Whiped 8 or 10 for weight to day."[103] The final entry referred to a failure to meet the daily poundage quota for cotton picked.

A few dismal methods describe how most whippings were carried out, aside from the spontaneous lashes inflicted in the fields. "The usual mode of punishing the poor slave was," wrote ex-slave Austin Steward, "to make them take off their clothes to the bare back, and then tie their hands before them with a rope, pass the end of the rope over a beam, and draw them up till they stood on the tips of their toes. . . . Thirty-nine was the number of lashes ordinarily inflicted," using whips made of several strands of rawhide.[104] An outside tree branch might work as well as an inside beam. At times the slave was left suspended for hours after the whipping ended; at others salt water might be rubbed into the wounds. Many plantations had a post secured in the ground to which slaves were tied and whipped. A wooden paddle was sometimes substituted for the whip, a device that left fewer scars that lowered a slave's auction block value. The paddles had a striking surface about three inches wide and eighteen inches long with small holes drilled through it. "The persons who are thus flogged," an ex-slave recounted, "are always stripped naked, and their hands tied together. They are then bent over double, their knees

Flogging with a paddle left fewer scars than lashing with a leather whip. CREDIT: *SLAVERY IMAGES.*

are forced between their elbows, and a stick is put through between the elbows and the bend of the legs, in order to hold the victim in that position, while the paddle is applied."[105]

A few masters employed more inventively cruel methods of discipline. A former slave recalled, "A large farmer, Colonel M'Quiller in Cashaw county, South Carolina, was in the habit of driving nails into a hogshead so as to leave the point of the nail just protruding in the inside of the cask; into this, he used to put his slaves for punishment, and roll them down a very long and steep hill."[106] A particularly gruesome account of punishment is provided by ex-slave James Williams of a bondsman who was staked to the ground by forked sticks over his neck, ankles, and wrists. "The overseer then sent for two large cats," Williams' narrative states. "These he placed upon the naked shoulders of his victim, and dragged them suddenly by their tails downward. At first they did not scratch deeply. He then ordered me to strike them with a small stick after he had placed them once more upon the back of the sufferer. I did so; and the enraged animals extended their claws, and tore his back deeply and cruelly as they were dragged along it."[107] The slave was then whipped and, Williams wrote, after being placed in stocks for three days, died.

William Poe, a slave-owning native of Richmond, recounted that Benjamin James Harris, a wealthy tobacconist of that city, "whipped a slave girl fifteen years old to death. While he was whipping her, his wife heated a smoothing iron, put it on her body in various places, and burned her severely. The verdict of the coroner's inquest was, 'Died of excessive whipping.' He was tried in Richmond, and acquitted. I attended the trial." Harris was later accused of a second slave murder and again acquitted, "because none but blacks saw it done," and they could not testify in court against a white man.[108]

———

Thomas Jefferson knew whereof he spoke in attributing "a perpetual exercise of . . . the most unremitting despotism" to those who owned other human beings as property.[109]

The killing at times could take a casual, almost offhand aspect. One morning on a Mississippi plantation while the overseer was calling the slaves together to give orders, one narrative reads, "a slave came running out of his cabin, having a knife in his hand and eating his breakfast. The overseer seeing him coming with a knife, was somewhat alarmed, and instantly raised his gun and shot him dead. He said afterwards, that he believed the slave was perfectly innocent of any evil intentions, he came out hastily to hear the orders while eating. *No* notice was taken of the killing."[110]

The *Lynchburg Virginian* reported on the fate of a slave owned by William Mays and two sons of William Payne who were bird hunting on Mays's plantation. When the Payne sons reached the tobacco house, one with a string of pigeons and the other with none, the slave, not named in the report, had the impudence to ask of the one with an empty string where his pigeons were. "He replied that he killed none," the newspaper recounted, "but could kill him (the negro), and raised his gun and fired. The load took effect in the head, and caused death in a few hours. The negro was a valuable one. Mr. Mays had refused $1,200 for him."[111] The loss of the investment was evidently more salient news than the murder.

In North Carolina the *Wilmington Advertiser* ran an insert in 1838 reading, "$100 will be paid to any person who may apprehend a negro man named Alfred. The same reward will be paid for satisfactory evidence of his having been killed." A similar insert ran in an 1836 edition of the South Carolina *Charleston Courier*, reading, "$300 REWARD. Ranaway from the subscriber, his two negro men, Billy and Pompey. Billy is twenty-five years old, and known as the patroon of my boat for many years. In all probability, he may resist; in that event, $50 will be paid for his head."[112]

The killing was not all one-sided. The slave's ultimate expression of resistance was murdering the master. Such cases are comparatively rare, especially in contrast to the number of slave killings, but they appear throughout the antebellum period. One involved a slave named Austin in Independence County, Arkansas, in 1853. After he had "talked improperly to his master," according to the court record, Austin expected a beating but vowed "that he would not be taken by his master or anybody else."[113] The next day, after bundling up some clothes with the possible intent to run away, he returned to his work in the woods, carrying an ax. His master and some other men, including Hiram Payne, pursued him. When found, Austin said he would kill anyone who tried to touch him and refused to put down the ax. When Payne tried to hit him with a plank, Austin swung his ax, hitting Payne in the skull severely enough that Payne died a few days later. Austin was hanged for the crime.

In early 1858 in Meriwether County, Georgia, an overseer named Jenkins told a slave named Sarah to put down a fence rail she was holding because he was going to whip her. She did so, but Jenkins grew frustrated after two switches he was using to beat her broke. He grabbed her from behind. She swung a knife over her shoulder, severing Jenkins's carotid artery. He bled to death. Sarah was hanged.[114]

Ailey, a teenage slave girl in Jasper County, Georgia, was also hanged. Her crime arose in November 1853 when her mistress, Edna McMichael, berated her for missing a stich in her weaving and slapped her. Ailey responded by grabbing Mrs. McMichael by the throat, throwing her to the floor, and suffocating her. Ailey was executed the following spring.[115]

When they occurred, these types of cases, including reports of kitchen slaves poisoning meals prepared for the master and his family, sent shivers through the planter class like some faint but continuous background dirge. Not all slaves understood their role in the patriarchal paradigm.

A notorious case, both for its protracted court proceedings and its widespread publicity, involved a slave girl named Celia that has best been recounted by historian Melton A. McLaurin.[116] She was about fourteen years old when Robert Newsom, who owned a few slaves on his 800-acre farm in Callaway County, Missouri, bought her in 1850. His wife had died the year before. That the sixty-year-old Newsom purchased her for sex was made clear when he got her to his home and raped her.[117] He built her a brick house of her own, apart from the slave quarters and some fifty yards from his own home, where she eventually began raising two children, probably his, while working as his cook. By 1855 she had formed a relationship with a slave named George, who threatened to break off with her unless she stopped having sex with Newsom. She tried to avoid him, attempted to enlist the aid of his two daughters to dissuade him, feigned illness to discourage him. On the night of June 23, 1855, Newsom went to the brick house for her. She was standing near the fireplace, a stout wooden stick placed close by. When he demanded sex, she struck and killed him with two blows with the stick.

Celia then decided to erase any evidence of the killing. She shoved his body into the fireplace and throughout the night kept pushing the corpse into the tended flames until nearly nothing was left but ash and some bones. Those she crushed, burying some within the house. By morning Newsom had apparently disappeared, perhaps on some errand where he might have been waylaid by criminals. Suspicious neighbors and local authorities eventually unraveled the case, finding buttons from Newsom's coat in the fireplace and pieces of bone in the house. She was eventually convicted at trial, escaped jail with possible help from her lawyers, and only after the state supreme court denied an appeal was she executed on December 21, 1855.

The morning after the killing Celia called Newsom's grandson Coffee Waynescot into her house. She offered him two dozen walnuts to clean the ashes out of her fireplace. While the boy was pouring the remains from the fireplace into a bucket, a thin cloud of ash rose in the air about him. As Celia well knew, Coffee was breathing in the ashen remains of his cremated grandfather whom she had killed.[118]

CHAPTER 6

Slave Revolt and State Nullification

GOD HIMSELF decreed a righteous destiny for Nat Turner. From childhood on, Nat was convinced of it. When he was about four years old, Nat's parents came to believe that he must have been touched by the divine after he recited details of an incident that had occurred before he was born. He had a quick mind and early on developed a powerful religious bent. He was reserved to the point of austerity, did not drink alcohol or swear, and as he grew to manhood "avoided mixing in society and wrapped myself in mystery, devoting my time to fasting and prayer."[1]

Nat Turner was born in 1800, the same year Gabriel Prosser planned insurrection in Richmond. Like Gabriel, Nat Turner was a slave, first the property of Benjamin Turner, then of his son Samuel, then of Thomas Moore. When Moore died, his wife, Sally, married Joseph Travis, a local wheelwright, who moved onto his wife's place a few miles from the North Carolina border in Southampton County, Virginia. Nat was a plowman. He learned to read and devoted himself to the Bible, in time becoming a respected if aloof preacher among other slaves in the remote backwater of southeastern Virginia.

As he worked in the fields one day, a voice came to Nat, as if on the wind, calling him to follow the scriptural admonition, "Seek ye the kingdom of Heaven and all things shall be added to you."[2] For two years Nat prayed over the questions posed by Christ's Sermon on the Mount verse in Matthew 6:33, trying to understand what *was* the kingdom of heaven and *how* was one to seek it out. Slowly the revelation came to him that the kingdom was where oppression was forever banished. Even more, to find it Nat turned not to the Christ of mercy and love, but the Christ of Revelations, who would descend from heaven to redeem the faithful and punish the unbelievers amid fire and devastation. Nat knew that he "was ordained for some great purpose in the hands of the Almighty."[3]

While still in service to Samuel Turner, Nat ran away when he was placed under a new and harsh overseer. His father had escaped slavery years earlier, disappearing north, never to he heard of again. But after about thirty days of hiding in the woods, Nat returned. Nat explained that he had come back in compliance with the stricture of Luke 12:47, "For he who knoweth his Master's will, and doeth it not, shall be beaten with many stripes, and thus have I chastened you."[4] His fellow slaves mocked Nat for not completing his escape. Samuel Turner likely comforted himself with the thought that Nat's devotion to the true word had returned him to his proper place. That thought was in one sense true, as Nat himself acknowledged.[5] But in another sense, Samuel Turner was not Nat's master. Nat's master was God. Nat had not been commanded to seek the things of this world, but the kingdom of heaven. And the words in that part of the verse he recited, "thus have I chastened you," were not the Lord's words in Luke. They were Nat's. He had to return, and he must be chastened as was Christ, for he had a mission assigned to him by God.

Soon afterward, when he was twenty-five years old, Nat experienced another vision in which "I saw white spirits and black spirts engaged in battle, and the sun was darkened—the thunder rolled in the Heavens, and blood flowed in streams—and I heard a voice saying, 'Such is your luck, such you are called to see, and let it come rough or smooth, and you must surely bear it.'"[6] As he contemplated this vision, Nat realized that the Holy Spirit was in him, that he had been made perfect. Another vision came to him three years later, telling him that upon a sign from heaven he was to take up the yoke Christ had borne for the sins of man, "for the time was fast approaching when the first should be last and the last should be first."[7]

The first heavenly sign that a new day of judgment was at hand occurred with a solar eclipse in February 1831. Nat confided in but four fellow slaves who were already convinced that he was a prophet. They secretly recruited about twenty other slaves to Nat's cause. They had no great need for planning. God was in control of events. On Nat's order,

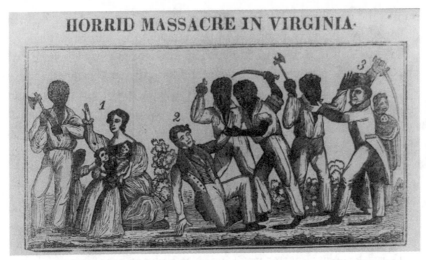

Composite images of Nat Turner's revolt. COURTESY OF THE LIBRARY OF CONGRESS.

the uprising was set for July 4, then delayed, and finally confirmed in mid-August when a prominent black spot appeared on the sun.[8] On the afternoon of Sunday, August 21, 1831, Nat met his confederates at Cabin Pond less than a mile from Joseph Travis's home. They were Hark Travis, Henry Porter, Samuel Francis, and Nelson Williams. Two newcomers were also present, Jack Reese, and the man who more than any other would wield the blade of vengeance, Will Francis. They ate, planned, drank brandy—Nat excepted—and waited until after midnight.

The goal of their endeavor was never made clear: perhaps to hack their way to the hamlet of Jerusalem and then to the vast Dismal Swamp some twenty miles to the east, perhaps just to let events unfold according to a plan already written in heaven. Their first objective, however, was obvious: Joseph Travis and his family.

On reaching the Travis home at about 2 a.m., Nat, using a ladder, gained entry through a second-floor window. Letting in the others, Nat and Will Francis went to the main bedroom. Nat swung his hatchet at Joseph's head, but the blade glanced off. Will finished the job with a single ax blow. He then hacked Sally Travis to death. Two children were murdered. After the marauders left, one circled back to kill Travis's infant son, who had been forgotten in the initial round of bloodletting. The pattern was set: murder all whites encountered, men, women, and children.[9]

The killings were not acts of personal vengeance for Nat, although he had cause, having endured whipping in the past and seen his wife sold south. He bore no grudge against Joseph Travis, instead recalling that Travis "was to me a kind master, and placed great confidence in me; in fact, I had no cause to complain of his treatment to me."[10] Nat was, rather, the agent of God, the Old Testament God of wrath, the God who commanded Ezekiel to go through Jerusalem and "slay utterly old and young, both maids, and little children, and women."[11]

In darkness, now armed with a sword and on horseback, Nat briefly drilled his little army and marched them to the next victim some 600 yards distant. Salathiel Francis was dragged out of his home and hacked to death. After slaughtering three more whites on another farm at daybreak, Nat's forces divided, with him pushing forward to Mrs. Catherine Whitehead's place. Will Francis decapitated her with a broad ax. Her son, three of her daughters, her grandchild, and her mother were killed. Margaret, the fourth daughter, attempted to run off. Nat himself caught up with her and beat her to death with a fence rail. She was the only person to die by Nat's hand during the revolt.

As Nat's forces moved north from farm to farm, then east toward Jerusalem across the Nottoway River, they grew to about forty in number, recruited along the way, many of them on horseback. Other slaves had run off rather than join Nat's forces. Some attempted, and at least one was successful, in hiding their masters. Word of what was happening began to spread. Church bells tolled. White men armed themselves, assembled on horseback, and began hunting the killers. News reached Jerusalem, where the river bridge was barricaded. Word of the revolt got to Richmond by evening, where Governor John Floyd called out the militia, sending them south toward Southampton County before daybreak the next morning.

Nat had taken to riding at the rear of his army, reunited after separating earlier, sending his best forces on horseback at full gallop at their victims "to prevent their escape and strike terror to the inhabitants."[12] The worst of it all occurred at Levi Waller's plantation. He had been alerted to the danger while away from the house and managed to hide, first in a clump of weeds just before the horsemen descended, then in an orchard as they hit their mark. As he later testified, Waller watched as his wife was slashed to death and two of his daughters had their heads chopped off. Another daughter crawled up into a clay chimney in the house and survived. Several children from a nearby school were at the house. Ten of them were decapitated, their mangled bodies thrown together in a bloody pile. By the time Nat arrived, many of the insurgents were drunk with brandy taken from Waller's still. As is written in Deuteronomy 32:25, "the sword without, and terror within, shall destroy both the young man and the virgin, the sucking also with the man of gray hairs."

Within minutes of Nat's departure, a group of about twenty armed whites came upon the horror at Waller's home. Another posse of perhaps forty men was in nearby pursuit. By the time the first party reached Jacob Williams's place, they found Williams's wife and three children dead and his overseer disemboweled. Nat got to Rebecca Vaughan's home about noon, where, as he later recalled of his various encounters with the aftermath of the revolt, he felt "a silent satisfaction" at seeing that his men, now numbering close to sixty, had hacked her, her son, and her niece to death.[13]

By about noon, after ten hours of unresisted killing, some of the white militia came upon Nat's forces and opened fire. In this first exchange of rifle shots, no one was apparently killed, but the revolt began to disintegrate. Nat and a remnant of his forces lurched east, but realizing that the road to Jerusalem was blocked, swung south and by nightfall had turned north again, evading the white patrols, and recrossed his original line of march to wind up in some woods near Thomas Ridley's farm. More of his forces deserted overnight. During a skirmish on Tuesday, Will Francis was killed. By nightfall Nat was alone. He finally made his way back near Joseph Travis's home, where the revolt had begun. He hid out for ten weeks until he was found and peacefully surrendered on October 30.

Throughout the day Tuesday and to the end of the week the militia hunted down, captured, or killed nearly all the insurgents. Fifty-three Blacks were jailed, and in a rampage of fury, as many as 200 other Blacks, both slave and free, were murdered.[14] The revolt's death toll was placed at fifty-seven, a majority of them women and children. Whites in Virginia and much of the rest of the South were traumatized.

A rumor that Wilmington had been sacked and 2,000 Blacks were on the march resulted in North Carolina's militia being called out. Many Blacks were arrested. Three were executed.[15] An unreported number of Blacks suspected of revolt in Macon, Georgia, were killed. Rumors of rebellion swept Alabama and New Orleans. In Boston, William Lloyd Garrison's recently launched abolitionist newspaper, *The Liberator*, declared, "The fact must now be self-evident to the dullest observer, that the lives of the planters are in imminent peril—*and they know it.* . . . Not one of them rests easy upon his pillow at night—dismay is universal."[16] In Petersburg, Virginia, an Englishman who had commented that as men, Blacks were entitled to freedom, was stripped naked, whipped, and left to walk to Richmond, where he booked fare to New York.[17] Essentially no record exists of the revolt's direct impact on the nation's enslaved population. Word of it undoubtedly spread through the slave grapevine to the remotest plantations, word that Black men had arisen in arms against their servitude, and that they had, if only for a matter of hours, been free. That news must have been, in the same moment, both inspiring and chilling.

In subsequent trials, seventeen Blacks were sentenced to death, with the remainder of those arrested being convicted and sold south, acquitted, or discharged. In his jail cell awaiting trial, Nat Turner dictated his *Confessions* to lawyer Thomas R. Gray. They quickly appeared in pamphlet form and were sold throughout the country. While transcribing the account, and perhaps expecting some expression of remorse, Gray asked Nat if he did not now find himself mistaken. "Was not Christ crucified," Nat answered.[18] Nat Turner was executed on November 11. His body was dissected for medical study.

~

In Richmond, Governor Floyd confided to his diary, "Before I leave this Government, I will have contrived to have a law passed gradually abolishing slavery in this State, or at all events to begin the work of prohibiting slavery on the West side of the Blue Ridge Mountains."[19] The owner of a dozen slaves, Floyd came from the western Allegheny Mountains region of Virginia, where slavery had not assumed anything like the scale that dominated the tidewater and piedmont eastern parts of the state. In his December annual message to the legislature, Floyd laid out a series of new measures to suppress slaves but also opened the door to state support for a removal and deportation plan for free Blacks.

The House of Delegates that heard his message had been elected under voting reforms adopted in an 1829 revision of the state constitution. The lopsided power granted to the slaveholding counties under the old constitution had been shifted to give greater power to western counties in the Shenandoah Valley and Trans-Allegheny regions. Even with the reform, the eastern portion of the state held seven more, and the western region seven fewer seats in the House of Delegates than would have been allocated in an equally apportioned one-man-one-vote system of white male suffrage.[20] Virginia had the largest slave population of any state in the union, a distinction it would carry into the Civil War. Some 470,000 Blacks were held in bondage in 1830, amid a white population of just under 700,000. But slaves outnumbered eastern Virginia's 376,000 whites by 40,000. Another 40,000 free Blacks lived there. To the west, 318,000 whites lived among 53,000 slaves and 6,340 free Blacks.[21]

A committee, heavily weighted in favor of slaveholders, was appointed in the House of Delegates to report on issues relevant to the just-crushed insurrection. It found it "inexpedient" to act on the underlying issue of slavery. Shunning the issue was not acceptable to a significant portion of public opinion nor to many House members. Thomas Ritchie's *Richmond Enquirer* demanded to know whether some plan could be "firmly and deliberately introduced, for striking at the roots of the evil . . . for reducing surely but quietly, the number of our slaves?"[22] Thomas Jefferson's grandson stepped forward to propose a remedy. Thomas Jefferson Randolph offered a motion to seek voter approval for a plan that would have all slaves born after July 4, 1840, turned over to the state and hired out to work. Under this plan women would be granted freedom at age eighteen and men at age twenty-one, and the income from their work would be used to pay for their mandatory deportation for destinations such as Liberia in Africa. His plan

Thomas Jefferson Randolph.
SOURCE: WIKIMEDIA COMMONS/
PORTRAIT BY CHARLES WILSON
PEALE, MONTICELLO DIGITAL
CLASSROOM.

included giving slaveholders the right to sell their state-held property before they reached the age of emancipation.

What followed was an open legislative debate on slavery, unprecedented then or later in southern history. William Preston declared to the House that "for near 200 years, the thoughts, words and actions of Virginians have been suppressed, and that a solemn silence has closed the mouth and stifled all investigation of this subject . . . [but] the spell is broken, and the scales have been lifted from our eyes."[23] The *Enquirer* printed the debates. Copies of several of the speeches were published for wide distribution. Breaking the seal of silence was an outrage to some, Petersburg delegate John Thompson Brown lamenting "We are, by this act, to make public confession of our fears—to acknowledge that the sense of security is gone—to announce to the slave, that the principles of natural justice entitle him to freedom."[24] The *Enquirer's* Thomas Ritchie was denounced as "an apostate traitor."[25]

The case for Randolph's gradual abolition plan was put graphically by delegate John Chandler, who compared slavery to a merchant who "has a large quantity of gunpowder in his store: its explosion would endanger the town—can he not be compelled to remove it to a place of safety?"[26] Slavery's danger to the white community was a consistent theme in the emancipationists' argument. Society has a paramount right to protect itself from destruction, delegate Charles Faulkner said, even at the sacrifice of private property. Speaking directly to slaveholders, he said, "There is no obligation upon society to continue your right one moment after it becomes injurious to the best interests of society: nor to compensate you for the loss of that, the deprivation of which is demanded by the safety of the state."[27] Western delegate William B. Preston from Montgomery County believed "The slave has a *natural* right to regain his liberty." The primary issue for him, however, was that "when the public necessity demanding their emancipation is greater than the public necessity of their retention of slaves," the legislature can repeal the statute that makes them slaves.[28]

Emancipation, compounded with no compensation for the lost labor, struck slaveholders as madness. In a lengthy mid-January 1832 speech, delegate John Brown dissected the plan. Virginians had yet to be convinced, he said, of any necessity of surrendering $100 million worth of slave property and "voluntarily embracing pauperism." The entire plan was "visionary and impracticable." Referring to the writings of the Sage of Monticello, he said Thomas Jefferson's desire to see an end to slavery was no more than a "daydream" set against the hard reality that to free Virginia's slaves without compensation "will shake this ancient commonwealth to its centre; it will sever it in twain." Examined on its own terms, he continued, the plan "is not to have any visible effect for a quarter of a century" while every slave born before July 1840 and ineligible for emancipation would be "transformed into a dark, designing and desperate rebel."[29]

The plan's flaws were evident. Eastern Virginia's slaveholders were implacably opposed to it. The first trickle of emancipation and deportation would not begin until July 1858 for women, three years later for men, and could take well into the twentieth century to reach its final goal. Scant attention was paid to the prospect that the plan would set off a wave of slave selling by owners set on cashing out before emancipation deadlines were reached.

William H. Brodnax offered a middle way. A plantation owner with twenty-six slaves, the lawyer-politician had commanded part of the militia sent to quash the Southampton revolt. Believing that slavery was "a transcendent evil," he thought the shock of emancipation could be avoided by first concentrating on getting rid of Virginia's free Blacks. He calculated his plan to the penny. For a thirty-cent per person annual tax on whites, enough money could be raised to deport and resettle 6,000 free Blacks annually, eliminating all of them from the state within ten years. The free persons of color would have no say in the matter. With this phase of the work in train, he proposed, deportation of emancipated slaves might commence. Perhaps Virginia's share of federal land sale income could be added to the kitty.[30]

Delegate Thomas Marshall, who favored the deportation plan, made a rare confession. The eldest son of the chief justice of the Supreme Court said that because Virginia's slaves were "perfectly happy" and treated with "indulgent kindness," it was not for their sake that abolition was desirable. Instead, he explained, the institution should be gradually eliminated because "it is ruinous to the whites—retards improvement—roots out an industrious population—banishes the yeomanry of the country—deprives the spinner, the weaver, the smith, the shoemaker, the carpenter, of employment and support." In surveying the state, he saw that "there is no diversity of occupations, no incentive to enterprise. Labor of every species is disreputable, because performed by slaves. Our towns are stationary, our villages almost everywhere declining: the general aspect of the country marks the curse of a wasteful, idle, reckless population."[31] It was an extraordinary public admission of how the master class's grip on slavery impoverished a wide swath of non-slave-owning white Virginia.

By the time Randolph took the floor to answer his critics, he was visibly weary. "I have had such a host upon me, that I must be excused if I cannot recollect whence every shot has come," he said. Realizing that his effort encompassed a broader scope than Virginia only, he said, "I cannot concur with the hopeless, ultra-absolutism of the South." He foresaw "as inevitable in the fullness of time, a dissolution of this Union."[32] He was defeated.

In the end, the General Assembly found that interference with slavery in Virginia was inexpedient but gave vague sanction to some effort at deportation, which produced scant results. What they did agree upon were new slave-suppression laws aimed at keeping Blacks illiterate and restricting their ability to congregate or to worship. Similar statutes followed from Maryland, Delaware, Georgia, North and South Carolina, and Louisiana.[33] Two years after the Virginia debate, Tennessee briefly considered emancipation during its 1834 constitutional convention. The matter was shuffled to a committee that issued a report defending slavery, while the convention adopted measures to forbid the legislature from emancipating slaves without their owner's consent and disenfranchising all free Blacks.[34] The South's brief consideration of an alternative to slavery sputtered out, never to be rekindled. No other course was open but to embrace slavery, and that embrace, the white South would discover, required expanding slavery.

—◦—

"One nation, indivisible" is a core phrase in the pledge of allegiance that schoolchildren across the United States recite daily. Its matching phrase, "with liberty and justice for all," rounds out the inclusiveness of the republic's founding principles.*

The concepts are so plain and so long and often repeated as to have become part of the nation's political genetic makeup. It was not always so. An equally well-established concept is that the Supreme Court is the final arbiter, short of amendment, of the Constitution. That was not always so. The people of this country traveled a long and arduous path in determining for themselves that the United States is, in fact, one nation and that that nation is, in fact, indivisible. The Constitution does not itself definitively establish either concept. Controversy and conflict would ultimately make them so. On a parallel path, the Supreme Court's supremacy was not fully agreed upon until after the issues of a single, indivisible nation were resolved. The pledge of liberty and justice for all is incomplete and ongoing.

---

*The words "under God" were added in 1952.

The first major clash over the meaning of nationhood occurred during the nullification crisis of 1828 to 1833. The role of the high court was folded into that controversy. South Carolina's assertion, at first, and enforcement by state law later on, of a right to nullify law passed by Congress and signed by the president provided the controversy's framework. Not all of the essential questions were settled at that time. Instead, after coming to the brink of armed conflict, divergent interpretations of the Constitution's fundamental meaning were laid out, North and South, that would become causes of, and only be settled by, civil war. The word "slavery" was rarely invoked during the six years of controversy, but slavery provided the relentless gyre that nearly hurled the union into dissolution during the crisis. Slavery was South Carolina's underlying cause to run the risk of declaring where federal authority ended and states' rights prevailed.

The doctrines that justified South Carolina's challenge to federal authority were laid out decades earlier in Thomas Jefferson's and James Madison's Kentucky and Virginia Resolutions of 1798 and Madison's Report of 1800. Those documents posited the Constitution as a compact among the states, limiting the federal government's authority to enumerated powers, and explicitly giving states authority to interpose against Congress if it exceeded its delegated powers. From Jefferson's first administration forward, what was widely called the "Spirit of '98" contained in those documents served as the guidebook to constitutional interpretation for much of the nation. Written in defiance of an attempt to suppress a free press and grant the president unilateral authority to arrest and deport aliens, the "Spirit of '98" became the bulwark of states' rights, local control against federal intrusion, and limited government as the surest shields for freedom and liberty—and for slavery. The "Spirit of '98" was not an inflexible catechism, even for its authors. Jefferson had purchased the Louisiana Territory despite there being no enumerated power to do so. During their presidencies, both he and Madison accepted the Bank of the United States that lacked direct constitutional sanction. But the "Spirit of '98" defined the bedrock principles first of Jefferson's Republican Party, then of its Democratic Party successor that came to power with the rise of Andrew Jackson.

At the conclusion of the War of 1812, the nation finally transferred its gaze from across the Atlantic back onto the continent, where four issues dominated the political agenda for decades. The first was removal of Native Americans west of the Mississippi River that had nearly universal approval among white Americans for its ends, even as the means of war, forcible removal and strong-arm peace treaties, drew criticism. The remaining three issues of tariffs, internal improvements, and sales of the nation's vast domain of public lands were intertwined.

The "Spirit of '98" would be tested, stretched, and invoked in the struggle over those issues as advocates of states' rights and adherents of a more aggressive national agenda to direct and propel the nation's growth vied for the upper hand. Tariffs protecting local manufactures were of prime concern in New England and Pennsylvania. More ardent states' righters in the South resented tariffs that entailed higher costs for imported goods with no recompense to their region that was largely bereft of any manufacturing base. Internal improvements encompassed a host of subsidiary questions involving military preparedness in terms of coastal security and transportation, and whether a coherent system of roads and canals should be directed and paid for by the national government, or left to local control. The disposal of public lands, vital to the West, brought with it a similarly complex set of issues. Should the land be given to the states, or sold high or low, and if sold, should the income flow directly to the states, or be allocated to federally directed projects, or projects designed by the states? Both improvements and public land disposal were further enmeshed in bifurcated constitutional mandates in which the national government had enumerated authority to make all necessary regulations for the territories but arguably was limited to militarily justified security measures in the states.

In all of these issues, states' rights and limited versus expansive government were in play. In addition, they provided the frame within which the North and South competed for allegiance of the West and, with it, dominant influence on the national stage. The era in which these issues played out is the most prominent in which the nearly unseen influence of slavery exerted its gravitational pull on public debate and decision. Ultimately the struggle produced something approaching—but never quite achieving—a solid South and a generally ruling Democratic Party that favored suppression of the slavery issue via the states' rights doctrine. That dynamic led to the emergence of opposition in the form of the Whig Party, which was later subsumed by the Republican Party that united the North and West to win the presidential election of 1860. In the opening decades of the 1800s, as Congress and the nation sorted through the choices, tensions over tariff policy funneled directly onto South Carolina, tipping off the nullification crisis. By the end of that crisis, not only tariff policy, but its sister issues of internal improvements and public land disposal, would be set on a path that endured up to the Civil War.

Thomas Jefferson signed the nation's first major federally directed internal improvement project into law. Jefferson approved the Cumberland Road in 1806, and the project was built between 1811 and 1832. Also known as the National Road, it was a 620-mile link from Cumberland, Maryland, on the Potomac River, through Pennsylvania, western Virginia, across Ohio and Indiana, and westward into Illinois.

In his 1816 annual message, Jefferson's successor, James Madison, spoke favorably of a national internal improvements program. This led John C. Calhoun, a young congressman from South Carolina, to draft the Bonus Bill, a measure to fund improvements with income from a bonus to be paid by the Bank of the United States for subscription purchases. "We are under the most imperious obligation to counteract every tendency to disunion," the nationalist Calhoun told Congress. "The more strongly are we bound together; the more inseparable are our destinies," he said. "Let us then, bind the Republic together with a perfect system of roads and canals."[35] In this stage of his career, Calhoun was a nationalist largely on military security grounds. He saw the Bank of the United States as central to a secure currency, roads and canals as essential to military transport in time of war, and protective tariffs as needed to avoid reliance on foreign imports that could be cut if conflict arose.

Stunningly, Madison vetoed the bill, citing the "Spirit of '98's" tenet against going beyond enumerated powers. A year later Senator Nathaniel Macon wrote confidentially to a close friend "I must ask you to examine the constitution of the U.S. . . . and then tell me if Congress can establish banks, make roads, and canals, whether they cannot free all the Slaves in the U.S."[36] Resistance to the use of unenumerated powers was the surface contention; slavery was the undertow, the deep current.

By 1820 a bill was introduced to build federal toll gates to fund needed repairs along the Cumberland Road. President Monroe vetoed the measure, writing that such unenumerated authority could only be authorized by a constitutional amendment. He did support, however, a general survey bill to allow the national government to draw up plans for a system of roads and canals. During debate on that measure, Virginia Senator John Randolph warned "If Congress possesses the power to do what is proposed by this bill, they may . . . emancipate every slave in the United States." He speculated that to do so, Congress might "hook the power upon the first loop they find," such as the preamble's "to promote the general welfare" clause, or the war-making power.[37] He was prescient. Nearly four decades later, Lincoln justified the Emancipation Proclamation as a necessary war measure.

The passing of the Revolutionary War generation with John Quincy Adams's 1824 election ushered in a new, and brief, era in which the fear of consolidated government did not preoccupy the president. Adams wanted a vigorous national government. He favored ambitious advances for internal improvements, education, and scientific research, among other measures. The term "American System", which Kentuckian Henry Clay coined, was deployed as the slogan for a coordinated agenda favoring the Bank of the United States, protective tariffs, internal improvements, and public land sales to pay for them. No national system of internal improvements ever emerged, however, either during Adams's presidency, or in the nineteenth century. Andrew Jackson destroyed the Bank of the United States, protective tariffs were slashed after the nullification crisis, and although a host of improvements were funded by land sales and grants, they were essentially a hodgepodge of locally designed and built projects devoid of coherence.[38]

In the years immediately preceding the nullification crisis, two lengthy and widely distributed pamphlets appeared that both captured and propelled public sentiment in much of the white South, particularly in South Carolina. Whitemarsh Seabrook's 1825 *The Critical Situation of the Slave-Holding States*, printed in Charleston, was a jeremiad against northern plots to interfere with southern slavery. His underlying warning was that "the tenure by which we hold our slaves, is daily becoming less secure." He inveighed against a plan that Ohio's legislature put forward for gradual emancipation and deportation using treasury funds, and another that Senator Rufus King offered in Congress to devote all revenue from public land sales to slave emancipation, possibly to be linked to setting aside territorial lands far to the west to relocate them.

Seabrook viewed with the deepest suspicion plans that he believed northern meddlers hatched for congressional support of Colonization Society efforts to relocate free Blacks in Africa. His pamphlet evoked words that Patrick Henry spoke in Virginia's convention to ratify the Constitution. The great patriot had warned that proposed powers of defense and general welfare will operate on the minds of legislators "to see if they have power of manumission. . . . May they not pronounce all slaves free, and will they not be warranted by that power? . . . The paper speaks to the point. *They have the power in clear unequivocal terms; and they will clearly and certainly exercise it.*"[39]

Even more influential were a series of essays titled *The Crisis: or, Essays on the Usurpations of the Federal Government*, printed anonymously in 1827 in the *Charleston Mercury* and later published as a pamphlet. South Carolina sea-island planter and lawyer Robert Turnbull wrote *The Crisis* as a definitive attack against protective tariffs and internal improvements. He warned that in all the states, except those in the South, "the people have no fears whatever from the exercise of implied powers of Congress on any subject." If the South continued to acquiesce in allowing Congress to exercise "powers which belong not to it," he wrote, on tariffs, internal improvements, "and other schemes of the Northern People . . . we shall soon find that we shall be for them 'hewers of wood and drawers of water.'" We may discover, he continued, "that under phraseology of the term 'general welfare' in the Constitution, Congress may be propelled by public opinion of the North, to regulate our domestic policy." The North, he wrote, was determined "to extirpate from the body politic, what is regarded by them as a crying evil and as a canker." Constitutional construction that allowed for "the encouragement of domestic manufacture, and the construction of national roads and canals . . . is *Usurpation.*" Citing Madison's Report of 1800 on the requirement that powers be enumerated, *The Crisis* declared, "The words 'Canals' or 'National Roads,' or 'Internal Improvements,' are not to be found in the Constitution." Congressional or court sanction of them had rendered the Constitution "A DEAD LETTER—It may mean ANY THING, or it may mean NOTHING."[40]

A year later Congress passed what became universally known in the South as the Tariff of Abominations, including hikes on import duties of up to 50 percent. The stage was set for the nullification crisis.

Andrew Jackson and John C. Calhoun were the principal antagonists. They had much in common. Both were southerners of Scots-Irish parentage born within a few hundred miles of one another. Jackson came from poverty. Calhoun was from a more established family. Both became planters and slave owners, Jackson master to upwards of 150 slaves on his Tennessee plantation named the Hermitage, Calhoun owning dozens of Blacks at his Fort Hill, South Carolina, estate. The two men resembled each other, with hawk-like faces topped by a shock

Andrew Jackson. COURTESY OF THE NATIONAL ARCHIVES.

John C. Calhoun. COURTESY OF THE LIBRARY OF CONGRESS.

of swept-back hair that as they grew older imparted visages of biblical prophets. When the controversy began in 1828, Jackson had just been elected president with Calhoun his vice president. Both claimed allegiance to the Jeffersonian tradition of limited government enshrined in the "Spirit of '98." Throughout the controversy, both were driven by sharply divergent visions of how best to preserve the Union, Jackson upholding the binding power of majority rule, Calhoun contending for broader protection of minority rights.

When Jackson was a boy during the Revolutionary War, one of his brothers died from exhaustion after fighting in a battle with the British. Jackson and his older brother John joined the American forces and were captured. When they refused to blacken an officer's boots, they were each struck severely with a sword. Released to their mother in an exchange, Andrew walked barefoot and feverish for forty-five miles with her back to their home, escorting the badly injured John on horseback. John died soon thereafter, as did his mother, who had been tending American prisoners of war in Charleston, South Carolina. Andrew was fifteen years old, his experience with war, death, illness, and suffering just beginning.[41]

Jackson earned a reputation as a quick-tempered man of rash habits and a love of fast horses while establishing himself as a planter and political figure at his adopted home at the Hermitage near Nashville, Tennessee. In 1806 he challenged Charles Dickinson to a duel over what began as a horse-racing debt but sank to aspersions on Jackson's wife, Rachel, a transgression that was then and forever utterly unforgivable for him. They had been married when Rachel mistakenly believed that a divorce from her first husband had been finalized. Dickinson was a crack shot. Jackson let him fire first, counting on a miss by too quick a shot under pressure. The ball struck home, in Jackson's chest, breaking two ribs and lodging near his heart, where it remained throughout his life.

But he stood his ground, aimed, and pulled the trigger. The hammer misfired. The duel might have ended at that point, but Jackson and his seconds insisted on the unwritten rule that a mechanical failure of the hammer could not be counted as a shot. Dickinson, called back to his mark, stood defenseless. Coolly, Jackson aimed and fired, striking his opponent in the stomach with a shot that blew a large hole in his back. He died a short time later. Afterward, Jackson's visceral hatred for his opponent was revealed in his remark: "I should have hit him if he had shot me through the brain."[42] One crossed Andrew Jackson at one's own peril.

More bloodshed followed with Indian wars and the climactic battle of the War of 1812 that propelled the military leader known as Old Hickory onto the national stage as the Hero of New Orleans. Andrew Jackson was legend in life.

John C. Calhoun earned his status as legend more slowly. He shared Jackson's unflinching determination in adversity, but his weapon was his mind. His driving ambition was tied to his acute intelligence and, beyond that, to a righteous conviction in the infallible truth of his own conclusions. His fierce contempt for lesser mortals made some men fear and others idolize him as he rose from congressman to secretary of war, vice president under John Quincy Adams, and vice president-elect under Jackson. As it developed over time, his driving insight was that the political bargain fashioning the Democratic Party on the basis of suppressing the slavery issue to join the North and South in gaining national dominance was flawed. The bargain was too flimsy. Ultimately, he was convinced, northern abolitionists would prod the North to interfere with slavery, and ultimately the North was sure to have majority power in Congress over the South to get its way. Instead of a pact of silence over slavery, Calhoun believed that the South must confront the North with enforceable demands to secure to the minority what he called its "peculiar institution"—meaning slavery—and with it its entire way of life.

Jackson's 1828 victory over John Quincy Adams was decisive nationally and crushing in the South. He took all eleven slave states, except Maryland, where the Electoral College delegates were split. In addition, he won four of the thirteen northern states, took a majority of New York's delegates and one in Maine. Yet even before he took office, his vice president-elect Calhoun had anonymously authored the first chapter in the nullification crisis.

By the mid-1820s, South Carolina began a plunge into political paroxysm driven by fear of being isolated, outnumbered, and surrounded by forces determined to degrade and destroy it. An avalanche of incendiary rhetoric intended to create frenzy fed the fear. Denmark Vesey's failed rebellion had implanted the most primal of fears in a state where nearly 56 percent of the population was Black and that had the highest proportion of slave-to-free population in all the southern states.[43]

Rufus King's Senate proposal to devote funds for emancipation and resettlement, which disappeared almost as soon as it was introduced, fed the flames. The Colonization Society's plea for national funding to deport free Blacks provided more kindling. In the Senate, that plan led South Carolina's Robert Hayne to forecast "If this policy should ever be adopted by this Government, they will go directly into the market, as the purchasers of our slaves, for the purpose of emancipation and transportation."[44] James Henry Hammond's *Southern Times* exploded: "It ruins our property; it breaks down our individual rights; it destroys our political security; it sweeps away our Constitution; it dissolves our Union; it annihilates the last hope of self-government on earth."[45]

The proposal went nowhere in Congress. In practical political terms, fears over King's proposal and funding deportations were phantoms, but they provided grist to incitement. "We shall ere long be compelled to calculate the value of our Union," South Carolina College president Dr. Thomas Cooper shouted out to a large 1827 gathering in Columbia. His words stoked a militancy that first divided, then consumed, his state. His cold prescription "to calculate the value" of union was heard and remembered to the north. "The question . . . is fast approaching," Cooper said, "to the alternative of submission or separation."[46] A year later, in a state legislative debate, Thomas T. Player intoned that the Tariff of Abominations "is only preparatory to ulterior movements, destined by fanatics and abolitionists to subvert the institutions and established policy of the Southern country."[47]

In mid-1828 Calhoun stepped in, as much to quell fanaticism in his state as to lay down a marker to confront the North. Without disclosing his authorship, he wrote the *South Carolina Exposition*, a lengthy and densely reasoned argument that the entire tariff system was unconstitutional, basing his conclusion on those first put forth in Jefferson's and Madison's 1798 Kentucky and Virginia Resolutions.[48] Although the Constitution granted power to impose tariffs, he argued, that power did not extend to doing so by an enumerated authority to protect or benefit any section of society. The right to judge such infractions belonged to the states. Their power extended to nullifying congressional overreach. Crucially, the *Exposition* was accompanied only by a protest that South Carolina lodged in Congress against such usurpation, not by state action to actually declare any law "null, void, and of no force or effect," in Jefferson's "Spirit of '98" terms. An alerted Congress and an about-to-be inaugurated states' rights president could remedy the error and avert the danger.

That did not happen. Jackson proceeded with a states' rights attack on vestiges of the American system and signaled his disdain for the Bank of the United States, but tariff reform was left in abeyance. His relationship with his vice president disintegrated over perceived slights to his and his late wife's honor and issues relating to his conduct as a military commander in Florida in 1818 while Calhoun was secretary of war. In South Carolina, the state's leading nullifier, George McDuffie, harangued an audience that the tariff was a "system of stupendous oppression" and that "the Union, such as the majority have made it, is a foul monster."[49] The schism between Jackson and Calhoun was exemplified in brief toasts they offered during an 1830 Jefferson birthday celebration. "The Federal Union—it must be preserved," the president said. "The Union—next to our liberties the most dear," Calhoun replied.

A few months later Calhoun revealed the source of his concern over the unresolved tariff issue. "I consider the Tariff, but the occasion, rather than the real cause of the present unhappy state of things," he wrote to a friend. "The truth can no longer be disguised, that the peculiar domestick institutions of the Southern States" placed them in a position in which "if there be no protective power in the reserved rights of the states, they must in the end be forced to rebel or submit."[50] At nearly the same time, James Hamilton Jr., South Carolina's governor, wrote a public letter declaring "I have always looked to the present contest with the government, on the part of the Southern States, as a battle at the out-posts, by which, if we succeeded in repulsing the enemy, *the citadel would be safe.*" Putting the contest on the grounds of slavery, he wrote, would be the last option "on which the South ought to desire to do battle; that however we might be united at home, we should have few confederates abroad—whereas on the subject of free trade and constitutional rights, we should have allies throughout the civilized world."[51] States' rights was the preferred defensive cloak to disguise the citadel of slavery.

Keeping his battle to protect slavery and the white South at the outpost of the tariff issue, Calhoun openly declared his support for nullification in a July 1831 Fort Hill address. He based his stance on Madison's Virginia Resolution declaration of a state's right to interpose against congressional usurpation. For his part, the aging Madison spent much of the remainder of his life protesting that the Virginia Resolution and his Report of 1800 did not mean what the words in them said they meant. His writing had been "misconceived," the constitutional architect protested; the Virginia Resolution was no more than a remonstrance directed at Congress.[52]

His pleading could not wipe away the Report of 1800's declaration that the Constitution was a compact among states, and in the case of Congress overreaching its enumerated powers "it follows of necessity that there can be no tribunal, above their authority, to decide, in the last resort, whether the compact made by them be violated," and for them to decide "in the last resort, such questions as may be of sufficient magnitude to require their interposition."[53] The leading nationalist during the Constitutional Convention, who then became one of the principal expounders of the states' rights doctrine that defined Jeffersonian democracy, reverted to his origins. In his *Advice to My Country*, written in 1836 as he was dying, Madison pleaded that "the Union of the States be cherished and perpetuated."[54]

In late June 1832, Congress acted. The Tariff Act of that year reduced overall revenues, lowered many rates to 25 percent, but largely retained 50 percent tariffs on imported cottons, woolens, and iron.[55] Events unfolded quickly thereafter. In November, a convention elected on the call of the South Carolina legislature passed a nullification ordinance declaring the Tariff Acts of 1828 and 1832 unconstitutional, "null, void, and no law, not binding upon this State."[56] The legislature was instructed to enact statutes to enforce the ordinance. Should the federal government attempt coercion to collect the tariffs, South Carolina would secede from the union and stand ready to fight for its independence. To leave room for compromise, the ordinance was not to go into effect until February 1. Calhoun joined ranks with his state, writing a friend "The question is no longer one of free trade, but liberty and despotism. The hope of the country now rests on our gallant little state. Let every Carolinian do his duty."[57] Later in December, Calhoun resigned his office, returned to South Carolina, and was elected to the Senate.

In a nation of more than 13 million people, the pro-nullification members of the state convention that thrust the country toward dissolution and war were elected by approximately 25,000 South Carolina white male voters.[58]

Jackson's initial public response was decidedly low key. In his December 4 annual message, he urged that tariffs be "gradually diminished," in part to alleviate "a spirit of discontent and jealousy dangerous to the stability of the Union." Manufacturers protected by high tariffs, he said, "cannot expect that the people will continue persistently to pay high taxes for their benefit." Midway through the message he expressed his "painful duty to state" that opposition to the tariff system that could "endanger the integrity of the Union" had arisen in one section of the country. He hoped for a peaceful resolution and was confident that existing laws were adequate to deal with the immediate situation. Should additional measures be needed, he would advise Congress. The message was a states' rights platform. He disparaged the Bank of the United States, offered assurance that the national debt, still lingering from the War of 1812, would soon be paid off, and said that national improvement projects required an authorizing constitutional amendment. Because the "speedy settlement" of public lands was in the national interest, they should be sold at a price to cover expenses only and not viewed as a source of future revenue. After all, he noted, the nation's population was its true wealth and strength, "and the best part of that population are the cultivators of the soil." John Quincy Adams, then a member of the House from Massachusetts, later examined those words carefully. In conclusion, the president urged adoption of policies to make the national government "so simple and economical as scarcely to be felt."[59] Limited government would prevail.

The hammer fell a week later. Jackson presented a sweeping denunciation of nullification and secession in a December 10 proclamation. He declared "the power to annul a law of the United States, assumed by one state, *incompatible with the existence of the Union, contradicted expressly by the letter of the Constitution, unauthorized by its spirit, inconsistent with every principle on which it was founded, and destructive of the great object for which it was formed. . . .* Disunion by armed force is *treason.*"[60]

He was even more combative in private. In a letter to Martin Van Buren, by 1832 his vice president-elect, shortly after the proclamation was issued, Jackson wrote that if South Carolina "authorizes twelve thousand men to resist the law, I will order thirty thousand to execute the law." In a second letter, he informed Van Buren "I expect soon to hear that a civil war of extermination has commenced. I will meet all things with deliberate firmness and forbearance, but woe, to those nullifiers who shed the first blood."[61]

A month after the proclamation, Jackson sought congressional approval for a Force Bill giving him authority to use land and naval forces to enforce the law. General Winfield Scott had already been placed in command of several military companies reinforcing the garrisons at Fort Moultrie and Castle Pickney in Charleston harbor. Robert Hayne was among the officers drilling South Carolina militia in anticipation of invasion. The nation seemed within days of conflict. Both sides drew a breath of caution. Jackson instructed Scott not to initiate a fight. South Carolina pushed back the nullification deadline until after Congress' March adjournment.

As he had during the Missouri crisis, Henry Clay next stepped in to fashion a compromise diffusing the situation. A bill lowering tariffs to 20 percent by 1842 and expanding the list of items to be free of tariffs was cobbled together and received final congressional approval on March 1, immediately before the Force Bill was passed. South Carolina rescinded its nullification ordinance. The crisis passed. As a final gesture of defiance, South Carolina nullified the Force Bill, which had already been rendered moot.

The nullification crisis was a political drama in which the nation's fate was at stake. The constitutional debate during the crisis helped define the Civil War's causes. As arguably the single most important debate about constitutional meaning ever held in Congress and the nation, it also left imprints that endure to this day.

Among all the participants, John C. Calhoun left the most extensive record of his quest to redefine the Constitution in his *South Carolina Exposition*, the Fort Hill address, two speeches in the Senate, and two volumes of constitutional exegesis published after his death. He proceeded from the self-perceived vantage point of his own superior intellect. On completing one of his nullification essays, Calhoun wrote that it "will forever settle the question, at least, as far as reason has anything to do with settling political questions."[62] Just as Newton and Galileo had used the power of analysis to reduce "the most complex idea into its elements," political science, too, he informed the Senate, was "subject to laws as fixed as matter itself, and . . . as fit a subject for the application of the highest intellectual power."[63] From this lofty eminence, Calhoun applied his conclusions to the Constitution rather than drawing them from it, thus denying himself that document's authority. The flaw of this method quickly showed itself, leading Calhoun in mid-debate to redefine the remedies drawn from his conclusions.

His premise was that the nation was on "the verge of civil war," and he spoke to offer a remedy to preserve the union.[64] That some of his most radical adherents then and later wanted dissolution is true, yet it is equally true that Calhoun desperately desired to hold the union together but to do so on terms acceptable to the white southern minority.

Calhoun opened his argument on the Senate floor before a packed gallery by positing "The great question at issue is, where is the paramount power?" Power, he continued, resides in the people, and crucially under the American Constitution with "the people of the States, as constituting separate communities." The people acting in their state capacities, he said, had not only formed "the Union, of which the constitutional compact is the bond," but their sovereignty under it was unimpaired: "Not a particle resides in the Government; not one particle in the American people collectively." Although the people of the states had delegated part of their sovereign power in forming the Constitution, he said "to delegate is not to part with or to impair power."[65] Sovereignty "is in its nature indivisible," Calhoun maintained.[66] Under this doctrine, the people in each state, acting in convention, retained sovereign authority to "be controlled or resumed at pleasure."[67] Calhoun's inescapable conclusion was that "our system is a union of twenty-four sovereign powers."[68]

Earlier, in his Fort Hill address, Calhoun had invoked the 1798 Virginia Resolutions' doctrine that states had the right of interposition against overreaching acts of the national government. "This right of interposition," he had written, "thus solemnly asserted by the State of Virginia, be it called what it may—State-right, veto, nullification, or by any other name—I conceive to be the fundamental principle of our system."[69] To draw fundamental principles not from the organic law of the Constitution, but from a document originating in a single state more than a decade later, proved to be the weak link in Calhoun's chain of reasoning.

Back on the Senate floor, having defined sovereign power in terms nowhere acknowledged in the Constitution, Calhoun turned to deciding who could rightfully judge abuse of it. He drew directly from Madison's Report of 1800, which found that "the states, then, being the parties to the constitutional compact, and in their sovereign capacity, it follows of necessity that there can be no tribunal, above their authority, to decide, in the last resort, whether the compact made by them be violated."[70] As Calhoun had noted in the *South Carolina Exposition*, Madison's report held that the state's right to be final arbiter "must extend to . . . the judiciary as well as . . . the executive, or the legislature."[71] The Supreme Court "is destitute of the least particle of sovereign power," Calhoun told the Senate, because its authority was delegated by the states that retained their full sovereignty unimpaired and indivisible.[72] Each state, not the Supreme Court, was the Constitution's final arbiter. That this assuredly would produce a crazy quilt of conflicting state interpretations of national law was not included in Calhoun's remarks.

Calhoun's formulation of undiminished state sovereignty had implications for the concepts of both nationhood and citizenship. It followed, he said, that "no such community ever existed as the people of the United States, forming a collective body of individuals in one nation, and the idea they so united by the present constitution . . . is utterly false and absurd."[73] As to being a citizen of the United States, Calhoun said that although he did not "object to the expression" if that "meant a citizen at large, one whose citizenship extended to the entire geographical limits of the country, without having a local citizenship in some State or Territory . . . not a single individual of this description could be found in the entire mass of our population."[74] Citizenship was a state, not a national attribute.

Having defined the Constitution as a compact among twenty-four sovereign states, Calhoun began propounding remedies to the current crisis. In his January 1833 Senate address, he first outlined what sounded like a rolling series of state conventions to decide disputed issues. Comparing the states to stockholders, he proposed that they meet under constitutional sanction, presumably the clause requiring assent by three-quarters of the states to ratify an amendment, to give direction to the corporate directors, the national government.[75] He did not dwell long on this concept, perhaps because there was no assurance three-fourths of the stockholders would converge on the same remedy, or that if they did each sovereign state would retain the right to reject it, or because if a multitude of disputes arose, a multitude of ongoing state conventions would be required to consider them.

Instead, Calhoun quickly turned to offering three resolutions to quell the controversy. Congress should first declare that the United States "are united as parties to a constitutional compact" in which the union "is a union between the States ratifying them." Next, Congress should consent that the states delegated certain powers to the national government and in cases where it attempted to exercise undelegated powers, its acts "are unauthorized, and are of no effect." Finally, Congress must resolve that any assertion that the people of the United States are or ever were "formed into one nation or people," or that the states had not retained their full sovereignty including their right of final determination, are "without foundation in truth," and that any "erroneous" contrary claim was "unconstitutional."[76] Calhoun knew that the votes to pass these resolutions did not exist. They were not pursued. But he had laid down his marker.

In the days immediately following his January address, it is reasonable to speculate that even Calhoun realized his grand intellectual construct was flawed. The constitutional mandate that all laws be uniformly applied to all states was impossible to reconcile with the power of each state to decide which laws or Supreme Court decisions were valid. Laws and treaties passed under the Constitution were the supreme law of the land, and oaths required of state officials to uphold the Constitution were binding—only until they were not under Calhoun's addendum to the Constitution. Two ironies are apparent in Calhoun's exertions over political theory. First, instead of an iron chain of logic often attributed to him, Calhoun's conclusions came in sometimes contradictory fits and starts. His *South Carolina Exposition* specifically refers to "the division of the sovereign power between the state and general government," a position he wholly abandoned by 1833 with his assertion that "not a particle" of sovereignty resided in the national government.[77] The second great irony of Calhoun's thinking is that for one whose primary objection was to the exercise of undelegated powers, he derived both his conclusions and remedies from supposed rights of the states that are nowhere enumerated in the Constitution. As historian William W. Freehling has noted, Calhoun "defended the consent of the governed at the expense of destroying the power to govern; he proposed conserving the Union with principles which would have destroyed it."[78]

In February 1833 Calhoun returned to the Senate to state his case anew. His target was majority rule. This was his third attempt at remedy following his vague formulation of continuous state conventions and three resolutions that had no hope of passage. He began by asserting that it was "the opinion of a large majority of our country . . . that the very *beau ideal* of a perfect Government was the Government of a majority, acting through a representative body, without check or limitation of its power."[79] Such a government, he maintained, would inevitably fracture into a majority interest of takers and a minority interest of payers, leading in train to corruption, anarchy, and despotism. He ignored the layers of the Constitution's checks and balances designed to protect minorities. Instead, he argued, even in a system granting limited powers, a majority ignoring those limits would trample a minority that had no right "to enforce the restrictions imposed by the constitution on the will of the majority."[80]

As proof of his case, Calhoun pointed to experience. "That our Government," he said, "has been gradually verging to consolidation, that the constitution has gradually become a dead letter . . . so as practically to convert the General Government into a Government of an absolute majority, without check or limitation, cannot be denied by anyone."[81] He was specific about the divide between the majority thirteen free and minority eleven slave states. The tendency of the conflict, he said, "is between southern and other sections. The latter, having a decided majority, must habitually be possessed of the powers of the Government."[82] This conflict, he continued, created the necessity of "giving to each part the right of self-protection."[83]

He then posited a remedy totally novel to the Constitution. Instead of having the twenty-four states governed by the will of the majority, in cases "tending to bring the parts into conflict" he proposed a new scheme. In such instances, Calhoun said, "take the will, not of the twenty-four as a unit, but that of the thirteen and that of the eleven separately, the majority of each governing the parts; and, where they concur, governing the whole; and where they disagree, arresting the action of the Government." The concept of the concurrent majority was born. The minority would have the self-protection of veto power over the majority. Years later, in refining his plan, Calhoun wrote that gridlock resulting from such a system need not be feared, because the threat of it and subsequent anarchy would compel the two sides to compromise.[84]

A final tenet of Calhoun's thinking, one that survived him, was the right of each sovereign state to secede from the constitutional compact if it so chose. A natural corollary to this portion of the compact theory was that the government had no countervailing right to resist secession by force.[85] Ironically, the right of peaceful secession, to which Calhoun devoted little attention, survived the nullification debates as one of the major lessons that the white South drew from them.

＊

Andrew Jackson's contribution to the constitutional debate centered on his December 1832 proclamation, weeks before Calhoun's concurrent majority proposal. The president had one distinct advantage over his adversary. Jackson grounded his argument in the Constitution itself. The document offered to the country by the Founding Fathers had assumed reverential status almost as soon as it was ratified. Speaking of the "sacred awe" in which the Constitution was held, Jackson made full use of it against Calhoun's intellectual inventions. "We have hitherto relied on it as the perpetual bond of our union," he said. "We have received it as the work of the assembled wisdom of the nation. We have trusted to it as to the sheet anchor of our safety in stormy times."[86]

Jackson also employed a second advantage. Calhoun's argument was a dry, legalistic pronouncement that read like the political equivalent of a mathematical formula. Jackson spoke directly to the people. Old Hickory, whose patriotism and readiness to die if need be for his country were unquestioned, assembled the people around him by his language as if counseling with them in their own homes. The proclamation is studded with reference to his "fellow citizens," and phrases like "the momentous case is before you," "whether your sacred Union will be preserved," "are you ready to risk all," and "examine them carefully—judge for yourself."

The contrast with Calhoun could not have been clearer. The South Carolinian did not ask people to judge for themselves, but to recognize they were being instructed by a personage of superior intellect. Finally, Jackson draped himself in the Jeffersonian tradition but did so as a steward rather than critic of the Constitution. "No one, fellow citizens," he wrote, "has a higher reverence for the reserved rights of the states than the magistrate who now addresses you. No one would make greater personal sacrifice, or official exertions, to defend them from violation; but equal care must be taken to prevent, on their part, an improper interference with, or resumption of, the rights they have vested in the nation."[87]

The proclamation, first drafted by Jackson's secretary of state, Edward Livingston, went straight to the core issues of nullification, secession, and union. Nullification was founded on the proposition, Jackson declared, "that any one state may not only declare an act of Congress void, but prohibit its execution," a claim that amounted to permitting "a state to retain its place in the Union, and yet be bound by no other of its laws than those it may choose to consider as constitutional."[88]

But the Constitution itself, he continued, "does not contain the absurdity of giving power to make laws, and another power to resist them." During the ratification process, no state was "under the impression that a veto on the laws of the United States was reserved to them." Nothing in the Constitution and "not a syllable uttered" in the state ratifying conventions questioned the validity of "the explicit supremacy given to the laws of the Union over those of the states."[89] Not only does the document declare in express terms that "the laws of the United States, its Constitution, and treaties made under it, are the supreme law of the land," but it requires state officials to take an oath to uphold the Constitution.[90] Because discretion to pass laws on such things as revenue and tariffs must exist somewhere, he wrote, the Constitution "has given it to the representatives of all the people" in the House of Representatives where revenue measures must originate, "checked by the representatives of the states" in the Senate, "and by the executive power," holding a veto.[91]

The proclamation essentially read back to the people what they could readily read for themselves in the Constitution. His case was not one of interpretation or invention, but of the document's commonsense meaning. In cases of disputed constitutionality, Jackson explained, the Constitution offers two avenues of appeal, "one to the judiciary, the other to the people and the states," referring to the right to vote officials into or out of office, or to amend the fundamental law.[92] Turning yet again to the document itself, Jackson reminded his fellow citizens "The Constitution declares that the judicial powers of the United States extend to cases arising under the laws of the United States."[93]

In turning to secession, Jackson had to deal with the twin issues of who formed the Constitution and the nature of sovereignty. The Constitution "forms a government, not a league," he wrote, "in which the people of all the states collectively are represented" and acts directly on the people as individuals, not upon the states.[94] A right to secede rests, he wrote, "on alleged undivided sovereignty of the states, and on their having formed, in this sovereign capacity, a compact which is called a Constitution, from which, because they made it, they have a right to secede."

This was Calhoun's doctrine, drawn from Jefferson's and Madison's writings. The states formed the union by creating the Constitution. A self-evident iron law of nature decreed that sovereignty is indivisible: not a particle can be surrendered or alienated. Jackson posed the rather obvious alternative that sovereignty need not be indivisible, that sovereignty over one sphere of activity could be vested in one place and sovereignty over a different sphere of activity vested in another. Calhoun's iron law was a phantom. "The states severally have not retained their entire sovereignty," he wrote; "in becoming part of a nation, not members of a league, they surrendered many of their essential parts of sovereignty" including the rights to make war, conclude peace, write treaties, and levy taxes. In thus doing so "they became American citizens."[95]

The states retained all the powers they did not grant, he wrote, "but each state, having expressly parted with so many powers as to constitute, jointly with the other states, a single nation, cannot from that period, possess any right to secede, because such secession does not break a league, but destroys the unity of a nation." A state might break from the union as a revolutionary act, just as the colonies broke from Great Britain by revolution, he wrote, but "to say that any state may at pleasure secede from the Union, is to say that the United States are not a nation."[96]

Jackson granted that a party to a compact containing no sanction may leave it without consequences. "A government, on the contrary," he stated, "always has a sanction, express or implied . . . by the law of self-defense, to pass acts for punishing the offender." The Constitution, he maintained, granted express power to do so under the authority "to pass all laws necessary to carry its powers into effect."[97] These were conclusions of interpretation, and as self-evident as they may seem to some, the Constitution itself contains no express language regarding secession or authority to suppress it.

Jackson's definition of the union was also an exercise in interpretation, as the Constitution contains no definitive language resolving the issue. Jackson maintained that the union existed prior to the Constitution. Ultimately, whether or not the union predated the Constitution is a matter of interpretation, and either position can be argued with reason.[98]

By taking the position that the union came first, however, Jackson undercut Calhoun's essential postulate that the states created the union by ratifying a constitutional compact. "We declared ourselves a nation," Jackson wrote, in the 1777 Articles of Confederation. "In the instrument forming that Union," he continued, no state could legally annul an act of the Continental Congress. The document was titled Articles of

Confederation and Perpetual Union, its preamble expressly noted that the delegates agreed "to certain articles of Confederation and perpetual Union," and Article XIII of it states that their provisions "shall be inviolably observed by every state, and the Union shall be perpetual."[99]

The Constitution, he continued, was written to correct the Confederation's defects and, as its preamble states, "to form a more perfect union." How could it then be conceived, Jackson asked, that an instrument intended "to form a more perfect union" was intended to be construed as "a form of government dependent for its existence on . . . the prevailing faction of a state? Every man of plain, unsophisticated understanding . . . will give such an answer as will preserve the Union."[100] Jackson concluded "We were the United States under the Confederation; and the name was perpetuated, and the nation rendered more perfect, by the Federal Constitution. In none of these stages did we consider ourselves in any other light than as forming one nation."[101] The only means to dissolve that union were by an act of the whole people, revolution, or rebellion. Jackson had laid down his marker.

In the event, neither documents nor interpretation decided the issues. The right to secede and the meaning of union were decided by the people, or more precisely by that part of the nation that prevailed in the Civil War.

John Quincy Adams's role in the nullification crisis is often overlooked or underplayed. His presidency had largely been a brief transition from the revolutionary generation to the Jacksonian era that followed him. At the age of sixty-four in 1831, he began the most productive part of his political career representing his Massachusetts district in the House for the following seventeen years. His contribution during the nullification debate is notable for two reasons. The interpretation he gave to the Constitution forecast the present after generations of laissez-faire government were cast aside in the wake of the Great Depression. In pushing back hard on Calhoun's narrative of a beleaguered white Southern minority, Adams also forecast the Slave Power doctrine that helped reshape antebellum politics in the 1840s and give rise to the Republican Party in the 1850s. Diminutive, bookish, and with a canny sense of how to use his lone spot in the House to rivet national attention, the aging Adams displayed a backbone of iron and a depth of rhetorical passion that distinguish him to this day.

Adams thought Jeffersonian democracy was too timid a use of constitutional power and too much local control of democracy a dangerous thing. He favored vigorous government that gave direction to the temporary clamoring of a boisterous people. "The constitution itself is but one great organized engine of improvement—physical, moral, political," he wrote during the crisis. He held that the exercise of power is "essential to the welfare and prosperity of the whole people . . . and that to refrain from the exercise of power would be a dereliction of duty in Congress itself, and treachery to the trust committed to them by the people." He derided the government's "chaining its own hands" in deference to the "doctrine of abdicating powers arbitrarily designated as doubtful."[102]

These ideas did not sway Adams's contemporaries, but they resonated with new leadership that came to power 100 years later. At about the same time, Adams grumbled in his private journal, "Democracy has no forefathers, it looks to no posterity." Left to itself, the democratic impulse "is swallowed up in the present, and thinks of nothing but itself," ruled in the end by "the maxim of leaving money in the pockets of the people."[103] He unabashedly wanted tariff revenue and public land sales income to promote large projects to chart the nation's future. He could not have been more at odds with Jackson's statement of his own principles: that the government's true role "consists in leaving individuals and States as much as possible to themselves—in making itself felt, not in its power, but in its beneficence; not in its control, but in its protection; not in binding the States more closely to the center, but leaving each unobstructed in its proper orbit."[104] The two men's conflict over government's proper role persists to the present.

Addressing the nullifiers, Adams, like Jackson, placed the union's origin before the Constitution, preceding even the Declaration of Independence. By the time the colonies asserted their independence, it was as "a primitive social compact of union," he said, and from "the hour of that Declaration, no one of the States whose people were parties to it, could, without violation of that primitive compact, secede or separate from the rest." Like Jackson, Adams declared that the Constitution was created by the people acting jointly, not as separate residents of sovereign states.

The claim to a right of nullification, he said, rests on the "hallucination of State sovereignty." One would look in vain in the Constitution, or the constitutions of the individual states, he said, for authority "for one State of this Union, by virtue of her sovereignty, not only to make, but to unmake the laws."[105] On the House floor he pointed to the Constitution's opening words, "We the People." "If the words meant any thing at all," he said, "they declared explicitly that that constitution was the work of the people of the United States." Those contending for a state compact theory, he continued, were arguing that the Constitution "was the work, not of the people, but of their attorneys." The founding document, he declared, was "the act of the people collected in separate communities, but forming one people, whose sanction alone gave the constitution all its power."[106]

More than mere legal argument, however, Adams injected a dose of invective into the nullification debate. His vehicle was a May 1833 minority report he wrote for the House committee on manufactures. In it he stood Calhoun's premise of an abused South on its head and attacked President Jackson for supporting southern domination of the national agenda. Jackson had opened himself to the assault, no doubt inadvertently, in his annual message observation that "cultivators of the soil" were "the best part" of the nation's population. His words could have as easily been spoken by Jefferson.

However, if one part was the best, Adams reasoned, then another part must be the worst. That part could only be the handicraftsmen, mechanics, and wage laborers in the nation's towns and cities, the manufacturing interests of the North. The consequences flowing from favoring one part of the country over the rest, Adams continued, were evident in the administration's policies: "abandonment for the future of all appropriations [for] internal improvement, . . . total dereliction of all protection to domestic industry, . . . denunciation of the Bank of the United States."[107] The North, not the South, was beleaguered. Andrew Jackson wielded the cudgel. In reducing the "General Government to a simple machine," Adams charged Jackson with being the central figure by which "the highest interests" of the manufacturing section of the country "may be sacrificed."[108]

For whom was the sacrifice being made, Adams asked. Not for the actual cultivators of the soil, because a vast proportion of them were slaves. No, Adams asserted, Jackson was reserving the honor of being the best part of the population, "the basis of society, and true friends of liberty" to the "the wealthy landowners," the nation's "landed aristocracy."[109] Slaveholders stood on the pedestal of honor.

Adams then pivoted to describing Calhoun's thesis, in its own terms, as "a collision of sectional interests between the slaveholding and the exclusively free portions of the country . . . an opposition of interests between servile and free labor." South Carolina's complaint, he said, was that free states benefited from the tariff to the detriment of slave states. "The foundation of the argument is an irreconcilable opposition of interests between two of the great masses of population constituting the Union," Adams said. "This opposition of interests is geographical, the division line being that between the States where the population is entirely free, and those where the population consists of masters and slaves; the divisions are of North and South."[110] Without actually using the term, Adams had described a house irreconcilably divided against itself.

The predominance of power in this system, Adams continued, lay in the South. The possession of some two million slaves gave the South $600 million in wealth the North did not possess. The Constitution's three-fifths clause to count slaves in representation in the House gave the South twenty-two extra votes, he said, and "in the next Congress, it will amount to twenty-five." By shifting revenue to tariffs, rather than direct taxation as Adams claimed was originally envisioned in adopting the three-fifths clause, the South gained further advantage, paying less in tariffs than it would under a direct taxation system. The South's disproportionate voting power in Congress and the Electoral College, he continued, "has secured to the slaveholding States the entire control of the national policy, and almost without exception, their possession of the highest executive office of the Union," including ten victories for slaveholding candidates in the nation's twelve elections for the presidency.

The exceptions, he did not need to note, were his father and himself. He also did not note, but could have, that the current Speaker of the House, the president of the Senate, and five chairs of the Senate's top seven committees came from slave states. Calhoun's depiction of the white South as an abused minority was a travesty, Adams argued. On top of all this, Adams railed, a group of South Carolina voters, amounting to less than the population of New York City, then presumed to nullify "the whole code of revenue laws of the United States . . . and declares that, if an attempt is made to execute the laws of the Union within the State . . . South Carolina will secede from that Union."[111]

The entire foundation of the nullification doctrine, he said, was "falsified logic, falsified history, falsified constitutional law, falsified morality. . . . All, all is false and hollow." And for what, he asked, "is this enormous edifice of fraud and falsehood erected? To rob the free working man of the North of the wages of his labor; to take money from his pocket, and put it into that of the Southern [slave] owner."[112] Calhoun's framework of an abused Southern minority now had a match in Adam's argument that a southern Slave Power ran roughshod over the land of free soil and free labor.

The first word and the last in the nullification debate, aside from the anonymous *South Carolina Exposition*, went to Daniel Webster. He had entered the Senate from Massachusetts as the controversy first arose. His reputation preceded him, probably the nation's finest constitutional lawyer whose pleadings made their way into the language of Supreme Court decisions. His presence was imposing: stout, grim of countenance, a massive bald forehead, and deep-set piercing eyes. He had penchants for alcohol, gambling, and sumptuousness far beyond his income. Daniel Webster was a conservative, of old Federalist stock, but keen to court the West whose votes might someday help realize his ambition to attain the White House. He was also a leather-lunged orator, perhaps the best ever to set foot in the Senate, who could hold an audience spellbound for hours on end.

Webster's 1830 Senate debate with Robert Hayne was a masterwork of drawing the South Carolinian away from his chosen ground of Western land policy and onto the Bay Stater's own turf of constitutional interpretation, where he savaged the flaws of nullification in defending the Union. Two years later, when the crisis had fully erupted, Webster used

Boston's famed Faneuil Hall to denounce the doctrine as "nothing more nor less than resistance by *force*—it is disunion by force—it is secession by *force*—it is Civil War."[113] He regarded slavery "as one of the greatest of evils," but referring back to the 1790 House report that concluded Congress had no authority over emancipation in the states, said, "The domestic slavery of the South I leave where I find it—in the hands of their own Governments."[114]

In February 1833, after Calhoun had delivered his closing address propounding his concurrent majority theory, Webster took the floor to close the debate. Like Jackson, he would draw his argument from the Constitution itself, and like both Jackson and Adams, he held that the union predated that document. As far back as 1774, he said, the colonies had been, in some measure, united together. Prior to the Articles of Confederation, "they had declared independence jointly, and had carried on the war jointly, both by sea and land, and this, not as separate States, but as one people."[115] The language used in drafting and approving the Constitution, he said, was of "adopt," "ratify," "ordain," and "establish." For South Carolina to secede, he said, "she must show that she has a right to reverse what has been ordained, to unsettle and overthrow what has been established, to reject what the people have adopted, and break up what they have ratified. . . . In other words, she must show her right to make a revolution."[116]

Webster then focused on Calhoun's compact theory of government, derived from the "Spirit of '98." He asked if the Constitution calls itself a compact, answering, "Certainly not. It uses the word 'compact' but once, and that is when it declares that the States shall enter into no compact." Was it a league or a confederacy among states? "There is not a particle of such language in all its pages," he said; "it declares itself a constitution . . . a fundamental law . . . expressly declared to be the supreme law."[117] Turning to the preamble, Webster declared that the words "We the People of the United States, do ordain and establish this constitution" would have to be stricken from the document before any "human argument can remove the popular basis on which the constitution rests" and make it a compact among the states.[118] Webster wove popular origin and union together into a single concept. "No ingenuity of argument, no subtlety of distinction," can evade the truth, he said, "that, as to certain purposes, the people of the United States are one people. They are one in making war, and one in making peace: they are one in regulating commerce, and one in laying duties of impost. The very end and purpose of the constitution was to make them one people in these particulars."[119] Further, he maintained, the Constitution "regards itself as perpetual and immortal. . . . The instrument contains ample provisions for its amendment, at all times, none for its abandonment, at any time. It declares that new States may come into the Union, but does not declare that old States may go out."[120]

The proposition that states had the final right to judge constitutional interpretation was Webster's next target. Because the Constitution granted Congress legislative power, and the Supreme Court judicial power, "the inference is irresistible," he said, that a government thus created "by the whole and for the whole, must have an authority superior to that of the particular government of any one part." Laws passed by Congress would be "idle ceremony," he said, if any one of the twenty-four states could overrule them. In a government granted legislative authority to be the supreme law of the land and judicial authority to decide all cases arising under the Constitution, he argued, "the inevitable consequence is, that the laws of this legislative power, and the decisions of this judicial power, must be binding on and over the whole."[121]

All arguments referring the constitutionality of acts of Congress to state decision were efforts, he said, "to supersede the judgement of the whole by the judgement of a part." Calhoun's doctrine rejected, he said, "the first great principle of all republican liberty; that is, that the majority must govern. In matters of common concern, the judgement of a majority must stand as the judgement of the whole." To enact a law, Webster noted, a majority of the people represented in the House, a majority of the states represented in the Senate, and the president, selected by a plan compounding both principles, must agree. "Within the limits and restrictions of the constitution," he said, "the Government of the United States like all other popular Governments, acts on majorities."[122]

In further accord with Jackson, Webster adopted a limited and divided role for the delegation of sovereignty. He noted that, unlike any

European power, in the United States sovereignty resided in the people alone under a written constitution. The document recognized two distinct, but not adverse, governments at the national and state levels. "Each has its separate sphere," he said. "It is a case of a division of powers between two Governments, made by the people, to which both are responsible ... and neither can call itself master of the other; the people are masters of both."[123]

Referring directly to Calhoun, Webster said that "the current of his opinions sweeps him along, he knows not whither." The results of his doctrine would be that "Virginia may secede, and hold the fortresses in the Chesapeake. The Western States may secede, and take to their own use the public lands. Louisiana may secede, if she choose, form a foreign alliance, and hold the mouth of the Mississippi."[124] In Webster's view, under such conditions the union would be no more that "a rope of sand."[125]

Twenty-seven years later, Abraham Lincoln, then president-elect, asked his law partner, William Herndon, to bring him copies of the Constitution, Jackson's proclamation, and Webster's reply to Hayne as among the few documents he consulted in drafting his first inaugural.[126] Working alone in an upstairs room across the street from the State House in Springfield, Illinois, he wrote the address. The words he wrote then would become in large measure the words by which we understand now the constitutional principles contested for in the nullification crisis.

"I hold," he said, "the Union of these States is perpetual. ... Perpetuity is implied, if not expressed, in the fundamental law of all national governments," no government ever having "a provision in its organic law for its own destruction." Further, he recalled, the Articles of Confederation were formed to create a perpetual union. He then drew directly from Jackson, writing, "One of the declared objects for ordaining and establishing the Constitution was '*to form a more perfect Union.*' ... But if destruction of the Union by one or by a part only of the States be lawfully possible, the Union is less perfect than before the Constitution, having lost the vital element of perpetuity." He next reasoned that although one party to a contract may violate it, it required all parties to rescind it. "It follows from these views that no State upon its own mere motion can lawfully get out of the Union; that resolves and ordinances to that effect are legally void, and that acts of violence within any State or States against the authority of the United States are insurrectionary or revolutionary, according to circumstances."[127] By this view, Lincoln held that the union was unbroken and that the war that followed was a rebellion. The union was one and indivisible.

Webster's finest hour came in the peroration to his reply to Hayne. He asked that when his eyes last saw the sun's light, it be not "shining on the broken and dishonored fragments of a once glorious Union." Rather he asked that they behold the ensign of the republic:

> *Still full high advanced, its arms and trophies streaming in their original lustre, not a stripe erased or polluted, not a single star obscured—bearing for its motto, no such miserable interrogatory as,* What is all this worth? *Nor those other words of delusion and folly,* Liberty first, and Union afterwards—*but every where, spread all over in characters of living light, blazing on all its ample folds, as they float over the sea and over the land, and in every wind under the whole Heavens, that other sentiment, dear to every true American heart—*Liberty *and* Union, *now and forever, one and inseparable.*[128]

In country stores, in villages and towns, on farms in the West and across the North, Webster's speech was read and pondered, republished in newspapers and distributed in 40,000 pamphlets. What resonated most was the rally point of union. Tens of thousands of the young men who later made up the Union Army were taught as schoolchildren to recite Webster's closing words from memory, as did generations of schoolchildren after them.

One result of the Civil War, historian Garry Wills has written, was that the United States became a singular, not a plural.[129] Prior to the war, Jackson wrote, "To say that any state may at pleasure secede from the Union, is to say that the United States *are* not a nation." Had that sentence been written after the war, it would have been rendered as "To say that any state may at pleasure secede from the Union, is to say that the United States *is* not a nation." The seed of that simple transformative concept, and the consequences flowing from it, was sown during the nullification crisis.

Just as the Missouri debates exposed most of the causes of the Civil War to come, the nullification debates forecast what has become the modern understanding of nationhood and key constitutional norms. Jackson's and Webster's formulation of one, indivisible union in which nullification and secession are unallowable are now norms, not propositions. The Supreme Court's authority as final constitutional arbiter is undisputed today. Adams was prescient in seeing the Constitution as intended to be used actively to pursue broad national interests, a view adopted by Franklin D. Roosevelt and continued ever since. Even part of Calhoun's theory survives. Drawing from his mentors, and the established practice of government, Lincoln contended that majority rule "is the only true sovereign of a free people."[130] That principle held, with few if significant exceptions, up to the twenty-first century.

At the beginning of the millennium, however, the Senate abandoned majority rule. In its place, the Senate adopted the practice that sixty votes in the 100-member chamber are required to pass nearly all significant legislation. Because the majority party rarely commands sixty votes among its own members, the new rule requires some degree of minority consent. Instead of the concurrent majority Calhoun espoused, the Senate now functions—at least as of this writing—by what may be termed a concurrent minority: sufficient minority party votes to reach the crucial sixty-vote threshold. In this sense Calhoun, too, may be said to have forecast a key principle by which Congress operates. His prediction that compromise, not gridlock, would flow from additional minority protections may be judged from the record, a subject beyond the scope of this work.

In its immediate aftermath, the nullification crisis produced near unanimity on one topic, but fractured results between the North and West, and the white South on the rest. Nullification was rejected across the nation, except by a minority of ultraradical diehards. Virginia's General Assembly put the case more mildly than some, but clearly, in a resolution reading, "They continue to regard the doctrines of State Sovereignty and State Rights," as embodied in the "Spirit of '98," "as a true interpretation of the Constitution . . . but they do not consider them as sanctioning the proceedings of South Carolina."[131] Mississippi was blunt, adopting a resolution declaring "We are opposed to Nullification. We regard it as heresy, fatal to the existence of the Union."[132] Alabama, North Carolina, and Maryland, among the southern states, passed similar resolves. But absent from them, as distinguished from resolutions adopted in the North, was endorsement of Jackson's proclamation or condemnation of secession. The last resort, as Madison and Jefferson envisioned, of a state to constitutionally break its ties to the union, remained.

Senator George M. Bibb of Kentucky expressed the ambivalence of many southerners in a speech during the nullification debates. "I wish it to be distinctly understood," he said, "that, while I concur in the doctrines of the Virginia and Kentucky Resolutions of 1798, 1799, and 1800, I do not mean to approve the time, manner, and occasion in which South Carolina has applied them in practice." The great conservative principles of "this holy text" were liable to abuse "in the hands of indiscreet and heated partisans." But, Bibb added, South Carolina was acting "upon the existence of the principles, that, in pursuit of happiness, 'the powers of Government may be re-assumed by the people.'"[133] South Carolina may have acted rashly on nullification, but the right of peaceful, constitutionally sanctioned secession was undiminished.

Devotion to the union continued to pervade the white South, but room for moderation was closing. Calhoun's and South Carolina's militancy spread even as the nullification doctrine did not. The white South, it was clear to all, was and would continue to comprise a minority of the states. Her safety, and especially that of slavery, required that she act in unity, as a bloc, in the face of all future threats.

A different view took hold in the North and in the West. The union came to be seen as an end in itself, not just as means to the ends of security and prosperity under a government based on individual liberty. Nullification and secession were unacceptable within the union, the one having no constitutional sanction, the other amounting to rebellion, or treason.

CHAPTER 7

Abolitionists and Proslavery

CHARLESTON POSTMASTER Alfred Huger knew he had trouble on his hands when stacks of abolitionist newspapers arrived by packet ship from New York at his office on July 29, 1835. The nearly 1,000 copies of *The Emancipator*, *The Slave's Friend*, *Human Rights*, and *Anti-Slavery Record* were addressed to nearly every prominent citizen in the city and many others farther off. Huger knew that whites who received these newspapers would view them as packets of contagious disease delivered to their doorsteps. Some copies, which in white southern eyes preached license to murder their masters, might even fall into the hands of their own slaves. To bide time Huger separated the abolitionist newspapers from the rest of the mail, locked his office for the night, and went home.

Robert Payne, returned to South Carolina from his Senate duties, and a group of irate citizens who had caught wind of the arrival solved Huger's problem for him. They broke into the post office during the night and seized the offending material. The next night, amid impassioned speeches and the whoops and chants of an assembled crowd lit by the glow of a bonfire, the newspapers and effigies of northern abolitionist leaders went up in flames.

A fire of indignation swept Charleston, already primed by news accounts of a vast Mississippi slave revolt plot that had been met with dozens of reported lynchings.[1] A citizens' committee was set up, which Payne headed, to confront the crisis. Arriving ships were searched at dockside for abolitionist cargo. The committee expressed its "utmost indignation and abhorrence" at incendiary abolitionist attempts to undermine slavery with fatal consequences to white society. In this crisis, the committee urged northerners "to put down" antislavery societies and for states in the North to prevent them from interfering with slavery, or risk

"THE CERTAIN DESTRUCTION OF THE UNION."[2] Echoing that call, the legislature passed resolutions urging northern states to suppress abolition societies and to "make it highly penal to print, publish and distribute newspapers" calculated "to excite the slaves of the Southern States to insurrection and revolt."[3]

The frenzy spread to other southern states that had been targeted with abolitionist mailings. South Carolina's legislature was joined by those in Georgia, Mississippi, and Virginia in passing laws and resolutions to stamp out the danger. Committees of Safety were formed. Post offices, ships carrying mail, stages, and quarters where Blacks lived were searched. Spanning nearly every southern state, some 150 rallies of angry citizens were reportedly held to denounce the mailings and demand measures to stop them.[4] The *Charleston Southern Patriot* made clear that "those states whose *peculiar institutions* are involved in hazard, must *take the law into their own hands. Extreme cases require extreme remedies.*"[5]

In Washington, D.C., Postmaster General Amos Kendall wrote to Huger, who had described receiving newspapers that were "insurrectionary in the highest degree." Kendall recognized that a higher law motivated by patriotism could override obligations to deliver the mail, especially of the type that Huger described.[6] President Jackson favored passing a bill to outlaw mailing incendiary publications. He also urged that if such material was mailed, the names of subscribers be published in local newspapers. John C. Calhoun proposed that local postmasters be prohibited from delivering mail proscribed by state law.

Although Congress did deliberate, none of those measures went beyond the rhetorical stage. Instead, southern postmasters adopted an informal policy to censure the mail at their own discretion. As the New York Abolition Society, which had initiated the campaign, realized that its missives were destined for the dead-letter box, the effort was discontinued. A new method designed to convulse the white South, gain publicity, and draw membership soon presented itself.

A stigma as the white South's chief tormentor quickly attached to William Lloyd Garrison. His effigy was one of those burned in Charleston.

William Lloyd Garrison.
COURTESY OF THE LIBRARY
OF CONGRESS.

This development was ironic, because the abolitionist mailing campaign neither involved his newspaper, *The Liberator*, nor was his idea. Garrison was accorded lead status in the white South's pantheon of detested agitators for Black freedom because his voice was uniquely focused and strident. History continued the Garrisonian legend while transforming it into his being the unparalleled leader of the cause of Black freedom. This development was ironic, too, because Garrison became increasingly isolated as the abolitionist movement grew while others charted a path infusing northern political thought with the conviction that slavery was a danger to the nation.

Garrison was born in Newburyport, Massachusetts, in 1805. Descended from indentured servants, abandoned by his father, enduring long separations from his mother, he lived in poverty well into adulthood. When he moved to Baltimore, Garrison saw colonization as the best way forward for enslaved Blacks. While there, he was befriended by William Watkins. In their conversations Watkins, a free Black prominent in the community, converted his young friend to the righteousness of abolition, complete and immediate freedom for all slaves.

Both men were undoubtedly influenced by the 1829 publication of David Walker's *Appeal*, a seminal work by a free Black man. His denunciation of the colonization movement was unequivocal. "America is more our country," Walker wrote, "than it is the whites—we have enriched it with our *blood and tears*. The greatest riches in all America have arisen from our blood and tears:—and will they drive us from our property and homes, which we have earned with our *blood*?" Far more threatening to the master class was Walker's direct appeal to enslaved Blacks to throw off their chains, stand as men, and confront their jailers. "Remember Americans," he wrote, "that we must and shall be free and enlightened as you are, will you wait until we shall, under God, obtain our liberty by the crushing arm of power? Will it not be dreadful for you? I speak Americans for your own good. We must and shall be free I say, in spite of you. . . . And wo, wo will be to you if we have to obtain our freedom by fighting."[7]

As a Black man, Walker had no difficulty in thrusting straight to his point without the temporizing by whites about entailed obligations and the need for compromise, accommodation, delay, and deference. He created for those such as Garrison a clear light to the truth. He also wrote in the age when the British Parliament was debating slavery and was soon to pass the Abolition Act of 1833 ending slavery, with some exceptions, throughout the empire. The tide was turning, or so it seemed, and Garrison was determined to help make it happen.

His vehicle was *The Liberator*, the newspaper he began printing in Boston in 1831 with the base of his subscribers in the Black community there. As Garrison's voice spread, so did the antislavery movement in the North. The base of 200 antislavery societies in early 1835 just before the mailing campaign began expanded to 527 a year later.[8] The opposite trend swept the South. Not a single antislavery society existed there by 1837, according to the estimate of a movement leader, where 106 had functioned a decade earlier.[9]

Garrison's determination was matched by his intensity. "It is useless to mince the matter," he wrote early in his career. "The people must be divided into two classes only, on the subject of slavery. And who do not lift up a warning voice against the infernal system, or who cravenly skulk away from the conflict, or who expend their whole philanthropy in groans,—whether they know it or not, whether they believe it or not,—are directly the advocates of oppression; and they alone are its enemies, whose practices correspond with their professions."[10] These words were mild compared to Garrison's ever-sharpening rhetoric. In full stride his voice became "the seven unloosed Apocalyptic thunders" that made men tremble.[11]

His logic knew no nuance. As slavery was a sin, then the only remedy was to abolish it immediately. His colleague John Greenleaf Whittier wrote "We do not talk of *gradual* abolition, because, as Christians, we find no authority for advocating a *gradual relinquishment of sin.* We say to slaveholders—'Repent NOW—*today*—IMMEDIATELY.'"[12] In unremittingly condemning not only the sin of slavery, but those who practiced or accommodated it as sinners, Garrison commenced three decades of clawing at the nerve endings of white southern honor. No person in American history has been as hated, with deep-seated personal disdain, as was Garrison in the white South.

But the objects of Garrison's derision knew no sectional boundary. His absolutism swept all before it. Democratic and Whig politicians wedded to cross-sectional party platforms that accommodated slavery were execrable. That closed the door to working within the political parties, the moral abyss of gradualism. A church that did not adopt his doctrine was a "synagogue of Satan." He ultimately denounced the Constitution, with its slavery compromises, as "a covenant with death and an agreement with hell" and burned a copy of it at a Fourth of July celebration in 1854. As his close associate Wendell Phillips accurately observed "merciless and incessant criticism . . . was his only means of agitation."[13]

And that greatest of Garrison's strengths was also his greatest weakness. As he drove sin and sinners, politicians and the clergy before him, he also drove away a large swath of the North, where he was widely seen as a fanatic agitating a reckless cause.

The fury that greeted the abolitionist mailings in the white South was matched during the late 1830s with the fury of northern mobs that attacked abolitionists, their printing presses, and the free Black communities in their midst. Three months after the initial flare-up in Charleston, Garrison barely escaped with his life when a Boston mob ransacked the offices of *The Liberator*. The same day in Utica, New York, a meeting of the state abolition society was disrupted. That night a mob, abetted by local officials, broke into the offices of the antislavery newspaper the *Oneida Standard and Democrat* and scattered the printing type onto the street. A year earlier, Arthur Tappan, president of the American Anti-Slavery Society, had seen his home in New York City broken into and the furniture burned in the street. The mailing campaign had been Tappan's idea. During three days of rioting, mobs numbering an estimated 7,000 had assaulted free Blacks in the streets and attacked their homes, businesses, and churches until the militia was called out to quell them.

In Ohio, abolitionist James Birney's press for *The Philanthropist* was destroyed twice by mobs in 1836. To the south in St. Louis, Elijah P. Lovejoy saw the press for his newspaper *The Observer* thrown into the Mississippi River in July. When he moved shortly afterward to Alton, Illinois, another mob smashed his press there. Lovejoy's antislavery sentiment was passionate. "My soul detests it," he wrote. "My heart sickens over it; my judgement, my understanding, my conscience, reject it, with loathing and horror."[14] Lovejoy's writing also contained a decided streak of anti-Catholicism, a trait shared by the Whig party that drove many recently arrived Irish Catholics into the Democratic Party and away from abolitionism. Lovejoy's scorn was driven by papal doctrine from Rome that suffering the wrong of slavery was preferable to the social turmoil that would arise from opposing it.[15] In the late summer and early fall of 1837, mobs broke into *The Observer*'s offices and twice destroyed its printing press. Finally, on November 7 yet another mob destroyed the paper's press.

Dred Scott
SOURCE: *SLAVERY IMAGES*

Henry Clay addresses the Senate during the 1850 Compromise debate. Daniel Webster is shown seated in the mid-left foreground. John C. Calhoun is standing to the right of the presiding officer's chair. The scene takes place in the Old Senate Chamber. SOURCE: LIBRARY OF CONGRESS.

This satire of the relationship between Thomas Jefferson and Sally Hemings was published in 1804. SOURCE: AMERICAN ANTIQUARIAN SOCIETY.

The white South's idealized image of slavery as captured in this 1841 image by E. W. Clay. *America*. SOURCE: EDWARD WILLIAMS CLAY, CIRCA 1841.

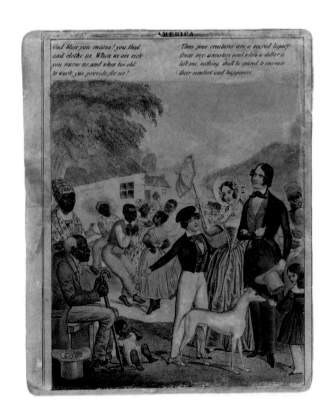

Thomas Jefferson from painting by Thomas Sully. SOURCE: LIBRARY OF CONGRESS.

George Washington at the Constitutional Convention. SOURCE: ALAMY STOCK PHOTO.

Allegorical image of America's manifest destiny. SOURCE: LIBRARY OF CONGRESS.

Lovejoy was shot to death in the melee. All those charged in the incident were acquitted. At a meeting concerning Lovejoy's murder, one of those present, a man named John Brown, stood up to declare "Here, before God, in the presence of these witnesses, from this time, I consecrate my life to the destruction of slavery."[16] John Brown kept his pledge.

Northern white antagonism to abolitionism was founded in large part on fear of job competition with free Blacks and the movement's message that Blacks should have equal status in civil society. A group of white laborers petitioned the Connecticut legislature in 1834 "to control the labor of free Negroes in the state and to stop the activities of the abolitionists," whose purpose was "to sow the seeds of insurrection and civil commotion in the nation, and acquire for [Blacks] equal civil and political privileges with ourselves."[17] In New York City, in 1830 nearly all household servants were free Blacks, but within two decades Irish servants there exceeded the free Black population by ten to one.[18] White workers moving grain, livestock, and other goods south along the Ohio and Mississippi Rivers feared that abolition would disrupt that trade and eventually lead to a mass influx of Blacks to compete for their jobs.

When the Anti-Slavery Convention of American Women met in the just-completed Pennsylvania Hall in Philadelphia in May 1838, a riot broke out. The *Pennsylvania Freeman*'s print shop was destroyed, bricks were hurled through the hall's windows, and the building was finally burned to the ground. The rash of northern riots and attacks on antislavery newspapers in the late 1830s was far outnumbered by assaults on individual abolitionist speakers.[19] Stephen S. Foster, an ardent Garrisonian, was one of them. He chose the novel course of rising uninvited during a church service to disclaim on slavery's evils. For doing so, he was bodily ejected from one church twice on the same day. The title of his pamphlet, *The Brotherhood of Thieves: Or a True Picture of the American Church and Clergy*, shows he did not believe that the evil was confined to the South. He was thrown out of at least twenty-four churches, jailed four times, and nearly lynched once for proclaiming that America's government was "a wicked and nefarious conspiracy against liberty of more than two million of our countrymen."[20] But he kept speaking.

Anti-abolitionists burned down the newly opened Pennsylvania Hall on May 17, 1838, in part because they opposed allowing women to address the audience assembled in the hall. COURTESY OF THE LIBRARY OF CONGRESS.

The abolitionists' answer to having their mailing campaign choked off by local postmasters was to switch the battle to Congress. Over eighteen months beginning in late 1835, the American Anti-Slavery Society gathered some 300,000 petitions.[21] They called for abolition of slavery in the District of Columbia and of the interstate slave trade; they pleaded against the annexation of Texas and for a ban on slavery in the territories. More to the point, they aimed at provoking the white South and awakening the North by agitating the issue in Congress. The white South was certainly primed to take on the abolitionist. Nearly a decade earlier, Robert Turnbull's widely read *The Crisis* had warned that any congressional slavery debate "will be the LANDING of an enemy" that "must be resisted. There must be no discussion. Discussion will cause DEATH and

DESTRUCTION to our negro property" that would be lured into revolt by talk of emancipation.[22]

By demanding silence, the white South fell into the trap of having to expend countless hours of congressional debate trying to justify and enforce it. The Senate's role in imposing a gag on slavery petitions was discussed earlier in this work. In the House, members were ensnarled in the controversy in session after session up to late 1844. In the process, ordinary citizens in the North were exposed to an unrelenting white southern attack on the constitutionally protected rights of freedom of petition, of speech, and of the press. Posed in this way, the peculiar institution took on a new dimension of Slave Power infringement on rights the North held dear. In response, northern Whigs in particular were joined by some Democrats in loosening their political embrace of their white southern confederates.

South Carolina's James Henry Hammond began the fight in the House in December 1835. He moved that slavery petitions be ignored by not receiving them.[23] His motion would shut the door to the normal practice of upholding the pretense of honoring petitions by receiving and then referring them to a committee that never acted on them. The ensuing debate engrossed the House for weeks. On February 1, 1836, Hammond took the floor to deliver his philippic demanding silence on slavery. His aim, admirably achieved, was to issue a warning throughout the white South that failure to rally to the most reactionary demands to choke off discussion was betrayal of white southern interests. Although Hammond failed to win his specific legislative goal, he succeeded on a broader front. He cut the ground out from under raising a moderate white southern voice on slavery and thus created the facade of a solid white South, whatever stilled misgivings might lay behind it. His tactic of intimidating white southern dissent into silence by labeling it as treasonous played out in future debates and came back to haunt him when the tide of secession swept the white South.

Hammond opened by describing the growth of abolitionism that "spreads like wildfire" with messages of infamy and insurrection. "I call on every slaveholder in this House, and in this country," he said, "to mark its fearful progress, and prepare to meet it. He who falters here or elsewhere, he who shrinks from taking the highest and the boldest ground at once, is a traitor! A traitor to his native soil! A traitor to the memory of those from whom he has inherited his rights! A traitor to his helpless offspring, who call upon him for protection!" He next leveled the white South's recurring threat, that the moment the House tries "to legislate upon this subject, it dissolves the Union." In that event he vowed to "go home to preach, and if I can, to practice, disunion, and civil war, if needs be."[24] Hammond's decision to reach instantly for extremes was deliberate. As his mentor, John C. Calhoun, had advised years earlier, the enemy must be met forcefully at the threshold.

Hammond coupled his disunion warning with a full-throated defense of slavery as a positive good. There is not "a happier, more contented race upon the face of the earth" than the white South's slaves, he said. "Lightly tasked, well clothed, well fed . . . their lives and persons protected by the law, all their sufferings alleviated by the kindest and most interested care, and their domestic affections cherished and maintained, at least as far as I have known, with conscientious delicacy." Any attempt at emancipation, however, "would be followed instantly by civil war between the whites and the blacks. A bloody, exterminating war."

What the white South wanted, he continued, was for the North to outlaw the publication and circulation of abolitionist tracts. This could be done without infringing freedom of speech or of the press, he said, because that "freedom means well-regulated freedom of speech, and not unrestricted licentiousness." Finally, the white South demanded "that these petitions be not received here." In a parting warning, Hammond said of the white South's institutions "We were born and bred under them, and will maintain them or die in their defense." Hammond's closing words are remarkable for their candor in disrobing slavery from its cloak of states' rights legitimacy and proclaiming clearly that slavery was the ground the white South stood on and would die for.[25]

By the end of the session, the House voted to table slavery petitions without further action for the remainder of the session. Only one of the fifty-five northern Whigs in the House voted for the measure, while nearly 80 percent of northern Democrats who answered the roll call approved it.[26] The vote meant that in the next congressional session the fight could begin anew. John Quincy Adams was prepared to be sure it did.

John Quincy Adams was a solitary figure in a profession where one usually thrived by being gregarious. He could be slashing in his invective, deliberate and unmovable in debate, infuriating to opponents, and an inspiration to his advocates. One House colleague described him as "fierce as ten furies, terrible as hell."[27] His long public record, taking a humble seat in the House after serving as president, added to his reputation as a devoted public servant. He was obstinate, of quicker wit than most, keen to the rules of procedure, of unquestioned personal probity, and believed that most of the House was composed of mediocrities. All these traits came into play as Adams approached the renewed House gag-rule debate late in 1836.

John Quincy Adams.
COURTESY OF THE
LIBRARY OF CONGRESS.

He began innocuously enough by offering a petition he said was from nine ladies in Fredericksburg, Virginia, calling for abolition of the slave trade in the nation's capital. It was immediately tabled. He next addressed the Speaker of the House, saying he had a petition in his hand, but before presenting it he asked that the Speaker decide whether it fell within the previously adopted gag rule. The petition, he said, was signed by twenty-two slaves.[28]

Furor instantly engulfed the House floor. Southerners were incensed by the notion that a petition written by slaves could be given any color of legitimacy in that august body. Congressman Julius Caesar Alford of Georgia shouted out that the petition should "be taken from the House and burnt. . . . There must be an end to this constant attempt to raise excitement, or the Union could not exist much longer." Congressman John Patton of Virginia intervened. He asked that Adams's petition from nine Fredericksburg women be taken off the table. He had been born in Fredericksburg, represented its citizens in the House, and was well acquainted with those who were respectable there. Patton wanted the House to know that the name of no "lady" from that town appeared on the petition. As to those who did sign it, Patton said he "did not believe there was a single one of them of decent respectability." In fact, Patton told the House, he recognized the name of one of the petition signers as that of a mulatto "of infamous character." Of the rest, he said, all were free negroes whom "he believed to be bad." The furor was compounded. Adams's affront of offering one petition from Black prostitutes and trying to offer another from slaves was too much to bear.

Congressman James Bouldin of Virginia proclaimed that unless the petitions were immediately rejected "the time had arrived when it was the business of Southern members to go home." A South Carolina member railed that the District of Columbia grand jury should indict Adams for promoting insurrection. Decorum was shattered. One observer later commented that the general agitation was as if a bunch of rattlesnakes had been unloosed at the members' feet. Adams was disgracing the House. Even some of his friends feared that he had gone too far. Congressman Dixon Lewis of Louisiana moved that the House censure Adams. By attempting to introduce a petition from slaves for the abolition of slavery in the District of Columbia, he said, Adams had "committed an outrage on the rights and feelings of a large portion of the people of this Union . . . and by extending to slaves a privilege only belonging to freemen, directly invites the slave population to insurrection."[29]

Adams sat quietly at his desk until the rant ran its course. Southerners in the House, he knew, had fallen into a well-laid trap. He rose to again address the Speaker. He had been accused of attempting to present a petition from slaves, he said, calling for the abolition of slavery in the capital. But that was not so. Adams asked the Speaker to confirm that he had not offered such a petition. He had merely held a piece of paper purporting to be a slave petition in his hand, asking the Speaker if it was within the rules to offer it. Further, Adams noted, the censure resolution would have to be revised. It claimed that the petition was for the abolition of slavery in the District. It was not. It called instead for the continuation of slavery there. His crime, Adams said, "has been for attempting to introduce the petition of slaves that slavery should not be abolished."[30] To prove his point, Adams continued, the House would have to read the document and to do that the House would have to receive it. The trap slammed shut. Southern outrage was suddenly cast in a new light as the foolishness of intemperate men. In an irony Adams did not discuss openly, the slave petition, which never was made public, was probably intended to trap Adams. The paper he held in his hand was most likely a fake meant to ridicule him if he did introduce it by calling for his expulsion from the House.[31] The trappee became the trapper.

Adams next turned his attention to the man seated at the desk immediately to his left, Congressman Patton from Fredericksburg. He acknowledged that he did not show the Fredericksburg petition to him before offering it. "I adhered to the right of petition," Adams began, "and let me say here that, let the petition be, as the gentleman from Virginia has stated, from free negroes—prostitutes he supposes. . . . Where is your law which says that the mean, and the low, and the degraded, shall be deprived of the right of petition, if their moral character is not good? Where, in the land of freemen, was the right of petition ever placed on the exclusive basis of morality and virtue? Petition is supplication—it is entreaty—it is prayer! And where is the degree of vice or immorality which shall deprive the citizen of the right to supplicate for a boon, or to pray for mercy? Where is such a law to be found?" Adams was hitting his stride. His true audience was not Congressman Patton or others in the chamber. He was speaking to the people at large who in the days to come would read and discuss what was said in Congress that day.

"There is no absolute monarch on earth," Adams said, "who is not compelled by the constitution of his country to receive the petitions of his people, whosoever they may be. . . . This is the law even of despotism. And what does your law say? Does it say that, before presenting a petition, you shall look into it, and see whether it comes from the virtuous, and the great, and the mighty? No, sir, it says no such thing; the right of petition belongs to all."[32]

Adams sat back down. Within the course of a few minutes, he had made his southern opponents look like fools. The censure motion was never put to a vote.

The widow Ann Spriggs ran a boardinghouse amid a row of four-story buildings along First Street Southeast directly across from the Capitol building, still under construction. John Quincy Adams was a frequent visitor, meeting with friends around the long dinner table tended by the free Black servants in Mrs. Spriggs's household and occasionally by slaves hired out to her. Two of them, in fact, disappeared from the boardinghouse only to be heard of later as having escaped to the North.[33] That was likely due to Joshua Giddings, Mrs. Spriggs' longtime boarder, a Whig member of Congress from Ohio, who had extensive contacts within the Underground Railroad that spirited slaves to freedom. Two of her other boarders, Joshua Leavitt and Theodore Dwight Weld, had similar contacts. Weld was a boarder only during parts of two congressional sessions. Leavitt's stay was longer. Adams dined at Mrs. Spriggs' to meet with these men and fellow antislavery Whig congressmen. Whig Representatives Seth Gates of New York and William Slade of Vermont were among those who, at different times and for different lengths of time, lived at her boardinghouse. When Abraham Lincoln began his single term in Congress in 1847, he lived there, too.

Congressman Joshua Reed Giddings of Ohio. COURTESY OF THE LIBRARY OF CONGRESS.

Theodore Dwight Weld. COURTESY OF THE LIBRARY OF CONGRESS.

Joshua Leavitt. COURTESY OF THE WIKI-MEDIA COMMONS. MATHEW BRADY PHOTO-GRAPH COURTESY OF SPECIAL COLLECTIONS, FINE ARTS LIBRARY, HARVARD COLLEGE.

Abolition House was the name by which Mrs. Spriggs's boarding-house was widely known in Washington. The political leadership of the nation's abolitionist movement lived there, with Adams as its fulcrum. Adams, Weld wrote, was "in a position to do for the Anti-Slavery cause by a single speech more than our best lecturers can do in a year."[34] Over a period of years plans were put in motion there that ultimately aimed at overthrowing the dominant two-party system and replacing it with an avowedly antislavery party in the North.

The mixture of Mrs. Spriggs' guests was ideally suited to the task. Adams provided prominence. Giddings, Gates, and Slade acted like entering wedges to split fellow northern Whig congressmen from the party's proslavery foundation. In the process they made northern Democrats nervous about their positioning, too. Weld and Leavitt were proven crusaders in the cause of abolition, although of different stripes. Weld's stay at Mrs. Spriggs's boardinghouse was brief but pivotal. He was close to Garrison in avoiding getting in league with political parties, but he advocated a path he called immediate gradualism, meaning "that at the earliest possible period consistent with the best good of the slaves, they should be fully emancipated."[35]

In 1839 Weld published *Slavery As It Is: Testimony of a Thousand Witnesses*, among the most scathing and influential of all abolitionist publications. Using southern newspaper accounts of killings and trials involving slaves, advertisements for slave sales and runaway slaves, and testimonials from observers in the South, the volume sold more than 100,000 copies in its first year of publication.[36] He had emerged into the abolitionist movement in 1834 as a leader of the Lane Rebels, a group of students from Lane Theological Seminary in Ohio who staged an eighteen-day debate there on slavery. He had been stoned giving abolitionist lectures. He married Angelina Grimké, a native of South Carolina and abolitionist writer and lecturer and women's rights advocate, who with her sister Sarah helped Weld write *Slavery As It Is*. After losing his voice and suffering a near breakdown, most of Weld's time was spent in exhausting work late into the night at the American Anti-Slavery Society's New York office.

Leavitt was a Congregationalist minister who helped found that society. He moved to Washington as editor of *The Emancipator*, the main competitor in both circulation and doctrine to Garrison's *Liberator*. He helped enlist Adams in his successful Supreme Court defense of kidnapped Africans who had been imprisoned after seizing control of the slave ship *La Amistad* and sought freedom and return to their home country. Above all, Leavitt provided the impetus behind political abolitionism, anathema to the Garrisonians, that first formed the Liberty Party, and later with influences from different sources the Free Soil and ultimately the Republican Party.

Mrs. Spriggs' boardinghouse was not without its tensions. Adams opposed abolition of slavery in the District over fear of the sectional turmoil it would entail, even as he was determined to give voice to petitions advocating it. His dinner companions, he confided in his diary, were "constantly urging me to indiscreet movements."[37] Leavitt lashed out in *The Emancipator* at Slade for political infidelity to the abolitionist cause. Giddings became his target for supporting southern sympathizers as Whig presidential candidates. But the group's common antislavery cause overcame their tactical differences.

The Twenty-Fifth Congress opened in late 1837 with a new House blowup when Congressman Slade offered two abolition petitions that prompted most of the southern delegation to walk out. Meeting in private they wrote and quickly rammed through a strict new gag rule providing that all petitions "touching the abolition of slavery . . . be laid on the table, without being debated, printed, read, or referred, and that no further action whatever shall be had thereon."[38] With that avenue closed to them, the Spriggs house strategists decided on a new target: Texas.

Their choice was apt. After bloody battles at the Alamo and Goliad, Texas rebels under General Sam Houston defeated the Mexican army at San Jacinto and declared the Republic of Texas in March 1836. Houston wanted the newly freed republic to be annexed to the United States, but late in his final term of office President Jackson offered recognition but not statehood. His successor, Martin Van Buren, continued the arms-length policy, realizing that Texas statehood would bring with it the divisive question of the extension of slavery. Knowing that any petition mentioning abolition or slavery was consigned to oblivion, Adams and his colleagues lit on a new strategy of offering petitions opposed to the annexation of Texas. The object of agitating against slavery would remain intact while the wording of the petitions avoided the new gag.

Adams was assisted in preparing his Texas strategy by Benjamin Lundy, a Quaker abolitionist who had a varied career in the cause as writer, lecturer, and publisher. Garrison had assisted Lundy in editing the *Genius of Universal Emancipation* in Baltimore before he moved on to Boston to publish *The Liberator*. A few years later Lundy traveled to Texas, collecting reams of material he later used to assist Adams and to write in 1836 *The War in Texas*. Lundy wrote the book before Houston's San Jacinto victory while Mexico still held the territory.

The Mexican government had outlawed slavery in 1829, although the statute was largely unenforced in the Province of Texas among white Americans who settled there. Annexationists aimed, Lundy wrote, to *"wrest the large and valuable territory of Texas from the Mexican Republic, in order to re-establish the* SYSTEM OF SLAVERY; *to open a vast and profitable* SLAVE-MARKET *therein; and, ultimately to annex it to the United States."* The slaveholders, Lundy charged, were determined to carry out a *"Grand Scheme of Oppression and Tyrannical Usurpation."*[39] By the time Adams took on the issue in the House, he was armed not only with hundreds of petitions signed by some 100,000 citizens, but with resolutions addressed to Congress from seven state legislatures opposing Texas's annexation. Unable to deflect them with the gag rule, southerners steered them to the Foreign Affairs Committee. That body, which southern members dominated, duly declared that no action need be taken on the state resolutions because no proposition for Texas statehood or annexation was before the House. It was a gag under a different guise but with the same result of no report and no debate.

During three weeks beginning in mid-June 1838, Adams used the morning hour of members' time to break the silence. One after another, for days on end, he presented the resolutions opposing annexation from Massachusetts, Vermont, Rhode Island, Ohio, Michigan, New York, and Pennsylvania to a restive House. The chamber's official journal, the *Con-*

gressional Globe, did not even print Adams's remarks. He had them published on his own. The whole affair, he said, from the gag rule on petitions to using the Foreign Affairs Committee as a burial pit for resolutions, exposed "the *encroaching character* of this *system of suppression*—applied at first, only to the subject of slavery and the slave trade, but gradually spreading and absorbing in its despotic interdict almost every *subject of petition*, and almost every *class of petitioners*, including, at last, the resolutions of sovereign States."[40]

President Van Buren's White House, "a Northern Administration with Southern principles" Adams called it, abetted the effort that included "a sectional combination of interests of the slaveholding against the free States."[41] He was renewing his argument during the nullification crisis that the slave South held inordinate sway in the nation's councils. Consolidating the concept into the charge that a Slave Power dominated the nation soon followed.

Introduction of the term "Slave Power" is attributed to Senator Thomas Morris of Ohio, who first used it during a gag-rule debate in that chamber in February 1839.[42] The term saturated the abolitionist press and over time became a northern proxy for a host of sins attributed to the white South. Resistance to the Slave Power was a central theme of the Republican Party that nominated Abraham Lincoln for the presidency in 1860. In Morris's terms, the "power behind the throne, greater than the throne itself . . . is the power of SLAVERY. . . aiming to govern the country, its constitution and laws." He pointed to the slave states' hold on the presidency, modifying Adams's characterization of Van Buren to "a northern man with southern feelings." The Slave Power, he continued, "has the cabinet of the President . . . five out of nine judges of the Supreme Court . . . the President of the Senate, and the Speaker of the House of Representatives." The aim of the southern Slave Power in league with northern financial power—an alliance of "the cotton bale with the bank note" Morris termed it—was "to live upon the unrequited labor of others . . . and bid defiance, as they hope, to free principles and free labor."[43]

Adams took up the theme in 1842 in fighting against the sixth gag imposed on the House, although this one only passed by two votes. The new gag was incorporated as House Rule 21, not merely a resolution. It adopted Hammond's original demand that instead of slavery petitions being received and then tabled, they be rejected out of hand. When Adams tried to evade the rule and open room for debate by lodging a petition to "immediately adopt measures peaceably to dissolve the Union," a censure resolution was moved against him.[44] His request that a committee report back denying the petition's request was not enough to forestall the censure motion.

Weld was enlisted to aid Adams's defense, working by day from an alcove in the Library of Congress, then conferring with Adams, Leavitt, and others at night at Mrs. Spriggs' to frame arguments and decide strategy. The attempt to silence him demonstrated, Adams said, "the existence of a conspiracy, in the House and out of the House, against himself, and through him, against the right of petition, and all the rights and liberties of the free people of this Union." The history of efforts to censure the mails, gag debate, and choke off petition, he said, "furnishes one of the strongest proofs of a great combination and conspiracy of the whole Southern portion of this Union to extend the laws of slavery through the free states."[45] Adams's defense against the censure motion, which ultimately went nowhere, provided him with time to warn northerners of Slave Power designs.

In refining their argument into an attack on the Slave Power, the collaborationists around Mrs. Spriggs' dining table accomplished two things. The abolitionists cause was intertwined with northern white concerns for their own freedoms and the future of free labor. Further, because both political parties depended on white southern votes to form national coalitions, both parties were implicated in the Slave Power's grasp for dominance. If enough northerners could be convinced by these arguments, the ground would be set for a political realignment.

—◦—

Carrying out the campaign in Washington depended on thousands of individuals across the North willing to put in the time and effort needed to circulate the petitions, gather the signatures, and spread the word. In 1837 the American Anti-Slavery Society in New York decided to refocus its efforts into a massive propaganda campaign. Weld and Leavitt were instrumental in the decision that by the end of the year, and for nearly a decade afterward, saw tens of thousands of petitions, literal wagonloads of them, flow into the nation's capital. They were gathered by members of state and local antislavery societies, including some 100,000 members. Those with the largest membership, some 20,000, were concentrated in upstate and western New York, followed by approximately 15,000 in Ohio. Thousands more members were spread across New England and the northwestern states.

The effort was deliberately targeted at rural farming communities where evangelicalism resonated after the Second Great Revival. In making their rounds, petitioners were instructed, "Neglect no one. Follow the farmer to his field, the wood-chopper to the forest. Hail the shop-keeper behind the counter; call the clerk from his desk . . . forget not the matron, ask for her daughter. . . . Explain, discuss, argue, persuade."[46] Antislavery petitions were placed in stores, banks, and churches, distributed at fairs, and circulated at meetings of all sorts.

Women did most of this work. Women, white and Black, formed auxiliary societies to state antislavery groups, met to divide up where to canvass, then righteously marched forth in the cause of freedom. In doing so, they altered the nation's political culture.

During the early era of abolitionism, women's rights to sign contracts, keep their wages, inherit property, or dispose of assets were taken over by their husbands upon marriage.[47] That began to change in the 1840s. Women could not vote. That did not change at the national level until 1920. During much of the antebellum era, the biblical admonition "Servants, obey your masters" applied to women as well as to slaves. Politics was a male domain.

At the same time, increasing numbers of northern women were finding ways to carve out their own spheres of independence and to earn their own incomes. Mill girls were hired by and lived in company-owned boardinghouses in New England and Pennsylvania mill towns. Women set up commercial farming operations to sell such items as butter and produce. Northern women living in cities hired out as seamstresses and in any number of domestic occupations.[48] A few even entered the professions of teaching at institutions of higher education and medicine.

Women had long been involved in political affairs, but only in a certain class of political affairs deemed suitable to their gender: aid for orphans and unmarried women, advocacy for temperance, assistance to the poor or infirm. By forming their own antislavery societies, gathering petition signatures—most of them provided by women, many from the mill girls whose income depended on southern cotton—running local libraries supplied with abolitionist literature, writing letters, raising funds, and especially speaking out against slavery at public gatherings, women crossed a political line. The abolitionist movement empowered women. They engaged as advocates for abolition in the deepest political cross-currents of their time. Their advocacy led directly to the women's suffrage movement that drew many of its early leaders from the ranks of women writers, authors, and editors, lecturers and organizers, who began their journey as agitators for abolition.

The prominence of women in the abolition movement gave male southern critics, whose patriarchal construct began with dominance over their wives and children, ample fodder for gender-based attacks. It also caused a division in the ranks of the abolition movement itself. Garrison was among those who welcomed women assuming leadership in the crusade that he saw as involving their own freedom as well as that of enslaved Blacks. Others, such as the leadership of the New York branch of the American Anti-Slavery Society, did not. Women gathering petitions was well and good, but the controversy that attached to women speaking and acting in the same roles as men, they felt, distracted from the movement's abolition message.

Angelina Grimké was among the women who played active public roles in abolitionism. She spoke at the Pennsylvania Hall the day the just-opened building was burned down in May 1838. She had married Theodore Weld the day before. Following the building's dedication, the next two days of meetings there were held as the Second Annual Meeting of the Anti-Slavery Convention of American Women.

Large crowds, including hecklers and occasional brickbat throwers, gathered outside each day. Tensions existed inside the convention, as well as on the streets, about women speaking "promiscuously" in public to an "amalgamated" gathering of men and women. The contingent from New

York, closer to the movement's clerical wing, opposed the practice. Those from Boston and in Philadelphia who aligned with Garrison favored it. The convention had held the issue at bay during its meetings, but a decision was made that it would not sponsor the next day's gathering on May 17, where women would address a mixed audience.[49] During the day a hostile crowd estimated at up to 10,000 surrounded the building. Grimké was among those who spoke, even as chunks of broken bricks occasionally crashed through the windows. That night, once the meeting was over, the crowd ransacked and then burned the building.

Grimké had been drawn to Garrison's adamant stand on abolition a few years earlier. In 1836 she wrote an *Appeal to the Christian Women of the South* reflecting those views. With support from Weld and Garrison, she and her sister Sarah were the first two women to attend a training conference held by the American Anti-Slavery Society. From there they took to the lecture circuit, attracting audiences by the boldness of women speaking out in public and the authenticity of their message, given that they came from a South Carolina slaveowning family.

Lucretia Mott was also present at Pennsylvania Hall in 1838. A native of Nantucket, Massachusetts, she began her career in the cause as a young Quaker minister traveling extensively with an antislavery message emphasizing the divine that existed in all people, women and men alike. Relocated in Philadelphia, she and her husband, James Mott, were among those who raised funds to build Pennsylvania Hall. She had helped found the female antislavery society there, working closely with Blacks and whites in the community and assisting runaway slaves. Her address at the hall was interrupted by brickbats breaking through the windows, but she continued to speak. As Pennsylvania Hall burned, she and her husband took Garrison and others into their home as guests, hoping that the mob would not next descend on them there.[50]

Two years later Mott left for London with Garrison to attend the World Anti-Slavery Convention as one of six female delegates. When that convention ruled against seating women delegates, Garrison joined her in a segregated area roped off to accommodate the women who were not allowed to vote on or address the proceedings. While there, Mott met Elizabeth Cady Stanton, who was in London on her honeymoon with

Lucretia Mott. COURTESY OF THE LIBRARY OF CONGRESS.

Angelina Grimké. COURTESY OF THE LIBRARY OF CONGRESS.

Sarah Grimké. COURTESY OF THE LIBRARY OF CONGRESS.

Lydia Maria Child. COURTESY OF THE LIBRARY OF CONGRESS.

Elizabeth Cady Stanton. COURTESY OF THE LIBRARY OF CONGRESS.

Susan B. Anthony. COURTESY OF THE LIBRARY OF CONGRESS.

her husband, Henry Stanton, an antislavery orator and journalist. She later described her meeting with Mott as "an entirely new revelation of womanhood."[51] They found themselves in agreement that the antislavery movement's principles of human and civil rights should apply not only to enslaved Blacks but to women as well. The idea arose of the need for a women's rights convention. They began a lifelong friendship.

Elizabeth Cady met Henry Stanton through his friendship with her cousin Gerrit Smith, who was later identified among the Secret Six who purchased arms for John Brown's 1859 raid at Harpers Ferry designed to spark a slave revolt.[52] At her wedding Stanton refused to use the words "promise to obey" because she believed that she was entering a relationship of equals. When the couple moved to Boston, they mixed and worked with a network of antislavery agitators including Garrison and Frederick Douglass, who had recently escaped from his bondage in Maryland. The couple later moved to Seneca Falls, New York.

Eight years after they had first discussed the idea, Elizabeth Cady Stanton organized the Seneca Falls Conference with Lucretia Mott and others, initiating the American women's rights and suffrage movement. Stanton made major contributions to the *Declaration of Rights and Sentiments* issued there. The document's proclamation of the equality of women with men and call for female suffrage gave early impetus to the decades-long drive that resulted in the 1920 constitutional amendment securing women's right to vote. Douglass was among the conference speakers. Three years after the conference, Stanton was introduced in Seneca Falls to the thirty-one-year-old Susan B. Anthony.

Born into a Quaker household in Adams, Massachusetts, Anthony gathered signatures on antislavery petitions in 1837 at the age of seventeen early in John Quincy Adams's campaign against the House gag rule. Several years later she moved with her family to a farm near Rochester, New York. Sunday dinners there could be like seminars on the nation's reform movement. Garrison attended at times, speaking not just about abolition but his convictions as a pacifist as well. For all the southern outrage that he incited slave insurrection, Garrison was unwavering on the path of nonviolence. Temperance was another topic of frequent discussion. Stanton was drawn to the issue and later became a leader in linking the women's and temperance movements together, in large part due to the physical and psychic abuse and the material damage drunken husbands inflicted on their wives and children. Frederick Douglass and his family, who lived near the Stanton farm, were frequent guests there.

After moving to Rochester, Douglass began publishing his first newspaper, the *North Star*, under the motto "Right is of no Sex—Truth is of no Color—God is the Father of us all, and we are all brethren." In 1856 Stanton became the American Anti-Slavery Society's state agent in New York, where she pursued women's rights and abolition of slavery together. After the Civil War, Anthony and Stanton forged the core leadership of the women's suffrage movement. Before then, while still in Rochester, that city had become one of the main transit points north for the Underground Railroad, centered in New York City. Both Anthony and Douglass assisted runaway slaves. One of Anthony's diary entries noted "Fitted out a fugitive slave for Canada with the help of Harriet Tubman."[53]

That entry points to an additional aspect of the abolitionist movement: the agency it gave to Black men and women in the fight to end slavery. Frederick Douglass and Harriet Tubman were among them. He became the most renowned abolitionist lecturer in the North. His *Narrative of the Life and Times of Frederick Douglass* was a best seller on its publication in 1848. The fuller chronicle of his life, *My Bondage and My Freedom*, first published in 1857, remains in print to this day. Scores of other Blacks who had escaped from slavery wrote or were assisted in publishing their own accounts that were distributed by the tens of thousands of copies throughout the North by abolitionist presses. Some of the escapes were accomplished alone, like the final one of Henry Bibb, after being captured and re-enslaved, that he recounted in a widely read 1849 narrative.[54] Other runaways were assisted by the Underground Railroad which was detested in the white South for its deliberate subversion of the fugitive slave laws.

The Underground Railroad in New York City was first organized by David Ruggles. A free Black man born in Norwich, Connecticut, Ruggles spent two years as a mariner before settling in New York. He ran a grocery store there and became an agent for *The Emancipator*. In 1833, when the New York Anti-Slavery Society created a Committee of

Harriet Tubman. COURTESY OF THE LIBRARY OF CONGRESS.

David Ruggles, flanked by New York Vigilance Committee and Manumission Society members, confronts a Virginia slaveholder. COURTESY OF THE LIBRARY OF CONGRESS.

Vigilance, Ruggles was put in charge. The committee's avowed aim was to assist Blacks who were kidnapped on the streets of New York from being shipped south into slavery. Just as well known, but not as openly described, was the committee's complicated work of creating a network, the metaphorical railroad, by which runaway slaves could safely reach the North. Ruggles's shipboard experiences along the eastern seaboard's port cities gave him a wealth of contacts among Black seamen and dock workers willing to assist in the work. Escaped slaves who made their way to Baltimore or Washington, D.C., were spirited to their destinations aboard ships and ferries bound for New York or Philadelphia. Some hid out in the cargo hold; others posed as crew members or were given protection by sympathetic ship captains. Frederick Douglass was one of those who used the Baltimore to New York sea-lane to find his way to Ruggles's door in September 1838. Ruggles hid and cared for him, gave him some cash, and arranged for Douglass's transit to New Bedford, Massachusetts. Sometime later Ruggles was present at Douglass's wedding. "He was a whole-souled man," Douglass later recalled of Ruggles, "fully imbued with a love of his afflicted and hunted people."[55]

Scraping up funds where he could, often living hand to mouth, Ruggles opened a bookstore and did printing jobs. He published antislavery tracts, some of which he wrote himself. In 1835 he wrote *The Abrogation of the Seventh Commandment*, an attack against religious justifications of slavery and the "licentiousness" of slaveholding society. "Would Northern Christian ladies," he asked, "for one day tolerate the adoption of a system, which would recognize as their domestic servants, the spurious offspring of their own husbands, brothers, and sons, borne under their own eyes by their constant female attendants?"[56] He edited and published his own antislavery newspaper, the *Mirror of Liberty*, for two years.

Ruggles's most influential publication, however, was his painstakingly compiled and frequently updated *Slaveholders Directory*. The work was a manifest of lawyers, judges, police officers, marshals, and others who were complicit in the kidnapping of free Blacks or amenable to helping capture runaway slaves. Ruggles learned from his grapevine along the city's wharfs and rail depots when slave catchers arrived from the South. He tracked them to where they boarded, confronted them with other

Black men in their attempts at apprehension, helped free those they had captured from their grasp, and not a few times had to fight his way out of a violent scrum. He called his work "practical abolition."[57] Within the city, Ruggles and the Vigilance Committee enlisted abolitionist lawyers to defend runaway and kidnapped Blacks. Outside the city, he built up a reliable network of contacts, couriers, and safe houses reaching west into Philadelphia, northward to Utica, Syracuse, and Rochester, and eastward along the coast from Norwalk to Boston.

His health failing and after a legal rift with the antislavery society in 1839, Ruggles left New York. He settled in Northampton, Massachusetts, where nine years later he died at the age of thirty-nine. Exactly how many Black men and women owed their escape to freedom, in some measure, to Ruggles in unknowable. He later estimated the number at about 600.[58] From the time Ruggles began the Vigilance Committee up to 1860, an estimated 3,000 to 4,000 runaways reached freedom through the Underground Railroad's central transit point in New York.[59]

In Philadelphia, a Vigilance Committee was created in 1838 modeled on Ruggles's example. The city's long Quaker antislavery tradition and its proximity to the Maryland border made it a natural destination for runaway slaves. By 1852 the committee had grown dysfunctional, and a reorganization was decided upon. William Still, then thirty-one years old, was made committee chair.[60] He was born in Medford, New Jersey, one of eighteen children of parents who had escaped slavery. He moved to Philadelphia, first finding work as a janitor and, later, a clerical assistant in the offices of the Pennsylvania Anti-Slavery Society. Nearly all the work done by Ruggles and other vigilance committees in Pittsburgh, Syracuse, and Detroit was done with scant attention to record keeping. Impressions drawn from the past of how the Underground Railroad operated, based on a core of Black men, assisted by Black women and whites, were recorded later.

The work was dangerous. Slave catchers in the North were just as ready to use violence as slave patrols in the South. Contacts with escaping slaves were often fleeting, a rendezvous at night, trekking across fields and along back roads in rain or snow, then a drop-off at the next safe house along the way. Writing down any of this carried the risk of its being seized and used in court against those violating the fugitive slave statutes. Most of the Underground Railroad's history, of those who ran it and those who reached freedom by it, has vanished. Historian Eric Foner has provided the best contemporary account in *Gateway to Freedom*.

One of William Still's contributions was to publish a history of what he experienced during his years with the Philadelphia Vigilance Committee. Published in 1872 from his own notes and records, some of them hidden away for decades, *The Underground Rail Road* provides vivid first-hand accounts of how the escapes were actually carried out. His record of an escape that began on Christmas Eve of 1855 is one of the most telling. Six slaves, two men on horseback and four others, including two women in a commandeered wagon, had traveled nearly 100 miles to the Cheat River in Maryland when they encountered six white men and a boy on the road. After a tense parley, both sides drew weapons. The fugitives swore

A BOLD STROKE FOR FREEDOM.

Depiction of Blacks escaping to freedom facing down armed whites from a scene described in William Still's book *The Underground Rail Road*. COURTESY OF THE LIBRARY OF CONGRESS.

they would not be taken alive. As he pointed the muzzle of his gun at one of the Black women, one of the white men said that he would shoot. She shouted, "Shoot, shoot, shoot," aiming her own double-barreled pistol back at him in one hand, holding a dirk in the other. She would rather die than surrender her flight to freedom.

Both sides backed off. The four Blacks in the wagon moved on. The two on horseback were soon captured, according to subsequent newspaper accounts that tell the story in similar detail. Frank Wanzer was one of the four who escaped, aided first by the Philadelphia and later by the New York Vigilance Committees until they reached sanctuary in Toronto. But the fate of his sisters, left enslaved in Virginia, haunted him. On his own, he made his way back by train and on foot, where he brought out one of his sisters and three others, risking a gauntlet of "assassins, prisons and penitentiaries, bailiffs and constables" to realize their freedom.[61]

Harriet Tubman understood the family ties that drew Frank Wanzer back into the land of slavery. After her own escape as a slave in 1849, Tubman returned to Maryland's eastern shore of the Chesapeake Bay repeatedly to lead members of her own family out of slavery. She made the clandestine journey thirteen times or more, helping some seventy Black men and women including her own kin to reach freedom. She aided several dozen more with information about escape routes and safe houses along the Underground Railroad to the north.[62]

No one in American life better epitomized the model of "practical abolition," or was more willing to run the risks needed to achieve it, than Harriet Tubman. She was born Araminta "Minty" Ross on a Maryland plantation, probably in 1822, the fifth of nine children of the slaves Harriet Green and Ben Ross. She was beaten so badly as a child house servant that the scars on her back lasted for life. A head injury suffered as a girl left her with lifelong spells of suddenly falling into a deep sleep. She heard voices in her mind, suffered incapacitating headaches, and late in life bit down on a bullet as a doctor sawed through her skull in an operation to ease the suffering. As a field hand she plowed and chopped wood. In 1844 she married John Tubman, a free Black, taking on her mother's name of Harriet. By the early 1840s she was hiring herself out, becoming resourceful enough to buy her own pair of oxen and a wagon to take on plowing jobs or haul timber and other products. In the process, she came to know the back roads and stream crossings, the inlets where flat-bottomed boats and ferries docked, the pilots and seamen who ran them, and the free and enslaved Blacks who lived throughout Dorchester County's Chesapeake Bay area. It was as if she was unintentionally creating a mental map of the area studded with contact points where free Blacks lived and how plantation slave quarters were laid out.

In 1849, on learning that her owner intended to sell her, Tubman escaped, making her way to Philadelphia. Almost immediately she decided to go back to begin bringing her brothers and sisters, their spouses and children, and eventually her parents to freedom in the North. Most of those she helped to free ultimately made their way to new homes in Canada. Tubman, however, maintained a home for nearly a half century near Auburn, New York, one sold to her by future Lincoln cabinet member William Henry Seward. The residences of both were Underground Railroad safe houses.

Historian Kate Clifford Larson has provided the best modern rendition of Tubman's life in her book *Bound for the Promised Land*. The accounts are harrowing. Tubman often began her journey by rail to Baltimore—once, at least, holding a pair of live chickens to pass as a servant on a routine errand. Making her way south to Dorchester County, Tubman linked up with those set for escape, often via coded messages exchanged in letters beforehand. She preferred making these runs during the winter months when the longer nights offset the discomforts of snow, sleet, and cold along the back roads and byways she traveled. Once, on reaching a stream in the night that the four men with her were reluctant to cross, she waded in water up to her shoulders to the other side, nearly catching pneumonia. The men followed. During another escape, she led three men who had bounties on their heads totaling $2,600, a hefty sum at the time, along with a woman whose master had given her infant child to his nephew as a gift before the younger man left for Missouri.

The North Star was Tubman's guide. She and those with her might have use of a wagon, or walked nearly 100 miles on an easterly route through Delaware north to Philadelphia, and then rode by rail on to New

York. Other escapes were made first by boat to Baltimore, then on to freedom in the North with the aid of conductors along the Underground Railroad. She had no time for whimperers. Tubman carried a pistol. She never used it against her pursuers but once pointed it at one of her weary charges, telling him "Brother, you go on or die."[63] As she saw it, "a live runaway could do a great harm by going back, but that a dead one could tell no secrets."[64]

Garrison called Tubman the Moses of her people, a name that stuck. After she agreed to help him plan his raid on Harpers Ferry, John Brown called her General Tubman. During the Civil War she served as a scout and spy for Union troops in South Carolina. After the war she became an advocate for Blacks' rights and women's suffrage. She died, surrounded by family and friends, in 1913.

The political agency the abolitionist movement gave to women contributed to its breakup. A convergence of reasons caused the schism. Garrison's strident attack on the clergy was one. He attacked some of them as "blind leaders of the blind, dumb dogs that cannot bark, spiritual popes . . . they love the fleece better than the flock."[65] Boston churches closed their doors to Garrison. Those seeking to make headway with political abolitionism chafed at Garrison's singular demand for immediatism. The American Anti-Slavery Society's petition push in the rural North had decentralized its power. To top it off, the society was broke. Garrison's effort to elect a woman to the business committee split the society's 1840 convention and the movement with it. He held on to what amounted to a shell organization while his opponents formed the American and Foreign Anti-Slavery Society. For the next two decades leading up to the Civil War, Garrison and his followers were essentially little more than a highly vocal rump group within abolitionism, a decided minority of those dedicated to the cause.[66]

The Liberty Party also emerged from the breakup in 1840, a presidential election year. Led by Leavitt and others, the party nominated James G. Birney for president. Birney, a Kentucky native and Alabama lawyer and planter, was already deeply skeptical of slavery when in 1834, following a long correspondence with Weld, he freed his slaves, declared for abolition, and began printing his own newspaper, *The Philanthropist*, in Cincinnati. The party was a loose amalgam of interests. Political abolitionists in Washington, D.C., and New York City were joined by most city Blacks and a swath of evangelicals in northern farming communities around a platform centered on opposition to the Slave Power broadly projected as threatening to northern economic and political interests.

President Martin Van Buren was nominated for a second term by the Democrats, but after the economic collapse following the Panic of 1837, his reelection prospects, which were dismal to start with, never improved. William Henry Harrison was the Whig choice for president, with Virginian John Tyler his vice-presidential running mate in a campaign that still ranks as one of the nation's most content-free festival of political fluffery on record. Harrison's success as an Indian fighter in defeating the Shawnee at the Battle of Tippecanoe was inflated to Jacksonian proportions of military prowess. The candidate's chief object during the campaign was to say as little as possible.

The campaign, on the other hand, celebrated Old Tippecanoe's rise to martial fame from humble log cabin origins and his common man's taste for hard cider straight from the barrel. Bands and floats carrying log cabin replicas and plenty of hard cider paraded past bonfires at night and led the way to barbecues during the day, where more hard cider flowed freely. No matter that instead of humble beginnings, Harrison was born into the Virginia aristocracy, his father a signer of the Declaration of Independence, and that the old warrior was a teetotaler. The campaign was a joyful farce. The Whigs won resoundingly, taking both houses of Congress and the presidency. The Liberty Party trailed far behind, gaining only 7,000 votes. But a fuse had been lit that soon would lead to a national blowup over Texas.

"Liberty and equality are new things under the sun," George Fitzhugh wrote in a pamphlet published in 1850. He was right. The North American experiment in government based on those principles were of recent origin. Great Britain only approximated the model with its mixture of

George Fitzhugh. SOURCE: WIKIMEDIA
COMMONS/ENCYCLOPEDIA OF VIRGINIA.

monarchy and parliament. As Fitzhugh saw it, the "experiment has
already failed."[67]

Fitzhugh was among the white South's leading proslavery intellects
and writers. Of relatively modest means, he practiced law and wrote
voluminously for various southern periodicals from the bat-infested Port
Royal, Virginia, mansion he shared with his wife. His main contribution
was not simply to justify slavery, but to condemn the entire structure of
northern freedom. Not only was slavery a positive good, he maintained,
but the liberty and equality practiced in the North were an absolute
disaster. Fitzhugh switched the onus of perceived evil away from slavery
and onto the North. His premise was that the Enlightenment attempt
to "establish a new order of things on the ruins of feudalism" was a bust.
Freeing labor from capital, he argued, unleashed class conflict in which
workers were ground down and left without security by a more powerful moneyed class able to bid down wages to secure even greater power.

Social conflict prevailed in this system that would inevitably lead to mass upheaval and the system's overthrow.

By contrast, he continued, white southern society in which capital owned the labor of slaves "is a natural, healthy and contented state. Such was very much the condition of society in middle and southern Europe two centuries ago, before feudalism disappeared and liberty and equality were established."[68] His critique of the North was premature but prescient. A dominant trend in the American experience for nearly a century after the Civil War was the conflict between labor and capital that culminated in the redefinition of government and capitalism by the 1930s, averting the upheaval that Fitzhugh predicted.

The more relevant point in Fitzhugh's time was his argument that the white South's slave-based hierarchy was a superior form of social organization, conferring mutually reciprocal responsibilities on slaves and masters, thus providing stability and assuring economic progress. From this perspective, the white South's peculiar institution need not be bemoaned as a burden entailed from the past but the modern iteration of accumulated social wisdom stretching back for millennia. This was unapologetic ground on which to stand. Much of the white South, especially the planter elite, adopted it.

To modern eyes, the white South's proslavery arguments look like layers of exculpatory plaster troweled over the face of slavery and the white supremacist doctrine it was based upon. Proslavery doctrine existed for all of about twenty-five years. It did not have a deep temporal foundation or a long-tested structure of practice. The doctrine, rather, was whipped together quickly to meet a crisis of conscience and outside attack. It collapsed within the lifetimes of most of those who built it. It relied on a legacy of presumed Arcadian pastoralism reflected in the white South's construct of a harmonious patriarchy between slave and master. The construct was a myth and the doctrine a delusion. While they existed, both deepened their hold on much of the white southern imagination even as the crisis between slave and free grew more acute.

Forays into proslavery argument arose in the Missouri statehood crisis and from such southern leaders as James Henry Hammond early in the House gag-rule debates. The first full-length exegesis of proslavery doctrine came from the pen of Thomas R. Dew. A professor and later president of the College of William and Mary, Dew wrote his seminal work in the wake of the Virginia Assembly's emancipation debates of 1831–1832. His *Review of the Debate* unleashed a torrent of slavery justifications that poured forth from the white South's intellectual elite in books, pamphlets, and essays appearing in the *Southern Literary Messenger, Southern Quarterly Review, De Bow's Review,* and other leading publications and newspapers in the South.

Unlike abolitionist writings directed both north and south to respectively persuade and provoke, the onrush of proslavery argument was directed mainly at the master class of planter elites. The North paid scant attention, often to the disgruntlement of the white southern intelligentsia. As if emerging from a chrysalis, proslavery thought first shucked off the old necessary evil, entailed burden construct, then developed a biblical and historical rational of validity, and finally transformed itself into the full-blown vision of white southern society being the realization of divinely inspired morality and proper social organization: the doctrine of white supremacy.

Dew's early condemnation of the slave trade as a palpable evil would not stand the test of time in the antebellum white South. But much of the rest of his thinking did. His principal object was to prove that every "plan of emancipation and deportation . . . is *totally* impracticable." To reach this conclusion, he first trotted out the already familiar proslavery concepts of historical precedent and biblical sanction that generations of white southerners would be able to recite by rote as occasion arose. Both the historical citadel of democracy and its standard of empire and order were based on slavery. "In the ancient republics of Greece and Rome," he wrote, "where the spirit of liberty glowed with most intensity, the slaves were more numerous than the freemen." This historical precedent extended further back to the chosen of God. "Slavery was established and sanctioned by Divine Authority," Dew wrote, "among even the elect of Heaven—the favored children of Israel, Abraham . . . the chosen servant of the Lord, was the owner of *hundreds* of slaves." From these depths of human experience, Dew reasoned, "Well then might we have concluded . . . *that* [slavery] *marked some benevolent design and was intended by our Creator for some useful purpose.*"[69]

The Creator's design was evident to Dew. Slavery, he wrote, was "the principal means for impelling forward the civilization of mankind." By its agency primitive man was tamed, his "habits of indolence and sloth" destroyed, and his character of "improvidence and carelessness" eradicated. That some savages did not survive the process of breaking and taming them was unfortunate, Dew allowed, but in the end, civilization prospered from the bounties of the labor of those who did. Under slavery, "man no longer wanders through the forest in quest of grain," he wrote. As a result, the woman "is relieved from following on his track," and instead "becomes the cheering and animating centre of the family circle." Dew clearly confused the roles of white and Black women in drawing this portrait. Slave women had to follow in the furrow tracks plowed by men before them. Be that as it may, in Dew's benign world, once savages were broken and tamed, "time is afforded for reflection and the cultivation of all those mild and fascinating virtues, which throw a charm and delight around our homes and firesides, and calm and tranquillize the harsher tempers and more restless propensities of the male."[70] Civilization thrives.

Turning to the more immediate situation in the South, Dew curtly dismissed free Blacks as "the most worthless and indolent of the citizens of the United States . . . the very *drones* and *pests* of society." The fewer of them, the better. He then proceeded to demonstrate that slaves are "not only *economically* but *morally* unfit for freedom." Kept right where they were, however, Dew wrote, "we have no hesitation in affirming, that throughout the whole slave holding country, the slaves of a good master, are his warmest, most constant, and most devoted friends. . . . A merrier being does not exist on the face of the globe, than the negro slave. . . . Why, then, since the slave is happy, and happiness is the great object of all animated creation, should we endeavor to disturb his contentment by infusing into his mind a vain and indefinite desire for liberty?"[71]

Dew's white supremacist construct, and that of the host of proslavery writers who followed him, was an illusion, but seductive enough to capture much of the white southern mind. Aspiration replaced reality. The benign master and contented slave, bonded by mutual affection and ordered in a hierarchical structure of reciprocal responsibilities, became the white South's model of slavery, making what it wanted to see what it did see.[72] One reality that was more difficult to obscure was Thomas Jefferson's legacy of words.

Those pesky words again that would not go away: the boisterous passions slavery aroused in masters, the Creator's certain judgment in the scales between slave and master, and especially the proposition that all men are created equal and are endowed with unalienable rights to life and liberty.

It is commonplace now to think or speak of rights to life and liberty as God (no matter how that word is defined) given, or as birthrights of citizenship. The state may abuse or trample upon these rights, but they still adhere. Contemporary America has lost a sense of just how revolutionary this Enlightenment concept was in the early republic, or, indeed, in the world. The proposition of unalienable rights is an expression of faith, no matter how much its authors derived it from reason. It has no empirical foundation. It is declared to be self-evident. Upon this declaration of faith, the Founders created a government intended to operate as far as possible on reason, employing checks and balances to prevail over the buffeting of private ambitions and popular passions. Yet as respected as the Constitution is as a reasoned guide to self-government, faith that every individual is born equal and has unalienable rights to life, liberty, and the pursuit of happiness remains the animating impulse of the American experience. The white South struggled to overcome, redefine, or eliminate that faith expressed in Jefferson's words for the Blacks living among them.

"Who taught me to hate slavery and every other oppression," Ohioan Thomas Morris asked of his Senate colleagues in 1839. "*Jefferson*, the great and the good Jefferson," he answered. "Yes, *Virginia Senators*, it was your own Jefferson, Virginia's favorite son; a man who did more for the natural liberty of man, and the civil liberty of his country, than any man that ever lived in our country; it was him who taught me to hate *slavery*; it was in his school that I was brought up."[73] No accusation hurled at the slave South was more telling, and perhaps none was more often repeated, than that framed in Jefferson's words. Southern proslavery writers, such as professor of moral philosophy William A. Smith, strove to counter them. "Let us then free ourselves," he wrote. "Let us free the country, of the domination of Mr. Jefferson's philosophy, because it is false . . . and the opposite is true, namely, that the great abstract principle of domestic slavery is, *per se*, RIGHT."[74]

The bare assertion that Jefferson was wrong was not sufficient for Albert Bledsoe. He wrote his nearly 400-page *An Essay on Liberty and Slavery* to make his case. Born in Kentucky, Bledsoe attended West Point with Robert E. Lee and Jefferson Davis, and as a lawyer in Illinois practiced alongside Lincoln and Stephen A. Douglas. He later served as assistant secretary of war in the southern Confederacy. Bledsoe was a professor of mathematics at the University of Virginia when he penned his essay. In it he systematically deconstructs Jefferson's logic and then reassembles it to prove that a natural law of unalienable rights to life and liberty does not exist.

Albert Bledsoe. SOURCE: WIKIMEDIA COMMONS/HATHI DIGITAL TRUST LIBRARY.

He began by turning on its head the Lockean notion of natural rights existing independently of the state. The civil state, he argued, is the author and protector of liberty because, in a state of nature, humans are subject to the brute force of the strongest and, therefore, unable to exercise any right to liberty. The civil state and its authority, he continued, derive from a "decree of God" and an "ordinance of heaven." By restraining tyranny, good government "introduces liberty into the world." By this logic, liberty is not an unalienable right because it is a right given by a divinely ordained state, which creates the order needed to have and enjoy it.

Although all would agree that the state cannot justly take life or liberty without sufficient cause, Bledsoe continued, "the general good is the sole and sufficient consideration which justifies the state in taking either the life or the liberty of its subjects." It follows that when the general good demands a law to deprive a person of freedom, "then such a law is just and good." The truly unalienable right is that conferred "by the Creator, and Governor of the universe" for society "to make such laws as the general good demands. . . . All individual rights are subordinate to this inherent, universal and inalienable right. . . . Hence, if it be shown that the public good, and especially the good of the slave, demands such a law, then the question of slavery will be settled."[75] Bledsoe then drew on the plethora of historical, biblical, and other proslavery arguments to show that the good of white southern society and of slaves themselves did indeed justify slavery. Unalienable rights to life and liberty did not belong to the individual. They belonged to the state. By Bledsoe's standard of the general good, a whole class of people could justly be deprived of their liberty in perpetuity without any one of them being found guilty of any offense.

It is beyond the scope of this work to reflect fully on how views such as those of Bledsoe saw twentieth-century expression in the extermination of undesirables in Nazi-occupied Europe or forced sterilizations of "defectives" in the United States. They both boil down to state supremacy over individual rights. It is enough to say that Jefferson's, not Bledsoe's, words have, so far, survived in this country as a foundation of faith in unalienable individual rights upon which a government based on reason exists.

The white South's immediate judgment on Bledsoe, which gushed from the pages of *De Bow's Review*, found that his work was of "such signal success that not a thread of reason is left" to support abolitionist vituperation. "Accept this theory," the journal continued, "and all the declamation about the original right of liberty, about primeval equality of men, becomes vain twaddle."[76] The Jefferson problem was solved, at least for those who did as *De Bow's* recommended.

As proslavery thought evolved, the institution's historical and biblical justifications were augmented with the argument that it also elevated barbaric Africans to the plain of Christianity, offering them some hope for the salvation of their souls. By the 1850s, however, proslavery writers employed these postulates less frequently as the theory that slavery was a necessary and superior form of social organization took hold. This late strain of the argument not only rejected universal liberty as a failed experiment, but that depicted its embrace of the hierarchical system ruled by the planter aristocracy as implicitly antidemocratic. Slavery ceased to exist before the latter tendency was fully played out, but the indictment of a wage—as opposed to a slave—labor system had resonance even in the North.

"Is there any law in the North requiring those who receive the benefit of the poor man's labor to support him when he is past his labor," the *New York City Working Man's Advocate* asked of its readers in 1844. The capitalist, the paper growled, "has a lash more potent than the whipthong to stimulate the energies of his white slaves: the fear of want." Given this situation, the *Advocate* wanted to know "how much better, then, is the condition of some of our white laborers than some of our black southern slaves?"[77]

These were precisely the points George Fitzhugh was making to his white southern readers to extol slavery there as superior to wage labor in the North. "From their own mouths," he wrote of northerners, "we can show free society to be a monstrous abortion, and slavery to be the healthy, beautiful and natural being which they are trying, unconsciously, to adopt."[78] This strain of rhetoric that marked the late stage of proslavery writings by Fitzhugh and others fed directly into the northern Slave

Power warning that the South intended not only to extend slavery indefinitely, but to have it dominate the entire nation.

Fitzhugh was avowedly reactionary. He drew his exemplar from feudal society that predated the Enlightenment and projected what he saw as his native Virginia's benign form of slavery as the model that pervaded the entire South. Conservatives who guarded the true structure of social order, he wrote, "fight under the banner of faith, wholly rejecting reason when it conflicts with faith in the experience, the lessons, and the authority of the past."[79] That experience showed that compared to the "short-lived experiment of free society," Fitzhugh wrote, "slave society is co-extensive with man in time and space." Further, the history of free society was a catalog, in his estimation, of "crime, famine, ignorance, anarchy, infidelity and revolution."[80]

Fitzhugh's condemnation of the northern free-labor system was absolute. "The free laborer rarely has a house and home of his own," he wrote in his definitive *Sociology for the South or the Failure of Free Society*; "he is insecure of employment; sickness may overtake him at any time and deprive him of the means of support; old age is certain to overtake him, if he lives, and generally finds him without the means of subsistence." As to the southern Black, Fitzhugh held, "he is but a grown up child, and must be governed as a child." Harkening back to Bledsoe's argument, Fitzhugh wrote that the improvidence of Blacks gave society "the right to prevent" them from becoming a social burden "and can only do so by subjecting him to domestic slavery." In the final analysis, he wrote, "the negro race is inferior to the white race." Blacks would be crushed by free competition, he continued, or be "devoured by savages and cannibals" if returned to Africa, while "his slavery here . . . christianizes, protects, supports and civilizes him."[81] This was white supremacists' racism in full flower.

Just as slavery was the Blacks' salvation, Fitzhugh wrote, so, too, was it for northern laborers. Following his own argument to its logical conclusion, Fitzhugh wrote that "the principle of slavery is itself right and does not depend on difference of complexion."[82] An 1856 *Charleston Standard* article that reflected Fitzhugh's thought propounded "Slavery is the natural and normal condition of the *laboring* man, whether WHITE or *black*. . . . Master and slave is a relation in society as necessary as that of parent and child; and the Northern States will yet have to introduce it. Their theory of free government is a delusion."[83] Fitzhugh put the case just as clearly, writing "A state of dependence is the only condition in which reciprocal affection can exist among human beings—the only situation in which the war of competition ceases, and peace, amity, and good will arise. . . . Slavery is natural and necessary, and will in some form insinuate itself into all civilized society."[84]

Fitzhugh's advocacy for white slavery did not gain traction in the white South. What did take firm hold was his argument and that of other proslavery writers that the North's system of free labor and universal liberty was a failure. As the 1850s came to a close, a northern sentiment, fueled by abolitionists, that the entire white South—not just its peculiar institution but the whole region—was alien and threatening, was matched by a similar sentiment in the white South toward the North. The indictments each hurled at the other ultimately created the perception of two distinct peoples, two nations antagonistic to one another, a perception that contributed to the impending onslaught of war.

CHAPTER 8

Texas

THE SWEEPING Whig victory of 1840 did not turn out as planned. A month after his inauguration President Harrison died of what his doctors thought was pneumonia but was more likely septic shock from severe intestinal inflammation. The Virginian John Tyler took over. Tyler bolted from the Democrats when Andrew Jackson prepared to use force against South Carolina's threat of nullification. Whig strategists nominated him for the second spot thinking that as a states' rights slaveowner he would draw southern votes while posing no danger in a job that had little power. He is the only American president who later in life switched his allegiance to a foreign government, serving in the Provisional Confederate Congress before his death in 1861.

Early in his White House tenure Tyler, dubbed His Accidency by many, vetoed Whig legislation shepherded through Congress by Henry Clay. In short order all but one of his cabinet members resigned as the Whigs abandoned him. Tyler was a president without a party. But he was not a president without a purpose. That purpose was to annex Texas, the shaky republic still technically at war with Mexico whose disputed boundaries by its own reckoning covered nearly 400,000 square miles of land.

The road to civil war ran through Texas. The turn the nation took in thrashing out the Texas question was the tipping point in setting in motion a series of events that led inexorably to the conflict.[1] A process emerged from the political maneuvering, Texas statehood, war with Mexico, and acquisition of new territory that altered the nation. Part of the process was a perception that evolved and hardened throughout the 1850s, precipitated by events the Texas controversy initiated. A conviction grew in the North that the white South was not simply seeking to be left unmolested with its slave property. Instead, the Slave Power was increasingly seen as determined to expand slavery indefinitely, demanding finally that even free states could not prohibit the entry of slaves within their borders. This perception, in turn, eroded the alliance that Jefferson initiated of the planters of the South and the plain Republicans of the North, created Jackson's Democratic Party, and prodded the Whigs to forge cross-sectional bonds creating a second party with legitimate national aspirations. Ultimately the Whigs collapsed. Democrats in the North broke from their brethren in the South. A new sectional alliance took hold in the North leading to Lincoln's Republican Party victory in 1860. And the war came.

The struggle over Texas also came at a time when another process began to grip the nation's imagination. Manifest Destiny, as it came to be called, was the belief that the United States was ordained to expand to the Pacific coast and, in the process, spread white America's civilizing and Christianizing influence across the continent. "By the right of our manifest destiny," John O'Sullivan wrote in an 1845 editorial coining the phrase, the United States was entitled to "overspread and to possess the whole continent which Providence had given us for the development of the great experiment of liberty and federative self-government entrusted to us."[2]

Congressman William Giles of Maryland became exuberant when he contemplated the prospect of pushing westward by acquiring territory claimed by Mexico. "We must have it," he told Congress. "Every consideration of national policy calls upon us to secure it. We must march right out from ocean to ocean. . . . We must march from Texas straight to the Pacific Ocean and be bounded only by its roaring wave. We must admit no other Government to any participation in this great territory. It is the destiny of the white race: it is the destiny of the Anglo-Saxon race."[3] Despite resistance from leaders such as John Quincy Adams and Daniel Webster, the tide of Manifest Destiny, promising outlet for the immigrants flowing into the North and fresh land for planters in the South, swept along most of the nation in its wake.

President Tyler had a more personal stake in westward expansion. With no party to back him, Tyler reasoned that he could fashion a winning reelection coalition behind a policy to annex Texas to the union. The policy was sure to entice votes from the South. Properly framed, it could enlist enough northern support to ensure victory in the 1844 election. Tyler opened secret negotiations for a treaty of annexation with the Republic of Texas in 1843. He found his architect for the public presentation of his plan in Mississippi Senator Robert J. Walker. A Pennsylvania native and transplanted Mississippi slaveholding planter, Walker had supported Jackson during the nullification crisis and won his Senate seat in 1835 as a unionist candidate. In that same year, his brother transferred to him some 31,000 acres of land that he had acquired near San Antonio, helping to make Walker a zealous proponent of Texas annexation.[4]

Early in 1844 a *Letter of Mr. Walker of Mississippi Relative to the Reannexation of Texas* appeared first in newspapers, then in a widely distributed pamphlet. The letter was a masterstroke of appeal to all shades of opinion. Texas was to be reannexed, framing the issue as reclaiming something once owned. That was untrue despite Walker's claim that, as secretary of state, John Quincy Adams had exchanged a Louisiana Purchase claim to Texas in return for Spain's cession of the Florida territory. No such title to Texas under the Louisiana Purchase ever existed.

The senator then laid out the dangers to be avoided and benefits gained by acquiring Texas. Without annexation, Britain was sure to become the republic's patron, thus surrendering "the mouth of the Mississippi, the command of the Mexican gulf, and finally Texas itself into the hands of England," he wrote. The opportunities of annexation, however, extended to all in the union. New markets for northern merchants would open to be supplied by northern shipping. Vast stretches of fertile land would become available to southern planters. That outlet would negate a looming danger for the North. If slavery was confined and ultimately collapsed due to soil exhaustion, he warned, "three millions of free blacks would be thrown all at once . . . upon the States of the North," where they would live by theft or charity. "A few might earn a wretched and precarious subsistence by competing with the white laborers of the North," he wrote, "whilst the poor-house and the jail, the asylums of the deaf and dumb, the blind, the idiot and insane, would be filled to overflowing." By funneling slaves to the west, however, Walker foresaw that "they would be diffused gradually through Texas into Mexico, and Central America." Within a decade after annexation, he predicted, Delaware would be free of slaves, Maryland would soon follow, and slavery would be greatly diminished in Virginia and Kentucky.[5]

Not everyone was convinced. Alabama Senator Arthur Bagby noted "The idea of slavery going off by a sort of insensible evaporation into the great desert between Texas and Mexico is, to say the least, preposterous."[6] But Walker's case of something for everyone, whatever its logical fallacies, factual inaccuracy, and blatant racism, had the advantage of telling many people what they wanted to hear. His *Letter* was widely embraced in newspaper editorials and gained purchase among those already inclined to follow Manifest Destiny into Texas.

As annexation worked its way into the mix of presidential election issues, Henry Clay, the presumptive Whig candidate, and Martin Van Buren, seeking to regain the White House atop the Democratic ticket, made their views on it public. By coincidence, both men's letters expressing those views appeared on April 27, the same day a leaked text of Tyler's proposed treaty of annexation with Texas and an explanation of it to the British ambassador were made public. Both candidates stumbled badly. The leaked documents, casting annexation as unequivocally necessary to expand slavery, caused an uproar. Clay came out against annexation but hedged his stance by saying that he could be persuaded otherwise if it could be done without provoking Mexico into war. Later, belatedly realizing how popular annexation had become in the white South, Clay attempted to revise his position. It still amounted to a full straddle. He was caught between northern Whigs opposed to slavery's expansion and southern Whigs demanding it. Clay protested that far from catering to northern abolitionist sentiment against annexation, he sought to protect the union from those advocating measures that could dissolve it. "I should be glad" to see annexation, Clay wrote, if it could be done without war and on just and fair terms.[7]

Depending upon from which section of the country one viewed it, Clay was either beholden to the Slave Power or insufficiently zealous for white southern interests. Van Buren's stumble was worse, at least in immediate political terms, although not for his later reputation. The white South was the Democrats' base. In a prolix letter to a Mississippi congressman, Van Buren urged the same caution over annexation as he had exercised in not pursuing it as president. Annexation might be desirable, he wrote, but should be moved forward only if it became necessary to forestall foreign intervention or could be achieved without disruptive consequences. The man who had fashioned the Democratic Party on the basis of northern accommodation to white southern interests could not now raise his voice in favor of what the white South at that moment wanted most. His break with the Democratic Party was set in motion.

Thomas Ritchie, his friend and partner in creating the party, wrote from Richmond "I am compelled to come to the conclusion that we cannot carry Virginia for you."[8] Van Buren had expressed his own sense of estrangement two years earlier, writing from New York, "The truth is, that the Democrats of this State have suffered so often, and so severely in their advocacy of Southern men, and Southern measures, as to make them more sensitive in respect to complaints of their conduct from that quarter, than I could wish."[9]

Clay's and Van Buren's attempts to distance themselves from annexation coincided with the revelation that the Tyler administration considered it essential to protecting slavery in the South. The declaration came in a letter Secretary of State John C. Calhoun wrote to Britain's minister to Washington, Richard Pakenham. Up to that moment, Tyler's case for annexation had been consistent with Senator Walker's argument that it would serve the entire nation's interests. Calhoun's letter changed that. The South Carolinian had taken over the state department only weeks earlier following the untimely death of his predecessor. His letter to Pakenham expressed deep concern that Britain was attempting to make the abolition of slavery in Texas a condition to recognize the republic's independence. Assurances from America's ambassador to Britain that that was not the case made no difference to Calhoun. If slavery was abolished in Texas, Calhoun wrote, inroads against it in the white South were sure to follow. The United States, he continued, had no choice but to protect itself against such danger. The treaty of annexation, enclosed with his missive, was the result.

Calhoun next launched into a lengthy exposition arguing that free Blacks in the North were far more subject to poverty, deafness, blindness, insanity, idiocy, and crime than the South's slaves who enjoyed "a degree of health and comfort which may well compare with that of the laboring population of any country in Christendom." Slavery, the secretary informed the minister, "is in reality a political institution, essential to the peace, safety and prosperity of those States of the Union in which it exists."[10]

Calhoun's motives for making protection of slavery, and by obvious extension the expansion of it into a new state in Texas, have been debated for decades. In one sense he may have been emphasizing the marker he laid down during the nullification debates of his insistence that the North unequivocally embrace the white South's right to its slaves by creating a reliable congressional balance between northern and southern interests. More immediately, he may have been aiming a shot at his longtime rival, Martin Van Buren. Once the Pakenham letter went public, the New Yorker would be hard-pressed to take a position on Texas that would hold the Democratic Party's cross-sectional coalition together even if he won over enough southern delegates to gain the party's presidential nomination.

Going into the 1844 election, the fledging Liberty Party stuck by James Birney as its nominee. The Whig convention that opened in Baltimore on May 1 proceeded quickly to nominate Clay by acclamation. The delegates chose to ignore the sectionally divisive Texas issue by passing a platform endorsing Clay's American System of internal improvements and tariffs around which the Kentuckian had originally cobbled together the party.

Two weeks later the Democrats gathered, also in Baltimore, a city symbolically situated as a meeting place between North and South. Van Buren, though hobbled by the distraction of Texas, was confident of victory. The party's two-thirds rule, which Van Buren originally designed to assure that the nominee could draw cross-sectional support, had been laid aside. Van Buren knew he had a majority of the delegates. At this point the machinations began. Tyler's friend and Texas stalking horse Senator Walker of Mississippi and fellow Senator James

Buchanan of Pennsylvania, who was eyeing the nomination for himself, worked the delegations to reinstate the two-thirds rule.

On the first ballot, Van Buren won his expected majority but fell short of two-thirds support. His position deteriorated from then on. On the ninth ballot, James K. Polk of Tennessee won the nomination. He had traveled to Baltimore through the Hermitage, where Old Hickory laid the mantle of Young Hickory on his upstart protégé. Although he was coming off twin defeats in bids for the governorship, Polk had served in Congress as Speaker of the House and later as governor of Tennessee. He had stood by Van Buren early in the convention, making him acceptable to the New Yorker when concession became unavoidable.

Most important, Polk captured the sentiment of the hour. He was a spread-eagle advocate of Manifest Destiny, the widely popular cause that suffused slavery within a wider vision of conquering the entire continent between the still amorphous borders of Mexico and Canada. Polk stood

James K. Polk.
COURTESY OF THE
LIBRARY OF CONGRESS.

for Texas annexation and the "reoccupation" of Oregon, where American land claims stretched north through much of the current province of British Columbia. His stance had the symmetry of promising new territory to add both free and slaveholding states to the union. Polk's stand on Texas also gave Tyler a graceful way to bow out of the race that he never had any chance of winning.

When the votes were in, Polk won in a nail-biter. With 2.7 million votes cast, his 38,000-vote plurality over Clay hinged on New York. In that state Polk won by just over 5,000 votes while the Liberty Party captured its largest state tally, just under 16,000 votes. The lesson many Whigs drew was that antislavery Liberty voters had cost them the election. Despite the victory, northern Democrats had reason to worry, too. Antislavery sentiment in parts of Ohio, New York, and New England, although not carrying a majority, was apparent. Polk had run behind the Democratic ticket in several key districts. Open alliance with white southern interests was becoming a liability. The old coalition had held together, eking out a victory, but cleavages began to appear.

Before Polk's inauguration and the convening of a new Congress, the lame-duck session of the old Congress met to complete its work. On the House side, one of the first items of business, on a motion made by John Quincy Adams, was to repeal the gag rule.[11] Tellingly, the repeal passed with the support of nearly 80 percent of the North's Democrats, no longer willing to bear critics at home for suppressing petitions that the white South found distasteful. Old Man Eloquent had fought through nine years of House debate to earn the victory. Just over three years later, he suffered a massive cerebral hemorrhage while casting a vote on the floor. He died two days later, on February 28, 1848, in the Speaker's Room at the Capitol.

President Tyler also had business to complete before he left office. The Whig-dominated Senate had predictably rejected his Texas annexation treaty earlier in the summer. While he still held power, Tyler decided to bypass the constitutional process by which a two-thirds Senate vote was required for treaty ratification. Instead, he sought majority votes in both houses of Congress to approve the annexation of Texas. A welter of proposals sprang from that process.

The bill the president signed on March 1, 1845, was actually two incompatible pieces of legislation, one from the House and one from the Senate, with a provision that the president could decide which one to pursue. The House, where the Democrats had regained a lopsided majority in the 1842 elections, passed a straight-up annexation bill to bring the whole area of Texas into the union, with borders to be decided later. The Senate measure, fashioned with help from Democrats loyal to Van Buren's wing of the party, accepted annexation but only if it was based on further negotiations.

John Niles, a Connecticut senator who had served in Van Buren's cabinet, expressed the frustration among his colleagues, writing "There have been enough northern democrats who have sacrificed themselves to southern interests and I do not wish to see any more."[12] The plan was that Polk would be the president to decide which version to adopt. Senators of Van Buren's stripe were given the impression that the president-elect favored their approach. Tyler signed the bill on March 1. He then stole a march on Polk.

The day before leaving office, he dispatched an envoy to Texas empowered to seek annexation based on the House section of the bill. Polk could have recalled the envoy after he was sworn in the next day, but he did not. Polk was as determined as Tyler to complete the business in Texas, then deal with the consequences later. The new president turned to the two men who had torpedoed Van Buren during the Baltimore convention, installing Senator Walker as treasury secretary and Senator Buchanan as secretary of state. Van Buren's recommendations for presidential appointment were largely shunted aside. The war department went to Van Buren's New York rival, William Marcy. Over the coming summer, Texas voters approved Tyler's offer, which Polk had endorsed. In December 1845 the Lone Star State, with slavery sanctioned by its constitution, entered the union as the twenty-eighth state.

Just two matters remained unresolved. Mexico had never extended recognition to the Texas Republic, let alone to its entering the union. Even if that issue could be resolved, none of the three parties involved had yet agreed with any of the others just what territory fell within the borders of Texas. Mexico claimed that the western border of Texas ran along the

Nueces River. Texas held that the line was a good deal to the west along the Rio Grande, although it had no government offices or agents there. It also claimed a large chunk of what later became New Mexico and portions of the future states of Oklahoma, Kansas, Colorado, and Wyoming. The statehood bill had omitted any delineation of just what Texas was.

Van Buren had urged negotiations all along, knowing that placing Texas annexation ahead of securing Mexican agreement to both recognition and borders was a path to war. In February, Van Buren had written to Polk's soon to be navy secretary George Bancroft, warning him that care must be taken to avoid war about "which the opposition shall be able to charge us with plausibility, if not truth, that it is waged for the extension of slavery." If that happened, Van Buren continued, northern Democrats would "be driven to the sad alternative of turning their backs upon their friends, or of encountering political suicide with their eyes open."[13]

Instead, while Texas proceeded with its own process to accept annexation, Polk directed General Zachary Taylor in June to take 4,000 troops to Corpus Christi, where the Nueces River flowed into the Gulf, and await further orders. He also dispatched an envoy to Mexico, prepared to offer $2 million to settle all claims and throw the purchase of California into the deal. The shaky Mexican government, knowing that it could not withstand a humiliating concession to the United States, refused to receive the envoy, who stayed in the country nonetheless.

Polk's aims were clear. He wanted not only Texas but the whole of Mexican territory, clear to the Pacific Ocean. In March 1846, to up the pressure, Polk ordered General Taylor to cross the Nueces strip and march his troops 150 miles across the disputed territory to the bank of the Rio Grande. U.S. naval ships closed the river's outlet to the Gulf. Taylor aimed his cannon at the buildings in Matamoros across the river, where Mexican forces had begun to mass. "We have not one particle of right to be here," Colonel Ethan Allen Hitchcock, a member of Taylor's staff, wrote in his diary. "It looks as if the government sent a small force on purpose to bring on a war, so as to have a pretext for taking California and as much of this country as it chooses."[14]

That is what happened. On April 24 a firefight broke out when a squadron of sixty-three U.S. dragoons was sent to confront a detachment of Mexican cavalry that had crossed the river north of the town. Eleven U.S. troops were killed. The remainder surrendered. In Washington, D.C., Polk had already decided to ask Congress for a declaration of war. After word reached him of the firefight near Matamoros, he sent Congress a message on May 11 seeking approval to fight a war already existing because Mexico "has invaded our territory and shed American blood upon the American soil."[15] His war declaration was attached as the preamble to a bill to fund the needs of U.S. troops already in the line of fire, making it virtually politically impossible to vote against the measure. Congress acquiesced. The war was on.

To prosecute the war, however, the president first had to resolve the dispute with Britain over Oregon. As a candidate, Polk had favored insisting on America's claim to all the jointly occupied Oregon territory north to a border at fifty-four degrees thirty minutes latitude. Less than a month after the war with Mexico began, Polk resolved the Oregon dispute by agreeing with Britain to a border from the Continental Divide along the forty-ninth latitude that divides Canada from the United States to this day. The British also got Vancouver Island. The border Polk agreed to was nearly 375 miles south of the position he had claimed two years earlier as rightfully American territory when seeking votes from northern expansionists eager to get their share of Manifest Destiny and new free states added in the bargain.

To many northerners, particularly to Democrats in New York still aligned with Van Buren, the pattern could not have been clearer. Their champion had been sabotaged at the Democratic nominating convention. The plan to negotiate for Texas annexation to which they believed Polk had committed himself had been abandoned within hours after he assumed office. Southern stalwarts and northern proslavery sympathizers filled the cabinet that excluded Van Buren's friends after they had carried New York as the keystone to the president's election. American claims to Oregon territory had been signed away. A war with Mexico they sought to avoid was in full swing, presaging a landgrab that might extend slavery to the Pacific. The Slave Power had the bit in its teeth under James K. Polk. At least such was the pattern clear to many.

Historical hindsight has smoothed over many of those sharp edges. Polk had entered the Democratic convention hoping to be Van Buren's vice-presidential nominee, not his usurper. The cabinet picks were not deliberate rebuffs. The president seems not to have known that Marcy, his choice for the war department, was the former president's New York political enemy. The decision to push forward on Texas was driven by concern that prolonged negotiations would draw in the British and possibly lose the prize. Polk did provoke the war with Mexico. As has been noted, he was preparing a war declaration before he learned of the deadly skirmish near Matamoros. He did intend from the outset to use the conflict to demand Mexican land concessions clear to the Pacific. He held a single-minded conviction that his presidency's central mission was to make Manifest Destiny real in the far west. That given, Polk could hardly risk provoking a second war with Britain over the Oregon territory that included what is now the state of Washington, so U.S. concessions there were merely realpolitik.

The white South was not anxious for war—far from it. Calhoun, a senator once again in 1845, had abstained from the vote on the original war authorization bill, fearing that a landgrab in Mexico itself would bring more nonwhites into the population and that the conflict would be politically divisive. Once U.S. troops were engaged, however, the white South rallied to the flag. This more nuanced view of events largely dissolves any conscious Slave Power conspiracy. It is more the view of history, however, than of Polk's detractors who experienced the events.

Eight weeks after the war began, an obscure freshman congressman from northeastern Pennsylvania found the vehicle that galvanized the North's frustrations. Thirty-one-year-old David Wilmot introduced a proviso to the administration's $2 million request for funds to be used in facilitating negotiations with Mexico.[16] The money, as was widely understood, was to acquire from Mexico as much territory as possible beyond Texas's amorphous borders. The Wilmot Proviso provided for the prohibition of slavery in all territory thus acquired. Four days later, on August 12, the House

David Wilmot. COURTESY OF THE LIBRARY OF CONGRESS.

passed the proviso by an eighty-three to sixty-four vote.[17] Wilmot was a Democrat. His measure drew not only Whig support, but assent from other northern Democrats as well. The measure was essentially defensive, a way to counter Slave Power expansionism. The Democrats who supported it were signaling in the most politically decisive way possible that the era of accommodating the white South for the sake of intersectional comity was over. A transformational era in American life began.

The reasons for Wilmot's action had as much lasting influence as the action itself. "I have stood at home, and fought," he told the House in 1847, "against the Abolitionists of the North. . . . I have no squeamish sensitivities on the subject of slavery—no morbid sympathy for the slave." He and other northern Democrats supported Texas statehood and the war to secure it knowing full well that Texas was a slave state. The California and New Mexican territories were another question entirely. Under Mexican law, slavery was prohibited in that territory.[18]

"All we ask in the North is, that the character of its territory be preserved," he said. "There is no question of abolition here, sir. It is a question whether the South shall be permitted, by aggression, by invasion of right, by subduing free territory and planting slavery upon it, to wrest this territory to the accomplishment of its own sectional purposes and schemes?" In words that presaged the 1860 Republican campaign platform, Wilmot said "I am one . . . of those who believe that the future destiny and glory of this Republic depend in a great measure upon letting [slavery] remain within its present limits."[19] In words reflecting the racism of many who, then and later, supported an end to slavery's expansion, Wilmot said "I make no war upon the South, nor upon slavery in the South. . . . I plead the cause and the rights of white freemen. I would preserve to free white labor a fair country, a rich inheritance, where the sons of toil, of my own race and own color, can live without the disgrace which association with negro slavery brings upon free labor."[20]

A decade of abolitionists' emancipation rhetoric had penetrated hardly at all in the North, and virtually not at all among northern Democrats. What did take hold was the abolitionist accusation that the Slave Power aimed at the peculiar institution's untrammeled expansion at the expense of free white labor in free white territory.

Congress adjourned before the Senate could act on the Wilmot Proviso. In the following session, Van Buren ally Congressman Preston King of New York reworked the proviso to ban slavery from all future territorial acquisitions, not just those anticipated from Mexico.[21] During debate on the measure Joseph Root, a Whig member from Ohio, taunted northern Democrats who might side with the white South. They must know, he said, "that any northern man whose vote should be given against the North on that question, must make up his mind to have the scorn and execration of his constituents; to hang his head in shame before his old neighbors; nay, to make his wife ashamed of him." While southerners "were very confident of their power to manage both their black and white slaves," he was there to tell them, "the North never would, never could suffer another foot of slave territory, or another slave State to come into this Union."[22] He was prescient. After Texas had gained statehood more than a year earlier, no new slave states or slave territory entered the union. From then on, the white South's only path to expanding slavery would be to pry open the right to take slaves into free states or territory or to acquire wholly new lands such as Cuba or other parts of Mexico.

A revolt welled up as the proviso debate progressed, a revolt that made many northerners begin rethinking old political loyalties. The revolt did not instantly overthrow the existing party structure that dated back to Jackson's 1828 election. That did not come until years later. Most apparent during the debate was a new determination among northern Whigs and Democrats, conspicuously led by Van Buren's wing of the party, to be on the right side of history concerning slavery's expansion. Congressman King put the case in straightforward terms. "Shall the territory now free which shall come to our jurisdiction be free territory, open to settlement by the laboring man of the free States," he asked, "or shall it be slave territory given up to slave labor? One or the other it must be; it cannot be both." Behind that assertion lay a second premise. "The labor of the free white men and women, and of their children," King continued, "cannot and will not eat and drink, and lie down, and rise up with black labor of slaves: free white labor will not be degraded by such association."[23] For most northerners, King could just as well have spoken of Black labor, whether free or slave.

The familiar complaint of disproportionate slave-state representation also arose. Let slavery stand where it already existed, Massachusetts Congressman George Ashman said "until God in his Providence shall move the hearts of the people to blot it out. But gentlemen . . . who wanted to make new slave States, new Senators, new Representatives, based on slavery, could not expect . . . northern men to stand quietly by" and let it happen.[24] "Sir, *we want no more of that*; and, with the help of God and our own firm purpose, we will have no more of it," Ohioan Robert Schenck told the House.[25]

These were arguments against slavery's expansion, not for its abolition. "It is not a question of Abolitionism," Ohio Democrat Jacob Brinkerhoff said. "We propose nowhere to abolish slavery, or to interfere with it where it exists—nowhere, sir." But as to the new doctrine, that slavery is a positive good and "is to be extended and perpetuated," Brinkerhoff was adamant. "Sir," he said, "we abominate, loathe, abhor the doctrine. The whole people of the North abominate, loathe, abhor the doctrine."[26] As if to put a seal on northern sentiment, New York Democrat Sidney Lawrence introduced resolutions opposing slavery's expansion from ten state legislatures, including Vermont, New York, Pennsylvania, Rhode Island, Ohio, New Jersey, New Hampshire, Michigan, Massachusetts, and Maine.[27] A new standard had been raised around which northerners could rally. End slavery's expansion. Let it stand where it existed, the Constitution recognized it, but do not allow it to grow.

The white South's response in the House ran true to form but was muted in comparison to the onslaught from the North. Congressman Alexander Stephens's reply was typical. The Georgia congressman later became the Confederacy's vice president. He forecast the union's dissolution in response to northern aggression. That threat was predictable, but his address to the House also carried a tone of resignation. "I would rather that the southern country should perish," he said, "that all her statesmen and all her gallant spirits should be buried in honorable graves, than submit for one instant to degradation."[28]

Alexander H. Stephens.
COURTESY OF THE LIBRARY OF CONGRESS.

In the Senate, John C. Calhoun viewed the revolt in the House with deepening concern. His long-held conviction was being vindicated that a cross-sectional Democratic Party was too weak a reed upon which to stake white southern fortunes. As he contemplated his response, fifteen slave states, counting Delaware and Maryland, held a majority in the Senate over thirteen free states. With several northern senators staunchly loyal to the cross-sectional pact, Wilmot's Proviso never had strong Senate support. What Calhoun feared was the future. Four days after the House passed its second version of the proviso, Calhoun took to the Senate floor with a plan. He opened by noting of the slave states "already we are in a minority," referring to membership in the House and in the Electoral College. In point of fact, the slave states had been in a minority in both institutions since the First Congress convened in 1790.

But Calhoun had a broader perspective in mind. Excluding slavery in all future territorial acquisitions would give free states a "monopoly of the public domain," he said, at the expense of the slaveholding states. As he surveyed that territory, Calhoun calculated that twelve to fifteen new states could be created from it. When that occurred the government, he concluded, "will be entirely in the hands of the non-slaveholding States—overwhelmingly." The South Carolina sage demurred from ascribing the exclusionist policy to "blind fanaticism" in the North. Whatever its origins, the policy "is a scheme," he said, "which aims to monopolize the powers of this Government and to obtain sole possession of its territories." He had turned the Slave Power argument on its head. The white South was the besieged one, soon to be defenseless prey to northern antagonism. He then issued a warning, saying "the day that the balance between the two sections of the country—The slaveholding States and the non-slaveholding States—is destroyed, is a day that will not be far removed from political revolution, anarchy, civil war, and widespread disaster."[29]

To forestall that and to save the union, Calhoun next introduced four resolutions. His case rested on the proposition that the territories were "the common property" of the states, the partners making up the union, not the property of the United States as a single entity. From this premise it followed that the national government was no more than an agent for the states and had a positive duty to protect the rights of citizens from all states to enter any of the territories freely, with their property. South Carolina Congressman Robert Barnwell Rhett had made a similar argument a few weeks earlier.[30]

The core of Calhoun's remedy was a resolution declaring unconstitutional any law that would "deprive the citizens of any of the States of this Union from emigrating, with their property, into any of the territory of the United States."[31] Thomas Hart Benton of Missouri, who followed Calhoun on the Senate floor, dismissed the resolutions as a "string of abstractions" offered "to set the world on fire."[32] Calhoun's plan was never put to a vote. Others would not be so dismissive. Alabama lawyer and planter William Lowndes Yancey soon took up the concept of unobstructed emigration, with freedom for the migrant to bring his property with him, into any territory within the United States. The common property rationale evolved into a white southern mantra. The Supreme Court examined the issue more than a decade later in the *Dred Scott* case.

With Calhoun's presentation, the debate produced two competing concepts. Northern Whigs and Van Buren Democrats, influenced by the Slave Power argument, demanded an end to slavery's expansion. The South's leading radical countered with his plan to allow emigration with slave property into all the United States' territory. That proposition was more of a marker than a legislative initiative that stood any chance of becoming law.

The remaining Democrats, the party of President Polk, needed to find a third way. Vice President George Dallas hit upon it in a speech he delivered in Pittsburgh in September 1847. "The very best thing which can be done" about slavery, he said, "will be to let it alone entirely—leaving to the people of the territory to be acquired, the business of settling the matter for themselves."[33] This was old wine in a new bottle, a variant of the Missouri Compromise provision allowing new states south of the compromise line to decide for themselves whether to adopt slavery, the option that was then considered certain.

A few months later Daniel Dickinson took up the idea in the Senate. Dickinson came from the anti-Van Buren wing of New York's Democratic Party, the Hunker faction that had long before decided that silence was Congress's best policy on slavery. He was for leaving "local communities, territories as well as States, to consult their own interests, wishes, and sense of propriety, and to erect or prohibit, continue or abolish, such institutions as may not be repugnant to the principles of the Constitution."[34] In a subsequent address he elaborated on the concept, explaining that the "principle that a distant people, in the formation of a government, need a master to administer restrictions to preserve them from running headlong to ruin in their policy, is founded in a distrust of popular intelligence and virtue." Instead, a policy of popular control "would give to the people of the Territories the rights that belong to them; would turn the vexatious and agitating question of slavery out of Congress, where it has no business, and should never have entered."[35]

A freshman Senator from Illinois, Democrat Stephen A. Douglas, liked the idea of letting the people within the territories "form a constitution and State government as they please."[36] In the run-up to the 1848 presidential election, Michigan Senator Lewis Cass, who was seeking the Democratic nomination, laid out one of the earliest articulations of what would later become known as the doctrine of popular sovereignty. After reviewing the reasons why Congress had no proper role in deciding slavery's status in the territories, he wrote "I am in favor of leaving to the people of any territory, which may hereafter be acquired, the right to regulate it for themselves."[37] The doctrine gave Democrats a policy that could plausibly maintain the cross-sectional alliance. It offered the white South the prospect of slavery's expansion while telling the North that it might also be banned. The doctrine never gained broad support among white southerners who fully grasped that it did not contain the guarantee for slavery's expansion they sought. Stephen Douglas, however, eventually based his political career on being the champion of popular sovereignty, the policy to extract slavery from congressional agitation, calm the country, avoid civil war, and possibly win him the White House.

William Lowndes Yancey also occupied himself with writing a new slavery doctrine in the run-up to the 1848 presidential election. Born in Georgia, as a child following his father's death Yancey was transplanted to Troy, New York, where he was raised by his mother and the Presbyterian Reverend Nathan Sydney Smith Beman. Beman was an ardent

William Lowndes Yancey. COURTESY OF
WIKIMEDIA COMMONS/SOUTHERN HISTORI-
CAL COLLECTION, WILSON LIBRARY, UNIVER-
SITY OF NORTH CAROLINA AT CHAPEL HILL.

abolitionist and friend to such members of the cause as Theodore Weld.
He was also a dictatorial, demanding, and abusive husband and father.[38]

By the age of nineteen, Yancey had made his way back to the South,
where as a resident of Greenville, South Carolina, he openly defended
the union during the nullification crisis. He moved from Greenville to
Cahaba, Alabama, but on a visit back to South Carolina, Yancey shot
and beat a man to death outside a tavern in a fight that vaguely traced
its origins back to the white southern code of honor. Convicted of man-
slaughter, he was freed from serving his full prison sentence by a pardon
from the governor.

He returned to Alabama, setting himself up as a lawyer, newspaper
editor, and planter in the town of Wetumpka and won election to the
Alabama house of representatives and senate. From his youthful days as
a nationalist, Yancey had grown consistently more conservative, his exposure to white southern thought drawing him ever more firmly into the
states' rights camp. As he became active in public affairs, Yancey displayed
a gift for eviscerating sarcasm delivered with calm repose and extraordinary skill as an orator. He fairly mesmerized audiences.

In 1844 he was elected to the House of Representatives where, after
his first speech from the floor, he was challenged to a duel by a member

who was the object of Yancey's derision. In the subsequent face-off both men fired and missed.[39] In Washington, D.C., Calhoun befriended Yancey. He also began a long association with Robert Barnwell Rhett Sr., who shared Calhoun's common property theory. Within a few years Yancey and Rhett became two of the white South's leading "fire-eaters," radical advocates for secession. In 1846 Yancey resigned from Congress, relocating to the Alabama capital in Montgomery, his reputation for recklessness, enormous rhetorical gifts, and growing radicalism for the white southern cause following him.

In preparation for the 1848 presidential election, Yancey wrote the Alabama platform, a set of resolutions intended for adoption by the state Democratic Party in preparation for the May national nominating convention. The platform was both an attack on, and alternative to, the doctrines of ending slavery's expansion and popular sovereignty. Drawing directly from Calhoun's common property resolutions concerning acquired territory, Yancey's version sought assurance "securing an entry into those territories to all the citizens of the United States, together with their property of every description." Adoption of such an assurance would negate any congressional authority to ban slavery in acquired territories.

Next, Yancey's resolutions addressed a pair of related problems. One was the normal practice of continuing to recognize, after acquisition, laws existing in a territory before its acquisition. If this practice held, the Mexican ban on slavery in California and New Mexico would remain in effect after acquisition by the United States. The second problem was what white southerners saw as a Trojan horse lurking inside popular sovereignty. The question centered on whether territorial officials could ban slavery before writing a constitution prior to seeking statehood. The distinction was not an esoteric one. Years might typically pass between the formation of a territorial government and a petition for statehood. If slavery could expand into a territory before a statehood constitution was written, the path was clear to do so. Once established in a territory, slavery would almost certainly be immune from a state constitutional provision banning it.

In the resolutions, Yancey devised his own Trojan horse to deal with the issue. His version was dressed in the reasoning that because territorial governments were agents created by the national government, any action by a territorial government to ban slavery went beyond the scope of delegated constitutional authority. He argued that a territorial government could not do anything the national government was barred from doing. To deal with the problem of Mexico's preexisting slavery ban, Yancey's resolutions provided that "the rights of the Southern people should not be endangered during the period the territories shall remain under the control of the U.S." They then went further to introduce Yancey's Trojan horse.

The 11th Resolution focused on any territorial action prior to the adoption of a constitution seeking statehood. It declared unacceptable any action that restricted citizens from any state "from removing to, or settling in such territory with his property, be it slave property or otherwise." The platform was, in effect, a manifesto of white southern demands to assure slavery's expansion. To enforce these demands, Yancey's resolutions provided that *under no political necessity whatever* would the Alabama delegation support the nomination for president or vice president of any person who did not oppose "either of the forms of excluding slavery from the territories of the U.S. mentioned in the resolutions, as being alike in violation of the constitution, and of the just and equal rights of the citizens of the slaveholding States."[40]

With Yancey's contribution, three competing approaches for dealing with slavery in acquired territory were on the table. The Van Buren wing of the Democratic Party, and many northern Whigs, backed a congressional ban on slavery in the territories to assure that it would not expand but be contained where it already existed. Other Democrats, attempting to retain a base in the South, supported popular sovereignty. Calhoun's common property doctrine and the Alabama platform offered a path to assure slavery's expansion. As it turned out, these three approaches to dealing with slavery dominated American politics up to 1860. In that year the Alabama platform proved to be the tipping point in shattering the Democratic Party and assuring the election of Abraham Lincoln. A dozen years before the Civil War began, the basic terms of the debate leading up to it were set by the controversy over Texas.

At the same time that Yancey was preparing the Alabama platform, the war with Mexico came to an end with the signing, in February 1848, of the Treaty of Guadalupe Hidalgo. Polk, after considerable arm-twisting, had gotten his funding bill to pay for Mexican cessions through Congress, shorn of Wilmot's proviso. The U.S. military had beaten Mexico into submission. New Mexico was easily overrun by General Stephen W. Kearny. The flamboyant General John C. Frémont, with help from the navy, subdued California. General Taylor worked his troops north along the Rio Grande before striking south into Mexico, where his forces held the field after the battle of Buena Vista. Colonel Henry Clay Jr., Henry Clay's son, died there. General Winfield Scott led his forces in an invasion on the Gulf coast at Vera Cruz, then marched west, winning victories at Cerro Gordo and Jalapa before finally entering Mexico City. A year after it began, the war turned sour. Reports emerged of U.S. troops dying of disease and incidents of rape and murder of Mexican civilians. Newspaper accounts of at least twenty-five Mexican civilians being massacred by a detachment of U.S. soldiers at Agua Nueva shocked the nation. By the time it was over, more than 12,500 American troops and at least 25,000 Mexicans had died in the struggle.[41]

But President Polk got what he wanted. For a payment of $15 million, Mexico acknowledged Texas's Rio Grande border and ceded all of what is present-day California, Nevada, and Utah, most of New Mexico, Arizona, and Colorado, and parts of Oklahoma, Kansas, and Wyoming. With the 1854 Gadsden Purchase of 30,000 square miles of southern New Mexico and Arizona, the deal was complete. Including Texas, the United States gained just under 950,000 square miles of land. Mexico was reduced to 45 percent of its previously held and claimed land area. The United States' holdings stretched from sea to sea.

"The members here are divided into the propagandists of slavery, and the advocates for freedom," Joshua Giddings told the House in February 1848. The Ohio Whig was also looking to that year's presidential campaign. "The old party lines are becoming indistinct and uncertain," he said. "New political associations are forming, and have been for years, and the trammels of party are often broken, and their influence disregarded."[42] He was looking, in part, to the final Wilmot Proviso vote in the House, in which all northern Whigs and twenty-two northern Democrats broke with the white South in unsuccessfully voting for it. He was also expressing a conceptual transformation, which more than a decade of abolitionist agitation engendered. Their antislavery, pro-Black argument had been run through the political grist mill and emerged in the North as an anti-expansion and pro-white agenda.

The challenge for abolitionists was whether to embrace the change. Some, such as William Lloyd Garrison, brooked no deviation from the true path, denouncing compromise and the political process that produced it. Others, such as Leavitt and Theodore Weld, were prepared to accept partial victory as a foothold for future gains. As Boston native Charles Sumner saw it, "there is no *real* question now before the country except the Slave Power." His vision may have been saturated by his ardent convictions, but Sumner foresaw the transformation of political parties "in which there shall be one grand Northern party of Freedom."[43] He would soon join with others in an attempt to bring that vision to life.

In May the Democrats got the race for the presidency in full motion with their Baltimore nominating convention. The assembly endured insurgencies from the left and the right before deciding on a candidate decidedly of the middle. Before the convention, the New York state party convention had split into Van Buren's Barnburner faction that supported the Wilmot Proviso and the Hunker faction that did not. The national convention voted to seat both delegations, at which point the Barnburners walked out. Van Buren, architect of the Democrats' cross-sectional coalition, ruefully wrote his son "The unavoidable tendency of the slave question to break the party as a national one [is] something but imperfectly understood by the generality of the northern people."[44] The insurgency from the right came when William Lowndes Yancey moved the adoption of a truncated version of his Alabama platform. Resoundingly defeated, he and a few supporters walked out of the convention. The delegates soon settled on Michigan Senator Lewis Cass. The campaign took his popular sovereignty message to the North, arguing that it would allow for the prohibition of slavery in the territories, and to the white South, suggesting that it could accomplish exactly the opposite.

In June the Whigs held a less-contentious nominating convention in Philadelphia. Henry Clay had thought that this would finally be his year to lead the party he had created to the White House. But his own words crippled him. Before the war ended, Clay had come out against the expansion of slavery in new territories. That position won him plaudits in the North and a cold shoulder in the white South. The convention delegates, dominated by white southerners, above all wanted a winning candidate. To achieve that, they turned to the formula that had worked for them in 1840: a military hero with indistinct political views.

Zachary Taylor, the hero of Buena Vista, was their man. His southern credentials were impeccable. Taylor was a Virginia native who owned a large slave plantation in Louisiana. His military record was even better,

Zachary Taylor. COURTESY OF THE LIBRARY OF CONGRESS.

stretching back to the War of 1812 and service in the Second Seminole War, where he earned national attention as Old Rough and Ready. Buena Vista, a battle largely fought by subordinates acting beyond the reach of his direct command, added fresh luster to his martial fame.

As a citizen he had never voted. While directing military operations in the Mexican War, he had parried overtures from Whigs and Democrats alike with the posture that he was a man above parties and factions. He had the added attraction of being plain spoken and without pretention. In short, Taylor was a man of proven devotion to his country upon whom the electorate could project varying shades of political conviction. The convention helped to ensure that result by adopting no platform. Taylor was nominated on the fourth ballot. To secure sectional balance, New Yorker Millard Fillmore was named the vice-presidential nominee.

What happened next was the coalescence of an amalgam of seemingly disparate political forces into a short-lived but influential third party. Political abolitionists joined with the fragments of northern Whigs and Democrats who had been knocked out of their party's traditional orbits of cross-sectional harmony by controversies over the war and slavery's expansion. Salmon Chase played a significant role in stitching together the new party. An Ohio lawyer, Chase had won a reputation as one of the nation's leading defenders of fugitive slaves and those who aided them. In 1840 he abandoned the Whigs to help form the Liberty Party in Ohio. By 1848 he saw an opening to take advantage of the fissures that had calved northern Democrats from their traditional loyalties, win over disaffected Whigs, and unite them with political abolitionists like himself into a common front. He reached out to Van Buren to test the water. He persuaded the Liberty Party's presidential nominee, who had been selected the year before, to be ready to step aside if efforts to create a broader-based antislavery party proved successful. Building on conventions in Utica, New York, among the Barnburners and in Worcester, Massachusetts, of dissident Conscience Whigs, Chase engineered a call for a coalition convention in Buffalo on August 8. Twenty thousand people showed up.

Van Buren's Democrats had the heft of numbers while Liberty Party members and their Whig allies such as Giddings, known as Conscience

Whigs, carried the distinction of being the original standard-bearers of the antislavery cause confronting the Slave Power. Frederick Douglass and Henry Bibb addressed the mass gathering to roars of approval and applause. A committee of 500 was formed to draft a platform and rivet the factions together. The Free Soil Party was born, uniting the North's support of free white labor with opposition to slavery's expansion into the territories. Van Buren accepted the convention's presidential nomination, made unanimous on a motion offered by Joshua Leavitt. That decision was balanced by the choice of Conscience Whig Charles Francis Adams, John Quincy's son, as vice president.

Chase led in drafting the platform. "We accept the issue which the Slave Power has forced upon us," the document stated, "and to their demand for more Slave States and more Slave Territory, our calm but final answer is, No more Slave States and no more Slave Territory."[45] A Garrisonian call for immediate and complete abolition was never considered. Nor did the platform take a position on racial equality or women's rights. It pledged noninterference with slavery in the states where it already existed. The federal government, the platform stated, had a duty "to relieve itself from all responsibility for the existence or continuance of slavery" wherever it had constitutional power to do so, a pledge to fight for abolition in the nation's capital.[46] A call for free grants of land to settlers in the public domain rounded out the platform planks.

Under these pledges the party entered the fray under the banner of Free Soil, Free Speech, Free Labor, and Free Men. However the final ballots might be cast, for the first time a face was put on an avowedly antislavery, sectional political party drawing support, however fragile, from diverse strands of northern opinion. As *The Emancipator* summed up, "the Barnburners have their choice for the Presidency, the Conscience Whigs theirs for the Vice Presidency, and the Liberty men have their principles—the platform."[47]

The 1848 presidential election was the first in which all votes were cast on the same day, November 7. No candidate won a majority. Taylor eked out a slim plurality with 1.36 million votes against Cass's 1.22 million but a strong Electoral College majority of 290 to Cass's 127. Van

Buren, who did not carry a single state, trailed with 10 percent or just under 300,000 votes. Chase won election to the Senate as a Free Soiler, as did nine of the party's House candidates. Van Buren undoubtedly drew votes away from Cass, but not enough to support a contention that the Free Soil Party was decisive in swinging the election to Taylor. Rather, it may be said in retrospect, the voters generally ran true to form, adhering to well-established voting patterns, unswayed by furor over slavery.

In another light, it may be said of the 1848 election that it was one of those comparatively rare events in which party leaders were ahead of public opinion, rather than scrambling to catch up with it. Slavery in territories hundreds, even thousands, of miles off remained an abstraction compared to the immediate, daily concerns of most voters, North or South. Party leaders and power brokers saw it differently. The fissures caused by the controversies surrounding the war with Mexico may have been at the margins, but they were real and portentous. The Whigs fielded a candidate of safe white southern credentials but politically innocuous enough not to offend the North. The Democrats chose a campaign that could essentially speak out of both sides of its mouth to different constituencies in the North and the white South. The dynamic in both cases was to obscure or bridge differences over slavery that remained as real after Election Day as before it. The Free Soil Party sought to exploit the rift.

The election marked a directional shift, initial and partial but real, in the nation's party structure. With its base in the North, the Whigs could hardly expect to survive by appeals to the white South. The Democrats had gotten a taste of the difficulty inherent in uniting two regions with a growing divergence over slavery's expansion. The Free Soil Party presented a model that rejected regional coalition in favor of a sectional one. The tectonic plates of American political structure were shifting.

The discovery of gold at Sutter's Mill in Coloma, California, brought urgency to deciding how to organize the newly acquired territories. The Gold Rush that discovery set off in January 1848 funneled some 300,000 foreign and domestic immigrants into the territory who were soon demanding congressional action on a territorial government and statehood. The stage was set for the Compromise of 1850.

CHAPTER 9

The Last Great Compromise
and Bleeding Kansas

THE WEATHER WAS miserable in the nation's capital when Henry Clay called unannounced at Daniel Webster's Massachusetts Avenue home in the early evening of January 21, 1850. The two political warriors, Clay, at seventy-two, and Webster, sixty-eight, had much in common. Stretching back nearly forty years, both had held public office as representative, senator, and secretary of state, each winning national prominence in the process. Both had failed in their ambitions to win the presidency. Both had lost sons in the Mexican War. Neither man had long to live.

In an hour-long discussion, Clay laid out a plan to resolve the issues regarding slavery, North and South, that had festered unresolved since Texas gained statehood. The Kentuckian appeared feeble, coughed constantly, and was almost exhausted as he spoke, symptoms of the tuberculosis that ultimately killed him.[1] He needed Webster to risk his reputation for the sake of a compromise to save the union. To work, Clay's plan required two major concessions from the North: a readiness to abandon the Wilmot Proviso's slavery ban in territory acquired from Mexico and support for a new fugitive slave law. With the backing of a man of Webster's stature those concessions might gain just enough support to pass Congress. Taking that stand would certainly unleash fierce northern attacks.

As they spoke, both men agreed that, in practical terms, slavery was never likely to take hold in either the New Mexico or Utah territories. If the white South could be brought on board with concessions on the Wilmot Proviso and fugitive slaves, the North could win its prize of seeing California quickly admitted to the union as a free state. The question Clay posed was whether Webster was willing to lead the fight for such a compromise in the face of northern brickbats. Before the hour was out, Webster said that he was, "no matter what might befall himself at the North."[2]

Nine days later Clay introduced his compromise proposals in the Senate, the third and final time after Missouri and the nullification crisis that he stepped into the breach as healer between the nation's regional antagonists. In doing so he inaugurated the greatest set piece of high political drama in the history of Congress. With the nation's fate in the balance, the Senate triumvirate of Clay, Webster, and John C. Calhoun expended their last great oratorical broadsides in the cause of public service. The contest riveted the nation. In its course the triumvirate's successors stepped forward from the South, the North, and the West: the mentally and physically rigid proslavery senator from Mississippi, Jefferson Davis; the shrewd and occasionally rash antislavery senator from New York, William Seward; and the prophet of the balm of popular sovereignty to soothe slavery agitation, the Little Giant, five-foot-four-inch tall Senator Stephen A. Douglas of Illinois.

The effort came none too soon. The nation faced a real threat of civil disorder, possibly including disunion. The congressional session opened with a three-week, fifty-nine-ballot snarl over the House speakership decided amid grating sentiments over slavery and sectionalism. After barely forming a territorial government in the Oregon territory, Congress was stalled and fed up with the entire basket of issues pending from Texas: southern members over demands for the Wilmot Proviso, northern members over demands that territories be treated as common property, as open to slaveowners as to anyone else. Texas was threatening to settle its border dispute with New Mexico with gunfire. President Taylor countered by contemplating having U.S. troops open fire on the Texans unless they drew back on their still-unresolved border demands. A decades-old refrain of white southern threats to break up the union was finding its match in the North. "If by your legislation you seek to drive us from the territories . . . thereby attempting to fix a national degradation upon half of the States of this Confederacy, *I am for disunion*," thundered Georgia Congressman Robert Toombs.[3] "I deliberately say," Horace Mann, John Quincy Adams's successor in the House, told his colleagues, "better disunion, better a civil or a servile war—better anything that God in his providence shall send, than an extension of the boundaries of slavery."[4] Early in 1850 Georgia Congressman Alexander Stephens, one of the white South's more thoughtful and moderate voices, wrote, "A dismemberment of this Republic I now consider inevitable."[5]

The problem was exactly what John C. Calhoun had been predicting for three decades. The white South was outnumbered, and the numbers were getting worse. Not only that, but at the same time, just as Calhoun had predicted, abolitionist voices were growing louder and resonating among Whigs and even northern Democrats who opposed slavery's expansion. In the Senate, it was true that slavery existed in half of the thirty states represented, but Calhoun ranked Delaware and Maryland as doubtful. The numbers in the House of Representatives were more indicative. From holding just over 40 percent of the House seats in 1800, the South had slipped to 31 percent in 1850. If doubtful Delaware and Maryland were excluded, the number dropped to 28 percent. Calhoun's South Carolina fell from nine House seats in 1810 to six in 1850. Mighty Virginia was down to thirteen House members in 1850 from a high of twenty-three in 1810.[6]

Those figures reflected the population trends across the country. By mid-century the fifteen slave states had a white population of just below 6.5 million, less than half the more than 13 million whites in the free states. The South's slave population was 3 million.[7] The parity white southerners had counted on in adopting the Constitution was shattered. Prospects in the immediate future were even more dire. All the territories lined up for statehood were free and likely to stay that way. Not a single new slave state lay on the horizon. After California's entry, a host of new free states were in embryo on the free side of the Missouri Compromise line. What had seemed like a white southern victory when the deal was struck to bring Missouri in as a slave state now appeared ready to yield nothing but deepening the white South's minority rank among increasingly hostile free states to the north and to the west. A metaphor was gaining traction in the country that the North's intent was to surround the South with free states so that it, like a scorpion surrounded by a ring of fire, would sting itself to death.

To make matters worse, the white South was shocked to learn that their slaveholding plantation-owner president was unreliable on slavery. "The people of the North," President Taylor said in the summer of 1849, "need have no apprehension of the further extension of slavery."[8] The old general was considering ways to bring California and New Mexico in as free states. He was even willing to accept the Wilmot Proviso if Congress passed it. Mississippi led the white southern reaction. Its call for a southern states convention in Nashville in June 1850 was quickly endorsed by sister slave states. Secession, all knew, would top the agenda. By the winter of 1850, when Henry Clay appeared at Daniel Webster's door, the union was in peril.

"At this moment we have in the legislative bodies of this Congress, and in the States, twenty-odd furnaces in full blast in generating heat, and passion, and intemperance, and diffusing them throughout the whole extent of this broad land," Clay said in explaining his compromise plan before a packed Senate gallery. His object was nothing less than "to settle all the controversial questions arising out of the subject of slavery."[9] Clay's main proposals to accomplish that were to admit California as

Daniel Webster. COURTESY OF THE LIBRARY OF CONGRESS.

Henry Clay addresses the Senate during the 1850 Compromise debate. Daniel Webster is shown seated in the mid-left foreground. John C. Calhoun is standing to the right of the presiding officer's chair. The scene takes place in the Old Senate Chamber. COURTESY OF THE LIBRARY OF CONGRESS.

a free state, organize the New Mexico-Utah territories without slavery restrictions, and pass a new fugitive slave law more amenable to the white South. Ancillary provisions fixed the borders of Texas (essentially along their current lines) while assuming the state's public debt and protecting the interstate slave trade from congressional interference. A ban on the slave trade, but not slavery itself, within the District of Columbia was tacked on as a sop to the North.[10]

"What do you want?" Clay asked in a plea to the North. "Do you want that there shall be no slavery introduced into the territories acquired by the war with Mexico? Have you not your desire in California? And in all human probability you will have it in New Mexico also. What more do you want? You have got what is worth more than a thousand Wilmot

Provisos."[11] Clay was repeating the conclusion that he and Webster had agreed upon in their private January meeting: as a political principle, the Wilmot Proviso was attractive to the free states, but in practical terms it was unnecessary because all of the territory acquired from Mexico was virtually certain to enter the union as free states at all events. In closing his speech delivered over two days in early February, Clay implored the members, and the country at large, to pause "at the edge of the precipice, before the fearful and disastrous leap is taken in the yawning abyss below."[12]

For white southerners such as Mississippi's Senator Jefferson Davis, Clay's compromise was too little, too late. He saw "sectional domination" in it, "nothing short of conquest on the one side, or submission on the other." As if auditioning for the role as Calhoun's successor, Davis recalled the South Carolinian's main line of argument by warning that without a realignment of the balance of power "the great purposes of this Union could never be preserved, the Confederacy must be short-lived, and PERISH."[13]

Calhoun's turn came on March 4. Gaunt, too ill from tuberculosis to speak for himself, he was brought onto the Senate floor in a wheelchair. There his friend Senator James M. Mason of Virginia read his speech for him, a final grim prediction of disunion. The great cause of the nation's discontent, as Calhoun saw it, was that "the equilibrium between the two sections in the Government" that had existed when the Constitution was ratified "has been destroyed." The government itself was the agent of that destruction. First the Northwest Ordinance, then the Missouri Compromise, and most recently the organization of the Oregon territory had all taken "territories belonging to slaveholding powers, and open to the emigration of masters with their slaves" and converted them into exclusive bastions of freedom.

His reasoning was arguably legitimate, if one accepts the plausibility of slaveholders being ready to march their chattel into Minnesota or Montana but for the shackles of government-imposed bans on slavery. But whether the white South had been dispossessed of something it had never actually possessed was beside Calhoun's point that the white South was outnumbered. In his eyes, "what was once a constitutional Federal Republic is now converted, in reality, into one as absolute as that of the

Autocrat of Russia, and as despotic in its tendency as any absolute Government that ever existed." To this burden was added a constant agitation for the abolition of slavery that unless stopped would leave nothing "to hold the States together except force." A glimmer of hope for continued union existed, Calhoun argued, but only on conditions beyond attainment: slavery agitation must cease, fugitive slaves be faithfully returned, the white South given equal rights in all acquired territory, and the Constitution amended to somehow restore the equilibrium that existed when the nation was founded.[14] Calhoun objected, in short, to the nation's entire course of history over the previous six decades.

Calhoun's terms were a demand, New York Senator William Seward replied, "to convert the Government from a national democracy, operating by a constitutional majority of voices, into a Federal alliance, in which the minority shall have a veto against the majority." Invoking words that

William H. Seward. COURTESY OF THE LIBRARY OF CONGRESS.

his predecessor, Rufus King of New York, had spoken during the Missouri crisis, Seward asserted that "there is a higher law than the Constitution" compelling the choice of freedom over slavery in the territories. If that choice drove some states to break up the union, Seward warned, "there can be no peaceful dissolution . . . [and] dissolution, happen when it may, will, and must be revolution."[15]

Later in the congressional session, Seward defined the nation's sectional divide more broadly than it had ever before been portrayed in Congress. The rift, instead of being confined to specific episodic differences over freedom and slavery, was, in fact, a far deeper current that affected all aspects of American life. "Slavery and freedom," Seward said, casting his gaze back to the nation's founding, "are conflicting systems, brought together by the Union of the States, not neutralized, nor even harmonized. Their antagonism is radical, and therefore perpetual. Compromise continues conflict, and the conflict involves, unavoidably, all questions of national interest—questions of revenue, of internal improvement, of industry, of commerce, of political rivalry, and even all questions of peace and war."[16] Slavery warped all aspects of national life; even those not ostensibly attached to it were bent by its influence. If that be true, it was little wonder that citizens in all sections increasingly saw division, and war with it if necessary, as unavoidable.

By early March President Taylor was privately talking about imposing a blockade on southern harbors to "save the union" from those determined to bring on civil war.[17] Weeks of congressional debate had done more to sharpen than to bridge sectional differences. Avowed secessionists such as William Lowndes Yancey in Alabama and Robert Barnwell Rhett Sr. in South Carolina were looking to the June Nashville Convention, rather than anything Congress might do, to settle the issue. The Mississippi legislature approved $200,000 for "necessary measures for protecting the state."[18] At this point, with discord wavering on a line between rhetoric and action, Daniel Webster stepped forward to make good on his promise to Henry Clay.

"I wish to speak today," Webster said in opening his March 7 address, "not as a Massachusetts man, nor as a northern man, but as an American. . . . I speak today for the preservation of the Union." Calhoun, who died before the month was out, was brought into the Senate chamber in a wheelchair to hear his old adversary's remarks. Webster opened with a low-key rendering of the long-past failed expectation that outlawing the African slave trade would lead to the gradual extinction of slavery. He traced the expansion of slavery up to Texas's statehood in 1845. At that point he began the core of his argument.

With the admission of Texas, Webster said, not a single acre of land was left within control of the union geographically suited for slavery. Invoking an undefined "irrepealable law" of nature, Webster argued that the chapter was closed and the books settled as to slavery's expansion. It had nowhere else to expand because the climate and soil of all the remaining lands could not sustain plantation slavery. Given this "fixed fact" of nature, there was no need for a Wilmot Proviso to exclude slavery from territory where it would never take hold in the first place. In organizing the New Mexico territory, Webster pledged, "I would put in no Wilmot proviso" that could only serve as a taunt or reproach to "wound the pride" of white southerners.[19] He had redeemed the first part of his January pledge to Clay.

He turned next to the second part of that pledge: to enacting a new fugitive slave law. For nearly all Americans the territories were distant places. Slavery was a distant institution for northerners. The capture of runaway slaves or the kidnapping of free Blacks accused of being fugitives occurred in northern cities and rural communities where the event was direct, not distant. Slave catchers were despised. One did not have to be an abolitionist to deplore using the judicial process to send a person living in freedom into bondage. "There has been found in the North," Webster said, "a disinclination to perform, fully, their constitutional duties, in regard to the return of persons bound to service, who have escaped into the free States. In that respect, it is my judgement that the South is right, and the North is wrong."

A decade later Abraham Lincoln repeatedly made the same case, but the Civil War ultimately obliterated arguments about returning fugitive slaves. Webster, and Lincoln after him, did no more than reassert allegiance to a key compromise clause in the Constitution. In doing so, however, they pledged themselves to the document's most morally repugnant obligation. Further, the fugitive slave clause's benefit to slaveholders was not the only reason that the white South valued it. The clause was the North's test of acceptance of the white South. Even beyond that, its language most closely approached, and in many white southern minds embraced, a constitutional acceptance of the right to property in man.

Webster had to live with the consequences of his words. He was excoriated in the North. His political career was wrecked badly enough that he soon accepted a cabinet position rather than run for reelection to the Senate. "The South," Webster said in binding himself to Clay's agenda, "has been injured in this respect, and has a right to complain; and the North has been too careless of what I think the Constitution peremptorily and emphatically enjoins upon it as a duty." Having cast his lot, Webster went a step further. Northern abolition societies, he argued, "have produced nothing good or valuable." Their agitation, by "good" but "misled" people, had instead resulted in slaves being "bound more firmly than before; their rivets . . . more strongly fastened."[20]

He closed on the thought that had convinced him that new concessions to the white South were preferable to the alternative. There could be no such thing as peaceable secession, Webster believed. He saw "as plainly as I see the sun in heaven" that disruption of the union "must produce such a war as I will not describe." Facing this prospect, he concluded, "Never did there devolve, on any generation of men, higher trusts than now devolve upon us for the preservation of this Constitution."[21]

Webster's March 7 address is arguably the single most consequential speech ever delivered in Congress. His words did not cure the malady, but they did break the fever. As seen in the white South, the North's leading political figure, Yankee to the core, had yielded to their principal demands, rejecting the hated Wilmot Proviso, embracing the return of fugitive slaves, and disparaging abolitionists. The wind was taken out of the Nashville Convention's sails. Secessionists went into retreat. More moderate voices across the country spoke with greater confidence. Compromise seemed possible. A reasonable reading of history is that Webster, and the ultimate success of the Compromise of 1850, meant that secession and war did not then occur. A decade later, when they did occur, the North had so gained in power and four of the border slave states had so diminished their alliance with the white South that the outcome for union was greatly enhanced. The price Webster paid when he offered compromise where he otherwise saw conflict was a moral oblique that attaches to his name to this day.

Webster's speech, however, did not secure the compromise. Clay and a Committee of Thirteen fashioned most of the provisions into a single omnibus bill that began to draw critics from every quarter. In the midst of this process, President Taylor died after falling ill at a Fourth of July celebration after consuming raw fruit and iced milk. His death was fortuitous for the compromise because his successor, Millard Fillmore, favored it where Taylor had not. After Clay retreated to Newport to recuperate from exhaustion, Senator Stephen A. Douglas made a move as obvious as it had been ignored. He drew the crucial lesson from Clay's Missouri Compromise. As chair of the committee on territories, he broke the omnibus bill into its separate provisions; then, with support from Fillmore, he built majorities for each separate piece where no majority existed for the whole. By mid-September the entire package of legislation, passed by sectional votes in each instance, was approved by Congress and signed by the president. The Compromise of 1850 was law.

The Fugitive Slave Law was onerous to the North. It passed the Senate only because several northern members abstained from voting while sulking outside the chamber during the roll call. Its provisions were draconian. Accused fugitives were denied the right to a jury trial. Cases were decided by court-appointed commissioners who received $10 for each fugitive returned to slavery and $5 each for those who were not. Federal marshals were empowered to summon local citizens to assist in the capture of suspected runaway slaves. The judgment of the Reverand Nathaniel Colver of the Tremont St. Church in Boston was representative of much of northern opinion. Enforcement of the Fugitive Slave Law, he said, "would be the commission of a monstrous crime."[22]

As Douglas and the measure's supporters framed the compromise, the white South's offsetting concession to the North was the immediate admission of California as a free state. This concession was more in the nature of recognition of reality as the people of California had approved a state constitution prohibiting slavery well before the statehood portion of the compromise was passed. The add-on of banning the slave trade in Washington, D.C., took the chained coffles out of sight of the Capitol by pushing the trade into neighboring Maryland and Alexandria.

The heart of the compromise was contained in the two nearly identically written bills organizing the New Mexico and Utah territories.[23] The wording of these measures was fought over for months before passage. The bills, as Douglas and his supporters saw them, enshrined popular sovereignty, or the right of local control in the territories. The white South saw the prevailing principle as the nonintervention of Congress into territorial matters of local government.

Either way, the Wilmot Proviso's territorial ban on slavery was rejected, eliminating a congressional stamp of slavery's illegitimacy that was an affront to white southern honor. Specifically, the law provided that either New Mexico or Utah could be admitted to statehood with or without slavery as its state constitution provided at the time of entry. More important, the bills stipulated that the "legislative power of the Territory shall extend to all rightful subjects of legislation, consistent with the Constitution." This meant that territorial legislatures were free to act or not to act on slavery as they chose and when they chose. The "consistent with the Constitution" phrase implied the ultimate jurisdiction of the Supreme Court over whatever laws the territorial legislatures enacted. The implication was made explicit by another provision allowing any court decisions regarding title to slaves—a ban on property in man, for instance—to be appealed directly to the Supreme Court. Unstated, but packed within this language, was that the Supreme Court could decide whether Congress had the constitutional authority to grant a territorial legislature power to act on slavery.

The New Mexico and Utah bills did, it is true, provide that the governor or the Congress could override decisions of the territorial legislatures. These checks, however, were intended to provide against the possibility that a Mormon-controlled territorial legislature in Utah would sanction polygamy. The clear implication at the time was the law's broad intent to punt the issue of slavery, should it arise in either territory, to the Supreme Court, keeping both Congress and the president, who appointed territorial governors, out of it.

In the nation at large, the minutia of obscure legal provisions was lost entirely in an overwhelming sense of relief that disaster had been averted and a possible long-term settlement on slavery had been reached in the Compromise of 1850. Both sides had wounds to lick, but each side could extol its share of victory. Northern Democrats, in particular, could return to their constituents, arguing that the principle of local control by which slavery could be prohibited was triumphant. Southern Democrats, in particular, could tell their constituents that the right of slaveholders to enter the territories acquired from Mexico with their slaves had been vindicated. Secessionists who had been on the rise were held at bay. When a South Carolina state convention meekly held that secession was not expedient, Robert Barnwell Rhett Sr. resigned from the Senate in disgust.

The Democrats, led by Douglas, were the chief political victors, as became clear in the 1852 elections. Gone from the stage that they had dominated from the early 1800s were the triumvirate of Clay, Webster, and Calhoun. Ascendant was Stephen A. Douglas and his cause of popular sovereignty. They both remained dominant until events proved that popular sovereignty destroyed every politician who embraced it.

Harriet Beecher Stowe was one northerner affected by the new Fugitive Slave Law. Expression born of righteousness ran in her family. The Beechers were prominent New England religious leaders in the cause of abolition. Harriet also had the advantage of attending the Hartford Female Seminary, where she received an advanced education denied to most women of her era. She and her husband, Calvin Ellis Stowe, opened their home as a way station on the Underground Railroad when they lived in Cincinnati. While there she may have witnessed a slave auction during a visit in Kentucky. The time she spent in the border region between free and slave states exposed her not only to slavery and those seeking to escape it, but also to a sensibility for southern whites far more nuanced than the stereotypes common to her New England upbringing.

By 1850 she was living in Brunswick, Maine, and was an occasional contributor of fictional pieces to the *National Era*, the antislavery weekly

Harriet Beecher Stowe.
COURTESY OF THE LIBRARY
OF CONGRESS.

newspaper Gamaliel Bailey then edited in Washington, D.C. In March of 1851 she wrote him that she was preparing a story that might run through three or four issues.[24] She had been circling a major project on slavery for the past year, stirred in part by the compromise debates in Congress. The Fugitive Slave Law in particular roused her, with its sheer injustice, the destruction of families, and, pointedly for her, its cost to the minds and souls of those who profited from it as traders in the traffic. By June of that year, the first installment appeared of what quickly became America's most sensational creative narrative of the century.

Uncle Tom's Cabin continued in serialization to the following March, when it was published as a book that sold 300,000 copies in the country within a year, nearly three million over its full run, and just over that total number in sales abroad.[25] Stowe made slavery vivid. Judged hopelessly sentimental and melodramatic by later generations of critics, *Uncle Tom's*

Cabin has more recently been cast as the most powerful political narrative of its time that also happened to be written by a woman.

Stowe wrote that she intended to create pictures to bring slavery alive. In doing so she created stereotypes that live to this day, beginning with her title character, Uncle Tom, the servant who bears abuse with loyal servility. Her message was the ultimate triumph of Christian love, a higher law that even the worst of slave traders and slaveowners came to obey. To the North, Stowe's work inspired a visceral disgust with slavery and its practitioners among a wide swath of the population, particularly women, who had not before given great heed to life on the other side of the Mason-Dixon line. *De Bow's Review* deemed the "influence of her book at the South is evil, and evil only." Most cutting, the review found, was Stowe's charge of injustice and inhumanity, not against the institution, but directly against the whites who lived by it. "Every word Mrs. Stowe says against us is utterly and ridiculously confutable," the journal complained.[26]

The significance of the *Review's* conclusion is that the injury Stowe inflicted was "against us," not "against slavery," against the honor, morality, and Christian worthiness of individual white southerners. The *Southern Literary Messenger's* editor sought a review of *Uncle Tom's Cabin* "as hot as hell-fire, blasting and searing the reputation of the vile wretch in petticoats who could write such a volume."[27] Many such efforts were made, including a series of books depicting contented slaves within the patriarchal embrace of the big house and its master. But the damage was done, the insult received. The white South had to widen the scope of its frustrated contempt beyond New England's moral snobbishness to include much of the North as a whole.

The breakup that the Compromise of 1850 avoided was followed by the anticlimax of the presidential election two years later. Just as the nation sought a political ebb tide after the great surges of the Missouri Compromise and the nullification crisis, so, too, the nation sought calm after the storm of 1850. The Free Soil Party that had helped legitimate northern opposition to Slave Power expansion virtually collapsed after Martin Van

Buren's son led the New York Barnburners back into the Democratic Party. Banking the fires of sectional conflict, the two major political parties chose war heroes over policy choices to attract voters.

General Winfield Scott was the Whig standard-bearer. Because the party's southern wing insisted on a platform endorsing the 1850 Compromise, and Scott would not do so personally, the party was left with a candidate unacceptable to the South running on a platform unpalatable to the North. The surface contradiction ran straight through the withering party as a whole. Texas and the political baggage that came with it had created the Conscience Whigs in the North, whose antislavery beliefs separated them from their southern partisans. By 1852 the Whigs were no longer a viable cross-sectional party. By 1856 they would no longer be a political party at all.

In contrast, the Democrats were united. Their forty-ninth ballot choice of dark horse Franklin Pierce, a former New Hampshire senator and Mexican War brigadier general, was a trademark blend of the northern man with southern principles. Just as Martin Van Buren had patented that mixture in creating the Democratic Party, Stephen Douglas updated it to meet the demands of his own times. Both men were primarily political strategists. Van Buren ultimately came to believe that his creation betrayed him. The framework he perfected was to suppress agitation about slavery. Only later was it evident that the framework came at the cost of accommodating the white South's desire for a grip on the levers of power out of proportion to its share of the population. That model ceased to work as the nation was forced to confront the choice between slavery and freedom in the territories acquired from Mexico. The 1850 Compromise was Stephen Douglas's framework to avoid dealing with the issue. His model retained cross-sectionalism by replacing Van Buren's worn-out embrace of suppression with a new standard of popular sovereignty meant to yank slavery from the national agenda by placing it safely out of the way at the local level.

In 1852 the Democrats rode that formula to one of the most crushing triumphs in American electoral history. Pierce carried twenty-seven states, winning 254 electoral votes. Scott carried four with forty-two votes.[28] The Democrats also won a better than two-to-one majority in the House and thirty-eight of the sixty-two seats in the Senate. Even in victory, however, the structural rot was evident. In all but two of the sixteen northern states, Pierce had failed to gain a majority of the votes, winning only by pluralities.

～～

The election results may have lulled Stephen Douglas into believing that he could achieve a grand design that turned out to be one of the greatest political blunders in American history, the Kansas-Nebraska Act. Several factors motivated the Little Giant to take the biggest risk of his political career. A chance to win the presidency was one. So was the prospect of considerable financial gain. California statehood and the organization of the New Mexico, Utah, and Oregon territories presented the nation with its next great challenge: how to tie the pieces together.

Stephen Douglas became a railroad man. Immediately after passage of the 1850 Compromise, Douglas steered a bill through Congress authorizing what became the 700-mile-long Illinois Central Railroad, the first line using grants of public lands that were, in turn, sold to finance the enterprise. That legislation had a southern component of an additional line all the way to Mobile, Alabama, but little of that road was completed before the Civil War. Douglas was keenly aware that the politician who engineered the far-grander feat of forging a transcontinental railroad linking the Atlantic to the Pacific would have a strong suit to play in a presidential election. The businessman who placed the right bets on where the link might be formed stood to gain handsomely. Douglas invested in that future, placing his bets on a northern rail route.[29]

Rail proponents backed several different routes, with railheads beginning in New Orleans, St. Louis, or Chicago, among other cities. As Congress mulled the matter, a sectional roadblock emerged. The white South was ready to filibuster any rail line, and the prosperity likely to go with it, through territory where slavery was banned. That meant that nearly all of the remaining Louisiana Purchase territories were off limits as long as the Missouri Compromise of 1820 stood. The bulk of that land was then lumped together in what was called the Nebraska Territory, running from the current southern border of Kansas all the way north through Nebraska

and the Dakotas to Canada. Slavery was banned in the Nebraska Territory because all of it was north of the dividing line between slavery and
freedom that the Missouri Compromise had established. The white South
had northern rail proponents, including Douglas, over a barrel. After he
steered the Kansas-Nebraska Act to passage, Douglas claimed, "I had the
authority and power of a dictator throughout the whole controversy in
both houses."[30] In the process by which the bill was enacted, however, the
white South extracted from Douglas its full measure of vengeance against
the Missouri Compromise's hated restrictions.

The chief extractor was Missouri Senator David Rice Atchison.
"Bourbon Dave" to his friends, Atchison was a behind-the-scenes deal
maker, next in line to the presidency as president pro tempore of the Senate following the death of Vice President William King, and a member
of the F Street Mess, slavery's answer to Mrs. Spriggs' Abolition House.
Atchison's F Street boardinghouse messmates included the Senate's slave
state chairman of the foreign relations, finance, and judiciary committees.

David Rice Atchison.
COURTESY OF THE LIBRARY
OF CONGRESS.

As 1854 approached, Atchison faced a tough reelection battle at home. To win that, he wanted credit for removing the thorn that had festered in the white South's side for more than three decades: repeal of the Missouri Compromise. That, in turn, could serve twin purposes. With Kansas on Missouri's west flank open to slavery, a transcontinental railhead at St. Louis could begin its route to the Pacific through newly designated slave territory. Repeal, the first step to establishing slavery in Kansas, would also make Missouri's slaveholders less apprehensive that their chattel only need but cross the border to gain a foothold to freedom. Atchison was blunt with Douglas. The Little Giant was told that if he was unwilling to acquiesce, Atchison was ready to resign as president pro tempore, take over Douglas's chairmanship of the committee on territories, and do the job himself.[31]

On January 4, 1854, Douglas reported a bill out of his committee to organize all remaining Louisiana Purchase territory based largely on language identical to that in the Compromise of 1850 organizing the New Mexico and Utah territories. The key provision was that states formed from the territory could join the union, with or without slavery, as their constitutions provided at the time of entry. Atchison and the South informed Douglas that this was not enough. Because the Missouri Compromise banned slavery in the Nebraska Territory, waiting for a constitutional sanction until a territory was on the cusp of statehood was certain to result in a free state. Claiming that language that should have been in the bill was dropped due to a clerical error, Douglas quickly came back with a second version allowing the territorial governments to permit or prohibit slavery as they saw fit.[32]

The white South again informed Douglas that this was not enough. The Missouri Compromise ban would still apply until a territorial government sanctioned slavery. To stand a chance of survival, slavery had to be established before the legislature took it up. The bill's next iteration took the crucial step of declaring the Missouri Compromise "inoperative."[33] But the South informed Douglas that this was not enough. "Inoperative" was a vague term. Finally, early in February, a bill emerged that Senator Atchison and southern Democrats were prepared to support. It declared the Missouri Compromise "inoperative and void."[34]

Along the way the Kansas Territory was delineated, with borders corresponding to the present state. All involved recognized that if slavery was to be extended, it would happen in Kansas, immediately west of slaveholding Missouri, and not in Nebraska or the Dakotas that were still Indian country. The provision from the 1850 Compromise was tucked into the package calling for direct appeal to the Supreme Court of court disputes over slavery. Douglas and his supporters went to great lengths arguing that when Congress passed the Compromise of 1850, it intended that the bill's principles be applied to the remainder of the Louisiana Purchase territories. That the record did not support their contention did nothing to lessen their vehemence on the issue.[35]

Above all, Douglas proclaimed that popular sovereignty triumphed once again as it had four years earlier. Turning decisions about slavery in the territories over to the people living there set aside the constitutional error of allowing Congress to intervene and thereby provoke divisive national agitation over the issue. Popular sovereignty, he contended, solved the national controversy over slavery by safely turning it over to the people to decide at the local level. Douglas could not have been more wrong. He knew, in his own words, that overturning the Missouri Compromise "will raise a hell of a storm," having himself once termed that measure "a sacred thing, which no ruthless hand would ever be reckless enough to disturb."[36]

For starters, Douglas's plan, instead of subduing, immediately intensified national agitation over slavery. His bill was a "gross violation" of the "sacred pledge" embodied in the Missouri Compromise, according to appeal signed by several northern antislavery leaders, including Senators Salmon Chase and Charles Sumner. They denounced the measure as an "atrocious plot" to compel passage of the nation's commerce "between the east and the west for hundreds of miles through a slaveholding region" that would "subject the whole country to the yoke of a slaveholding despotism."[37]

The northern charge that the Slave Power was engaged in a conspiracy wider than whatever part of it was prominent at the moment dated back to the annexation of Texas. From the Kansas-Nebraska bill forward, the theme of a white southern plot to insinuate slavery at every turn gained increasing purchase to the North. "Slavery must now become general, or it must cease to be at all," Ohio's Senator Ben Wade said, expressing a second theme of all or not at all that began to take hold in the North. Sounding genuinely shaken as he addressed the Senate, Wade said, "The Missouri compromise has been regarded, as far as I know, from that time to this, as having a character not much less important or sacred than that of the Constitution itself." He did not believe that "this Union can survive ten years the act of perfidy that will repudiate the great compromise of 1820."[38] The actual breakup occurred four years earlier than Wade forecast.

Wade was also right about the standing of the Missouri Compromise as akin in stature, at least in the North, to the Constitution itself. That struggle laid to rest northern apprehension that slavery could ever creep above the thirty-six-degree, thirty-minute north latitude compromise line. However much abolitionists decried the abominations of slavery and the immorality of slaveholders, northern citizens felt protected from its direct influence by the wall of separation between freedom and slavery created by the 1820 compromise. The Kansas-Nebraska bill did not just breach that wall; it obliterated it. Several years later Abraham Lincoln captured something of how shaken the North was by the rejection of the Missouri Compromise when he wrote that it "took us by surprise— astounded us. . . . We were thunderstruck and stunned, and we reeled and fell in utter confusion."[39] He made the impact seem biblical in its proportions, and for many northerners, it was. For one, Lincoln's stale political career took on new life. As he reentered the public arena, Lincoln carried with him the themes of a Slave Power conspiracy and of a union as a house divided that eventually must be either all one or the other, either wholly free or wholly slave.

Douglas crafted the Kansas-Nebraska Act in closed committee sessions, convinced that so long as he could get the southern leadership behind the measure, the Democrats' lopsided majorities in Congress would assure its passage and a compliant president would sign it into law. He was right, but the bill sustained one final round of criticism just before the Senate vote. That debate's contrast with the themes deployed in the Missouri Compromise is notable.

In 1820 much hairsplitting was done over constitutional legalities. Making a choice between free and slave labor was prominent. White Southern threats of disunion were commonplace. In 1854 the battle was reduced to stark terms, and the most forceful threats came from the North. The contest, Senator Seward said, "involves a moral question. The slave States so present it. They maintain that African slavery is not erroneous, not unjust, not inconsistent with the advancing cause of human nature. . . . On the other hand, we of the free States regard slavery as erroneous, unjust, oppressive, and therefore absolutely inconsistent with the principles of the American Constitution and Government." Speaking as a Whig who would become a Republican in less than two years, he continued, "This antagonism must end either in a separation of the antagonistic parties—the slaveholding States and the free States—or, secondly, in the complete establishment of the influence of the slave power over the free—or else, on the other hand, in the establishment of the superior influence of freedom over the interests of slavery."[40]

Massachusetts Senator Charles Sumner was hardly less threatening. He spoke as a member of the Free Soil Party who would soon become a Republican. The Kansas-Nebraska bill, he said, "annuals all past compromises with slavery, and makes all future compromises impossible. Thus it puts freedom and slavery face to face, and bids them grapple." He foresaw that day when the North would rise up to throw off the Slave Power's "wretched despotism," and the fugitive slave law would become a dead letter. "Everywhere within the sphere of Congress," he said, "the great *Northern Hammer* will descend to smite the wrong; and the irresistible cry will break forth, 'No more slaver States.'"[41] These words and countless others like them, both spoken and written, convinced the white South that the soon-to-be-created Republican Party had malign intent against it, no matter how much some of its later leaders such as Lincoln tried to dissuade the thought.

For his part, Douglas preemptively hurled the charge of treason at those engaged in forming a new sectional coalition as a result of the disruption that the Kansas-Nebraska bill caused. "We have been notified," he said, "that the old political parties are to be dissolved, and that the northern Whigs, disaffected Democrats, Abolitionists, and Free-Soilers, are to be fused and amalgamated into a sectional party, and marshalled under the black flag of Abolitionism!" The most die-hard slaveholder could not have said it better.

Moreover, aside from the "black flag of Abolitionism" hyperbole, Douglas was right. The only thing missing was the name—Republican—that the new party would adopt. Once formed, Douglas charged from the Senate floor, its purpose would be to "contemplate civil war, servile insurrection, and disunion. I do not hesitate here, in the presence of its leaders and confederates, to denounce the scheme as involving treason in its most revolting form, and men who encourage or countenance it are guilty of treason against the Constitution and the Government of the country."[42] Words like these made men like Lincoln see the Little Giant as hardly more than a demagogue.

On May 25, 1854, at the close of debate, the Senate approved the final bill that had already passed the House.[43] President Pierce signed it into law five days later. In each house, southern Democrats and Whigs voted in near unanimity for the bill, and all northern Whigs and Free Soilers voted against it. The most pronounced division occurred among northern Democrats, who split forty-four to forty-four in the House and fifteen in favor and five opposed in the Senate.[44] That division was stark evidence that Democratic viability as a cross-sectional party was beginning to disintegrate.

The Kansas-Nebraska Act completed white southern victories in rolling back congressional stigmatization of slavery. No attempt was ever made to reverse the ban on the African slave trade, although some voices were being raised to do so. The Compromise of 1850 killed off the threat of the Wilmot Proviso and strengthened the Fugitive Slave Law. In the Kansas-Nebraska Act, the Missouri Compromise, an initially heralded white southern victory that had turned into wormwood, was repealed. Although they could not have then known it, the Kansas-Nebraska Act was also the last major white southern congressional victory after more than six decades of ascendancy.

Even with the victory, however, the white South was unsatisfied. Legislatively, white southerners wanted enactment of Calhoun's original claim that all territories were common property, not only open to slaveholders but requiring national protection of slave-owning property rights. In a broader sense, all the white southern victories drove off further what was wanted most. As Calhoun had realized, every white southern advance brought with it ever-louder accusations from northern abolitionists of white southern dishonor and moral debasement. The slave South could never achieve northern acceptance. Instead, the white South met ever-mounting rejection by an ever-widening segment of the North.

For Douglas, the Kansas-Nebraska Act was a Pyrrhic victory. The white South never trusted popular sovereignty. It wanted and achieved the effective repeal of the Missouri Compromise. Popular sovereignty prevailed in the Kansas-Nebraska Act but with its image thoroughly tarnished in the North as a cloak for slavery's expansion. By the time Douglas returned to Illinois in August, he claimed, "I could travel from Boston to Chicago by the light of my own effigy." Several days later, a Chicago audience shouted him off the platform; he was reduced to shaking his fists at them after declaring that he would explain the misunderstood principles behind the Kansas-Nebraska Act.[45]

The reckoning came due in the midterm congressional elections that took place between 1854 and 1855. Even before the Kansas-Nebraska Act passed Congress, a group of dissidents fitting Douglas's description of traitors met at a schoolhouse in Ripon, Wisconsin, and founded what they called the Republican Party. They chose the name in deference to the standard of liberty attributed to the political organization that formed around Thomas Jefferson. Their main strength, as their origin indicated, was in northwestern states.

In the northeast, the Know Nothing Party drew adherents with its xenophobic, anti-immigrant, anti-Catholic platform. The Know Nothings got their name from instructing members to reply "I know nothing" when asked about the organization's inner workings. On the ballot they appeared as the American Party. As Douglas forecast, the election produced an unprecedented amalgam of choices including new political entrées and a welter of fusion and coalition candidates among Know Nothing, Whig, Free Soil, and disaffected Democratic voters.

Opposition to the Kansas-Nebraska Act was the common theme that tied the coalitions together. The clearest message the election sent was of Democratic disaster. Northern Democrats lost sixty-six of their ninety-one House seats, a nightmare from which the party did not fully recovered until long after the Civil War.[46] Every northern Democratic member of the Senate who voted for the Nebraska-Kansas Act and ran in the midterms was voted out of office.

When the new Congress convened in December 1855, it was clear the Democrats had lost, but not at all clear who had won. The House had no majority party. The ensuing fight for the speakership demonstrated just how tangled the political realignment was and, in the end, sorted it out in the Republicans' favor. One era was ending and another beginning. During the previous three-and-a-half decades, slaveholders had held the speakership for thirty years. The House took two months and 133 ballots to select the new Speaker, the most contentious battle for that office ever. By the twenty-eighth ballot, a relatively obscure congressman from Massachusetts gained a lead but not a majority. Nathaniel P. Banks won his seat to the previous Congress as a Democrat and to the current one on the Know Nothing ticket. In the speakership contest, however, it was not Banks's position on Catholicism or immigration that distinguished him from other leading candidates, but his support for the Wilmot Proviso and his opposition to the Kansas-Nebraska Act that cleaved him from his closest contenders. Thus, the Democrat turned Know Nothing became the champion of the Republicans' call to end slavery's expansion.

Many northern Whigs underwent a similar transformation. The prolonged balloting stretched tempers thin. *New York Tribune* editor Horace Greeley was roughed up on the streets of Washington by an Arkansas congressman angered by the paper's treatment of his effort to undermine Banks.[47] An observer estimated that on one day, at least 300 loaded pistols were carried by those on the House floor and in the galleries.[48] The deadlock was resolved only after the House agreed to select the Speaker by a plurality, which Banks won with 103 votes against 100 for his closest rival. The victory, based on northern antislavery votes, marked "the commencement of a new era in our history," Greeley wrote in the *Tribune*.[49]

In the next election, Banks won as a Republican. Of the seventy-two House members who voted for Banks on the final ballot and ran for reelection, sixty-nine ran as Republicans.[50] Thurlow Weed, the New

York deal maker behind Senator William Seward, wrote emphatically, "This triumph is worth all it cost in time, toil, and solicitude . . . [for] the Republican party is now inaugurated. We can work with a will."[51]

Kansas brought something new to the conflict over slavery. White people had been killing Black people in North America, largely with impunity, for more than two centuries. Occasionally a Black person killed a white person. With Kansas, for the first time, white people began killing other white people over whether Black people should be allowed into the territory as slaves. The bloodletting was not unexpected. "Do you not see," Ohio Senator Ben Wade said during the Kansas-Nebraska debate, "that you are about to bring slavery and freedom face to face, to grapple for the victory, and that one or the other must die?"[52]

Horace Greeley. COURTESY OF THE LIBRARY OF CONGRESS.

As the Kansas-Nebraska Act was being debated, about 800 settlers lived in Kansas, a number that had increased to 8,601 when a census was taken in February 1855. Of that total, 2,905 were eligible to vote and 192 were slaves.[53] Most of the newcomers went there looking for farmland on which to build their own stake in life. Others went looking for a fight. In Massachusetts the New England Emigrant Aid Company sprang up to give encouragement and Sharp's rifles to those willing to settle in Kansas. The Platte Country Self-Defense Association arose in Missouri with the mission to remove emigrants sent to Kansas by northern aid societies.[54]

Mounted groups with similar aims that came to be known as Border Ruffians began marauding west of the Missouri River in the newly organized Kansas Territory. Missouri slaveowners were particularly anxious to prevent having a free state set up on their western border as a tempting escape route for their own slaves. Bourbon Dave Atchison, who had lost his Senate reelection bid but not his passion to extend slavery into Kansas, wrote "We are playing for a mighty stake, if we win we carry slavery to the Pacific Ocean."[55] In Alabama, Major Jefferson Buford, with rousing support from William Lowndes Yancey, set out from Montgomery leading 400 men to meet the abolitionist threat in Kansas.[56]

Slaveowners were the one group conspicuous by their absence in rushing into Kansas. The reason was obvious. Texas and Arkansas offered sufficient land to establish new plantations in safety while marching all of one's human capital into Kansas was fraught with risk. Many of the antislavery emigrants clustered in and around the town of Lawrence on the Kansas River about fourteen miles east of Lecompton, where a sizable portion of the proslavery forces gathered. Nearly all of what became known as the saga of Bleeding Kansas played out in a small portion of the territory, a half-moon arc of land south and within fifty miles of the two towns.

When newly appointed Governor Andrew Reeder arrived, he called for elections for the territorial legislature to be held in March 1855. A few months earlier, Border Ruffian intimidation and ballot stuffing had helped win the congressional delegate election for the proslavery candidate, who got nearly ten times more votes than his Free Soil opponent, including 604 votes in one district where the census showed only fifty-three voters resided.[57]

The March election was far more important. Delegates to Congress could talk, but legislatures passed laws. Men willing to pledge that they resided in the territory and intended to remain there were eligible to vote. Most were not even asked. A congressional investigating committee headed by Republican Congressman William A. Howard later compiled an account of the process. A day or two before the March 30 balloting, according to a typical rendition, men on foot, on horseback, or in wagons from Missouri began showing up at the wood-plank stores designated as polling places. One observer reported that 800 men a day were ferried across the Missouri River into Kansas for the three days running just before the election.[58] In Leavenworth, directly across the river, more than five times the number of voters identified in the census showed up at the polls. The Missourians were well supplied with liquor, Bowie knives, pistols, shotguns, and rifles. In most cases, their presence kept those planning to vote for Free-State candidates away from the polls. One man who said he was ready to take the voting eligibility oath was "dragged through the crowd away from the polls, amid cries of 'kill the damned nigger-thief.'"[59] Claiming "they had a right to vote, if they had been in the Territory but five minutes," many of those who came in from Missouri began the trek back there by the late afternoon or the next morning after the election.[60]

When it was all done, 6,307 votes were cast in the territory's eighteen districts. The congressional investigators found that 4,908 of those votes were cast illegally. In one district, all the votes cast went to the proslavery candidates, although only seven of them were cast by persons known to be legal residents there. In the Leavenworth district, 814 of the 964 votes cast were deemed fraudulent. Proslavery candidates won in all but one district, although in several of them the victors did not even reside there. The congressional investigators' majority report later declared that "the alleged Territorial legislature was an illegally constituted body, and had no power to pass valid laws."[61]

The newly elected legislature, however, met and proceeded to pass laws, several of them over vetoes by Governor Reeder, who soon resigned and joined the Free-State faction. The lawmakers made giving aid to a fugitive slave a capital offense, decreed two years' hard labor for writing or distributing antislavery material, and banned anyone who opposed slavery from sitting as a juror.[62] By December, the Free-State faction had set themselves up as an alternative government in Topeka with a constitution prohibiting slavery. President Pierce declared the territorial legislature legitimate and condemned the Topeka constitution.

The spark that ignited what was later called the Rape of Lawrence was struck when Franklin Coleman shot Charles W. Dow to death in the street with blasts from both barrels of his shotgun at Hickory Point, Kansas, on November 21, 1855. Coleman was proslavery. Dow was a recent arrival Free-State man, boarding at the home of one Jacob Branson, also of antislavery conviction. Coleman's dispute with Dow was about an overlapping land claim that had nothing to do with slavery, although their differences on that issue may have fueled Coleman's animosity. Late in the afternoon of the shooting Branson retrieved Dow's body, still lying in the street with eight slug holes in it, and took it to his home. Tension ran high between proslavery and Free-State men. Five days after the shooting, Sheriff Samuel Jones, staunchly proslavery, arrived with a small posse at Branson's home, where Branson was arrested on a "peace warrant." While escorting their prisoner to jail, however, Jones and his men were confronted in the road by a well-armed group of Branson's neighbors, who demanded his release. After some tense bickering, Jones relented. Branson then rode south with his rescuers to Lawrence, where he was taken in at the home of Charles Robinson, who had come to the territory as an agent of the New England Emigrant Aid Company.[63]

A standoff ensued that lasted for nearly six months. As many as 2,000 Border Ruffians and like-minded armed proslavery men camped out along the nearby Wakarusa River and began harassing the citizens of Lawrence. Wagons heading into or out of town were waylaid. Horses and oxen were stolen. Men were attacked and robbed along the roads, and Free-State sympathizers were threatened with violence if they did not leave the territory.[64] Finally, in early May, acting on indictments issued by a grand jury in Lecompton, a judge ordered that three Free-State leaders in Lawrence be arrested, two newspapers there be closed, and the Free State Hotel be shut down because it had been converted into a fortress intended to defy the law. On May 21 Jones, reportedly vowing to

Border Ruffians. COURTESY OF THE LIBRARY OF CONGRESS.

"take this damned town and blot it out," rode into Lawrence with some 700 men to execute the judge's orders.[65] Bourbon Dave Atchison, who had declared his readiness to "kill every God-damned abolitionist in the district," was at his side.[66] The hotel was burned down after being raked with cannon fire. The printing presses at both newspapers were thrown into the Kansas River, and several homes were burned or ransacked. One man died when part of the hotel wall fell on him.[67]

When the news reached New York, Horace Greeley's *Tribune* bannered it as "The War Actually Begun—Triumph of the Border Ruffians—Lawrence in Ruins—Several Persons Slaughtered—Freedom Bloodily Subdued."[68] The breathless account from the paper's on-the-scene reporter described men "firing at the houses with their artillery and freely entering and ransacking," while residents were "disarmed, robbed, plundered and shot down, under the color of law." A second report concluded that "no doubt but that the town is in ashes and many of its inhabitants butchered."[69] Similarly sensational accounts brought the news of the Rape of Lawrence to readers throughout the North.

In Kansas, when John Brown got the news, he and his command of some 100 Pottawatomie Rifles "traveled all night in the dark and at daybreak in the morning we were on top of the hills south of Waukarusa, where we could see Lawrence very distinctly," one of his sons later recalled. The Free State Hotel was still burning. Brown quickly decided on a plan of revenge for which his men would have to grind their broadswords sharp.[70]

⌐⌐

The day before Sheriff Jones attacked Lawrence, Massachusetts Senator Charles Sumner completed a two-day oration on the Senate floor in Washington, D.C., that he deemed "the most thorough & complete speech of my life."[71] In his era, erudite oratory required layering one's address with ample allusions to figures from ancient Greece and Rome. Sumner chose the role of Cicero denouncing the would-be Republic-smasher Cataline. A sprinkling of Latin in his speech was leavened by literary flourishes. Sumner picked *Don Quixote*, Ovid's *Metamorphosis*, and Milton's *Paradise Lost*, along with bows to Livy, Virgil, and Dante and several obscure historical and diplomatic references demonstrating the depth of his knowledge. The speech was baroque. It was also slashingly offensive.

Remains of the Free State Hotel in Lawrence, Kansas, after the May 21, 1856, attack.
SOURCE: WIKIMEDIA COMMONS/SKETCHED IN SARA T. D. ROBINSON'S *KANSAS, ITS INTERIOR AND EXTERIOR LIFE*, 1856

Sumner, a leading Republican, was in the forefront of northerners who made the transition from hating slavery to hating southern slaveowners. Among his address targets was South Carolina Senator Andrew Butler, whose offense was his role in crafting and passing the Kansas-Nebraska Act. Sumner's weapon was a continual insinuation about the slaveowner's appetite for sex with women forced into submission by bondage. The Crime Against Kansas, the title of his remarks, was "the rape of a virgin Territory, compelling it to the hateful embrace of Slavery." These words reached northern readers almost simultaneously with reports about the Rape of Lawrence. When he got to Butler, Sumner presented him as a deluded Don Quixote. "The senator from South Carolina," Sumner intoned, "has read many books of chivalry, and believes himself a chivalrous knight, with sentiments of honor and courage. Of course he has chosen a mistress to whom he has made his vows, and who, though ugly to others, is always lovely to him; though polluted in the sight of the world, is chaste in his sight;—I mean the harlot Slavery."[72]

Senator Charles Sumner of Massachusetts was beaten senseless on the Senate floor by Congressman Preston Brooks of South Carolina in 1856 to avenge the senator's scathing antislavery speech delivered days earlier. COURTESY OF THE BOSTON PUBLIC LIBRARY.

When Butler's cousin, thirty-seven-year-old Congressman Preston Brooks, also from South Carolina, read the speech, his first thought was to challenge Sumner to a duel. Brooks was no stranger to violence. He had been expelled from college for threatening local police with firearms and wounded in a duel that so injured his hip that he needed a cane to walk. Brooks's friend, fellow South Carolina Congressman Laurence Keitt, advised that as Sumner was not a gentleman, he did not merit the white southern code's remedy in matters of offended honor. Brooks decided instead to beat Sumner like a slave. His gold-headed walking cane would do the work.

Waiting until the galleries were clear of any women who might be offended by what was about to happen, Brooks approached Sumner on the afternoon of May 22 while he was writing at his desk on the Senate floor. Citing his duty to avenge the insult Sumner had done to his relative, Senator Butler, Brooks began beating Sumner savagely about his head and shoulders with his cane. Bleeding badly, in his effort to escape Sumner wrenched his desk from the bolts that held it to the floor. Keitt used a pistol to ward off other senators who started to intervene while Sumner crawled along the Senate aisle with Brooks continuously striking him until the cane broke.

Sumner did not resume his full-time role in the Senate until 1859. Brooks got off with a $300 fine on a misdemeanor charge. In applauding Brooks, the *Richmond Examiner* commented, "These vulgar abolitionists in the Senate are getting above themselves. They have been humored until they forget their position. They have grown saucy, and dare to be impudent to gentlemen."[73] Brooks resigned from the House to allow his constituents to pass judgment on his conduct. Back home, he told a gathering held to honor him that having been "a disunionist from the time I could think," the South's only hope "is in dissolving the bonds which connect us with the Government."[74] He was resoundingly reelected. The assault, in which Sumner became the North's martyr and Brooks the white South's hero, hit the nation as a presage of violence to come. In historian Joanne B. Freeman's words, "Sumner *was* the North suffering at the hand of the South and Brooks *was* the South enforcing its command."[75]

Two days after Brooks's revenge on Sumner, John Brown was ready at Pottawatomie Creek in Kansas to exact his revenge for the attack on Lawrence. The fifty-seven-year-old Brown had had his men sharpen their broadswords to avoid the alarm-raising crack of gunfire in the night. In the dark, at about eleven o'clock on May 24, Brown and seven of his men, four of them his sons and one his son-in-law, got to the Pottawatomie Creek cabin of James Doyle and his family. The Doyles were illiterate poor whites who owned no slaves but supported the territory's proslavery party.[76]

The elder Doyle and two of his three sons were forced out of the cabin. The following day, sixteen-year-old John Doyle found his father and his eldest brother, William, twenty-two years old, lying hacked to death in the road about 200 yards from the cabin. He found his other brother Drury, twenty years old, nearby in the grass. Drury's "fingers were cut off, and his arms were cut off; his head was cut open; there was a hole in his breast."[77] He had probably raised his arms to resist a sword stroke and been stabbed in the chest.

Brown's party split into two groups, one of them next making its way to the home of Allen Wilkinson, a proslavery member of the territorial legislature. Not even allowing him to put on his boots, Brown's men dragged Wilkinson about 150 yards from his house before they split his head open and stabbed him in the side.[78]

The final victim that night was William Sherman. His apparent offense was that his brother owned a store used as a meeting place by Major Buford's Georgia volunteers. His left hand was cut off, and his "skull was split open in two places and some of his brains was washed out by the water."[79]

The murders received national notoriety as the Pottawatomie Massacre, but Brown's role was obscured or covered up in many of the early accounts. Papers such as Greeley's *Tribune* did not want atrocities attributed to Free-State fighters. Greeley's correspondent, William A. Phillips, was, according to a colleague, one of a number of reporters who were Brown's "earnest supporters." John Kagi not only rode with Brown but was the Kansas correspondent for the *Washington National Era*.[80]

By autumn, under constant pursuit and with one son shot dead in a skirmish, Brown left the territory for his home in New York, vowing, "I will die for this cause. There will be no more peace in this land until slavery is done for."[81] He already had a new and far more dramatic plan in mind centered on Virginia and a federal armory there at Harpers Ferry.

Brown's departure came as newly appointed Governor John Geary managed to establish a sense of order in the territory by getting rough agreement on a truce between the hostile factions. While the political struggle continued, Bleeding Kansas ceased to be an open battleground. To a large extent the hostilities there had been a propaganda war fought by Greeley's *Tribune* and the rest of the antislavery press and, to a lesser extent, proslavery newspapers in the South. A modern assessment finds that during the territorial period, 157 violent deaths occurred in Kansas. Of those, fifty-six can reliably be attributed to political conflict or the slavery issue. The remainder came as the result of such things as fights, brawls, and land disputes.[82] That relatively low fatality count should not obscure the terror inflicted on a far-larger number of settlers who were wounded by gunfire, beaten up, saw their homes ransacked or burned down, their crops destroyed, and their livestock driven off, or had their lives threatened and children terrorized by an armed posse of night riders. The northern press, in particular, exaggerated the violence but did not invent it.

The autumn of 1856 also brought with it a presidential election. The newly minted Republican Party offered an avowedly sectional antislavery platform that kept its candidate off the ballot in most southern states. The Whig Party had vanished as a national force and the American, or Know Nothing, Party split into a proslavery southern faction and an anti-slavery northern contingent that merged with the Republicans. As their candidate, the Republicans chose the youthful John C. Frémont, idolized by the press as The Pathfinder for his daring expeditions into California and other regions of the West during the 1840s. He had famously helped secure California for the union at the outset of the war with Mexico, served the state briefly in the Senate, and was outspokenly in favor of Kansas as a free state. Less famous was the western trail of massacres Frémont's men inflicted on Native Americans, including the murder of at least twenty-one Klamath Indians and the destruction of their principal village for what was likely a mistaken belief that the Klamath had killed three of the Pathfinder's men.[83]

The Democrats resolved their dilemma over the unpopularity of President Pierce for the turmoil in Kansas by nominating a candidate who had been outside the country during the Kansas-Nebraska debate and subsequent territorial conflict. James Buchanan of Pennsylvania was the ultimate northern man with southern principles. He began his political career in the Senate by seeking accommodation with John C. Calhoun but was conveniently serving as minister to Great Britain while the turmoil over slavery flared in Kansas. By the mid-1850s the Democrats were the only party with national reach, with control resting securely in the southern wing. At their national convention, seventeen ballots were required to fend off bids by Pierce and Douglas before Buchanan won the nomination. The campaign quickly evolved into two separate races of Buchanan against Frémont in the North and Buchanan against ex-president Fillmore, the Know Nothing choice, in the South. Buchanan won by taking all southern states except Maryland and five northern states to the eleven that Frémont won. Given the northern preponderance in population and electoral votes, Republicans were quick to recognize that if they could but take Pennsylvania and either Illinois or Indiana in the next election while holding on to Frémont's gains, their candidate would win the presidency in 1860.

A few weeks after the election, the Supreme Court heard a case that had been initiated ten years earlier. Dred Scott, then held as a slave in Missouri, claimed that his prior residencies with his master in Illinois and later at Fort Snelling in the Wisconsin Territory entitled him to freedom. His claim was based on Illinois being a free state under the Northwest Ordinance and Fort Snelling being in part of the Louisiana Purchase where the Missouri Compromise banned slavery. Scott had both won and lost his case in earlier iterations before it reached the Supreme Court on appeal. The justices were initially prepared to dismiss Scott's claim on jurisdictional grounds. Chief Justice Roger Taney, however, saw an opportunity for the court to settle, once and for all, the fundamental issues involving slavery in the territories. As the Constitution's final authority, the court could put an end to the nettlesome questions Congress and the executive had failed to resolve. The decision would be the capstone to Taney's career on the bench that began in 1836 as President Andrew Jackson's appointment to succeed Chief Justice John Marshall. A native of Maryland, Taney had emancipated his own slaves and was widely considered a moderate within the Democratic Party.

The court reheard Scott's case in February shortly before Buchanan's inauguration. The president-elect, in fact, had prior word from a friend on the bench of what the court was about to decide. He had even written one of the four northerners on the court to persuade him to join the decision that the five southern justices supported.[84] In his March 4 inaugural, Buchanan alluded to slavery in the territories, saying that it was a judicial question "which legitimately belongs to the Supreme Court of the United States, before whom it is now pending, and will, it is understood,

Supreme Court Chief Justice
Roger B. Taney. COURTESY OF
THE LIBRARY OF CONGRESS.

be speedily and finally settled." Feigning no insight into the pending decision, Buchanan declared that "in common with all good citizens," he would "cheerfully submit" to the court's ruling whatever it might be.[85]

Two days later the decision was released. More accurately, Taney's decision along with seven separate written opinions were released, presenting legal snarls of concurrence and interpretation that persist to the present day.[86] These complications aside, the majority opinion Taney wrote constituted an across-the-board triumph for the white South's interpretation of how the framers had embedded slavery in the Constitution. In the first place, the high court found that as a Black man, Dred Scott was not a citizen of the United States and therefore had no right to bring a suit in federal court. Instead, as Taney read history, when the Constitution was written, Blacks were "considered as a subordinate and inferior class of beings who had been subjugated by the dominant race, and, whether emancipated or not, yet remained subject to their authority, and had no rights or privileges but such as those who held power and the Government might choose to grant them."[87] White suprem-acy was a constitutional doctrine. By it, Taney distinguished between national rights of citizens of the United States, to which Blacks had no entitlement, and local rights by which free Blacks might vote or serve on juries as residents of a given state. Instead of dismissing Scott's case for lack of jurisdiction at this point, Taney proceeded to lay down a far broader constitutional mandate.

The "right of property in a slave," Taney asserted, "is distinctly and expressly affirmed in the Constitution."[88] He derived this right from two of the document's clauses, the federal ratio's "all other persons" wording and the "such persons" wording used to describe fugitive slaves. In terms of slaves, Taney reasoned, the Constitution's "only two provisions which point to them and include them, treat them as property, and make it the duty of the Government to protect it."[89] Ever since it was announced, among the criticisms leveled at Taney's decision is that referring to enslaved Blacks as "persons" is not to "distinctly and expressly" confer a right to property in man. That the framers deliberately chose the word "persons" so as not to confer a right to property in man is a consideration that either did not occur to Taney or that he dismissed.

Next, in building the broadest proslavery case possible, the decision declared that the section of the Constitution granting Congress authority "to dispose of and make all needful rules and regulations respecting the territory . . . belonging to the United States" applied only to territory possessed at the time of ratification and then only in respect to matters of ownership and disposal. The immediate conclusion flowing from this reasoning was that Congress had no authority to deny slavery, a right conferred by the Constitution, in territories acquired after ratification, including those in the Louisiana Purchase. The Missouri Compromise was thus unconstitutional.

One farther step along this path that Taney took without concur-rence from his colleagues was that whatever Congress was barred from doing extended to any territorial legislature that Congress created. The *Dred Scott* decision was widely accepted as a marker for prohibiting territorial legislative bans on slavery. The decision did not touch upon the right of a territory or a state to ban slavery in its constitution. However, a logical final step that many feared could follow from Taney's reasoning was that if slavery was a right conferred and protected by the Constitution, then any sanction anywhere in the United States against it was of questionable validity.

Dred Scott's claim to freedom for having lived in territory where slavery was prohibited by the Missouri Compromise was dismissed. His argument for freedom based on having lived in Illinois was thrown out by the ruling that his status was determined by the laws of Missouri, to which he had returned, not by those of Illinois. He remained in bondage. In May of 1857, Scott was manumitted by his owner. He died a freeman a year later. Taney's ruling that Blacks were not citizens of the United States was overturned by passage of the Fourteenth Amendment in 1868 granting birthright citizenship.

Of immediate consequence, the *Dred Scott* decision knocked the stilts out from under Stephen Douglas's popular sovereignty case. To assure southern voters that he was on their side, Douglas had little choice but to hail the decision as "a proud monument" to the court's "greatness."[90] In truth, although phrased only as the chief justice's dicta, the ruling laid down the marker that territorial legislatures did not have the power to ban slavery—precisely the opposite premise posited by popular sovereignty. The Illinois senator devised a crutch to keep his case standing, as will be discussed in pages to follow, but the damage was done. Whatever luster popular sovereignty once had was tarnished. The decision also seemingly did irreparable damage to the Republicans' core argument that Congress must forestall slavery's expansion. Taney had shut and locked that door. As the *Louisville Democrat* put it in commending the decision, "what this tribunal decides the Constitution to be, that it is; and all patriotic men will acquiesce."[91] Republicans, and even many abolitionists, conceded that Congress had no power to interfere with slavery in states where it already existed. Taney ordered them to acknowledge that Congress also had no such power in the territories.

On a broader scale, the ruling reversed decades of practice since the Constitution's ratification that freedom was a national attribute and slavery a local one. By declaring a constitutional basis for property in man, Taney's decision made slavery the national standard and freedom a local prerogative of questionable validity. The cornerstone of the ruling, as Republican Senator William Fessenden saw it, was that "the Constitution of the United States recognizes slavery as property, and protects it as such. I deny it. It neither recognizes slavery as property, nor does it protect slavery as property."[92] His colleague Senator Henry Wise foresaw that the justices "have only got a step or two farther to go. They have only got to declare . . . that these views, legitimately carried out, would prevent the abolition of slavery in the States by the State constitutions."[93] For his part, President Buchanan was pleased with the court's "final decision" concerning slavery in the territories. "The right has been established of every citizen to take his property of any kind, including slaves, into the common Territories belonging equally to all the States," he said in his 1859 annual message. "Neither Congress nor a Territorial legislature nor any human power has any authority to annul or impair this vested right."[94]

Chief Justice Taney had vindicated John C. Calhoun's doctrine that the territories were common property into which a slaveowner could take his property without hindrance or sanction with assurance of constitutional protection. Remaining to seen was which slaveowners might actually go there and what protections their property might receive.

———

In Kansas, the new president appointed a new governor. Robert J. Walker was a familiar Democrat with a record of effectiveness. He had served Mississippi for a decade in the Senate, written the famous public letter *Reannexation of Texas*, helped maneuver James K. Polk's presidential nomination, and served in his cabinet as treasury secretary. A Pennsylvania native transplanted to the South, Walker saw Kansas as his route to the White House. Presiding over the territory's peaceful entry into statehood would be a national testament to his abilities at healing cross-sectional disputes. He did not last out the year.

Walker started well enough. As one skilled in high-stakes politics, before leaving for his new post Walker secured Buchanan's public endorsement that a proposed state constitution be submitted for approval or rejection to the voters in Kansas in a free and fair election. Once on the scene, he wrote Buchanan that of the territory's 24,000 inhabitants, he estimated 17,000 were antislavery and more than 15,000 were Democrats. The obvious inference was that Kansas could not be safely brought into the union as a slave state, but it could become a reliable Democratic one. Contrary to Walker's musings, the events that unfolded over the next year broke up the Democratic Party's foundational cross-sectional status, split Douglas from Buchanan, and pushed Kansas statehood back by more than two years.

Walker arrived too late to exert influence over the election of delegates to a state constitutional convention in which only about 20 percent of the eligible voters, the solidly proslavery contingent, participated. He did unravel some of the most egregious fraud in the October elections for a new legislature, with the result that both houses of that body had antislavery majorities. His object was to clear a path by which the majority might work its will. The majority, however, declined to accept his advice when the constitution that proslavery delegates drafted came up for a highly circumscribed vote. By November, those delegates meeting in Lecompton were well on their way to drafting a constitution to be included with the territory's congressional application for statehood. Their work was, as expected, a starkly proslavery document. In words Roger Taney might have endorsed, the Lecompton constitution provided that "The right of property is before and higher than any constitutional sanction, and the right of the owner of a slave to such and its increase is the same, and as inviolable, as the right of the owner of any property whatsoever."[95]

Free Blacks were to be excluded from the new state entirely. Other provisions covered the structure of government, poll taxes, public improvements, banks, education, a bill of rights, and other matters. The most crucial provision was how the proposed constitution was to be submitted to the voters. Instead of calling on them to accept or reject the entire document, voters were to be limited to adopting the constitution "with slavery," or adopting it "with no slavery."[96] In the event that a no-slavery choice was made, the owners of some 200 slaves already in the territory would continue unimpaired to hold all their rights to that property.

Free-State advocates vowed to boycott such an election. Walker was alarmed that the proposal went against the pledge he had secured to have

the entire constitution submitted to all the voters for ratification or rejection. He relented enough, however, to argue against a boycott, reasoning
with Free State advocates that once Kansas attained statehood, they would
have the majority needed to rewrite the constitution as they chose.

The antislavery leaders would have none of it. Everyone who watched
events in Kansas knew that the vote on Lecompton would be almost
entirely a proslavery affair, unrepresentative of majority sentiment in the
territory, even if technically in conformity with the law. At this point, the
Lecompton delegates set December 21 for the with- or without-slavery
election, and the antislavery legislature set January 4 for an election to
accept or reject the Lecompton constitution as a whole.

Walker headed back to Washington in an effort to personally convince Buchanan not to endorse the Lecompton constitution that all
informed observers knew would be ratified in its proslavery form. The
president saw it differently. Late in November, in consultation with a
phalanx of proslavery advisers in his cabinet, Buchanan decided to back
Lecompton. The white South wanted it. Technically its drafting and the
upcoming vote on it, however one-sided, were within the law. Prior to the
December 21 election, Buchanan could express readiness to accept whatever decision emerged from the polls in Kansas with the same apparent
ingenuousness that he declared his readiness to accept the Supreme
Court's decision prior to the *Dred Scott* ruling. This decision proved to be
a shattering blunder in Buchanan's presidency that almost unanimously
ranks as the worst in American history. Walker resigned. On December
3, Buchanan privately informed Douglas of his decision. The Illinois senator, aware that Free State sentiment ran high where he was soon to face
reelection, told Buchanan he would not support Lecompton. In reply he
received a presidential threat of political assassination.[97]

Five days later, in his annual message to Congress, the president
declared that although he would prefer that the entire constitution be
submitted to Kansas's voters, he was prepared to accept the upcoming
with-slavery or with-no-slavery vote.[98] In response Douglas, trying to
conceal his rupture with Buchanan, called on Congress to return the
Lecompton constitution, once it was received, for a vote to accept or reject
the entire document. His own sense of the matter was that in a fair elec-

tion, Lecompton would be rejected by a four-to-one vote. In the pending election, he said, "all men must vote for the constitution whether they like it or not, in order to be permitted to vote for or against slavery."[99]

The election was an anticlimax, with a predictable better than ten-to-one margin in favor of the Lecompton constitution with slavery.[100] Douglas again took to the Senate floor. "I have not become the mere servile tool of any President," he said, "as that I am bound to take every recommendation he makes." The split was out in the open as Douglas charged that "we are told we must force the Lecompton constitution down the throats of the people for the sake of peace" in a process that made a mockery of popular sovereignty.[101] Not long afterward, Douglas received a letter from Texas, warning, "I inform you as a friend that if you do not cease your hostility towards the Lecompton constitution in Kansas and vote for its reception you will not receive a corporal's guard in Texas in 1860 for president."[102]

The January 4, 1858, vote set by the antislavery legislature on Lecompton, which the proslavery forces boycotted, also had a predictable outcome: more than 10,000 opposed with fewer than 200 in favor. Congress ignored this result as it had the earlier Topeka constitution, of dubious legal origin, which Free State advocates had drafted. A debate ensued in which Congress returned the Lecompton constitution to Kansas, including an alluring land grant provision contingent on approval, for a ratification vote on the entire document. In August Lecompton finally died at its third stand at the ballot box with 11,300 voters opposed and 1,788 in favor.[103] Kansas's statehood was delayed until 1861 when it entered the union as a free state several weeks before the Civil War broke out.

For one senator, at least, the "whole history of Kansas is a disgusting one, from the beginning to the end."[104] Rather, what interested Senator James Henry Hammond of South Carolina was how all the clamor about fraudulent elections brought the two great contending forces of proslavery and antislavery face-to-face. From that point during the Lecompton debate, Hammond launched into one of the most remarkable speeches

James Henry Hammond. SOURCE:
WIKIMEDIA COMMONS/UNIVERSITY OF
ILLINOIS, URBANA-CHAMPAIGN.

ever delivered on the Senate floor. His Cotton Is King address overturned decades of conventions of white southern oratory. Instead of the jeremiads of Calhoun's brooding pessimism, or the all-too-familiar clenched fist avowals to die if need be in defense of white southern honor, Hammond offered defiant bravado as the true white southern creed.

If the slave states "never acquire another foot of territory," Hammond asked, was the 850,000 square miles already occupied not "enough to make an empire that shall rule the world?" Any talk of hemming in so great a territory, he said, like surrounding a scorpion by a ring of fire, "is absurd." Hammond was, for starters, throwing back into the North's face the call to end slavery's expansion. To do so would leave the white South with an empire large enough to rule the world. Within that territory, he said, "lies the great valley of the Mississippi, now the real, and soon to be acknowledged seat of the empire of the world," with sway as great as that of the Nile ever was. From that territory, he continued, the South could put a million men on its muster rolls, "a larger army than any Power on earth can send against her."[105]

Hammond proceeded to trace the source of this mighty empire's strength back to the South's economy. Using a metric that he termed "excess production," he calculated that the South was twice as productive as the North and had a higher production per capita rate than any nation in the world. With such overwhelming economic power, there need never be a dream of initiating war while the white South's fetching and carrying was done by the rest of the world. "Without firing a gun, without drawing a sword," Hammond asserted, "should they make war on us we can bring the whole world to our feet." Cotton was the special power that made the white South invincible. "What would happen if no cotton was furnished for three years," he asked. "England would topple headlong and carry the whole civilized world with her, save the South. No, you dare not make war on cotton. No power on earth dares make war upon it. Cotton is king."

Hammond's final step was to trace the power of cotton back to the logic of slavery. All social systems had a class "to perform the drudgery of life," he said, that formed "the very mud-sill of society." The white South, fortunately, had found "a race inferior to her own," he said, to perform society's mud-sill chores. They were called slaves in the South, but the North had them, too, because slavery "is everywhere; it is eternal." The North's slaves, he said, are the "whole hireling class of manual laborers. . . . The difference between us is, that our slaves are hired for life and well compensated. . . . Yours are hired by the day, not cared for, and scantily compensated." While the South's slaves were happy and content, he said, the North's mud-sill class had the power, if they realized it, to overturn the government and reconstruct society "by the quiet process of the ballot box." Having thoroughly established the white South's mastery,

Hammond delivered a final sentence of scorn to the North. "You are our factors," he said. "You bring and carry for us. . . . Suppose we were to discharge you; suppose we were to take our business out of your hands: we should consign you to anarchy and poverty."[106]

Hammond's speech was a brilliant feat of turning the tables on the North's perceptions of the white South's weaknesses. The *Charleston Mercury* declared that with "one bold stroke of Senatorial eloquence," Hammond had ascended "into the almost inaccessible niche occupied by Calhoun."[107] Left unnoted was that Hammond's address was also an elaborate exercise in fantasy and that, to some degree, the entire North-South, antislavery-proslavery conflict had taken on its own aspect of delusion.

A story that emerged from the war with Mexico had it that a celebrated general once declared to a Captain Duncan who commanded a battery of cannon, "Captain Duncan, fire! The crisis has arrived!" Captain Duncan, a stern and somber soldier, turned to his men and ordered them to fire. Upon hearing this, an old artilleryman walked up to Duncan and said, "Captain, I do not see any enemy within range of our guns; what shall we fire at?" "Fire at the crisis," Duncan replied. "Did you not hear the General say the crisis has come; fire at that!"

From the 1845 annexation of Texas onward, there was a lot of firing at the crisis from both the North and the white South. Also, from the annexation of Texas onward, not one square foot of soil was added to slavery's grasp in the United States and its territories. Henry Clay and Daniel Webster had been right when they consulted together privately at Webster's home on what became the Compromise of 1850. Slavery was not likely to gain a foothold in the territories acquired from Mexico, whether or not the Wilmot Proviso was adopted. They were not alone in that belief. Speaking of all the lands Mexico lost to the United States, Senator Douglas in 1850 said, "I think I am safe in assuming, that each of these will be free territories and free States, whether Congress shall prohibit slavery or not."[108] Even *De Bow's Review*, among the white South's most ardent champions, held in 1852, "We must in all candor say, that we think the limits of slave territory are fixed. California, New Mexico, and Utah, are, we think, already closed against the institution of slavery, and any other territories which we may acquire will share the same fate."[109] A few months later the journal openly expressed what many privately acknowledged: "It is exceedingly doubtful whether there ever will be another acre of land added to the slave territory of this continent."[110]

The bloody struggle over Kansas was comparable. No matter how many times a Lecompton constitution was put forward, or how much an administration supported it, slavery was never likely to thrive on the plains of Kansas. The situation was similar to that when Congress first legislated on governing the southern portion of the Louisiana Purchase, but in direct reverse. Washington might choose to outlaw slavery in the Purchase territories, but the people there had and were bound to keep slavery. As to Kansas, historian Charles Ramsdell insightfully observed, "the one side fought rancorously for what it was bound to get without fighting; the other, with equal rancor, contended for what in the nature of things it could never use."[111]

As was noted in these pages earlier, a slaveowner looking for new plantation lands had, for example, sufficient tracts of opportunities available in Texas or Arkansas. Given that option, it was beyond implausible that he would choose to risk his human capital and his fortune in a distant western territory filling up with Free State settlers. In Kansas, as it turned out, only two slaves were counted in the entire territory in the 1860 census.[112]

Though little noted then, or later, an element of unreality entered the intensifying debate over slavery in the decade preceding the Civil War. Like James Henry Hammond's escape into the fantasy of his Cotton Is King speech, partisans north and south chased phantoms—to some degree—in their denunciations of Slave Power conspiracies to overrun freedom or northern conspiracies to constrict slavery into its existing boundaries so that it, like a fire-encircled scorpion, would kill itself. Historians David M. Potter and his collaborator, Don E. Fehrenbacher, in their seminal study of the era, *The Impending Crisis*, note that the Compromise of 1850, the Kansas-Nebraska Act, and the *Dred Scott* decision "strangely combined theoretical significance with trivial consequences." For example, they observe that the *Dred Scott* decision "annulled a law which had in fact been repealed three years previously, and it denied freedom to the slaves in an area where there were no slaves."[113]

The enrapturement of fantasy reached its peak in various southern schemes to amass new plantation lands beyond the nation's existing borders.[114] The Democratic Party's platform in 1856 and 1860 obligingly included planks favoring acquisition of Cuba. As Mississippi Senator Albert Gallatin Brown expansively phrased it, "I want Cuba, . . . I want Tamaulipas, Potosi, and one or two other Mexican states; and I want them all for the same reason—for the planting or spreading of slavery."[115] Acquisition of Cuba had been on the agenda since Thomas Jefferson's day. During the Pierce administration, garbled authorization from the State Department led three of America's European ambassadors to produce the Ostend Manifesto. That document, named after the Belgium city where it was written, appeared to endorse a war with Spain if Madrid refused to sell Cuba to the United States.

The uproar the Manifesto caused at home made clear war for slavery would ignite massive northern opposition. Former Mississippi governor and congressman John Quitman concocted a scheme to finance an invasion of Cuba by a public bond offering during 1854. The idea fizzled out as it became clear that an invasion force would be met by armed resistance. William Walker was the most flamboyant of land-grabbers, an adventurer driven by his own taste for power but willing to tilt toward slavery if that advanced his purposes. After various scrapes in lower California and Sonora, Mexico, Walker briefly became president of Nicaragua before having to flee the country. He died facing a firing squad in Honduras in 1860.

The disconnect between rhetoric and reality during the 1850s is most easily observed, of course, in retrospect. Although slavery's expansion into Kansas and other territories may have been highly doubtful, the fear that it would do so unless vigorously opposed was quite real. For its part, the white South never had any need to doubt that the Republicans' ultimate goal was to celebrate the extirpation of slavery throughout the United States. The *Dred Scott* decision may have touched few slaves directly, but its declaration of a constitutional right to property in man sought to degrade freedom from a national standard to a local phenomenon. What the disconnect shows most clearly is that, in both the North and white South, the struggle between freedom and slavery had taken on an emotional intensity in which each side saw the other through the lens of its own formulation of reality. An emotional break between the two sides was the last measure needed to push rhetoric over the threshold into violence.

To James Stirling, a British observer at the time, the situation was clear. "A crisis is at hand," he wrote. "A spirit of disunion has taken possession of both parties; they regard each other with jealousy, if not dislike; and the language of the two geographical sections of the States savours more of the rancor of avowed enemies than the loving-kindness of brethren."[116]

CHAPTER 10

Lincoln and Secession

"I HAVE NEVER had a feeling politically, that did not spring from the sentiments embodied in the Declaration of Independence."[1] Abraham Lincoln offered that insight into his beliefs in 1861 after his election to the presidency on his way to Washington, D.C. Those pesky words again. The ones that would not go away. This time, however, the affirmation of equality and unalienable rights to life, liberty, and the pursuit of happiness was deployed by an individual who not only believed in them but also was as eloquent as Jefferson.

Both gregarious and intensely private, Lincoln was described by some who knew him best as a person who never fully revealed himself to anyone. As a self-taught individual, his approach was to carefully consider an issue from every angle. Only after thorough examination did he reach a conclusion. The conclusions thus reached were held to tenaciously. His mind, Lincoln once confided to a friend, was like a "piece of steel, very hard to scratch any thing on it and almost impossible after you get it there to rub it out."[2] One of those conclusions was that "he who molds public sentiment, goes deeper than he who enacts statutes or pronounces decisions. He makes statutes and decisions possible or impossible to be executed."[3] Lincoln put the Declaration's core proclamation through the process of his intense examination. He then used the result to mold public opinion about slavery.

In his 1858 campaign to unseat Senator Stephen A. Douglas in Illinois, Lincoln called on voters to judge slavery against the standard that the Declaration created. He could have assailed slavery for its catalog of human outrages. He rarely touched on these. He could have made the halt of slavery's expansion his campaign's central theme. That was, after all, the unifying message of the Republican Party that Lincoln had recently joined. Although Lincoln carried that message, he deliberately

Stephen A. Douglas. COURTESY:
LIBRARY OF CONGRESS.

chose to make the assertion in the Declaration of Independence of an
equality among individuals that entailed unalienable rights his campaign's moral underpinning and the ground on which to challenge Douglas. He did what is rarely done in a political context: instead of asking
voters to cast ballots based on their own narrow self-interest, he called
on them to register a moral objection to slavery based on the Declaration
of Independence.

At age forty-nine, Lincoln's once promising political career seemed
to be a washout. He had served four terms in the Illinois legislature more
than a decade earlier and a single term in Congress. By 1858, Douglas
was one of the most prominent public figures in the country. The two
men had known each other since the mid-1830s. Douglas had been
one of Mary Todd's suitors not long before she accepted Lincoln's offer
of marriage. As Douglas bounded forward in wealth, fame, and stature,

Lincoln receded to the sidelines of politics while building a law practice based in Springfield that earned him a favorable reputation that extended little beyond Illinois.

Douglas changed that with the Kansas-Nebraska Act's repeal of the Missouri Compromise. For many northerners, Lincoln included, over-turning the 1820 compromise was a stunningly unexpected shift from decades of containing slavery to suddenly opening it to expansion. From 1854 onward, Lincoln returned to the public arena to oppose Douglas, popular sovereignty, and the expansion of slavery. A lifelong Whig and champion of Henry Clay, Lincoln refused to join the fledging Repub-licans in 1854 due to his constitutional scruples over their advocacy of the repeal of the Fugitive Slave Act and other positions he viewed as too radical. During this period, he wrote to his former law partner, Joshua Speed, then living in Kentucky, that he acknowledged *"your* right and *my* obligations, under the constitution, in regard to your slaves. I hate to see the poor creatures hunted down, and caught, . . . but I bite my lip and keep quiet."[4] Lincoln's sense of slavery's essential injustice was perhaps conveyed most revealingly in a rare direct criticism of slaveholders:

> *They have him in his prison house; they have searched his person, and left no prying instrument with him. One after another they have closed the heavy iron doors upon him, and now they have him, as it were, bolted in with a lock of a hundred keys, which can never be unlocked without the concurrence of every key; the keys in the hands of a hundred different men, and they scattered to a hundred different and distant places; and they stand musing to what invention, in all the dominions of mind and matter, can be produced to make the impossibility of his escape more complete than it is.*[5]

By 1856, Lincoln had joined the Republicans, drawing some attention when he was nominated for vice president at the party's convention and came in a respectable second in the balloting.[6] By the time of Douglas's reelection bid, Lincoln was the consensus Republican challenger.

Lincoln was politically conservative in an era buffeted by radical and reactionary forces. From early in life as he rose from log cabin obscurity, he was also intensely ambitious. Unseating Douglas in the Democratic stronghold of Illinois would certainly propel Lincoln into presidential consideration two years later. Due to the state's weight in electoral vote calculations for that election, even a strong showing could bring him into consideration for the higher office. Pragmatism and the advice of his close political strategists urged Lincoln to play it safe: avoid taking risky or controversial stands while relentlessly hammering at Douglas and popular sovereignty's weakness as a cover for slavery's expansion. The first act in the 1858 campaign of the conservative, ambitious, and politically seasoned Lincoln was to reject that advice.

Lincoln opened his campaign in Springfield with the most radical speech of his political career. He had two objectives. One, which has been nearly forgotten over time, was to stanch rumblings among eastern Republicans prompted by newspaper editor Horace Greeley to consider embracing Douglas, given his split with Buchanan and his stand against the Lecompton constitution. The other, for which Lincoln is remembered to this day, was to fixate the campaign on the central issue facing the nation. On June 16, in response to his party's nomination, Lincoln delivered the House Divided speech.

He began with words adapted from Daniel Webster's second reply to Robert Hayne in 1830 at the outset of the nullification crisis. "If we could first know *where* we are, and *whither* we are tending," Lincoln said, "we could then better judge *what* to do, and *how* to do it." Under a policy designed to end slavery agitation, he said in reference to Douglas's Kansas-Nebraska Act, the agitation had not only not ceased but, instead, constantly increased. It would not cease, he continued, "until a *crisis* shall have been reached, and passed." He then invoked a biblical reference from Mark 3:25:

> *A house divided against itself cannot stand. I believe this government cannot endure half slave and half free. I do not expect the Union to be dissolved—I do not expect the house to fall—but I do expect it will cease to be divided. It will become all one thing, or all the other. Either the opponents of slavery, will arrest the further spread of it, and place it where the public mind shall rest in the belief that it is*

in the course of ultimate extinction; or its advocates will push it forward, till it shall become alike lawful in all the States, old as well as new—North as well as South.[7]

These words expressed Lincoln's examination from all angles of where the country was and a stark choice about where it must tend. His conclusion and the vividness with which he delivered it led some in the North who had long labored in the antislavery cause to begin thinking that the obscure Illinois lawyer might have the grit needed for a more important role in the national arena.

Greeley's *Tribune* ran the text in full. Even before it had become an issue, Lincoln had shaken off suspicion that he was too conservative in the old Whig style of accommodation to white southern sentiment to be trusted to stand firm against slavery in principle and the expansion of it in particular. That gain came at a cost, the one Lincoln's advisers had warned against. The southern press read his speech as advocating civil war and abolition. *Chicago Press and Tribune* chief editor John Locke Scripps wrote to Lincoln a few days after the speech that some of his friends "who want to be Republicans, but who are *afraid* we are not sufficiently conservative" objected to the "ultraism" in his remarks.[8] Lincoln was quick to reply that the speech neither asserted nor intimated "any power or purpose, to interfere with slavery in the States where it exists."[9]

Such distinctions were important. A few months later New York Senator William Seward's warning of an "irrepressible conflict" between North and South was seen not only as incendiary in the white South but by many Republicans as too radical. Although considered the front-runner for the Republican 1860 presidential nomination, Seward was so hobbled by the remark that he never fully recovered. For his part, Douglas easily characterized Lincoln as an abolitionist because making the nation all free could only be accomplished by ending slavery where it already existed. He leveled some variant of this charge repeatedly during the campaign.

The Springfield speech also contained a version of what Lincoln presented as having the appearance of a conspiracy. The plot, as he saw it, was to lull the North into accepting the tendency aimed at sanctioning slavery in all the states, old as well as new. Lincoln named those who were involved as Stephen, Franklin, Roger, and James—Senator Douglas, President Pierce, Chief Justice Taney, and President Buchanan.

The plan began by opening the territories to slavery with the repeal of the Missouri Compromise. In place of that sanction, Lincoln said, a doctrine of national indifference to whether slavery was voted up or down—popular sovereignty—was instituted. Following on that step, he continued, Presidents Pierce and Buchanan welcomed a high court ruling on whether slavery could be banned in the territories. When that decision came in Chief Justice Taney's *Dred Scott* ruling, both Douglas and the new president endorsed it. The last and still pending step, Lincoln said, was for "another Supreme Court decision, declaring that the Constitution of the United States does not permit a *state* to exclude slavery from its limits. . . . Welcome or unwelcome, such decision *is* probably coming, and will soon be upon us, unless the power of the present political dynasty shall be met and overthrown."[10]

Lincoln explained the unfolding of these events in detail, requiring the listener to hold all the pieces in mind in order to see the whole. But he provided those who heard or read his words, in a single sentence, his own summary in terms thoroughly clear to any citizen:

> *We can not absolutely* know *that all these exact adaptations are the result of preconcert. But when we see a lot of framed timbers, different portions of which we know have been gotten out at different times and places and by different workmen—Stephen, Franklin, Roger and James, for instance—and when we see these timbers joined together, and see they exactly make the frame of a house or a mill, all the tenons and mortises exactly fitting, and all the lengths and proportions of the different pieces exactly adapted to their respective places, and not a piece too many or too few—not omitting even scaffolding—or, if a single piece be lacking, we can see the place in the frame exactly fitted and prepared to yet bring such piece in—in such a case, we find it impossible to not* believe *that Stephen and Franklin and Roger and James all understood one another from the beginning, and all worked upon a common* plan *or draft drawn up before the first lick was struck.*[11]

Lincoln's implication of a Slave Power conspiracy was no more original than his analogy to a house divided. Others had invoked the biblical reference before Lincoln did in describing the nation's dilemma. A "scheme" to overturn the Missouri Compromise as a preliminary to declaring slavery legal in all states was laid out by Maine Senator William Fessenden several months before Lincoln spoke.[12]

Douglas dismissed the first of Lincoln's assertions, asking, "When did he learn, and by what authority does he proclaim, that this government is contrary to the law of God, and cannot stand? It has stood thus divided into free and slave States from its organization up to this day."[13] Tying the Little Giant to a Slave Power plot put Douglas on the defensive throughout the campaign, trying to deny what he could not disprove. Read carefully, Lincoln's words do not claim a conspiracy, only that the best way to understand events was to assume that one must have existed. Between 1854 and 1860, he made the claim in more than fifty speeches.[14]

That proslavery leaders with some northern support sought noninterference with slavery where it existed and its expansion where it did not is incontrovertible. That a plot existed to accomplish these aims, particularly among the men Lincoln singled out, is beyond dubious. Buchanan was out of the country when Douglas backed overturning the Missouri Compromise. His version of popular sovereignty was never trusted in the white South in the first place. Taney's *Dred Scott* ruling undercut Douglas by its implicit denial of a territorial legislature's authority to ban slavery. As noted earlier, some Republicans thought of accepting Douglas because of his open break with Buchanan over the Lecompton constitution. The prospect that the Supreme Court might broaden its sanction for slavery into free states would have required the unlikely declaration that states could not determine the status of slavery in their own constitutions.[15]

Nonetheless, a case that would have given the court an opportunity to establish the right of slaveowners to transit through free states with their human property was working its way through the legal system when Lincoln spoke in Springfield.[16] As for Lincoln, evidence that he believed the conspiracy charge can be found in a draft he made for a speech that reads "I clearly see, as I think, a powerful plot to make slavery universal and perpetual in this nation."[17]

Soon after Springfield, Lincoln was in Chicago, where his address on July 10 came as an impromptu response to Douglas's attack the night before on his House Divided speech. Lincoln was on the defensive, concerned that Douglas would gain ground by pointing out that freedom and slavery had existed in the republic from its inception so that claiming one or the other must prevail sounded like a call for abolition in the states where it existed. His reply reflected the belief that those who opposed slavery had comforted themselves with since the Constitution was written. Until the Kansas-Nebraska Act, Lincoln said, "the public mind did rest, all the time, in the belief that slavery was in course of ultimate extinction."

Although he had always hated slavery "as much as any Abolitionist," Lincoln said he had "always been quiet about it," believing that "everybody was against it, and that it was in course of ultimate extinction" until Douglas's bill overturned that belief. Citing the slave-free Northwest Ordinance and the constitutional clause used to outlaw the foreign slave trade, Lincoln asserted that the "framers of the Constitution intended and expected the ultimate extinction of the institution."[18] He had called for no more than what the framers had intended and had no inclination to interfere with slavery where it already existed. Lincoln was admitting to the same self-deception that northerners had indulged in for decades, despite the obvious thrusts toward slavery's expansion arising from the Louisiana Purchase, the 1820 Compromise's inclusion of Missouri as a slave state, and the admission of Texas, the largest slave state of them all. The Kansas-Nebraska Act may have finally shattered the illusion, but it had been an illusion at least since the white South began the transition to the cotton plantation economy.

Lincoln's Chicago speech also included one of his campaign's most forceful invocations of the Declaration of Independence. Surveying the crowd of several thousand people, he noted that perhaps half of them were immigrants or descended from European settlers who had arrived in America after the country won its freedom. They had no blood tie to the Revolutionary generation. But when they look at the words "We hold these truths to be self-evident, that all men are created equal," they claim a right to that moral principle "as though they were blood of the blood, and flesh of the flesh of the men who wrote that Declaration, and so they are," he said. "That is the electric cord in that Declaration that links the hearts of patriotic and liberty-loving men together, that will link those patriotic hearts as long as the love of freedom exists in the minds of men throughout the world."[19]

The Declaration's principle, he said, opposed the principle espoused over the ages by kings or men of one race who enslaved another "that says you work and I eat, you toil and I will enjoy the fruit of it." If the people accept the argument that "one man says it does not mean a negro, why not another say it does not mean some other man," where will exceptions to the Declaration stop, he asked. Rousing the crowd in his conclusion, Lincoln shouted out that if the Declaration was not true, who would be so bold as to tear it out from where it is found. With chants of "No," "No one" answering from the crowd, Lincoln declared "Let us stick to it then, let us stand firmly by it."[20]

The Chicago speech initiated what soon became a pattern of Lincoln traipsing along behind Douglas to take advantage of whatever residual crowds his opponent had gathered and to counter his attacks before they set in the public mind. While Lincoln traveled mostly alone in common rail passenger seats, Douglas toured the state with flare. The Illinois Central Railroad directors' private passenger car was at his disposal. A banner strung outside the baggage car proclaimed the presence of "S.A. Douglas, The Champion of Popular Sovereignty." A flatbed was armed with two small brass howitzers tended by a pair of red-clad, sword-carrying gunners who fired off the pieces to announce the great man's arrival.[21]

The people themselves, as was then the tradition, traveled by ox-drawn wagon or horseback to the town where the candidate and, quite likely, his trailing challenger were to appear. They camped out wherever convenient, socialized, occasionally got into scuffles with partisans on the opposite side, and made a day or two of the stay to hear both men out. Along with townsfolk, the crowds could run into the thousands. Douglas made up for his short stature with combative cockiness. The senator stamped his feet, unleashed sarcasm, and used years of experience as a public speaker to draw crowds to him while strutting about the stage like a Roman emperor, taking on hecklers in the crowd and blistering Lincoln with a flurry of charges. The Douglas that crowds saw then was a more seasoned version of a younger Douglas years earlier, just entering the House of Representatives, captured in a portrait written by John Quincy Adams:

> *His face was convulsed, his gesticulation frantic, and he lashed himself into such a heat that if his body had been made of combustible matter, it would have burnt out. In the midst of his roaring, to save himself from choking, he stripped off and cast away his cravat, and unbuttoned his waist-coat, and had the air and aspect of a half-naked pugilist.*[22]

Jefferson Davis simply dismissed Douglas as "our little grog-drinking, electioneering demagogue."[23]

The Little Giant's "most trenchant weapon" during the 1858 campaign, according to Chicago's *Press and Tribune*, was some variant of Lincoln favoring racial equality.[24] One example was Douglas's umbrage at his opponent's "preaching up this same doctrine of the Declaration of Independence that niggers were equal to white men."[25] The Little Giant wanted everyone in Illinois and beyond to know that he would have none of it. "I believe this government was made on the white basis," he said during the campaign. "I believe it was made by white men, for the benefit of white men and their posterity forever, and I am in favor of confining citizenship to white men, men of European birth and descent, instead of conferring it upon negroes, Indians and other inferior races."

To clarify his position, Douglas added, "I do not hold that because the negro is our inferior that therefore he ought to be a slave." Instead, he asserted, Blacks should "enjoy every right, every privilege, and every immunity consistent with the safety of the society in which he lives."[26] He skirted the issue of slavery with a public attitude that he did not really care about it one way or the other, the attitude underlying popular sovereignty that whether local people voted to embrace or reject it was of no national concern. He could not skirt the toll the campaign took on him physically. As the election drew near, Douglas, puffy and worn, gave a tell of his penchant for brandy by calling his opponent "Misha Linka." A newspaper reporter who covered him later wrote that during that time, Douglas was simply "drinking himself to death."[27]

Lincoln's disdain for Douglas stemmed, in large measure, from his belief that rejecting or accepting slavery did matter. In stating that he hated slavery "because of the monstrous injustice of slavery itself," Lincoln also declared that the supposed indifference of popular sovereignty was actually a "covert *real* zeal for the spread of slavery."[28] The path to slavery's expansion was opened by lulling people into indifference about it. Yet, however much Lincoln persisted in uncovering what he saw as popular sovereignty's real influence, Douglas's attacks found their mark.

Abraham Lincoln believed that by getting the central issue right, the rest of the pieces would fall into place. As a lawyer he was noted for dispensing with peripheral issues in a case while steadfastly maintaining his core argument. For Lincoln, the central idea behind American democracy was the Declaration's assertion of a universal equality endowing all with unalienable rights. He had examined the Declaration from all angles. The Constitution was the means of carrying out the national governance requirement of republican democracy. The Declaration articulated the self-evident truths behind it all. Yet for a man so well known for his close examination of all aspects of an issue confronting him, Lincoln was notably at a loss when considering what the application of the Declaration's principles should mean in the lives of Blacks in America. He was sure that "in the right to eat the bread, without leave of anybody else, which his own hand earns, *he is my equal . . . and the equal of every living man.*"[29] Beyond that, in Lincoln's mind during the 1850s, the Declaration's reach was not so certain. "If all earthly power were given me," he said, "I should not know what to do, as to the existing institution."[30] He supported colonizing free Blacks while recognizing that it was too cumbersome and costly to work.[31] He revealed some of his uncertainty in delving into what should be done with enslaved Blacks if they were freed.

> *What next? Free them, and make them politically and socially our equals? My own feelings will not admit of this; and if mine would, we well know that those of the great mass of white people will not. Whether this feeling accords with justice and sound judgment, is not the sole question, if indeed it is any part of it. A universal feeling,*

whether well or ill-founded, can not be safely disregarded. We can not,
then, make them equals.[32]

During the campaign Lincoln refused to sign a petition to repeal a state law forbidding Blacks to testify in court against whites. His close adviser David Davis urged Lincoln and all Republican candidates to "distinctly & emphatically disavow *negro suffrage*—negro[es] holding office, serving on juries, & the like."[33] Lincoln complied, saying at one campaign event "I am not, nor ever have been in favor of bringing about in any way the social and political equality of the white and black races—that I am not nor ever have been in favor of making voters or jurors of negroes, nor of qualifying them to hold office, nor to intermarry with white people." He then went further, saying that the physical difference between whites and Blacks—presumably meaning their skin color—made living together in equality impossible. This being so, he said, "while they do remain together there must be the position of superior and inferior." To loud cheers from the audience, he concluded, "I as much as any other man am in favor of having the superior position assigned to the white race."[34]

In these remarks, Lincoln was not only responding to Davis's prompting, but to such attacks from Douglas as "those of you who believe that the nigger is your equal and ought to be on an equality with you socially, politically, and legally; have a right to entertain those opinions, and of course will vote for Mr. Lincoln."[35] Douglas's thrusts moved Lincoln to acknowledge "very frankly that I am not in favor of negro citizenship."[36] When addressing how long the ultimate extinction of slavery might take, Lincoln offered that if done peacefully it might stretch out to "a hundred years at the least."[37]

Read together, these remarks by Lincoln leave behind tattered remnants of what the unalienable rights to life, liberty, and the pursuit of happiness might mean for Blacks once slavery was abolished. He left a crack open in the door to a broader understanding with qualifiers to his views about being in accord with justice and sound judgment, or being well or ill-founded. To what extent the remarks reflect bending to Douglas's race-baiting is not now possible to know. Just a year earlier in discussing his disagreement with the *Dred Scott* case, Lincoln had favorably cited Black voting rights in five states when the Constitution was adopted. He had also said that he wished the court had affirmed Dred Scott's citizenship at least as far as allowing him to obtain a hearing on whether or not he was free.[38] Read together without further context, these campaign remarks might fix an image of Lincoln as a racist incapable of growth.[39] That would be a mistake. Under Lincoln's leadership, or inspired by it, within ten years slavery was abolished and birthright citizenship became a constitutional guarantee.

The record of campaign speeches exists because Lincoln, persuaded by advisers, challenged Douglas to a series of debates. The Little Giant agreed to seven joint meetings beginning in Ottawa on August 21 and ending in Alton on October 13. Each man gave dozens of less-well-reported speeches, but the full-length newspaper accounts of the Lincoln-Douglas debates stand as one of the most famous political encounters of American history. Reprinted in eastern and other newspapers from transcripts prepared by Chicago reporters who covered the debates, they also gave Lincoln exposure to Republican opinion makers and voters far beyond Illinois. What struck them most forcefully was not Lincoln's equivocations. Abolitionists such as Garrison had long called for full social and political equality for Blacks. Seward was among political leaders who favored Black voting rights. Instead, what impressed much of the northern public beyond Illinois most clearly was the passion of Lincoln's conviction that slavery was a moral wrong in contradiction to the nation's founding principles.

At the campaign's close, Lincoln declared "The real issue in this controversy—the one pressing upon every mind—is the sentiment on the part of one class that looks upon the institution of slavery *as a wrong*, and of another class that *does not* look upon it as a wrong."[40] Douglas's popular sovereignty doctrine, he said, was attempting to promote a policy based on not caring "about the very thing that every body does care the most about."[41] The attempt to sweep slavery off the national agenda with the doctrine of indifference left no place to oppose it as a moral canker on the nation. In Lincoln's words:

You say it must not be opposed in the free States, because slavery is not here; it must not be opposed in the slave States, because it is there; it must not be opposed in politics, because that will make a fuss; it must not be opposed in the pulpit, because it is not religion. Then where is the place to oppose it? There is no suitable place to oppose it.[42]

To understand slavery as a national disgrace, one need only look to the Declaration's assertion that all men are created equal. Lincoln said he fought the exclusion of Blacks from the Declaration's embrace because that "evil tendency" was designed to dehumanize them while preparing the public mind "to make property, and nothing but property of the *negro in all the States of this Union.*"[43] Although Lincoln's view of the reach of the Declaration's unalienable rights was constricted, he did not see the document as a static memorial of a dead past. Rather, in Lincoln's eyes, the Declaration was a living instrument, to be applied by succeeding generations in the light of their own understanding of what its words meant. The founders, Lincoln said,

meant simply to declare the right, *so that the* enforcement *of it might follow as fast as circumstances should permit. They meant to set up a standard maxim for a free society, which should be familiar to all, and revered by all; constantly looked to, constantly labored for, and even though never perfectly attained, constantly approximated and thereby constantly spreading and deepening its influence, and augmenting the happiness and value of life to all people of all colors everywhere.*[44]

For Lincoln, the principles of the Declaration of Independence formed the ark that could most safely carry the nation into the future. Where those principles might take the republic could not be seen in advance, but they were the surest hold in which to make the journey. To Lincoln, in the years immediately preceding the Civil War, those principles meant that slavery was wrong and must at least be halted in its expansion. In later decades, although it has no constitutional grounding, the Declaration underpinned movements by women, Blacks, gays, and others to have themselves included among those who are created equal and are therefore endowed with unalienable rights. Lincoln's contribution, on examining the issue from all sides, was to take up the promise that Jefferson offered to make the self-evident truths of the Declaration the nation's compass guide.

Douglas won the election, or more accurately, just enough members of the new state legislature who supported him were elected to vote him a new term in the Senate. With his claim to leadership of northern Democrats validated, Douglas's next target was to win the party's presidential nomination.

A snare of his own creation lay in his path to that goal. During the campaign in the debate at Freeport, Douglas had answered a question Lincoln put to him. The challenger wanted to know if the people of a territory had any means to exclude slavery before adopting a state constitution. Regardless of what the Supreme Court decided, Douglas replied "the people have the lawful means to introduce it or exclude it as they please, for the reason that slavery cannot exist a day or an hour anywhere, unless it is supported by local police regulations."[45] His answer was not new. A year earlier he had said that although the Constitution granted the right to hold slaves in the territories "it necessarily remains a barren and worthless right unless sustained, protected and enforced by appropriate police regulation and local legislation presenting adequate remedies for its violation."[46] Slave-owning southerners did not like being told that one of their most cherished constitutional rights was worthless. Senator James M. Mason of Virginia put it directly to Douglas: "You have promised us bread, and you have given us stone; you promised us fish, and you have given us a serpent; we thought you had given us a substantial right, and you have given us the most evanescent shadow and delusion."[47]

That Douglas's observation was not a policy choice but a statement of fact made little difference. The Little Giant's reading of popular sovereignty meant the people could exclude slavery from the territories no matter what the Supreme Court said. Although Chief Justice Taney's decision may have left popular sovereignty only partially intact, Douglas was determined to hold on to the remnant in order to hold on to Illinois and, later, other northern Democrats who were increasingly none too partial to slavery's expansion into territory they or their children might

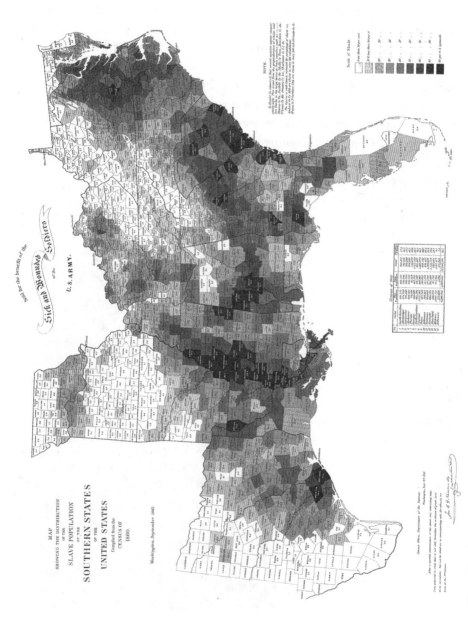

Slave density map in 1860. SOURCE: NOAA OFFICE OF COAST SURVEY.

one day want to homestead. To complete the record, Douglas went on to say during the campaign "I would not vote in Congress for any code of laws either for or against slavery in any territory."[48]

His stated reason for this stand harkened back to the bedrock of states' rights doctrine: that Congress had no authority to intervene anywhere on the subject of slavery, with the constitutionally mandated exceptions of fugitive slaves and the foreign slave trade. By this date, however, many white southerners were less interested in bedrock principles than in Congress intervening with a slave code to prevent territorial locals from nullifying what Chief Justice Taney had affirmed as their constitutional right to own slaves in the territories.

Mississippi Senator Jefferson Davis brushed aside decades of states' rights rhetoric about congressional nonintervention as "a thing shadowy

Jefferson Davis. COURTESY OF THE LIBRARY OF CONGRESS.

and fleeting, changing its color as often as the chameleon," and for nearly a decade past "woven into a delusive gauze thrown over the public mind."[49] In its place, Davis led the white southern charge for a congressionally mandated territorial slave code. In this regard, however, Davis and his colleagues were themselves a bit shadowy in that they never set down in writing what that slave code should say. They may well have realized that once congressional authority to intervene on slavery in the territories was granted, a majority of that body might include in the code such things as nonviolent treatment of bonded humans or rights to a certain standard of working conditions, food, housing, and clothing. So, Davis was content to fight for the idea, not its implementation, a bit like firing the cannon at the crisis.

A certain absurdity is obvious on the face of the slave code controversy. The white South was fighting for protections it refused to enumerate in order to uphold a right it had no prospect of ever exercising. As war drew unknowably closer, some of the rhetoric became detached from reality. While the North was pursuing the phantom of slavery's march into the territories, the white South was pursuing the phantom of a code to protect slavery where it never was going to exist. During the 1850s, dissent from Clay and Webster's belief that slavery would not expand into the territories at any event was the norm, not the exception. Lincoln called that notion "a palliation—a lullaby."[50] Jefferson Davis believed that even if the Arizona Territory, then part of the New Mexico Territory, was unsuitable for plantation slavery, slaves could be put to work mining gold and silver there somewhat along the model of ancient Rome.[51] Massachusetts Congressman Horace Mann wrote "Slavery depends not upon Climate, but upon Conscience."[52] And there was always the white southern dream of somehow acquiring Cuba, or a bit more of Mexico, or other lands in Central or South America. "In retrospect, the whole quarrel seems utterly senseless because nothing of practical value was at stake," historian Don E. Fehrenbacher has insightfully written of the slave code issue, which "makes sense only in the way that a chip on the shoulder makes sense—as a pretext for fighting, as the symbol of deep-seated antagonisms."[53]

The chip on William Lowndes Yancey's shoulder of his abusive abolitionist stepfather had grown from his youth into contempt for the North
and a zeal for white southern independence. From his vantage point in
Alabama, Yancey tucked away Douglas's rejection of a slave code for
future use. "The great mass of the States Rights men in the South," he
wrote, "have declared for protection to the right of the slaveholder in
the Territories by law of Congress against Abolition legislation, and will
sustain no party, be it national or sectional, which does not unequivocally
avow this doctrine." He saw the Republicans as "purely an aggressive
party—assailing a section which acts entirely on the defensive." In his
assessment, the Democrats could not count on carrying more than three
of the seventeen northern states in the upcoming presidential election.
The white South was further "assailed, in flank as it were, through the
Territories by Douglas and his followers." The remedy, he believed, was to
act as the colonists did before the Revolution. Committees of correspondence should be formed to warn of dire threats ahead until they so fired
the white southern heart that "at the proper moment, by one organized,
concerted action, we can precipitate the cotton States into a revolution."[54]

As Lincoln and Douglas geared up their campaigns in Illinois,
Yancey was selected to welcome guests to the Southern Commercial
Convention in Montgomery. The meeting was intended to promote the
use of southern ports for European shipping, but Yancey "immediately
turned it into a secession convention," according to a participant.[55] In
a torrent of eloquence unleashed over three days in the longest speech
of his life, Yancey foresaw the hour approaching when the white South
would have its own "independent sovereignty . . . which alone can be
the basis of a successful and permanent government."[56] He had invited
Robert Barnwell Rhett Sr., publisher of the *Charleston Mercury*, to the
convention. The sixty-four-year-old Virginia planter Edmund Ruffin
was also there, where he met Yancey for the first time. These three were
already recognized as among the South's leading "fire-eaters," the most
radical incendiaries for secession and the formation of an independent
white southern confederacy.

While in Montgomery, Ruffin convinced Yancey to help create a Southern League as a modern version of the Revolutionary era's committees of correspondence to prepare for secession. Sometime later Douglas described Yancey's intentions in a Senate address. "Yancey's whole plan," Douglas said, was "to wait in the Democratic party until the proper moment came for revolution; then plunge the cotton states into it; break up the party, and with the party," the union.[57] Little actually came of the Southern League, but the rest of Douglas's assessment of Yancey's revolutionary intent was remarkably accurate.

Yancey laid out his plan to precipitate secession in a July 1859 speech in South Carolina. At the Democratic convention in Charleston the following year, he said, states' rights men should demand a slave code platform plank. If Douglas's forces pushed that aside, Yancey said the states' rights delegates should bolt the convention, break up the Democratic party, and nominate their own candidate for president. With the Democrats split between Douglas and a states' rights candidate, "a black Republican may be elected," he warned. In that case, Yancey concluded, "the only hope of safety for the South is in a withdrawal from the Union before he shall be inaugurated; before the sword and the treasury of the Federal Government shall be placed in the keeping of that party."[58] He then set about implementing that plan.

John Brown also had revolutionary intent. After his return from Kansas to his home in North Elba, New York, he set out on a tour of northeastern states to solicit support for his latest, and last, plan to strike a hammer blow at the heart of slavery. In early 1858 he met with luminaries Ralph Waldo Emerson and Henry David Thoreau, among other prominent abolitionists, recounting his exploits in Kansas with the notable omission of his role in the murder of defenseless civilians in the dead of night near Pottawatomie Creek.

At the mansion of abolitionist Gerrit Smith, who had sold Brown the land for his home in North Elba, he laid out a plan involving the federal arsenal and armory at Harpers Ferry in Virginia. The town was situated on a neck of land in a mountain-rimmed bowl at the confluence of the Shenandoah and Potomac Rivers. Brown proposed to seize the federal facilities with a small band of handpicked recruits, raise a call for slaves to join him, and lead them in a great march south to throw off the shackles of bondage. Exactly how the slaves were to be alerted to join him, or how they would fend off the inevitable counterthrust from the militia and military, was left rather vague. Brown apparently envisioned a spontaneous chain reaction once his uprising began that would simply overwhelm opposition before it had time to organize. On hearing of the plan, Frederick Douglass thought it was madness. Federal troops would swiftly descend on the rail junction in response to an attack on a federal military installation. More convincing than his plan was the prophetic fervor of the man who proposed it. Brown radiated the convictions of one who is chosen to carry out a mission from God. He won over a core group of six abolitionist supporters, including Smith, who gave him $3,500 in the spring of 1859 to execute the plan.[59]

By summer Brown had inserted into Harpers Ferry one of his recruits, who blended in with the local population while gathering intelligence on how the raid's targets were guarded. In early July, Brown arrived at the isolated Kennedy farmhouse in Maryland about five miles from the town that served as his recruits' staging ground. In preparation for his assault on slavery, Brown declared himself commander in chief of the Provisional Army of the North and drafted a provisional constitution. The document's opening sentence pronounced slavery a barbarous "violation of those eternal and self-evident truths set forth in our Declaration of Independence."[60] John H. Kagi, the newspaper correspondent who had ridden with Brown in Kansas, was designated secretary of war. He was stationed in nearby Chambersburg, Pennsylvania, to take delivery of rifles and specially ordered pikes purchased with the patrons' donations. By fall Brown had twenty followers at the ready, fifteen of them whites, including two of his sons, five of them Blacks.

The raid began well after dark on the night of October 16. Brown's men walked as he drove a wagon holding the arms Kagi had delivered to the farmhouse. Curiously, the commander in chief had made no arrangements to bring food for his men along with the weapons. They cut telegraph lines on their way in. The town of about 1,300 residents was largely asleep. The watchman at the railroad and wagon bridge over the Potomac was captured and a pair of Brown's men deployed to guard the crossing. The bridge over the Shenandoah was similarly secured. The single watchman at the U.S. Armory grounds was quickly subdued, the area seized, and more men dispatched across the street to take the adjacent arsenal building. The armory was a large complex of buildings where small arms were manufactured for the military. Muskets and rifles were stored in the three buildings that made up the arsenal. Kagi and two others sped forward about a half mile up Shenandoah Street, where they took the rifle works. All the raid's main targets were now in Brown's hands, if only lightly defended. After midnight three white hostages, including the great-grandnephew of George Washington, and a few of their slaves were brought to Brown, who was stationed with the bulk of his men at the arsenal. He ordered the slaves, armed with pikes, to guard their masters. Brown next expected the spontaneous insurrection to break forth, ignited by his son Owen, who had been tasked with leading the first band of slaves into the town to meet their leader and receive arms. They were never aroused, and they never arrived.

At about 1:25 on the morning of the 17th, an express train from Wheeling halted in the town after the engineer saw that the bridge ahead was obstructed. When a pair of men from the train began to walk along the track to inspect the situation, Brown's men opened fire on them. The engineer backed the train off as Shepard Haywood, a free Black baggage handler, came walking along the track seeking the watchman. He was shot dead by one of Brown's men with a bullet in the back, the insurrection's first casualty. Not long afterward, a grocer named Thomas Boerley was shot dead, his body left in a pool of blood on the street. The gunfire aroused the town's folk and the local militia, who responded to rifle shots from Brown's men with return fire of their own. Inextricably, the train was not stopped as the engineer eased it forward over the Potomac bridge on its way eastward where a warning that Harpers Ferry was under siege was telegraphed to Washington.

By morning Brown was the one under siege, his men surrounded and under fire from their positions at the armory and the rifle works. In an attempt to exchange his hostages for free passage out of town, Brown sent Will Thompson to negotiate. He was seized, carried away, and later shot in the head before his body was dumped into the Potomac River. Next, Brown sent his son Watson and a second man, Aaron Stevens, under a white flag of truce. They were met by a hail of gunfire, wounding both men. Stevens lay in the street until carried to the railroad station where he received medical attention. Watson crawled back to the arsenal's engine house where Brown, several of his men, and the hostages with their guards took refuge.

Panicked, eighteen-year-old William Leeman, the youngest of Brown's army, ran out the back door, was pursued, and had his brains blown out. A half mile away down Shenandoah Street, Kagi and the two Black recruits with him were driven out of the rifle works. Kagi and Lewis Leary were killed by gunfire as they ran toward the riverbank. The second Black recruit, John Copeland, was captured, nearly lynched, then taken into custody by a law officer. Back at Brown's location the mayor, Fontaine Beckham, was shot dead as he walked toward the armory in what was probably an attempt to negotiate. Then it began to rain. Two of Brown's men took advantage of the mist to escape, get to the east bank of the Potomac in a small stolen boat, and make their way back to the farmhouse they had departed from several hours earlier.

The engine house that became Brown's fort was a brick structure with three large double doors made of oak. He was holed up there with the last four of his recruits who remained uninjured, his hostages now numbering eleven, and two of his sons, both of them wounded. They had no food. Worst off was Oliver Brown, shot during earlier skirmishing, bleeding badly, and, like his brother Watson, in intense pain. During the night Oliver begged his father to end his agony by killing him. Brown responded, "If you must die, die like a man."[61] Oliver was dead by daybreak.

At daybreak Brown saw a company of U.S. Marines deployed in front of the engine house. They had been dispatched by President Buchanan, who placed them under the command of Colonel Robert E. Lee. Lee had arrived by train from Washington during the night. He decided against an immediate assault out of concern for increased danger to the hostages during an encounter in the dark. By morning a dozen marines, led by Lieutenant Israel Green, were poised to make an assault using

Depiction of interior of the Engine House at Harpers Ferry before troops the broke door open. COURTESY OF THE LIBRARY OF CONGRESS.

sledgehammers to break open the doors and fixed bayonets to subdue the insurgents.

Before that, acting on Lee's orders, Lieutenant Jeb Stuart approached the engine house under a flag of truce. Brown opened the door a crack. Stuart handed him a note demanding his immediate surrender. When Brown replied that he would only accept terms allowing him and his men to escape, Stuart jumped away from the door and the assault team rushed the building. A heavy wooden ladder had to be used to batter open one of the doors. One marine was killed and another wounded in the attack. A glancing blow from Lieutenant Israel Green's dress sword left a deep wound at the back of Brown's neck. A second thrust bent the blade back double when it hit some solid object in the old man's clothing, so the officer beat Brown unconscious with the hilt of the weapon. All the hostages were safe. Brown was dragged outside where, once he regained consciousness, Lee ordered that he be given medical attention.

Lee's official report accounted for five civilians and one marine killed with nine others wounded, including one marine. Of the insurgents, he listed ten killed, including Watson Brown, who died two days after being wounded. Two others, including John Brown, were wounded.[62] Of the five insurgents who escaped and were never captured, three served in the Union army once the war came, including Owen Brown, Francis J. Mariam, and the free Black Osborne P. Anderson.[63]

With his capture, John Brown's raid was, in a real sense, just beginning. To the North, the deepest impression was created not by the details of the raid itself, but by Brown's stoic disdain for death as he knowingly took history's stage to play his role as martyr for freedom to the fullest. To the white South, reaction to Brown's raid came in ripples. The immediate concern that events at Harpers Ferry would incite slave uprisings elsewhere soon gave way to satisfaction that their nonoccurrence proved their slaves' contentment. In time the revelation of Brown's financing created a composite picture of him being the violent spearhead of a thrust jointly directed at the white South by abolitionists, Black Republicans, and the North generally. The *New York Herald*, a staunchly Democratic newspaper, pinned the blame on radical Republicans such as Senators Seward and Sumner, charging "They—not the crazy fanatic John Brown—are the real culprits."[64]

Brown was certainly fanatic. His messianic zeal to crush slavery was an obsession. He was not crazy. In interviews and statements from his capture up to his execution, Brown maintained a calm aloofness while clearly articulating his motives. He overruled his lawyers' advice to seek a stay of execution on the grounds of insanity, declaring "I am worth inconceivably more to hang than for any other purpose." His last message handed to a guard before facing the gallows on December 2 read "I John Brown am now quite *certain* that the crimes of this *guilty land will* never be purged *away* but with Blood."[65] On the day of his death, northern church bells pealed. On the same day abolitionist, essayist, philosopher, and poet Henry David Thoreau wrote "Some eighteen hundred years ago, Christ was crucified; this morning, perchance, Captain Brown was hung. These are the two ends of a chain which is not without its links. He is not old Brown any longer; he is an angel of light."[66] In much of the North, it was as if the ineptness and random murder of defenseless civilians during Brown's raid were washed away to reveal a prophet of the avenging hand of God.

The night before Brown's raid began, in Springfield, Illinois, Abraham Lincoln received a telegram from New York City.[67] The twenty-five-word message asked if Lincoln was willing to deliver a speech at Henry Ward Beecher's famed Plymouth Church in Brooklyn for an honorarium of $200. The request came from a group of the city's young Republicans who believed a western alternative to New York Senator William H. Seward was needed to head the party's ticket for the presidency in 1860. Lincoln was being asked to audition for the job before an audience of New York opinion leaders. He readily accepted.

Lincoln devoted more effort to preparing this speech than he did any other in his lifetime. The topic required meticulous research. His aim was to lay out an unassailable historical record proving that modern Republicans grasped hands in a direct link to a majority of the Constitution's framers in their call to halt slavery's expansion. In driving home that premise, Lincoln sought to give the fledging party being assailed for its radical ideas validation from those who founded the republic. In the process, he intended collaterally to strip Stephen Douglas's doctrine of indifference and Roger Taney's constitutional embrace of slavery of any veneer of credibility. He could not have set his sights higher.

Four and a half months after the initial invitation, Lincoln arrived in New York in late February with a new black suit, somewhat wrinkled from the train ride, and new boots that pinched his feet. The Republicans' presidential nominating convention was less than twelve weeks off. A few hours before delivering his speech Lincoln had his photograph taken at the New York studio of Mathew Brady, who captured a steady gaze from a tall man of middle age whose face reflected an inner sense of determination. The venue for his address, Lincoln learned, had been changed to Cooper Union, a free college in Manhattan for gifted students. The near-capacity audience in the Cooper Union's Grand Hall, which accommodated 1,800 people, paid twenty-five cents each for admission. The barons of New York's newspaper empires, along with opinion makers and regular citizens of all stripes, set aside a portion of the evening on February 27 to take the measure of this western newcomer for themselves.

Abraham Lincoln as photographed by Mathew Brady in his New York studio before Lincoln delivered his Cooper Union address. COURTESY OF THE LIBRARY OF CONGRESS.

As Lincoln began speaking, several in the audience suspected they were about to witness an awful embarrassment for a country lawyer far removed from his proper element. His high-pitched voice carried a distinct western twang. His shirt collar was too big, his pant legs too short. But those distractions quickly faded as Lincoln began to deliver what historian Harold Holzer has described as the "sledgehammer logic" of his argument.[68]

Lincoln first set himself firmly on the same ground Stephen Douglas had staked out in a speech the previous autumn in which, when speaking of slavery, he said "Our fathers, when they framed the Government under which we live, understood this question just as well, and even better, than we do now."[69] Time and again Lincoln invoked Douglas's words as he described in detail what the framers' understanding of slavery was as made evident in votes that they cast on it during their public careers.

Lincoln took the framers to be the thirty-nine men who signed the Constitution drafted at Philadelphia in 1787.

Three years earlier, his research showed, two of them—our fathers who understood this question even better than we do now—had voted in the Continental Congress to forbid slavery in the Northwest Territories. Three years later, two of them voted for the same ban in the Congress conducted during the Constitutional Convention. Two years after that sixteen of them—again, our fathers who understood this question even better than we do now—voted for the slavery ban in adopting the Northwest Ordinance in the First Congress under the Constitution. George Washington—one of the fathers who understood this question even better than we do now—signed it into law. Step by step, in meticulous detail, Lincoln traced the framers' votes in restricting slavery in legislation organizing the Mississippi and New Orleans territories and in the Missouri Compromise.

In totaling up the record, Lincoln found that a majority of twenty-one of the thirty-nine fathers who framed the Constitution demonstrated by their votes that they saw "no proper division of local from federal authority, nor any part of the Constitution, forbade the Federal Government to control slavery in the federal territories." To that majority, Lincoln said, could be added Benjamin Franklin, Alexander Hamilton, and Gouverneur Morris, among other framers, whose views on the question were well known even if they had not voted upon it.[70]

Shifting from scholarly discourse of the past to the political reality of the present, Lincoln then flung at his audience a challenge:

> But enough! Let all who believe that "our fathers, who framed the Government under which we live, understood this question just as well, and even better, than we do now," speak as they spoke, and act as they acted upon it. This is all Republicans desire—in relation to slavery. As those fathers marked it, so let it again be marked, as an evil not to be extended, but to be tolerated and protected only because of and so far as its actual presence among us makes that toleration and protection a necessity.[71]

Lincoln next turned to the white South's conviction, bolstered by the *Dred Scott* decision, that slaveholders had a constitutional right to take their chattel into the territories. The *Dred Scott* ruling, made "in a divided Court, by a bare majority of the Judges, and they not quite agreeing," Lincoln said, "was mainly based upon a mistaken statement of fact . . . that 'the right of property in a slave is distinctly and expressly affirmed in the Constitution.'"[72] No such distinct or express affirmation exists in the document, he said, because the framers intended "to exclude from the Constitution the idea that there could be property in man."[73] Once shown the error of its reasoning, Lincoln concluded somewhat weakly, it was reasonable to expect the court to reconsider its decision.

The white South's demand of the North, Lincoln said, was that the "whole atmosphere must be disinfected from all taint of opposition to slavery." It was useless to grope for some middle ground between the right and the wrong. Instead, Lincoln concluded, "LET US HAVE FAITH THAT RIGHT MAKES MIGHT, AND IN THAT FAITH, LET US, TO THE END, DARE TO DO OUR DUTY AS WE UNDERSTAND IT."[74]

The next morning the city's four major newspapers published Lincoln's speech in full, to be picked up and run by other papers around the country. The lawyer from Springfield was now under serious consideration for the presidency.

While Lincoln was preparing his Cooper Union address, William Lowndes Yancey was planning for the Democrats' nominating convention to be held in Charleston. Elected chair of his state's Democratic convention, Yancey led that group in January in adopting an Alabama platform updated from the 1848 original. The convention, as one participant later wrote, was dominated by secessionists.[75] The platform reaffirmed the territories as common property theme. A new plank was added that in modern terms would be termed a poison pill. It called for federal protection of slavery in the territories, the slave code provision that Stephen Douglas had pledged to oppose during his debates with Lincoln and elsewhere. Should the national convention refuse to adopt the principles of the Yancey-inspired document before nominating a candidate for president, the Alabama delegation was instructed to withdraw from the convention.[76] In addition, the state legislature passed resolutions calling on the governor to hold elections for a state convention in the event a Republican was elected president, with the unwritten understanding that the delegates would vote on a secession ordinance.[77]

A slave code was never a serious policy issue. Jefferson Davis, its leading Senate proponent, talked himself into a knot when confronted with a resolution declaring that conditions existed in the territories requiring such a code. "I rather think the necessity does exist," he said on the Senate floor, "but that is an opinion which I am not prepared now to declare as a fact."[78] Instead, the code was used as a device with which to break down the national Democratic Party into two sectional ones. If the national convention accepted Yancey's Alabama platform, neither Douglas nor the party's northern wing could go along with it. A sectional Democratic Party of the white South would be created. If the platform was rejected, the white South would bolt, making the Democrats a sectional party of the North. In either case, chances of a Republican victory would be enhanced. That outcome would, in turn, enhance chances that the Deep South would secede. Yancey was playing for stakes far beyond a platform plank or a presidential nomination. On the eve of the Charleston convention, the Georgia, Mississippi, Louisiana, Florida, Arkansas, and Texas delegations voted to stand by the Alabama platform.[79]

In a broader sense, a slave code was the chip on the shoulder, the proxy for decades of white southern realization that the compromises the North grudgingly conceded were a mere meal of ashes. The initially vaunted Missouri Compromise closed far more doors to slavery than it opened. The Compromise of 1850 produced a Fugitive Slave Law that returned few fugitive slaves, one new free state in California, and two more yet to come. The repeal of the Missouri Compromise in favor of popular sovereignty produced a system where a handful of local voters could overturn what the Supreme Court declared was a constitutional right. Since the admission of Texas to statehood in 1845, the white South had not gained a single acre for slavery while new free states arose in Iowa, Wisconsin, California, Minnesota, and Oregon. Abolitionists, as they witnessed at Harpers Ferry, were pushing their slaves toward rebellion, and a Black Republican might be elected president before the year was out. But first, Yancey had to deal with the northerner in his own ranks, Stephen Douglas, the leading contender for the Democratic presidential nomination.

The Democratic convention opened on April 23 as 304 delegates from all thirty-three states and more than 3,000 guests poured into a welcoming Charleston. A certain recklessness dominated the hour. Douglas's forces were confident that they had a majority of votes on the floor. They could even be content if a few southern states walked out, as their absence, they thought, could give the Little Giant a better chance of winning the two-thirds majority required for nomination. A rump group of establishment operatives tied to the Buchanan administration could even be content if the party split in two against a single Republican. Their reasoning went that if no candidate won an Electoral College majority, the decision would devolve onto a safely Democratic and sympathetically southern Senate after a too bitterly divided House failed to pick a victor.[80] Yancey's plan was the boldest of all: dominate or destroy being the public face of what others, then and later, saw as a deeper conspiracy to foment secession. That Yancey was drawing to an inside straight is near certain, as the majority of those within the Democratic Party as a whole, as well as within the slave states, at that hour stood by the union even in the face of secessionists' increasing stridency.[81]

The Douglas camp prevailed in an early decision to allow delegates from uninstructed states to vote as individuals, a move that assured their grip on a majority of votes from the floor. Secure on this front, they conceded the point that the platform be decided before the nominee was selected. In the platform committee, the white South held sway because each state held a single vote; and with votes from fifteen southern states, plus those from sympathetic delegates from California and Oregon, they commanded a one-vote majority. Following days of wrangling, the committee acknowledged that it was split and reported out two major competing platform planks. The majority report, with seventeen votes, included the substance of the Alabama platform. The minority report, with fifteen votes, dodged endorsing a slave code by pledging the party to abide by court decisions regarding property in the territories, a position anchored in the Compromise of 1850.[82]

At midday, Yancey took the convention floor for the first time. He opened by claiming to stand upon ground he had abandoned years earlier. "There is no disunionist," he said, in the Alabama delegation. Charges that they were disrupters or intent on breaking up the party or the union "I pronounce to be false," he soothingly assured the convention to a round of applause. But the party must "elevate itself," he warned, lest Alabama and the entire white South be forced to take their case for true adherence to the Constitution to the whole country. Warming to his case, Yancey continued, "Ours is the property invaded; ours are the institutions which are at stake; ours is the peace that is to be destroyed; ours is the property that is to be destroyed; ours is the honor at stake."

In reciting the white South's complaints against northern aggression, he recalled that the small band of abolitionists who he had seen "pelted with rotten eggs" when he was a schoolboy in the North had "grown and spread, until it is divided into three different classes, under different names, such as Abolitionists, Freesoilers and Squatter Sovereignty men." A conviction had grown in white southern minds, he cautioned, "that we are not safe in the Union, unless we can obtain your unequivocal pledge" to uphold what the white South saw as its constitutional rights. Yancey's closing stanza was a combination of white southern plea and conviction:

> *Hands off and let us work our own row in these Territories. If you beat us at the end you will be entitled to the palm of victory. If we beat you, we will give you good servants for life and enable you to live comfortably, and we will take your poor white man and elevate him from the office of boot-black, . . . [and] we will elevate him to a place amongst the master race and put the negro race to do this dirty work which God designed they should do.*[83]

"Tremendous cheering," according to the record of the event, greeted these words.

The platform fight continued through the weekend until on Monday, April 30, when the Douglas camp brought their majority vote on the floor to bear. The platform committee's minority report with no slave code provision was passed as the convention's majority report by a vote of 165 to 138. Realizing that the convention was on the verge of disintegration, the Douglas forces allowed a vote to remove the plank pledging the party to abide by court decisions regarding property in the territories. But this platform defeat for Douglas did not take away the defeat of the slave code plank. True to their January pledge regarding a slave code, the Alabama delegation walked out. They were followed by all but a few members of the delegations from Mississippi, Louisiana, South Carolina, Florida, Texas, and Arkansas. The next day most of the Georgia delegation quit, too.

The Democratic Party was rent asunder—ostensibly over the demand for protections for slavery where it did not exist, nor was ever likely to. From its origins in the national movement that supported Thomas Jefferson, the Democrats had tied the nation's sections together to govern the country during the majority of its first seventy years of existence. Robert Barnwell Rhett Sr.'s *Charleston Mercury* accurately assessed the consequence the day following the walkout: "The last party pretending to be a National party, has broken up; and the antagonism of the two sections of the Union has nothing to arrest its fierce collisions."[84]

By the time the shakeout from Charleston was complete, four political parties, two of them cobbled together for the occasion and all of them with only sectional appeal, put forward presidential candidates in the 1860 election. After the Deep South states walked out at Charleston, Douglas still could not garner a two-thirds majority for the nomination. A ruling from the chair declared that the necessary two-thirds must be of the whole number of original delegates, not just the number of those remaining after the walkout. The Douglas wing of the Democratic Party nominated the Little Giant after reconvening in Baltimore in June.

Five days later, the newly christened Southern Democrats held their own convention in Baltimore to nominate John C. Breckinridge. Their candidate was James Buchanan's vice president, a Kentuckian who had served in the House and the Senate. Breckinridge ran on a solidly pro-South platform, including planks favoring a slave code and annexation of Cuba. A vote for him was widely regarded as a proxy for secession, although he maintained his loyalty to the union throughout the campaign—a loyalty premised on national acceptance of the white South's view of slavery and the Constitution. More than a year later, he became a major general in the Confederate Army and toward the end of the conflict served as Jefferson Davis's secretary of war.

The residual southern forces, largely an agglomeration of ex-Whigs and Know Nothing voters, created the Constitutional Union Party. They nominated former senator and Speaker of the House John Bell of Tennessee as their candidate. Bell's platform was to stand foursquare in favor of the Constitution, the union, and the enforcement of the law, with no elaboration of what any of that might mean. A Bell vote was widely regarded as a proxy in favor of remaining in the union.

The Republicans held their convention in May at the Wigwam in Chicago, a temporary two-story structure made of wood that accommodated up to 12,000 people. Lincoln's campaign team made sure that the galleries were packed with their supporters. Thurlow Reed, the éminence grise of Senator Seward's campaign, arrived from New York with thirteen railcars of supporters, plenty of cash, and lots of liquor.[85] With the Democrats having just smashed up in Charleston, the Republicans were keenly aware the election was theirs to win if they simply avoided a candidate who drove voters away from him, rather than to him. Seward, whose political skill and years of labor in the antislavery cause made him the front-runner going into Chicago, carried a taint of radicalism—and the added taint of association with Reed with his reputation for backroom deal making. To win, the Republicans had to hold the North. To do that, they had to bring along the right combination of their southern tier of states, including Pennsylvania, Illinois, Indiana, and New Jersey. Seward failed to win on the first ballot and fell back a bit on the second. On the third ballot the delegates chose Lincoln, the more moderate candidate with the appeal of being a self-made man who had risen from a log cabin origin. The party platform declared that the maintenance of the Declaration of Independence's principles was essential to the nation's future. The Republicans stood against slavery's expansion as well as interference with it in states where it already existed.

In the North, Lincoln ran against Douglas. In the white South, Breckinridge ran against Bell. Lincoln did not even appear on the ballot in nine southern states. He captured all of the northern states except New Jersey, which he split with Douglas. In doing so he gained a solid majority of 180 Electoral College votes with just under 40 percent of the total 4,682,069 popular votes cast. Douglas trailed with just under 30 percent of the popular vote but won outright only in Missouri. Breckinridge carried eleven slave states with 18 percent of the vote. Bell received just over 12 percent of the vote in carrying Virginia, Kentucky, and Tennessee.[86]

As soon as he was declared president-elect, Lincoln received letters advising him to issue a placating message to the South to ease white southerners' worst fears of Black Republican intentions. At least from the time of his House Divided speech, Lincoln had been doing something quite close to that. From then to his election as president, Lincoln had largely stripped away all but the single pledge to stand against slavery's expansion and for defense of the union in the face of secession.[87] By 1860 one did not hear from him or his campaign the themes common to other Republican leaders of prohibiting the acquisition of existing slave territory such as Cuba, abolishing slavery in Washington, D.C., ending the interstate slave trade, banning slavery at U.S. arsenals and forts, or repealing the Fugitive Slave Law. Even his call to place slavery on the path to ultimate extinction was hardly a whisper by 1860.

He had winnowed his candidacy into the most moderate stance likely not to antagonize but to attract the greatest number of northern supporters. He had won on that platform. After the election, pleas that he chip away at the final bastion of opposing slavery's expansion sounded to Lincoln like a demand from those he defeated that he surrender. "Is it desired that I shall shift the ground upon which I have been elected," Lincoln asked in reply to one such request. "I can not do it." Any new public statement of his, Lincoln wrote, would be used to "make me appear as if I repented for the crime of having been elected, and was anxious to apologize and beg forgiveness."

His views, he continued, were readily obtainable by reviewing his earlier record, particularly from his 1858 debates with Douglas and the Republicans' 1860 platform. He had no desire to harass white southerners nor to interfere with slavery where it already existed. To a political ally in Washington, Lincoln wrote, "Prevent, as far as possible, any of our friends from demoralizing themselves, and our cause, by entertaining propositions for compromise of any sort, on '*slavery extension*'. . . . On that point hold firm, as with a chain of steel."[88]

— ❧ —

The 1860 election results are the best insight available into the nation's prevailing political attitudes at that moment. The 81.2 percent turnout, highest ever up to that point and only exceeded once in 1876, makes them more salient.[89] No popular vote totals are available for South Carolina because Electoral College delegates there were chosen by the legislature. The results from the remaining fourteen slaveholding states, however, reveal a remarkable depth of pro-union sentiment in the white South, particularly given that the union's breakup began within weeks of the election.

In the four border states that remained in the Union—Kentucky, Missouri, Maryland, and Delaware—the pro-union candidates, including Lincoln, who was on the ballot in all of them, polled 68 percent of the votes. In the four states that seceded after the war began with the firing on Fort Sumter in Charleston harbor—Virginia, Arkansas, Tennessee, and North Carolina—pro-union candidates received 51 percent of the vote. Holding out South Carolina as an exception, in the remaining six states that formed the initial Confederacy—all of them walkouts at the Democratic convention in Charleston—pro-union candidates polled a minority of 44 percent of the total vote. Overall, in the states that constituted the full Confederacy, again excepting South Carolina, 48 percent of the ballots cast in November 1860 were for candidates committed to upholding the union.[90] A fervor for secession unquestionably existed, especially in the white Deep South, but it had hardly swept all the slaveholding states on the day Abraham Lincoln was elected.

White southern unionism needs to be understood in context. In the five months leading to the outbreak of war, pro-union white southerners were, in broad terms, those willing to cooperate with efforts to save the republic by negotiating with the North a long-term settlement over slavery and the territories. A great many of these "cooperationists" were reluctantly ready to side with secession if such efforts failed. But they wanted the effort to be made. James Henry Hammond, South Carolina's firebrand in the Senate, counseled the white South "to fight the battle in the Union."[91] Secessionist "fire-eaters" such as Yancey, Rhett, and Ruffin knew striking quickly was a necessary strategy, that time was not on their side. A white southern convention to deliberate what negotiating alternative to dissolution should be presented to the North, followed by the inevitable delay in pursuing such talks, could more easily cool passions than excite them. The secessionists' best shot was to capitalize on the election of the Black Republican Lincoln by quickly precipitating the withdrawal of one Deep South state that would act like a magnet, just as in the Charleston walkout, tugging on the honor and interests of its slaveholding neighbors to follow suit. If a white southern Confederacy could be formed before the new administration gained hold of the levers of executive power, secession might even be accomplished without war.

Virginia "fire-eater" Edmund Ruffin.
COURTESY OF THE LIBRARY OF CONGRESS.

"When Lincoln is in place, Garrison will be in power," the *Southern Literary Messenger* exclaimed in promoting secession. "The only alternative left to us is this: *a separate nationality or the Africanization of the South.* . . . If we succeed in establishing, *as we shall*, a vast, opulent, happy and glorious slave-holding Republic, throughout tropical America—future generations will arise and call us blessed."[92] A paroxysm of apocalyptic nightmares was unleashed by the secessionist press and politicians predicting that without dissolution, the white South would be plunged into a St. Domingue-scale race war of murder, rape, and devastation. With Black Republicans in a majority, Georgia Supreme Court Justice Henry L. Benning warned, the white South "will have black governors, black judges, black legislators, black juries, black witnesses—everything black. . . . The consequences will be that our men will all be exterminated or expelled to wander as vagabonds over a hostile earth, and as for our women, their fate will be too horrible to contemplate even in fancy."[93] Fervid paranoia produced its intended effect of generating white southern hatred of the North as the premise to sustain secession. A glimpse into the depth that hatred could take is found in a prayer a Louisiana plantation overseer wrote in his journal in the summer of 1861: "My Prayer Sincerely to God," he wrote, "is that every Black Republican in the Hole combined whorl either man woman o chile . . . shal be trubled with pestilents and calamitys of all Kinds and Drag out the Balance of there existance in Misray and Degradation with scarsely food and rayment enughf to keep sole and Body to gather."[94]

The attitude of the white South, as expressed in November 1860, was quickly buffeted between moderates extolling caution and "fire-eaters" denouncing moderates as traitors while proclaiming jeremiads of ruin lest the South secede. The center did not hold.

President Buchanan contributed to a rapidly deteriorating situation when, in his December annual message, he blamed the "intemperate interferences of the northern people" for the white South's distress. He judged secession to be revolution but confessed that he could find no constitutionally sanctioned power for Congress or the Executive to compel a state to remain in the union.[95] His hand-wringing infuriated many northerners while emboldening secessionists.

South Carolina led the Deep South's rush to secession with a December 6 election of delegates to a state secession convention that voted 169 to nothing on December 20 to leave the union. On the recommendation of Robert Barnwell Rhett Sr.'s convention committee, South Carolina sent commissioners to seven other southern states to urge their secession and that they meet in Montgomery in February to form a new government. The idea took hold. Over the next four months, five of the seceding Deep South states sent fifty-two commissioners to other slave states with a mission to help convince them to leave the union.

The South Carolina convention also produced an address to the other slaveholding states justifying the break and urging them to join in a Confederacy of Slaveholding States. Their principal complaint was that the Constitution had been overthrown by a consolidated government ruled by a northern majority. "It is no longer a free Government, but a Despotism," the address proclaimed, which aimed next to overthrow slavery. "We prefer," the address continued, "our system of industry, by which labor and capital are identical in interest, and capital, therefore, protects labor."[96]

That framing "our system of industry" in this way literally excluded working people among the majority of white citizens who did not own slaves seemed to pass without notice. This omission is less surprising, given that 90 percent of the 169 convention delegates were slaveowners and that on average each owned just under sixty slaves.[97] The clear message from the delegates, an assembly primarily of wealthy, slaveholding planters and lawyers, was that to protect slavery, South Carolina must abandon the union and strike out on its own.[98]

South Carolina's secession convention was not the only reason in late 1860 that attention was riveted on Charleston. Three of the nation's nine coastal forts were located there. Beginning in late November, Major Robert Anderson, commanding the garrison at Fort Moultrie, repeatedly sought reinforcements. President Buchanan finally conceded to the request but was confronted with continuing delays presented by his War Secretary John Floyd of Virginia and other white southerners in his cabinet. One of them, Treasury Secretary Howell Cobb of Georgia, resigned on December 8. Two months later he began presiding over the convention that wrote the Confederate States Constitution. The day after Christmas, Anderson, acting under discretion given him by earlier orders, transferred his garrison from Fort Moultrie to the more readily defended Fort Sumter situated on an island of its own at the center of the entrance to Charleston harbor.

The transfer precipitated a cabinet crisis in Washington. Floyd demanded that Anderson be ordered to reverse himself. At this juncture Edwin M. Stanton, an Ohioan who had taken over as attorney general less than two weeks earlier, accused Floyd to his face of being a traitor.[99] The addition to the cabinet of Stanton and two other northerners came as Buchanan himself was being associated with treason. The president came perilously close to entering into direct negotiations with emissaries from Charleston on their demand that Anderson and his garrison be evacuated so that South Carolina's militia could occupy Sumter. Stanton warned the president that doing so would amount to a treasonous recognition of South Carolina's secession. Enmeshed in a financial scandal within his department as well as the cabinet brawl, Floyd quit on December 29 and returned to Virginia. Five months later he was a brigadier general in the Confederate Army. By year's end Buchanan, now under the influence of union supporters in his cabinet led by Stanton, ordered that reinforcements, ammunition, and provisions be sent to Anderson at Fort Sumter.

Attention quickly shifted to Mississippi, which held an election of delegates to a secession convention on the same day that South Carolina left the union. Senator Jefferson Davis had advised against immediate secession, but Governor John J. Pettus, declaring that the "existence or the abolition of African slavery in the Southern States is now up for final settlement" pushed ahead anyway. The 100 elected delegates, nearly all of them slaveowners, convened on January 7 and within two days had voted eighty-five to fifteen to secede.[100] A motion to submit the decision to the voters of Mississippi for ratification was rejected.[101] The convention's declaration of the causes justifying secession, Mississippi's version of a declaration of independence, proclaimed "Our position is thoroughly identified with the institution of slavery—the greatest material interest in the world."[102]

On the day that Mississippi voted for secession, the relief vessel that Buchanan had dispatched to Charleston withdrew after being fired upon as it approached the harbor. Word of that event reached delegates to Florida's secession convention in Tallahassee the following day as they prepared to vote on the issue. After hearing from Edmund Ruffin and rejecting a motion to submit their decision to a popular referendum, the convention delegates voted sixty-two to seven to quit the union.[103]

The following day, Alabama made its decision. William Lowndes Yancey had won his seat as a delegate to the state's secession convention despite being hanged in effigy by unionists in Athens, a town in the state's northern tier where slavery was far less prevalent than in the rest of Alabama. At one point during the convention, when concern was raised that the secessionists' margin of victory in the delegate elections was small, an angered Yancey took the floor. Denouncing opponents as "enemies of the State," he declared that victory by a single vote represented the sovereign will of the people. "There is a law of Treason," he shouted, "and those who shall dare oppose the action of Alabama, when she assumes her independence of the Union, will become traitors—rebels against authority, and will be dealt with as such."[104]

He reported the secession ordinance drafted by committee to the convention and later argued against submitting it to a popular referendum. Delay was unnecessary and dangerous. Yancey then joined the majority of delegates who voted, sixty-one to thirty-nine, to leave the union.[105] Reaching the goal he had nurtured for years he was greeted throughout Montgomery by cheers, fireworks, bonfires, cannon blasts, and church bells. Although he certainly could not have known it then, this was the pinnacle of his public career. Once the Confederacy was formed, Yancey and his hotheadedness were shipped off to Europe to plead the white South's case. On his return, he served in the Confederate States Senate until his death from kidney failure in the summer of 1863, two weeks before his forty-ninth birthday.

In Georgia, Judge William A. Harris set the tone for what followed. A native of the state, Harris was there as a commissioner from Mississippi, where he was a member of the state supreme court. The alternatives facing the white South, Judge Harris told the Georgia General Assembly, were a "*new union* with Lincoln Black Republicans and free negroes, *without slavery*; or, slavery under our old constitutional bond of union, *without* Lincoln Black Republicans, or free negroes either, to molest us." Speaking for Mississippi, he said, "She had rather see the last of her race, men, women and children, immolated in one common funeral pile, than see them subjected to the degradation of civil, political and social equality with the negro race."[106] Harris's remarks were well within the mainstream of the messages delivered by the commissioners first proposed by Robert Barnwell Rhett Sr. as South Carolina adopted succession.

The commissioners' role is best described by historian Charles D. Dew in his seminal work *Apostles of Disunion*.[107] He documents the centrality of slavery in their arguments to persuade other states to break their ties with the union. States' rights arguments were largely swept aside in their more urgent warnings of the imminent overthrow of slavery by Black Republicans, to be followed by the alternatives of amalgamation or an exterminating race war. Their appeals were to white southern honor, fear, and emotion regarding slavery rather than to states' rights political theories of consolidated government and enumerated powers. As one southerner put it in a late March address to the citizens of Alabama, "we have dissolved the late Union chiefly because of the negro quarrel."[108]

As Georgia Governor Joseph E. Brown put it in a special message to the legislature days after Lincoln was elected, as soon the Black Republicans assume control, "a hungry swarm of abolition emissaries, must be imported among us as office holders, to . . . corrupt our slaves . . . and do all in their power, to create in the South a state of things which must ultimately terminate in a war of extermination between the white and black races."[109] A meeting among legislators resulted in a near riot amid threats to blow out the brains of opponents hurled between secessionists and pro-union cooperationists members.

Although Georgia had more slaves and slaveholders than any other Deep South state, more than 60 percent of the white population did not own slaves. In the state's northern mountains and southeast pine barrens, there were hardly any slaves at all.

An election was finally held on January 2 for delegates to a state secession convention, the same day Governor Brown ordered the state militia to seize Fort Pulaski in Savannah harbor. Governor Brown refused to make the election results public until after the Confederacy was formed and only then claimed that secessionist candidates captured 58 percent of the vote. Recent research indicates that "the popular majority for immediate secession was paper thin, if it existed at all."[110] Once the convention convened, a motion to have a committee draft a secession ordinance passed on a 166 to 130 vote. The next day, January 19, delegates voted 208 to 89 to secede from the union. When state supreme court Justice Henry L. Benning, as a commissioner to Virginia, explained why Georgia had seceded, he said it "may be summed up in one single proposition. It was a conviction; a deep conviction on the part of Georgia, that a separation from the North was the only thing that could prevent the abolition of slavery. This conviction was the main cause."[111]

Of all the Deep South states, Louisiana was the most closely attached to the union. New Orleans merchants and bankers had commercial ties to the northern reaches of the Mississippi River. In the presidential election, the state had given 55 percent of its vote to Bell and Douglas. Shortly before Lincoln's election, Governor Thomas O. Moore wrote his South Carolina counterpart, "I shall not advise the secession of my state, & I will add that I do not think the people of Louisiana will ultimately decide in favor of that course."[112]

A month later he called for a state convention and endorsed secession. In the intervening period Moore, like others, was bombarded by a continuous stream of secessionist propaganda from press and pulpit that extolled disunion and stigmatized its opponents as submissionists.[113] The election results for convention delegates announced to the public showed that secessionist candidates took just over 54 percent of the vote with a turnout well below that recorded in November. Later research, however, trimmed that margin to just 52 percent.[114] The convention voted for secession 113 to seventeen on January 26. The slim margin of victory in the convention elections probably accounts for the decision not to submit the secession ordnance to a public referendum, although the state constitution required it.[115]

The Texas secession convention had no qualms about sending its ordinance dissolving the union to the voters for ratification. They had given Breckinridge his greatest margin of victory with 75 percent of their vote in November. That is not to say that Texas was without pro-union sentiment. A northern tier of counties where nonslave subsistence farming was the norm had experienced a recent influx of tens of thousands of German immigrants who were broadly antislavery and pro-union. Sam Houston, the state's aging but venerated governor, told a visitor that states seceding over slavery could expect no intervention from the English or French in support of their cause. The first shot fired in a civil war, he said, would sound slavery's death knell.[116]

Pushing aside such pro-union sentiment, the convention voted 166 to eight for disunion on February 1. South Carolina secession Commissioner John McQueen was present when the vote was cast. He told the delegates that the Black Republicans had been elected on a sectional platform of "the abolition of slavery upon this continent and the elevation of our own slaves to an equality with ourselves and our children."[117] A second commissioner, George M. Williamson of Louisiana, arrived in the state capital at Austin too late to address the convention. He did, however, address a letter to the convention's president stating that he looked forward to the creation of a white southern confederacy to "preserve the blessings of African slavery." His missive noted that his state and Texas were "peculiarly adapted to slave labor," making both states "deeply interested in African slavery" that was "absolutely necessary to their existence." All the slaveholding states, he wrote, were "bound together by the same necessity and determination to preserve African slavery."[118]

As historian Matthew K. Hamilton has noted, the arguments of all four of the secession commissioners who went to Texas "did not go beyond the desire to protect slavery."[119] In declaring the causes for secession, the convention pointed to the non-slave-holding states that had formed a sectional party "proclaiming the debasing doctrine of the equality of all men, irrespective of race or color." These northerners, the declaration continued in reference to John Brown, "have invaded Southern soil and murdered unoffending citizens." In a final charge against northerners, the document declared, "They have sent hired emissaries among us to burn our towns and distribute arms and poison to our slaves for the same purpose."[120] This accusation was based on a flurry of hysterical rumors that swept Texas in 1860, leading to dozens of Black lynchings based on false reports of arson and well poisonings.[121]

Elections were held and votes cast in other states during this period. On February 9 Tennessee decided against calling a secession convention with a decisive 55 percent of the statewide vote.[122] At the end of the month, North Carolina made the same decision to reject a state secession convention, although by a much slimmer margin. In Arkansas in mid-March, unionist candidates won just under 24,000 votes against 17,000 cast for secessionists for a state convention that voted thirty-five to thirty-nine against a secession resolution.[123] As tensions mounted over Fort Sumter, Virginia's convention that had been in session for weeks voted nearly two to one on April 4 in favor of a motion to not bring a secession resolution to the floor.[124] All four of these states joined the Confederacy after the war began.

"In *your* hands, my dissatisfied countrymen, and not in *mine*, is the momentous issue of civil war," Lincoln said in his inaugural address delivered on March 4 from the portico of the Capitol building that was still under construction. "The government will not assail *you*," he continued. "You can have no conflict, without being yourselves the aggressors."[125] When he was elected Lincoln may well have believed, as did many Republicans, that white southern threats of secession were no more than another round of threats to compel northern concessions. As South Carolina led the way to disunion, politicians in Washington cast about for a constitutional compromise to hold the republic together. Kentucky Senator John J. Crittenden convened a Committee of Thirteen on December 22, recommending to them six amendments to resolve the crisis. They essentially called for a Republican cave-in. The principal measure was an irreversible constitutional amendment extending the old Missouri Compromise line to California, thus envisioning new slave states in the New Mexico Territory or in land yet to be taken from Mexico or possibly even in Cuba.[126]

The effort collapsed within a week, as did a similar one in the House. Instead of bluff or compromise, seven states had left the union by the time Lincoln took office. The first word from Major Anderson at Fort Sumter that met Lincoln was that no fewer than 20,000 troops would be needed to effectively reinforce the garrison that had on hand sufficient provisions to last no more than six weeks.

A week after Lincoln took office, the seven states that had left the union adopted their own constitution. Fifty delegates, all but one of them slaveowners, meeting in Montgomery appointed a committee on February 4 to come up with a preliminary draft constitution. Within four days that task was complete. Robert Barnwell Rhett Sr. chaired a second committee to refine the draft that was adopted after debate on March 11. The Confederate States of America was created when Mississippi ratified the document on March 26.[127]

The Confederate Constitution was largely a cut-and-paste job from the original, including the Bill of Rights. The general welfare clause from the preamble was dropped, but the necessary and proper clause was not. Nothing was written into the document condoning a right to secession, but the intent "to form a permanent federal government" was explicitly recognized. So, too, was the state compact theory that Jefferson and Madison had advanced in 1798. The preamble refers to the white people of the Confederate States "each acting in its sovereign and independent capacity."[128] The foreign slave trade was prohibited. The ban was approved, according to a note sent by British representatives to London, to help persuade Virginia and Maryland to leave the union, too.[129] Provisions derived from states' rights doctrine included restrictions on or prohibitions of protective tariffs and government-sponsored internal improvements. Contrary to John C. Calhoun's articulation of states' rights, however, the new constitution retained the supremacy clause and appellate jurisdiction for a supreme court. The constitution was the law of the land, and the high court had authority of final determination. No provisions for a concurrent congressional majority were included. That presumably was unnecessary because slave states constituted the only majority in the new government.

The Confederate Constitution's most innovative provisions were those that abandoned states' rights altogether in creating a consolidated central government to protect slavery. The argument propounded by the white South for decades that Congress should have no authority to legislate for the territories was dropped. In its place, the new constitution

declared "Congress shall have power to legislate and provide governments for the inhabitants of all territory belonging to the Confederate
States" and in all such territory "the institution of negro slavery, as it now
exists in the Confederate States, shall be recognized and protected by
Congress and by the territorial government."[130]

To these positive powers protecting slavery was added a negative prohibition that the Confederate Congress was forbidden from passing any
"law denying or impairing the right of property in negro slaves."[131] With
this provision making ownership of another human being a constitutional right, the Confederate Constitution made slavery a national institution, not a local one. As described by historian Arthur Bestor, "with
respect to slavery the Confederacy was a unitary, consolidated, national
state, denying to each of its allegedly sovereign members any sort of local
autonomy with respect to this particular one among its domestic institutions."[132] When it came down to it, slavery trumped states' rights.

Three years after the Civil War ended, Alexander H. Stephens, the
Confederacy's vice president, wrote that "this whole subject of Slavery,
so-called, in any and every view of it, was, to the Seceding States, but a
drop in the ocean compared with . . . other considerations."[133] Lost Cause
advocates repeated that theme for generations. Barely a week after the
Confederate Constitution was adopted, however, newly installed Vice
President Stephens told a Savannah audience that the government's
"foundations are laid, its corner-stone rests upon the great truth, that the
negro is not equal to the white man; that slavery—subordination to the
superior race—is his natural and normal condition."[134] White supremacy,
not states' rights, Stephens proclaimed, was the Confederacy's rallying
ground. He was saying no more than what southern commissioners to
state secession conventions had been saying for months. A few weeks
after Stephens spoke at Savannah, Jefferson Davis, president of the Confederacy, said that slavery was endangered by "a spirit of ultra-fanaticism"
gripping the Republican Party. "A superior race," the president said, had
used slavery to transform "brutal savages into docile, intelligent, and civilized agricultural laborers."[135]

Leading up to secession and continuing into the Civil War, a widely
expressed white southern sentiment was relief at finally being free. In a

common refrain, a rebel soldier once wrote home of his pride in "Southerners battling for freedom and all that men hold dear."[136] What did this new freedom actually amount to, what rights did white southerners have in the Confederacy that they did not possess within the union? The *only* right expressly acknowledged in the Confederate Constitution that was not similarly expressed in the United States' Constitution, despite the *Dred Scott* ruling, was the right to own slaves and transport them into territory presumably to be acquired later. White southern soldiers fought for a variety of reasons, including what they saw as defense of their states from invading northern armies. But the white southern cry of fighting for freedom comes down in hard fact to fighting for slavery and the extension of slavery—except that with secession white southerners freed themselves from being accused of unchristian barbarity by their fellow countrymen. For many, that may have been the point.

At the White House, Lincoln was seeking a strategy to avoid a disgraceful abandonment of Fort Sumter or a federal initiation of hostilities. Shortly after taking office, only a single member of his cabinet, Postmaster General Montgomery Blair, was solidly behind reinforcing Major Anderson's garrison. Lincoln had bided his time. In the interim William Seward, former senator, Lincoln's main rival for their party's presidential nomination, and now secretary of state, pursued his own strategy. Through an intermediary, Seward had left Confederate commissioners sent to Washington with the impression that Sumter would soon be evacuated. No such decision had been made, but Seward believed he could engineer one.

On April 1 he sent a message to Lincoln complaining that the administration was "without a policy either domestic or foreign." To remedy this vacancy of policy, he proposed the abandonment of Sumter, the reinforcement of Fort Pickens in Savannah harbor, and steps to provoke a war with either Spain and France, or both. Patriotism rekindled by the peril of a foreign war, he reasoned, would bring the wayward southern states back into the fold. Finally, Seward none too subtly suggested that he would be best suited to lead the administration's efforts in these matters. Lincoln's understated reply the same day pointed Seward to his inaugural address for a statement of administration policy and assured the secretary of state that he, as president, would direct it.[137]

On April 6 an envoy was dispatched from Washington on Lincoln's orders with a message for South Carolina's governor. The missive advised that an attempt was soon to be made to supply Sumter with provisions, and if not resisted, no troops, arms, or ammunition would be sent to the fort.[138] When the message reached the Confederate government at Montgomery, Jefferson Davis and his cabinet suspected a double cross. Provisioning Sumter did not square with Seward's assurance of evacuation. Davis and his colleagues made a fateful decision. They ordered Brigadier General P. G. T. Beauregard, in command at Charleston, to demand the fort's surrender and, if that proved unsuccessful, to reduce it by force of arms. Davis was making the worst political mistake of his life: commanding that the white South be marked as the aggressor by firing the first shot while ratifying Lincoln's inaugural promise to them that "you can have no conflict, without being yourselves the aggressors."

Following a brief flurry of negotiation with Major Anderson, Beauregard ordered the cannonade of Fort Sumter to begin at 4:30 a.m. on April 12. After enduring nearly a day and a half of shelling, Major Anderson surrendered the fort on terms allowing his men to depart while firing cannon salutes. Two Union soldiers died in that exercise of honor, the only fatalities in the Civil War's first conflict. The following day Lincoln summoned 75,000 troops to be called up to defend the Union. The wavering southern states of Virginia, Tennessee, North Carolina, and Arkansas had the example of federal coercion to persuade them to secession and partnership in the Confederacy.

Edmund Ruffin was present in Charleston when the cannon fire commenced. The aging "fire-eater" had enlisted as a private in the Palmetto Guard. In that capacity, he was given the honor of firing one of the first shots hurled at the Union fort. Four years later on June 17, 1865, just weeks after Robert E. Lee surrendered the Army of Northern Virginia at Appomattox, Ruffin fired another shot. This one came after he had placed the muzzle of a rifle in his mouth.[139] In the time between those two shots, an estimated 750,000 Americans died in the Civil War.[140]

As a summary narrative of the role slavery played in American politics up to the Civil War, this work does not attempt a definitive answer to the question of what caused that war. Scholars have presented a variety of replies to that question.[141] In his second inaugural, Abraham Lincoln said everyone knew that somehow slavery caused the war. But just how, he did not attempt to say. At the conclusion of my own work, I can assert that slavery was at the core of it all, but the exact mechanisms elude my own precise definition. In identifying the cause of secession, one need look no further than the words of Alexander Stephens, the southern convention commissioners, and the remarks made by many of those who participated in those conventions: protecting slavery based on the doctrine of white supremacy was the cause for the breakup of the union.

In the many scholarly interpretations offered of the causes of the Civil War, the root of the matter, or at least part of it, lies in the white South's assertion of states' rights against consolidated government, *over slavery*; a broad sectional divide, *over slavery*; the breakdown in the 1850s of the second-party system, *over slavery*; defining sectionalism as clashing economic models, *over slavery*; a sectional clash of core values, *over slavery*; northern fear of white southern expansionism, *over slavery*; white southern outrage and assaulted honor, *over slavery*; the stumbling of inept politicians in handing an issue that threatened disruption, *over slavery*; the rhetoric of disunion finally risen to a plan for secession, *over slavery*; a clash over definition of property rights, *over slavery*; the resistance of Blacks *to slavery*.

Each route leads back to slavery. Each path can be presented with attributes of its centrality to answering the question, although the states' rights justification cannot bear scrutiny. This work, then, is the start of a journey of understanding, not the culmination of it, requiring not my judgment, but the reader's own.

Notes

Preface
1. Robert Pierce Forbes, *The Missouri Compromise and Its Aftermath* (Chapel Hill: University of North Carolina Press, 2007), 9.

Chapter 1: Slavery and the Constitution
1. Len Lamensdorf, *The Ballad of Billy Lee* (Santa Barbara, CA: SeaScape Press, 2012), 179. *The Ballad* is a novel based in large part on transcribed interviews *National Intelligencer* reporter Marcus Ames had with Lee in the summer of 1825. The context of one of those interviews places Lee in the convention meeting room, at least on occasion (p. 179). Lee was born in 1750, purchased by Washington in 1768, and in the general's service throughout the Revolutionary War. His work was curtailed by bad knees in 1789 shortly before Washington's inauguration as president. Washington died in 1799, Lee in 1828. Also see Joseph J. Ellis, *The Quartet Orchestrating the Second American Revolution, 1783–1789* (New York: Knopf, 2015), 147, who writes that Lee "stood behind his master's chair throughout the convention, tending to his personal needs."
2. See Clinton Rossiter, *1787: The Grand Convention* (New York: Norton, 1966), 72–73.
3. *The Papers of George Washington* (Confederation Series), edited by W. W. Abbot (Charlottesville: University of Virginia Press, 1995), March 31, 1787, 1:16.
4. Max Farrand, ed., *The Records of the Federal Convention of 1787*, 3 vols. (New Haven, CT: Yale University Press, 1966 edition of 1937 original), 1:605.
5. *Return of the Whole Number of Persons within the Several Districts of the United States*, Philadelphia, 1793.
6. Ibid., 4.
7. Ibid.
8. David Brion Davis, *The Problem of Slavery in the Age of Revolution, 1770–1823* (New York: Oxford University Press, 1999), 89.
9. George William Van Cleve, *A Slaveholders' Union: Slavery, Politics, and the Constitution in the Early American Republic* (Chicago: University of Chicago Press, 2010), 90, citing Robert William Fogel and Stanley L. Engerman, "Philanthropy at Bargain Prices: Notes on the Economics of Gradual Emancipation," *Journal of Legal Studies* 3, no. 2 (1974): 377–401.
10. *Historical Statistics of the United States 1789–1945* (Washington, DC: Government Printing Office, 1949), 26–27.
11. *Return of the Whole Number of Persons within the Several Districts of the United States*, 32.
12. Ibid., 49.
13. Ibid., 54.
14. Richard Beeman, *Plain, Honest Men: The Making of the American Constitution* (New York: Random House, 2009), 222.
15. Farrand, *Records of the Federal Convention of 1787*, 1:20.

16. James H. Hutson, ed., *Supplement to Max Farrand's The Records of the Federal Convention of 1787* (New Haven, CT: Yale University Press, 1987 edition of 1937 original), 26, emphasis in original.

17. Farrand, *Records of the Federal Convention of 1787*, 1:36.

18. Ibid., 1:48.

19. Ibid.

20. Ibid., 1:135. Emphasis in original.

21. Ibid., 1:136.

22. Ibid., 1:179.

23. Ibid., 1:181.

24. Rossiter, *1787 The Grand Convention*, 132.

25. Howard A. Ohline, "Republicanism and Slavery: Origins of the Three-Fifths Clause in the United States Constitution," *William and Mary Quarterly* 28, no. 4 (October 1971): 568–69.

26. Farrand, *Records of the Federal Convention of 1787*, 1:197–98.

27. Ibid., 1:193.

28. Ibid., 1:206.

29. Ibid., 1:201.

30. Ibid., 1:242.

31. Ibid., 1:486.

32. Ibid., 1:500–501.

33. Ibid., 3:190.

34. Ibid., 1:511.

35. Ibid., 3:56. Emphasis in original.

36. Ibid., 1:529–30.

37. Ibid., 1:531.

38. Ibid., 1:560, Gouverneur Morris.

39. Ibid., 1:561.

40. Ibid.

41. Ibid., 3:253.

42. Leonard L. Richards, *The Slave Power: The Free North and Southern Domination, 1780–1860* (Baton Rouge: Louisiana State University Press, 2009), 56–57.

43. Farrand, *Records of the Federal Convention of 1787*, 1:566.

44. Ibid., 1:567.

45. Ibid., 1:571.

46. See Donald L. Robinson, *Slavery in the Structure of American Politics, 1765–1820* (New York: Harcourt Brace Jovanovich, 1971), 195–96.

47. Farrand, *Records of the Federal Convention of 1787*, 1:578.

48. Ibid., 1:579.

49. See Michael J. Klarman, *The Framers' Coup: The Making of the United States Constitution* (New York: Oxford University Press, 2016), 273.

50. Farrand, *Records of the Federal Convention of 1787*, 1:587.

51. Ibid., 1:588.

52. David O. Stewart, *The Summer of 1787: The Men Who Invented the Constitution* (New York: Simon & Schuster, 2007), 120.

53. Farrand, *Records of the Federal Convention of 1787*, 1:593.
54. Ibid.
55. Ibid., 1:594.
56. Ibid., 1:595.
57. Ibid., 1:604.
58. Ibid., 1:605.
59. Merrill D. Peterson, *Thomas Jefferson & the New Nation* (New York: Oxford University Press, 1970), 283.
60. For the argument concerning treaty negotiation with Spain, see Van Cleve, *A Slaveholders' Union*, 158–67. Klarman, *The Framers' Coup*, presents a likely package of arguments, including the fugitive slave clause in the Constitution, 295–96.
61. Van Cleve, *A Slaveholders' Union*, 163.
62. Sean Wilentz, *No Property in Man: Slavery and Antislavery at the Nation's Founding* (Cambridge, MA: Harvard University Press, 2018), 74.
63. Farrand, *Records of the Federal Convention of 1787*, 2:182.
64. Ibid., 2:220.
65. Ibid., 2:222–23.
66. Ibid., 2:364.
67. Ibid.
68. Klarman, *The Framers' Coup*, 278.
69. Farrand, *Records of the Federal Convention of 1787*, 2:370.
70. Roy P. Basler, ed., *Collected Works of Abraham Lincoln*, 8 vols. (New Brunswick, NJ: Rutgers University Press, 1953), 8:333.
71. Farrand, *Records of the Federal Convention of 1787*, 2:371.
72. Ibid.
73. Ibid., 2:372.
74. Ibid.
75. Ibid., 2:371.
76. Ibid., 2:369–70.
77. Ibid., 2:373.
78. Ibid., 2:374. Emphasis in original.
79. Ibid., 2:375.
80. Ibid., 2:416.
81. Ibid., 2:417.
82. Wilentz, *No Property in Man*, 99.
83. Farrand, *Records of the Federal Convention of 1787*, 2:415.
84. See Stewart, *Summer of 1787*, 205. Beeman, *Plain, Honest Men*, puts the number of slaves imported to 1808 even higher, writing, "Between 1788 and 1808, the number of African slaves imported to the United States numbered something in excess of two hundred thousand, only about fifty thousand fewer than the total number of slaves imported to America in the proceeding 170 years," 333.
85. Farrand, *Records of the Federal Convention of 1787*, 2:453–54.
86. Ibid., 3:93.
87. Ibid., 3:211. Emphasis in original.
88. Ibid., 3:254–55.

89. Ibid., 3:161.
90. Basler, *Collected Works of Abraham Lincoln*, 3:539.
91. Farrand, *Records of the Federal Convention of 1787*, 3:325.
92. Beeman, *Plain, Honest Men*, 334, emphasis in original.
93. See Van Cleve, *A Slaveholders' Union*, 138 and 172.

Chapter 2: The Federalist Era

1. Designation of pro-administration Federalists or anti-administration/Antifederalists in the House and Senate of the first Congress is not a precise exercise. James Madison, for instance, who was Washington's close ally early on, is counted as an Antifederalist because of his later break with the administration. Being Antifederalist or anti-administration is not a synonym for having opposed the Constitution. Abraham Baldwin, a member of the House in the First Congress from Georgia, was a delegate to the Constitutional Convention and signed the Constitution, but he is counted as an anti-administration member in the sources used in this text. The figures and designations used here are from https://en.wikipedia.org/wiki/1st_United_States_Congress, which in turn are derived from Kenneth C. Martin, *The Historical Atlas of Political Parties in the United States Congress* (New York: Macmillan, 1982). Rudolph M. Bell, *Party and Faction in American Politics, 1789–1801* (Westport, CT: Greenwood Press, 1973), 252, counts thirty-nine members of the first House of Representatives as pro-administration and twenty-seven as anti-administration. Bell counts Benjamin Contee of Maryland as a pro-administration member of the House. Both the source used here and the online *Biographical Directory of the United States Congress* count him as anti-administration. Fergus M. Bordewich, *The First Congress* (New York: Simon & Schuster, 2016), 11, writes, without attribution, that self-described Federalists held twenty of the twenty-two seats in the Senate and forty-six of the fifty-nine original seats in the House, using membership totals before North Carolina and Rhode Island joined the union.
2. *Annals of Congress*, House of Representatives, 1st Congress, 2nd Session, 1225.
3. Ibid., 1240.
4. Edward S. Maclay, ed., *The Journal of William Maclay, United States Senator from Pennsylvania, 1789–1791* (New York, 1890), 196, online at Library of Congress, American Memory, http://memory.loc.gov/ammem/amlaw/lwmj.html.
5. George William Van Cleve, *A Slaveholders' Union: Slavery, Politics, and the Constitution in the Early American Republic* (Chicago: University of Chicago Press, 2010), 190.
6. *Annals*, House of Representatives, 1st Congress, 2nd Session, 1502.
7. Ibid., 1246.
8. W. E. B. Du Bois, *The Suppression of the African Slave-Trade in the United States of America, 1638–1870* (New York: Longmans, Green, and Co., 1904), 78.
9. Donald L. Robinson, *Slavery in the Structure of American Politics, 1765–1820* (New York: Harcourt Brace Jovanovich, 1971), 306.
10. *Annals*, House of Representatives, 1st Congress, 2nd Session, 1503.
11. Ibid., 1504. Smith's speech appears at 1502 through 1514, from which the excerpts in this text are drawn.

12. Ibid., 1505, 1508, 1509.

13. Ibid., 1506, 1512, 1510.

14. Ibid., 1508.

15. Ibid., 1505, 1509.

16. Ibid.; the committee report and the final report approved by the House appear at 1523–1525, and a side-by-side comparison appears in Du Bois, *The Suppression of the African Slave-Trade*, 78–80.

17. Howard A. Ohline, "Slavery, Economics, and Congressional Politics, 1790," *Journal of Southern History* 16, no. 3 (August 1980): 351.

18. James Madison to Robert Pleasants, October 30, 1791, *Founders Online*, National Archives.

19. "The Letters of William Loughton Smith to Edward Rutledge: June 8, 1789 to April 28, 1794," *South Carolina Historical Magazine* 69, no. 2 (1968): 108.

20. Ibid.

21. For an excellent review of the Davis case and passage of the Fugitive Slave Act, see Paul Finkelman, *Slavery and the Founders: Race and Liberty in the Age of Jefferson* (Armonk, NY: M. E. Sharpe, 2001, 2nd ed.), 81–104, upon which this text draws.

22. *Report of the Case of Charles Brown, A Fugitive Slave, Owing Labour and Service to Wm. C. Drury, of Washington County, Maryland* (Pittsburgh, PA: Alexander James, 1835), 36.

23. Manisha Sinha, *The Slave's Cause: A History of Abolition* (New Haven, CT: Yale University Press, 2016), 382.

24. Eric Foner, *Gateway to Freedom: The Hidden History of the Underground Railroad* (New York: Norton, 2015), 4.

25. Loren Schweninger, "Counting the Costs: Southern Planters and the Problem of Runaway Slaves, 1790–1860," *Business and Economic History* 28, no. 2 (Winter 1999): 268.

26. As cited in Thomas D. Morris, *Free Men All: The Personal Liberty Laws of the North, 1780–1861* (Baltimore: Johns Hopkins University Press, 1974), 32.

27. *Report of the Case of Charles Brown*, 39.

28. Emma Lou Thornbrough, "Indiana and Fugitive Slave Legislation," *Indiana Magazine of History* 50, no. 3 (September 1954): 203.

29. Joseph Nogee, "The Prigg Case and Fugitive Slavery, 1842–1850: Part I," *Journal of Negro History* 39, no. 3 (July 1954): 192.

30. *Prigg v. Pennsylvania* 41 U.S., Reports (1842) is among the most complex and controversial of all Supreme Court decisions. The view that it was an emphatically pro-slavery ruling is presented by Paul Finkelman, "Story Telling on the Supreme Court: Prigg v. Pennsylvania and Justice Joseph Story's Judicial Nationalism," *Supreme Court Review*, 1994 (1994): 247–94. A wholly different reading of the decision is presented by Leslie Friedman Goldstein, "A 'Triumph of Freedom' after All? Prigg v. Pennsylvania Re-Examined," *Law and History Review* 29, no. 3 (August 2011): 763–96.

31. Nogee, "The Prigg Case," 198.

32. Finkelman, "Story Telling," 288.

33. As cited in Nogee, "The Prigg Case," 202.

34. *Declaration of the Immediate Causes Which Induce and Justify the Succession of South Carolina from the Federal Union* (Charleston, SC, 1860).

35. *Annals of Congress*, House of Representatives, 14th Congress, 1st Session, 1117.

36. William C. Allen, *History of Slave Laborers in the Construction of the United States Capitol* (Washington, DC: Office of the Architect of the Capitol, 2005), 8.

37. James Sterling Young, *The Washington Community, 1800–1828* (New York: Harcourt, Brace & World, 1966), 31.

38. Don E. Fehrenbacher, completed and edited by Ward M. McAfee, *The Slaveholding Republic: An Account of the United States Government's Relations to Slavery* (New York: Oxford University Press, 2001), 60.

39. Walter C. Clephane, "The Local Aspect of Slavery in the District of Columbia," *Records of the Columbia Historical Society, Washington D.C.*, vol. 3 (1900): 227.

40. Worthington G. Snethen, *The Black Code of the District of Columbia* (New York: William Harned, 1848), 11.

41. Fehrenbacher, *The Slaveholding Republic*, 63.

42. Snethen, *The Black Code*, 18.

43. Ibid., 55.

44. Clephane, "Local Aspects of Slavery," 238–39.

45. Ibid., 236, citing a June 22, 1827, account in the *Alexandria Gazette*.

46. Ibid., 240. For dollar comparisons, see Robert Sahr's work at https://liberalarts.oregonstate.edu/sites/liberalarts.oregonstate.edu/files/polisci/faculty-research/sahr/inflation-conversion/pdf/cv2017.pdf.

47. Ibid., 235, citing a March 5, 1838, ad in the *National Intelligencer*.

48. For a full discussion of the District of Columbia antislavery petitions, see Mary Tremain, "Slavery in the District of Columbia," *University of Nebraska Seminary Papers*, 2 (April 1892).

49. *Register of Debates*, Senate, 24th Congress, 1st Session, 73.

50. Ibid., 74.

51. Ibid., 75.

52. Ibid., 79.

53. Ibid., 83.

54. Ibid., 84.

55. Ibid., 89.

56. Ibid., 94.

57. Ibid., 95.

58. Ibid., 652.

59. Ibid., 775.

60. Ibid., 774.

61. Ibid., 690.

62. Ibid., 810.

63. Ibid., 838.

64. Eli Whitney to Thomas Jefferson, November 24, 1793, *Founders Online*, National Archives, http://founders.archives.gov/documents/Jefferson/01-217-02-0407.

65. M. B. Hammond, *The Cotton Industry: An Essay in American Economic History, Part 1* (New York: MacMillan, 1897), 31.

66. Ibid., 32.

67. D. A. Tompkins, "The Cotton Industry," *Publications of the American Economic Association*, 3rd ser., vol. 5, no. 1. Papers and Proceedings of the Sixteenth Annual Meeting, part 1. New Orleans, December 29–31, 1903 (February 1904), 147.

68. Author's calculations from U.S. Bureau of the Census, *Negro Population 1790–1915* (Washington, DC: Government Printing Office, 1918), 53.

69. Ronald Bailey, "The Other Side of Slavery: Black Labor, Cotton, and Textile Industrialization in Great Britain and the United States," *Agricultural History* 68, no. 2, Eli Whitney's Cotton Gin, 1793–1993: A Symposium (Spring 1994): 50.

70. Du Bois, *The Suppression of the African Slave-Trade*, 152.

71. Bailey, "The Other Side of Slavery," British imports, 40; and exports' value, 48.

72. Tompkins, "The Cotton Industry," 42–43.

73. John Craig Hammond, "Slavery, Settlement, and Empire: The Expansion and Growth of Slavery in the Interior of the North American Continent, 1770–1820," *Journal of the Early Republic* 32, no. 2 (2012): 185.

74. Tompkins, "The Cotton Industry," 50.

75. Madison's role as a leading nationalist in the Constitutional Convention and a leading voice for states' rights by the end of the First Congress is the subject of a long-standing scholarly debate over whether he abandoned his former nationalist beliefs or was consistent in opposing a consolidation of federal power that was inherent in his concept of constitutional government from the outset. For a fuller discussion and the argument that Madison's opposition to Hamilton's economic agenda was consistent with his stance during the Constitutional Convention, see Lance Banning, "The Hamiltonian Madison: A Reconsideration," *Virginia Magazine of History and Biography* 92, no. 1 (January 1984): 3–28.

76. *Annals of Congress*, House of Representatives, 1st Congress, 3rd Session, 1946.

77. Ibid., 1987.

78. Ibid., 1941.

79. Ibid., 1989, 1994.

80. Ibid., 1955–56.

81. Thomas Jefferson to James Madison, October 1, 1792, *Founders Online*, National Archives, emphasis in original.

82. James Roger Sharp, *American Politics in the Early Republic: The New Nation in Crisis* (New Haven, CT: Yale University Press, 1993), 135.

83. Thomas Jefferson to George Washington, September 9, 1792, *Founders Online*, National Archives.

84. Thomas Jefferson to Philip Mazzei, April 24, 1796, *Founders Online*, National Archives.

85. See, for example, Lance Banning, *The Jeffersonian Persuasion Evolution of a Party Ideology* (Ithaca, NY: Cornell University Press, 1980), 14.

86. See, for example, James Roger Sharpe, *American Politics in the Early Republic*, 9–10, who writes, "The Republicans believed that they and they alone were the interpreters and translators of the wishes of a fictive sovereign people. But so did the Federalists. Under such circumstances, there could be little tolerance of opposition, for each proto-party was dedicated to the ultimate destruction of its political enemies, who were enemies of the people."

87. Banning, *The Jeffersonian Persuasion*, 42–69. The author is indebted to and has drawn upon this work for his own interpretation of Jefferson's opposition to the Federalist policies of Alexander Hamilton and his supporters.

88. James Madison to James Monroe, September 15, 1793, *Founders Online*, National Archives.

89. Thomas Jefferson to James Madison, September 1, 1793, *Founders Online*, National Archives.

90. John Taylor, *An Enquiry into the Principles and Tendency of Certain Public Measures* (Philadelphia: Thomas Dobson, 1794), 7; emphasis in original.

91. Ibid., 24.

92. Bray Hammond, *Banks and Politics in America from the Revolution to the Civil War* (Princeton, NJ: Princeton University Press, 1985), 123.

93. Ibid., 88.

94. Ibid., 125.

95. Ibid., 87.

96. Ibid., 30.

97. Ibid., 86.

98. Ibid., 85–86.

99. George Washington, *George Washington Papers, Series 2, Letterbooks 1754 to 1799: Letterbook 24, April 3, 1793–March 3, 1797*. 1793. Retrieved online from the Library of Congress, https://www.loc.gov/item/mgw2.024/.

100. Sharp, *American Politics in the Early Republic*, 158.

101. James Madison to James Monroe, September 15, 1793, *Founders Online*, National Archives.

102. Thomas Jefferson to John Taylor, June 4, 1798, *Founders Online*, National Archives.

103. Sharp, *American Politics in the Early Republic*, 190.

104. Douglas Bradburn, "A Clamor in the Public Mind: Opposition to the Alien and Sedition Acts," *William and Mary Quarterly*, 3rd ser., vol. 65, no. 3 (July 2008): 568.

105. Ibid., 591.

106. Sharp, *American Politics in the Early Republic*, 187–88.

107. Citations for Jefferson's draft of the Kentucky Resolutions are drawn from Thomas Jefferson, *The Works of Thomas Jefferson*, vol. 8, federal ed. (New York and London: Putnam, 1904–1905), http://oll.libertyfund.org/titles/805.

108. Sharp, *American Politics in the Early Republic*, 196.

109. Adrienne Koch and Harry Ammon, "The Virginia and Kentucky Resolutions: An Episode in Jefferson's and Madison's Defense of Civil Liberties," *William and Mary Quarterly* 5, no. 2 (April 1948): 157.

110. For the final version of the Kentucky Resolutions, see *Elliot's Debates*, vol. 4 (Philadelphia: Lippincott, 1861), 540–44.

111. Thomas Jefferson to James Madison, November 17, 1798, *Founders Online*, National Archives.

112. Thomas Jefferson to William Cary Nichols, November 29, 1798, *Founders Online*, National Archives.

113. For the final version of the Virginia Resolutions, see *Elliot's Debates*, 528–29.

114. James Madison to Thomas Jefferson, December 29, 1798, *Founders Online*, National Archives.

115. [Henry Lee], *Plain Truth: Addressed to the People of Virginia* (Richmond, 1799), 13–23.

116. Frank Maloy Anderson, "Contemporary Opinion of the Virginia and Kentucky Resolutions," *American Historical Review* 5, no. 1 (October 1899): 30–31.

117. Ibid., 51.

118. Alexander Hamilton to Theodore Sedgwick, February 2, 1799, *Founders Online*, National Archives.

119. Philip G. Davidson, "Virginia and the Alien and Sedition Laws," *American Historical Review* 36, no. 2 (January 1931): 336–42, makes the case that the Virginia arms and armory measures were unconnected to controversy over the Alien and Sedition Acts. James Roger Sharp, *American Politics in the Early Republic*, presents a contrasting argument, 203–6.

120. Thomas Jefferson to Archibald Stuart, February 13, 1799, *Founders Online*, National Archives.

121. Thomas Jefferson to Edmund Pendleton, February 14, 1799, *Founders Online*, National Archives.

122. Thomas Jefferson to James Madison, August 23, 1799, *Founders Online*, National Archives.

123. For the full text, see the Report of 1800, January 17, 1800, *Elliot's Debates*, vol. 4, 546–80.

Chapter 3: *Thomas Jefferson and the Empire of Liberty*

1. Thomas Jefferson to Henry Lee, May 8, 1825, *Founders Online*, National Archives, http://founders.archive.gov/documents/Jefferson/98-01-02-5212.

2. John Ferling, *Adams vs. Jefferson: The Tumultuous Election of 1800* (New York: Oxford University Press, 2004); and Edward J. Larson, *A Magnificent Catastrophe: The Tumultuous Election of 1800, America's First Presidential Campaign* (New York: Free Press, 2007) provide detailed narratives of the personalities and events of the 1800 election.

3. Thomas McKean to Thomas Jefferson, March 21, 1801, *Founders Online*, National Archives, http://founders.archives.gov/documents/Jefferson/01-33-02-0335.

4. See Garry Wills, *Negro President Jefferson and the Slave Power* (Boston: Houghton Mifflin, 2003), 2; and William W. Freehling, *The Road to Disunion, Volume I: Secessionists at Bay 1776–1854* (New York: Oxford University Press, 1990), 147.

5. Thomas Jefferson to Spencer Roane, September 6, 1819, *Founders Online*, National Archives, http://founders.archives.gov/documents/Jefferson/98-01-02-0734.

6. Thomas Jefferson to William Duane, March 28, 1811, *Founders Online*, National Archives, http://founders.archieves.gov/documents/Jefferson/03-03-02-0378. Emphasis in original.

7. Ibid.

8. "Empire of liberty" from Thomas Jefferson to George Rogers Clark, December 25, 1780, *Founders Online*, National Archives, http://founders.archives.gov/documents/Jefferson/01-04-02-0295; "has never been surveyed . . ." from Thomas Jefferson to James

Madison, April 27, 1809, *Founders Online*, National Archives, http://founders.archives
.gov/documents/Jefferson/03-01-02-0140.

9. Kevin M. Gannon, "Escaping 'Mr. Jefferson's Plan of Destruction': New England Federalists and the Idea of a Northern Confederacy, 1803–1804," *Journal of the Early Republic* 21, no. 3 (Autumn 2001): 414.

10. Thomas Jefferson, *Writings* (New York: Library of America, 1984), 492.

11. Thomas Jefferson to Isaac H. Tiffany, April 4, 1819, *Founders Online*, National Archives, http://founders.archives.gov/documents/Jefferson/98-01-02-0303.

12. Thomas Jefferson, *Writings*, first inaugural, 493–94.

13. Thomas Jefferson to Charles Yancey, January 6, 1816, *Founders Online*, National Archives, http://founders.archives.gov/documents/Jefferson/03-09-02-0209.

14. Thomas Jefferson to John Jay, August 23, 1785, *Founders Online*, National Archives, http://founders.archives.gov/documents/Jefferson/01-08-02-0333.

15. Jefferson, *Writings*, 290.

16. William Cohen, "Thomas Jefferson and the Problem of Slavery," *Journal of American History* 56, no. 3 (December 1969): 506.

17. Ibid.

18. Ibid., 290–91.

19. Thomas Jefferson to William H. Crawford, June 20, 1816, *Founders Online*, National Archives, http://founders.archives.gov/documents/Jefferson/03-10-02-0101.

20. Thomas Jefferson to Benjamin Austin, January 9, 1816, *Founders Online*, National Archives, http://founders.archives.gov/documents/Jefferson/03-09-02-0213.

21. Jefferson, *Writings*, 288.

22. Thomas Jefferson to Edward Coles, August 25, 1814, *Founders Online*, National Archives, http://founders.archives.gov/documents/Jefferson/03-07-02-0439.

23. Jefferson, *Writings*, 44.

24. Thomas Jefferson to Edward Coles.

25. Jefferson, *Writings*, 264.

26. Ibid., 270.

27. Thomas Jefferson to James Monroe, November 24, 1801, *Founders Online*, National Archives, http://founders.archives.gov/documents/Jefferson/01-35-02-0550.

28. Thomas Jefferson to John Holmes, April 22, 1820, *Founders Online*, National Archives, http://founders.archives.gov/documents/Jefferson/98-01-02-1234.

29. Thomas Jefferson to Edward Coles.

30. Jefferson, *Writings*, 115–16.

31. From Julian P. Boyd, ed., *The Papers of Thomas Jefferson*, vol. 1, 1760–1776 (Princeton, NJ: Princeton University Press, 1950), 243–47, as accessed online at the Library of Congress, www.loc.gov/exhibits/declara/ruffdrft.html.

32. Jefferson, *Writings*, 344.

33. Ibid., 264.

34. As quoted in William Cohen, "Thomas Jefferson and the Problem of Slavery," 510.

35. Thomas Jefferson to Chastellux, June 7, 1785, *Founders Online*, National Archives, http://founders.archives.gov/documents/Jefferson/01-08-02-0145.

36. Ibid.

37. As quoted in Paul Finkelman, *Slavery and the Founders: Race and Liberty in the Age of Jefferson*, 2nd ed. (Armonk, NY: M. E. Sharpe, 2001), 147, citing Boyd, *Papers of Jefferson*, 6:298.

38. Thomas Jefferson to James Madison, June 17, 1783, *Founders Online*, National Archives, http://founders.archives.gov/documents/Jefferson/01-06-02-0254.

39. Thomas Jefferson to John Jay, August 23, 1785.

40. Thomas Jefferson to Brissot de Warville, February 11, 1788, *Founders Online*, National Archives, http://founders.archives.gov/documents/Jefferson/01-12-02-0612.

41. Thomas Jefferson to George Logan, May 11, 1805, *Founders Online*, National Archives, http://founders.archives.gov/documents/Jefferson/99-01-02-1709.

42. Thomas Jefferson to William Armistead Burwell, January 28, 1805, *Founders Online*, National Archives, http://founders.archives.gov/documents/Jefferson/99-01-02-1057.

43. Thomas Jefferson to Charles Yancey, January 6, 1816.

44. Thomas Jefferson to James Heaton, May 20, 1826, *Founders Online*, National Archives, http://founders.archives.gov/documents/Jefferson/98-01-02-6127.

45. Christa Dierksheide, "'The Great Improvement and Civilization of That Race': Jefferson and the 'Amelioration' of Slavery, ca. 1770–1826," *Early American Studies* 6, no. 1 (Spring 2008): 184.

46. Thomas Jefferson to Edward Coles, August 25, 1814.

47. Thomas Jefferson to Reuben Perry, April 16, 1812, *Founders Online*, National Archives, http://founders.archives.gov/documents/Jefferson/03-04-02-0508.

48. Thomas Jefferson to Thomas Mann Randolph, June 8, 1803, *Founders Online*, National Archives, http://founders.archives.gov/documents/Jefferson/01-40-02-0383.

49. Thomas Jefferson to John Wayles Eppes, June 30, 1820, *Founders Online*, National Archives, http://founders.archives.gov/documents/Jefferson/98-01-02-1352

50. Jefferson, *Writings*, 270.

51. Thomas Jefferson to Henri Grégoire, February 25, 1809, *Founders Online*, National Archives, http://founders.archive.gov/documents/Jefferson/99-01-02-9893.

52. Ibid.

53. Jefferson, *Writings*, 265–70.

54. In 1802 journalist James T. Callender wrote a series of articles reporting that Jefferson had fathered children with Sally Hemings; see Paul Finkelman, *Slavery and the Founders*, 165 and 163–96 for his discussion of Jefferson, Hemings, and antislavery. For decades Jefferson biographers discounted that Jefferson had a sexual relationship with Sally Hemings. The issue was reintroduced to modern readers in Fawn M. Brodie's *Thomas Jefferson: An Intimate History* (New York: Norton, 1974). A seminal DNA study on the relationship is to be found in Eugene Foster et al., "Jefferson Fathered Slave's Last Child," *Nature*, 396 (November 5, 1998): 27–28. The most complete modern work on the topic is Annette Gordon-Reed, *The Hemingses of Monticello: An American Family* (New York: Norton, 2008). For a comprehensive study of the Jefferson-Hemings relationship, see *Report of the Research Committee on Thomas Jefferson and Sally Hemings*, Thomas Jefferson Memorial Foundation, January 2000, and http://www.monticello.org/plantation/hemings_resources.html.

55. As cited in Brenda E. Stevenson, "What's Love Got to Do with It? Concubinage and Enslaved Women and Girls in the Antebellum South," *Journal of African American History* 98, no. 1, special issue: "Women, Slavery, and the Atlantic World" (Winter 2013): 107.

56. As cited in Gordon-Reed, *The Hemingses of Monticello*, 326.

57. Ibid., 361.

58. See ibid., 657–59; and Paul Finkelman, *Slavery and the Founders*, 153–56.

59. Paul Finkelman, "Thomas Jefferson and Antislavery: The Myth Goes On," *Virginia Magazine of History and Biography* 102, no. 2 (April 1994): 154.

60. Robert E. Shalhope, "Thomas Jefferson's Republicanism and Antebellum Southern Thought," *Journal of Southern History* 42, no. 4 (November 1976): 555.

61. David Brion Davis, *The Problem of Slavery in the Age of Revolution, 1770–1823* (New York: Oxford University Press, 1999), 171.

62. Douglas R. Egerton, *Gabriel's Rebellion: The Virginia Slave Conspiracies of 1800 & 1802* (Chapel Hill: University of North Carolina Press, 1993).

63. James Monroe to Thomas Jefferson, September 15, 1800, *Founders Online*, National Archives, http://founders.archives.gov/documents/Jefferson/01-32-0094.

64. Thomas Jefferson to James Monroe, September 20, 1800, *Founders Online*, National Archives, http://founders.archives.gov/documents/Jefferson/01-32-02-0097.

65. As cited in Douglas R. Egerton, *Gabriel's Rebellion*, 151.

66. James Monroe to Thomas Jefferson, June 15, 1801, *Founders Online*, National Archives, http://founders.archives.gov/documents/Jefferson/01-34-02-0254.

67. Thomas Jefferson to James Monroe, November 24, 1801, *Founders Online*, National Archives, http://founders.archives.gov/documents/01-35-02-0550.

68. Douglas R. Egerton, "'Fly across the River': The Easter Slave Conspiracy of 1802," *North Carolina Historical Review* 68, no. 2 (April 1991): 109.

69. Egerton, *Gabriel's Rebellion*, 153–54; cited as enclosures with James Monroe to Thomas Jefferson, February 13, 1802, *Founders Online*, National Archives, http://founders.archives.gov/documents/Jefferson/01-36-02-0379.

70. Thomas Jefferson to James Monroe, June 3, 1802, *Founders Online*, National Archives, http://founders.archives.gov/documents/Jefferson/01-37-02-0430.

71. James Monroe to Thomas Jefferson, June 11, 1802, Library of Congress, http://loc.gov/resource/mtj1.026_0546_0549, advises Jefferson of the issue involving freeing slaves convicted of insurgency, yet Jefferson's letter to Rufus King in London, written a month later, makes no reference to the problem; Thomas Jefferson to Rufus King, July 13, 1802, *Founders* Online, National Archives, http://founders.archives.gov/documents/Jefferson/01-38-02-0052.

72. Christopher Gore to Thomas Jefferson, October 10, 1802, *Founders Online*, National Archives, http://founders.archives.gov/documents/Jefferson/01-38-02-0434. Gore was acting in place of Ambassador Rufus King, who was outside London when Jefferson's request was received.

73. Tim Matthewson, "Jefferson and the Nonrecognition of Haiti," *Proceedings of the American Philosophical Society* 140, no. 1 (March 1996): 24.

74. Thomas Jefferson to Albert Gallatin, December 26, 1820, *Founders Online*, National Archives, http://founders.archives.gov/documents/Jefferson/98-01-02-1705.

75. Egerton, *Gabriel's Rebellion*, 155–56.

76. General Assembly of St. Domingo, *A Particular Account of the Commencement and Progress of the Insurrection of the Negroes in St. Domingo*, 1791, 7–11.

77. Robin Blackburn, "Haiti, Slavery, and the Age of the Democratic Revolution," *William and Mary Quarterly*, 3rd ser., vol. 63, no. 4 (October 2006): 663.

78. Production figures from Donald R. Hickey, "America's Response to the Slave Revolt in Haiti, 1791–1806," *Journal of the Early Republic* 2, no. 4 (Winter 1982): 362; population figures from Donald L. Robinson, *Slavery in the Structure of American Politics, 1765–1820* (New York: Harcourt Brace Jovanovich, 1971), 362.

79. Hickey, ibid.

80. *City Gazette*, Charleston, SC, September 9, 1791.

81. Ashli White, "The Limits of Fear: The Saint Dominguan Challenge to Slave Trade Abolition in the United States," *Early American Studies* 2, no. 2 (Fall 2004): 363.

82. Timothy M. Matthewson, "George Washington's Policy toward the Haitian Revolution," *Diplomatic History* 3, no. 3 (Summer 1979): 332–33.

83. Hickey, "America's Response," 367.

84. Ibid.

85. Thomas O. Ott, *The Haitian Revolution, 1789–1804* (Knoxville: University of Tennessee Press, 1973), 114.

86. Matthewson, "George Washington's Policy," 334.

87. Robinson, *Slavery in the Structure*, 364.

88. Ott, *The Haitian Revolution*, 127.

89. Carl Ludwig Lokke, "Jefferson and the Leclerc Expedition," *American Historical Review* 33, no. 2 (January 1928): 324.

90. Tim Matthewson, "Jefferson and Haiti," *Journal of Southern History* 61, no. 2 (May 1995): 219–20.

91. Robert E. Bonner, *Mastering America: Southern Slaveholders and the Crisis of American Nationhood* (New York: Cambridge University Press, 2009), 8.

92. Ott, *The Haitian Revolution*, 182.

93. Peter S. Onuf, *The Mind of Thomas Jefferson* (Charlottesville: University of Virginia Press, 2007), 105.

94. Cited in Thomas Reinhardt, "200 Years of Forgetting: Hushing up the Haitian Revolution," *Journal of Black Studies* 35, no. 4 (March 2005): 256–57.

95. Bernard W. Sheehan, "Jefferson's 'Empire for Liberty,'" *Indiana Magazine of History* 100, no. 4 (December 2004): 352.

96. Thomas Jefferson to John Breckinridge, August 12, 1803, *Founders Online*, National Archives, http://founders.archives.gov/documents/Jefferson/01-41-02-0139.

97. *Annals of Congress*, 8th Congress, appendix, 1498.

98. Jon Kukla, *A Wilderness So Immense: The Louisiana Purchase and the Destiny of America* (New York: Anchor Books, 2004), 287, notes that the final borders of the Louisiana Purchase "comprised 529,402,880 acres," or $0.0282 per acre for the original purchase price of $15 million.

99. John Craig Hammond, "Slavery, Settlement, and Empire: The Expansion and Growth of Slavery in the Interior of the North American Continent, 1770–1820," *Journal of the Early Republic* 32, no. 2 (Summer 2012): 189.

100. *Annals of Congress*, 8th Congress, appendix, 1508.

101. Hammond, "Slavery, Settlement, and Empire," 187.

102. Ibid., 1523.

103. Ibid., 1503.

104. Lacy Ford, "Reconfiguring the Old South: 'Solving' the Problem of Slavery, 1787–1838," *Journal of American History* 95, no. 1 (June 2008): 103–4.

105. *Annals of Congress*, Senate, 16th Congress, 2nd Session, 77; and Ford, "Reconfiguring the Old South," 103.

106. Jed Handelsman Shugerman, "The Louisiana Purchase and South Carolina's Reopening of the Slave Trade in 1803," *Journal of the Early Republic* 22, no. 2 (Summer 2002): 264.

107. Thomas Jefferson to John Breckinridge, November 24, 1803, manuscript/mixed material. Retrieved from the Library of Congress, http://www.loc.gov/item/mtjbib012945.

108. Thomas Jefferson to Horatio Gates, July 11, 1803, *Founders Online*, National Archives, http://founders.archives.gov/documents/Jefferson/01-41-02-0004.

109. Author's conclusion from debate text in the journal of New Hampshire Senator William Plumber, recording remarks deprecating slavery from Senators Smith and Wright of Maryland, White of Delaware, Breckinridge of Kentucky, Anderson of Tennessee, Franklin of North Carolina, and Jackson of Georgia. The journal citations in this text are from Everett S. Brown, "The Senate Debate on the Breckinridge Bill for the Government of Louisiana, 1804," *American Historical Review* 22, no. 2 (January 1917): 340–64.

110. Brown, "The Senate Debate."

111. *Bureau of the Census, Historical Statistics of the United States, Colonial Times to 1970, Part 1* (Washington, DC: Government Printing Office, 1975), 28, with author's extrapolation from statistics for 1800.

112. Ibid., 345.

113. James C. Klotter, *The Breckinridges of Kentucky* (Lexington: University Press of Kentucky, 2006), 24.

114. Brown, "The Senate Debate," 345.

115. *Historical Statistics*, 32, as above.

116. Brown, "The Senate Debate," 355. Emphasis in original.

117. Ibid., 349.

118. Ibid., 347.

119. Ibid., 350.

120. Ibid., 351.

121. Ibid., 361.

122. Ibid., 354.

123. Ibid.

124. *Statutes at Large*, 8th Congress, 1st Session, 286.

125. Brown, "The Senate Debate," 353.

126. Hammond, "Slavery, Settlement, and Empire," 193.

127. *Annals of Congress*, Senate, 8th Congress, 1st Session, 244. The vote to approve the amendment in the Senate was eighteen in favor to eleven opposed. The measure would have failed without the eight favorable votes from Kentucky, Maryland, Delaware, Tennessee, and North Carolina.

128. *Statutes at Large*, 8th Congress, 1st Session, 289.

129. William C. C. Claiborne to James Madison, March 10, 1804, *Founders Online*, National Archives, http://founders.archives.gov/documents/Madison/02-06-02-0532.

130. William C. C. Claiborne to Thomas Jefferson, November 25, 1804, *Founders Online*, National Archives, http://founders.archives.gov/documents/Jefferson/99-01-02-0715. Emphasis in original.

131. *Annals of Congress*, 8th Congress, 2nd Session, appendix, 1619.

132. Ibid., 1606.

133. Hammond, "Slavery, Settlement, and Empire," 191.

134. John Craig Hammond, "'They Are Very Much Interested in Obtaining an Unlimited Slavery': Rethinking the Expansion of Slavery in the Louisiana Purchase Territories, 1803–1805," *Journal of the Early Republic* 23, no. 3 (Autumn 2003): 354, 356.

135. Thomas Jefferson, *Writings*, 528.

136. *Annals of Congress*, House, 9th Congress, 2nd Session, 168.

137. Ibid., 169.

138. Ibid., 174.

139. Ibid., 201.

140. Ibid., 477.

141. Ibid., 266.

142. Ibid., 238.

143. Robinson, *Slavery in the Structure*, 337–38.

144. W. E. B. Du Bois, *The Suppression of the African Slave Trade to the United States of America, 1638–1870* (New York: Longmans, Green, and Co., 1896), 128.

145. Matthew E. Mason, "Slavery Overshadowed: Congress Debates Prohibiting the Atlantic Slave Trade to the United States, 1806–1807," *Journal of the Early Republic* 20, no. 1 (Spring 2000): 60, citing Philip D. Curtin, *The Atlantic Slave Trade: A Census* (Madison, WI: Madison House, 1969).

146. White, "The Limits of Fear," 362.

147. Du Bois, *The Suppression of the African Slave Trade*, 117.

148. Ibid., 116.

149. Don E. Fehrenbacher, *The Slaveholding Republic: An Account of the United States Government's Relations to Slavery*, completed and edited by Ward M. McAfee (New York: Oxford University Press, 2001), 152.

150. David Head, "Slave Smuggling by Foreign Privateers: The Illegal Slave Trade and the Geopolitics of the Early Republic," *Journal of the Early Republic* 33, no. 3 (Fall 2013): 453, citing William C. Davis, *Three Roads to the Alamo: The Lives and Fortunes of David Crockett, James Bowie, and William Barret Travis* (New York: HarperCollins, 1998), 55–61. For dollar comparisons, see Robert Sahr's work at https://liberalarts.oregonstate.edu/sites/liberalarts.oregonstate.edu/files/polisci/faculty-research/sahr/inflation-conversion/pdf/cv2017.pdf.

151. Du Bois, *The Suppression of the African Slave Trade*, 123.

Chapter 4: The Missouri Crisis

1. Bureau of the Census, *Historical Statistics of the United States Colonial Times to 1970, Part 2*, Washington, DC, 1084.

2. *Annals of Congress*, House, 15th Congress, 2nd Session, 1166 introduction is noted, 1170 amendment wording is provided.

3. Ibid., 1170.

4. Ibid., 1214.

5. For full accounts of the Missouri controversy, see Glover Moore, *The Missouri Controversy, 1819–1821* (Gloucester, MA: Peter Smith, 1967); and Robert Pierce Forbes, *The Missouri Compromise and Its Aftermath: Slavery and the Meaning of America* (Chapel Hill: University of North Carolina Press, 2007).

6. *Annals*, House, 16th Congress, 1st Session, 998.

7. Ibid., 1377.

8. *Annals*, House, 15th Congress, 2nd Session, 1206.

9. *Annals*, Senate, 16th Congress, 1st Session, 184.

10. *Annals*, House, 16th Congress, 1st Session, 1375.

11. *Annals*, Senate, 16th Congress, 1st Session, 128.

12. Author's calculation from statistics in *Census for 1820* (Washington, DC: Gales and Seaton, 1821), 18.

13. Author's calculation from statistics in U.S. Bureau of the Census, *Negro Population, 1790–1915* (Washington, DC: Government Printing Office, 1918), 33.

14. Ronald Bailey, "The Other Side of Slavery: Black Labor, Cotton, and Textile Industrialization in Great Britain and the United States," *Agricultural History* 68, no. 2, Eli Whitney's Cotton Gin, 1793–1993: A Symposium (Spring 1994): 44–47.

15. *Richmond Enquirer*, December 11, 1819.

16. *Niles' Weekly Register*, 16 (August 14, 1820), 403.

17. *Annals*, House 15th Congress, 2nd Session, 1176.

18. *Annals*, House, 16th Congress, 1st Session, 1106.

19. *Annals*, House, 15th Congress, 2nd Session, 1178.

20. James Stirling, *Letters from the Slave States* (London: John W. Parker and Son, 1857), 65.

21. Rufus King, *The Substance of Two Speeches Delivered in the Senate of the United States, on the Subject of the Missouri Bill* (Philadelphia: Clark & Raser, 1819), 6–7.

22. *Annals*, House, 16th Congress, 2nd Session, 964.

23. *Annals*, House, 16th Congress, 1st Session, 1134.

24. Ibid., 1314.

25. Edwin C. Holland writing as a South Carolinian, *A Refutation of the Calumnies Circulated against the Southern & Western States Respecting the Institution and Existence of Slavery among Them* (Charleston, SC: A. E. Miller, 1822), 37.

26. *Boston Daily Advertiser*, November 16, 1819.

27. *Annals*, House, 16th Congress, 1st Session, 1070.

28. Ibid., 1357.

29. Ibid., 1112.

30. *Kentucky Reporter (Lexington, KY)*, February 16, 1820.

31. *Concord Observer*, February 14, 1820.

32. *Annals*, Senate, 16th Congress, 2nd Session, 392 and 395.

33. *Annals*, House, 16th Congress, 2nd Session, 992.

34. Ibid., 1179 and 1189.

35. Ibid., 1234.

36. Ibid., 1390.

37. Moore, *The Missouri Controversy*, 176.

38. *Kentucky Reporter (Lexington,KY)*, January 4, 1820.

39. *New Hampshire Patriot*, November 18, 1819, as cited in Moore, *The Missouri Controversy*, 186. Emphasis in original.

40. As cited in Lacy Ford, "Reconfiguring the Old South: 'Solving the Problem of Slavery, 1787–1838,' *Journal of American History* 95, no. 1 (June 2008): 105.

41. *Annals*, House, 16th Congress, 1st Session, 1391.

42. *Annals*, Senate, 16th Congress, 1st Session, 192.

43. Ibid., 348.

44. *New Hampshire Sentinel*, February 12, 1820.

45. Author's calculation from *Ninth Census, Volume 1* (Washington, DC: Government Printing Office, 1872), 7.

46. *Annals*, House, 16th Congress, 1st Session, 1011.

47. *Annals*, House, 15th Congress, 2nd Session, 1189.

48. *Annals,* House, 16th Congress, 1st Session, 1086.

49. *The Times (Hartford, CT)*, February 8, 1820, reprint from the *National Intelligencer*, Washington, DC.

50. Thomas Jefferson to Albert Gallatin, December 26, 1820, *Founders Online*, National Archives, http://founders.archives.gov/documents/Jeffersopn/98-01-02-1705.

51. *Annals*, Senate, 16th Congress, 1st Session, 174.

52. *Annals*, House, 16th Congress, 1st Session, 1378.

53. Ibid., 1534.

54. Thomas Jefferson to John Holmes, April 22, 1820, *Founders Online*, National Archives, http://founders.archives.gov/Jefferson/98-01-02-1234.

55. *Annals*, House, 16th Congress, 1st Session, 1210.

56. Ibid., 1354.

57. Ibid., 1109.

58. Ibid., 1397, emphasis in original.

59. Ibid., Kentucky Congressman Benjamin Hardin, 1076; Virginia Congressman Alexander Smyth, 994 and 1006; Delaware Congressman Louis McLane, 1153.

60. Ibid., 1388.

61. See chapter 1, 28.

62. *Annals*, House, 16th Congress, 1st Session, 1396.

63. See Sean Wilentz, *No Property in Man* (Cambridge, MA: Harvard University Press, 2018), 186–205, for discussion of the property in man argument in the Missouri Compromise debates.

64. *Annals*, House, 16th Congress, 1st Session, 946.

65. *New York Daily Advertiser*, January 19, 1820.

66. As cited in the *Philadelphia Weekly Aurora*, March 20, 1820.

67. *Annals*, House, 15th Congress, 2nd Session, 1204.

68. Ibid., Senate, 16th Congress, 1st Session, 175.

69. See Elizabeth R. Varon, *Disunion! The Coming of the American Civil War, 1789–1859* (Chapel Hill: University of North Carolina Press, 2008), 44–45. Varon describes five stages during which the language of disunion went from prophecy, to threat, to accusations of treasonous plotting, to a process of sectional alienation, and finally to a program for regional independence. The Missouri debates combined elements of the first four stages in that process.

70. *Annals*, House, 16th Congress, 1st Session, 1585.

71. *Annals*, Senate, 16th Congress, 1st Session 335.

72. *Annals*, House, 16th Congress, 1st Session 1016–19.

73. William W. Freehling, *Prelude to Civil War: The Nullification Controversy in South Carolina, 1816–1836* (New York: Oxford University Press, 1965), 78.

74. *Annals*, House, 16th Congress, 1st Session, 1024–25.

75. *Annals*, Senate, 16th Congress, 1st Session, 267–69.

76. Ibid., 279.

77. W. E. B. Du Bois, *The Suppression of the African Slave-Trade to the United States of America, 1638–1870* (New York: Longmans, Green, and Co., 1896), 152.

78. As cited in *Annals*, Senate, 16th Congress, 1st Session, 380.

79. *Annals*, House, 16th Congress, 1st Session, 1384.

80. Ibid., 1611.

81. See Ritchie Devon Watson Jr., *Normans and Saxons: Southern Race Mythology and the Intellectual History of the American Civil War* (Baton Rouge: Louisiana State University, 2008).

82. Freehling, *Prelude to Civil War*, 377, in endnote comment.

83. William Drayton, *The South Vindicated from the Treason and Fanaticism of the Northern Abolitionists* (Philadelphia: H. Manly, 1836), 106.

84. Ibid., 246.

85. Charles H. Wesley, "Negro Suffrage in the Period of Constitution-Making, 1787–1865," *Journal of Negro History* 32, no. 2 (April 1947): 166.

86. Joshua Michael Zeitz, "The Missouri Compromise Reconsidered: Antislavery Rhetoric and the Emergence of the Free Labor Synthesis," *Journal of the Early Republic* 20, no. 3 (Autumn 2000): 468.

87. See Don B. Kates Jr., "Abolition, Deportation, Integration: Attitudes toward Slavery in the Early Republic," *Journal of Negro History* 53, no. 1 (January 1968): 33–47.

88. *Annals*, Senate, 16th Congress, 1st Session, 217.

89. Alexis de Tocqueville, *Democracy in America*, 2 vols. (New York: 1835, 1840; reprint, 1990) I: 359.

90. *Annals*, House, 16th Congress, 2nd Session, 1228.

91. As cited in Larry H. Spruill, "Slave Patrols, 'Packs of Negro Dogs' and Policing Black Communities," *Phylon* 53, no. 1 (Summer 2016): 49.

92. As cited in Forbes, *The Missouri Compromise*, 98.

93. *Philadelphia Weekly Aurora*, April 10, 1820, citing letter by Charles Pinckney published in the *Charleston City Gazette*.

94. See Moore, *The Missouri Controversy*, 108–11, for an incisive analysis of the vote.

95. *Niles' Weekly Register* 6, no. 2 (March 11, 1820): 26. Emphasis in original.

96. Matilda Wildman Evans, "Elihu Embree, Quaker Abolitionist, and Some of His Co-Workers," *Bulletin of Friends Historical Association* 21, no. 1 (Spring 1932): 11. For the discussion of Elihu Embree in this text, the author drew on this source and on Asa Earl Martin, "Pioneer Anti-Slavery Press," *Mississippi Valley Historical Review* 2, no. 4 (March 1916): 509–28.

97. Martin, "Pioneer Anti-Slavery Press," 509–10.

98. Asa Earl Martin, "The Anti-Slavery Societies of Tennessee," *Tennessee Historical Magazine* 1, no. 4 (December 1915): 267.

99. Ibid., 527.

100. Richard H. Brown, "The Jacksonian Pro-Slavery Party," 273, in *New Perspectives on Jacksonian Parties and Politics*, edited by Edward Pessen (Boston: Allyn & Bacon, 1969).

101. *Richmond Enquirer*, March 7, 1820.

102. Rex Beach, "Spencer Roane and the Richmond Junto," *William and Mary Quarterly* 22, no. 1 (January 1942): 2. Also see Harry Ammon, "The Richmond Junto, 1800–1824," *Virginia Magazine of History and Biography* 61, no. 4 (October 1953).

103. Martin Van Buren to Thomas Ritchie, January 13, 1827, http://vanburenpapers.org/document-mvb00528, accessed July 31, 2020.

104. *An Account of the Late Intended Insurrection among a Portion of the Blacks of This City* (Charleston: A. E. Miller, 1822), 16–17.

105. Lionel H. Kennedy and Thomas Parker, eds., *An Official Report of the Trials of Sundry Negroes, Charged with an Attempt to Raise an Insurrection in the State of South Carolina* (Charleston, SC: James R. Schenck, 1822), 18.

106. Ibid., 26.

107. Ibid., 26–36.

108. Holland, *A Refutation of the Calumnies*, 12.

109. The most widely accepted account of the Vesey affair, and one that this text is indebted to and is broadly consistent with, is Douglas R. Egerton, *He Shall Go Out Free: The Lives of Denmark Vesey*, revised and updated edition (New York: Rowman & Littlefield, 2004). The primary source for the view that the Vesey conspiracy involved little more than talk among disgruntled Blacks and that the subsequent trials and executions were travesties based on manufactured evidence and testimony is Michael P. Johnson, "Denmark Vesey and His Co-Conspirators," *William and Mary Quarterly* 58, no. 4 (October 2001). Among the numerous scholarly papers on this subject, see Robert L. Paquette, "Jacobins of the Lowcountry: The Vesey Plot on Trial," *William and Mary Quarterly* 59, no. 1 (January 2002); Edward A. Pearson, "Trials and Errors: Denmark Vesey and His Historians," *William and Mary Quarterly* 59, no. 1 (January 2002); and Robert L. Paquette and Douglas R. Egerton, "Of Facts and Fables: New Light on the Denmark Vesey Affair," *South Carolina Historical Magazine* 105, no. 1 [Denmark Vesey] (January 2004).

110. Kennedy and Parker, *An Official Report*, 188.

111. As cited in Johnson, "Denmark Vesey," 939. Emphasis in original.

112. Kennedy and Parker, *An Official Report*, 102–3.

Chapter 5: Slavery—The Thing Itself

1. Herbert S. Klein, Stanley L. Engerman, Robin Haines, and Ralph Shlomowitz, "Transoceanic Mortality: The Slave Trade in Comparative Perspective," *William and Mary Quarterly* 58, no. 1 (January 2001): 97, for citation of 1839 estimate by Thomas Fowell Buxton. This article provides a base, with citations, for examination of mortality related to the Middle Passage.

2. Reverend S. H. Platt, *The Martyrs and the Fugitive, or a Narrative of the Captivity, Suffering and Death of an African Family and the Escape of Their Son* (New York: David Fanshaw, 1859), 22. Emphasis in original.

3. Sowande' M. Mustakeem, *Slavery at Sea: Terror, Sex, and Sickness in the Middle Passage* (Urbana: University of Illinois Press, 2016), 59.

4. Platt, *The Martyrs and the Fugitive*, 25.

5. William O. Blake, *The History of Slavery and the Slave Trade, Ancient and Modern* (Columbus, OH: H. Miller, 1860), Forgotten Books Reprint, 2017, 129.

6. Antonio T. Bly, "Crossing the Lake of Fire: Slave Resistance during the Middle Passage, 1720–1842," *Journal of Negro History* 1, no. 3 (Summer 1998): 181.

7. Sowande' Mustakeem, "'I Never Have Such a Sickly Ship Before': Diet, Disease, and Mortality in 18th-Century Atlantic Slaving Voyages," *Journal of African American History* 93, no. 4, Ending the Transatlantic Slave Trade: Bicentennial Research, Reflections, and Commemorations (Fall 2008): 485.

8. Blake, *The History of Slavery and the Slave Trade*, 290.

9. Ibid., 127.

10. See the Trans-Atlantic Slave Trade Database, http://slavevoyages.org/assessment/essays#, and http://slavevoyages.org/assessment/estimates.

11. Henry Bibb, *Narrative of the Life and Adventures of Henry Bibb, an American Slave* (New York: self-published, 1849), 103.

12. Gerald G. Eggert, "Notes and Documents: A Pennsylvanian Visits the Richmond Slave Market," *Pennsylvania Magazine of History and Biography* 109, no. 4 (October 1985): 572–73. Emphasis in original.

13. Alfred H. Conrad and John R. Meyer, "The Economics of Slavery in the Ante Bellum South," *Journal of Political Economy* 66, no. 2 (April 1958): 115.

14. For dollar conversions, see the work of Robert C. Sahr at https://liberalarts.oregonstate.edu/sites/liberalarts.oregonstate.edu/files/polisci/faculty-research/sahr/inflation-conversion/pdf/cv2017.pdf.

15. Jacob Stroyer, *My Life in the South* (Salem, MA: Salem Observer, 1885, new and enlarged edition), 16.

16. Kenneth M. Stampp, *The Peculiar Institution: Slavery in the Ante-Bellum South* (New York: Vintage Books, 1989 edition of 1956 original), 29.

17. Lewis Cecil Gray, *History of Agriculture in the Southern United States to 1860* (Washington, DC: Carnegie Institution, 1933), 529–30; Stampp, *The Peculiar Institution*,

30–31; and "The Non-Slaveholders of the South," *De Bow's Review* 30, no. 1 (January 1861): 67–68.

18. Daniel L. Fountain, "A Broader Footprint: Slavery and Slaveholding Households in Antebellum Piedmont North Carolina," *North Carolina Historical Review* 91, no. 4 (October 2014): 414. His works also suggests that "the beneficiaries of slave labor among the free population [both owners and family members] were far more numerous than historians have believed," 444.

19. Frederick Douglass, *My Bondage and My Freedom* (New York: Miller, Orton & Co., 1857), 328.

20. Robert S. Starobin, *Industrial Slavery in the Old South* (New York: Oxford University Press, 1970), 15.

21. Loren Schweninger, "John Carruthers Stanly and the Anomaly of Black Slaveholding," *North Carolina Historical Review* 67, no. 2 (April 1990): 177.

22. David L. Lightner and Alexander M. Ragan, "Were African American Slaveholders Benevolent or Exploitative? A Quantitative Approach," *Journal of Southern History* 71, no. 3 (August 2005): 551; figures from table 1, 556.

23. Stampp, *The Peculiar Institution*, 351.

24. L. Maria Child, ed., *The Patriarchal Institution as Described by Members of Its Own Family* (New York: American Anti-Slavery Society, 1860), 26.

25. Frederick Law Olmsted, *A Journey in the Seaboard Slave States* (Mount Pleasant, SC: Arcadia Press, 2017, reprint of 1856 original), 259.

26. Brenda E. Stevenson, "What's Love Got to Do with It? Concubinage and Enslaved Women and Girls in the Antebellum South," *Journal of African American History* 98, no. 1 (Winter 2013): 101.

27. James Mellon, ed., *Bullwhip Days: The Slaves Remember* (New York: Grove Press, 1988), 220.

28. H. Mattison, *Louisa Picquet, The Octoroon: or Inside Views of Southern Domestic Life* (New York: published by the author, 1861), 5.

29. Ibid., 18.

30. Stevenson, "What's Love Got to Do with It," 109.

31. Gray, *History of Agriculture*, 499.

32. Frederick Law Olmsted, *The Cotton Kingdom: A Traveller's Observations on Cotton and Slavery in the American Slaves States, 1853–1861* (independently published 2017 edition of New York: Mason Brothers, 1861, original), 373.

33. Ibid., 323–30.

34. Olmsted, *A Journey in the Seaboard Slave States*, 186.

35. Ibid., 212.

36. Charles Ball, *Slavery in the United States: A Narrative of the Life and Adventures of Charles Ball, a Black Man* (New York: John H. Taylor, 1837), 320.

37. Jeffrey R. Young, "Ideology and Death on a Savannah River Rice Plantation, 1833–1867: Paternalism amidst 'a Good Supply of Disease and Pain,'" *Journal of Southern History* 59, no. 4 (November 1993), mortality rates, 682; admonition to be kind, 675; reports to owner, 690.

38. Willie Lee Rose, *A Documentary History of Slavery in North America* (Athens: University of Georgia Press, 1999), 285.

39. *Compendium of the Seventh Census* (Washington, DC: Government Printing Office, 1854), 94.

40. Conrad and Meyer, "The Economics of Slavery in the Ante Bellum South," 105.

41. *Jackson Mississippian*, March 14, 1834, as cited in Edwin A. Miles, "The Mississippi Slave Insurrection Scare of 1835," *Journal of Negro History* 42, no. 1 (January 1957): 48–49.

42. William Kaufman Scarborough, *Masters of The Big House: Elite Slaveholders of the Mid-Nineteenth-Century South* (Baton Rouge: Louisiana State University Press, 2003), Natchez, 3; Marshall, 431; Cocke, 433.

43. Olmsted, *A Journey in the Seabord Slave States*, 26.

44. Stampp, *The Peculiar Institution*, 326.

45. Clement Eaton, *The Freedom-of-Thought Struggle in the Old South* (New York: Harper Torchbooks, revised and enlarged edition, 1964), 34.

46. Douglass, *My Bondage*, 108–10.

47. James Stirling, *Letters from the Slave States* (London: John W. Parker and Son, 1857), 59.

48. John W. Roberts, "Slave Proverbs: A Perspective," *Callaloo*, no. 4 (October 1978): 134.

49. Frederick Law Olmsted, *A Journey in the Back Country* (London: Forgotten Books, 2012, reprint of 1860 original published in New York by Mason Brothers), 81–82.

50. As cited in Olmsted, *A Journey in the Seaboard Slave States*, 213.

51. Stampp, *The Peculiar Institution*, 318. A sampling of the controversy involving slave mortality can be gathered from Peter Kolchin, "Review: Toward a Reinterpretation of Slavery," *Journal of Social History* 9, no. 1 (Autumn 1975); and Maris A. Vinovskis, "Review: The Demography of the Slave Population in Antebellum America," *Journal of Interdisciplinary History* 5, no. 3 (Winter 1975).

52. Conrad and Meyer, "The Economics of Slavery," 106, footnote 9.

53. Robert Collins, *Essay on the Treatment and Management of Slaves Written for the Seventh Annual Fair of the Southern Central Agricultural Society*, 2nd ed. (Boston: Eastburn's Press, 1853), 5.

54. Richard H. Steckel, "A Peculiar Population: The Nutrition, Health, and Mortality of American Slaves from Childhood to Maturity," *Journal of Economic History* 46, no. 3 (September 1986): 732–33.

55. Bibb, *Narrative*, 118.

56. Olmsted, *A Journey in the Back Country*, 82.

57. Ibid., 85–87.

58. Rose, *A Documentary History of Slavery*, 347.

59. Melton A. McLaurin, *Celia, a Slave* (Athens: University of Georgia Press, 1991), 23, citing Orville Vernon Burton, *In My Father's House Are Many Mansions: Family and Community in Edgefield, South Carolina* (Chapel Hill: University of North Carolina Press, 1985), 185–89; Carol Bleser, *Secret and Sacred: The Diaries of James Henry Hammond, a Southern Slaveholder* (New York: Oxford University Press, 1988), 17–21, 212–13; and Drew Gilpin Faust, *James Henry Hammond and the Old South* (Baton Rouge: Louisiana State University Press, 1982), 87.

60. Benjamin Drew, *The Refugee: Or the Narratives of Fugitive Slaves in Canada* (Boston: John P. Jewett, 1856), 30.

61. Douglass, *My Bondage*, 219.

62. Charles Ball, *Fifty Years in Chains or The Life of an American Slave*, edited by Isaac Fisher (New York: H. Dayton, 1860 reprint of 1837 original), 120–21.

63. Conrad and Meyer, "The Economics of Slavery," 104.

64. *American Slavery As It Is: Testimony of a Thousand Witnesses* (New York: American Anti-Slavery Society, 1839), 18, narrative of Reverend Horace Moulton.

65. Ball, *Fifty Years in Chains*, 128–29.

66. *De Bow's Review* 3, no. 5 (May 1847): 419–20.

67. Olmsted, *A Journey in the Seaboard Slave States*, 57.

68. John David Smith, "'I Was Raised Poor and Hard as Any Slave': African American Slavery in Piedmont, North Carolina," *North Carolina Historical Review* 90, no. 1 (January 2013): 18.

69. Mellon, *Bullwhip Days*, 146.

70. Michael Tadman, *Speculators and Slaves: Masters, Traders, and Slaves in the Old South* (Madison: University of Wisconsin Press, 1989), 160.

71. As cited in Thomas E. Will, "Weddings on Contested Grounds: Slave Marriage in the Antebellum South," *The Historian* 62, no. 1 (Fall 1999): 104.

72. Ibid., 100.

73. Bibb, *Narrative*, 15.

74. *St. Louis Observer*, May 7, 1835, as cited in Child, *The Patriarchal Institution*, 32.

75. Douglass, *My Bondage*, 146.

76. Gray, *History of Agriculture*, 513.

77. Nicholas May, "Holy Rebellion: Religious Assembly Laws in Antebellum South Carolina and Virginia," *American Journal of Legal History* 49, no. 3 (July 2007): 252.

78. Lunsford Lane, *The Narrative of Lunsford Lane, Formerly of Raleigh, N.C.* (Boston: J. G. Torrey, 1842), 21.

79. Harriet Jacobs, *Incidents in the Life of a Slave Girl*, edited by L. Maria Child (Boston: published for the author, 1861), 106.

80. Reverend Peter Randolph, *Sketches of a Slave Life: Or, Illustrations of the "Peculiar Institution"* (Boston: published for the author, 1855), 68.

81. Moses Grandy, *Narrative of the Life of Moses Grandy, Formerly a Slave in the United States of America* (Boston: Oliver Johnson, 1844), 10–11.

82. Ibid., 6.

83. Tadman, *Speculators and Slaves*, 5, 45, 170–71.

84. Ball, *Fifty Years in Chains*, 29–30.

85. Robert H. Gudmestad, *A Troublesome Commerce: The Transformation of the Interstate Slave Trade* (Baton Rouge: Louisiana State University Press, 2003), 47.

86. Child, *The Patriarchal Institution*, 20.

87. *Lexington Democratic Advocate*, February 14, 1855, as cited in Larry H. Spruill, "'Slave Patrols, Packs of Negro Dogs' and Policing Black Communities," *Phylon (1960–)* 53, no. 1 (Summer 2016): 53.

88. *American Slavery As It Is*, 11, narrative of Nehemiah Caulkins.

89. Drew, *The Refugee*, 68.

90. Olmsted, *A Journey*, 214–15.

91. As cited in Spruill, "Slave Patrols," 54.

92. Olmsted, *The Cotton Kingdom*, 281.

93. *American Slavery As It Is*, 46, narrative of Reverend William T. Allan.

94. As cited in Olmsted, *A Journey*, 474.

95. Sally E. Hadden, *Slave Patrols Law and Violence in Virginia and the Carolinas* (Cambridge, MA: Harvard University Press, 2001), 41.

96. Douglass, *My Bondage*, 92.

97. Herbert G. Gutman, *Slavery and the Numbers Game: A Critique of Time on the Cross* (Chicago: University of Illinois Press, 1975), 38.

98. Mellon, *Bullwhip Days*, 241.

99. Ibid., 243.

100. Stampp, *The Peculiar Institution*, 174. Emphasis in original.

101. Louis Hughes, *Thirty Years a Slave* (reprint of 1897 original), 5.

102. Zambia, *The Life and Adventures of Zambia, An African Negro King, and His Experiences of Slavery in South Carolina* (London: Smith, Elder and Co., 1847), 161.

103. Gutman, *Slavery and the Numbers Game*, 22–24.

104. Austin Steward, *Twenty-Two Years a Slave, and Forty Years a Freeman* (Canandaigua, NY: published by the author, 1867), 16–17.

105. Bibb, *Narrative*, 105.

106. Moses Roper, *Narrative of the Adventures and Escape of Moses Roper* (Berwick-Upon-Tweed, England: published for the author, 1848), 15.

107. James Williams, *Narrative of James Williams, an American Slave* (New York: American Anti-Slavery Society, 1838), 52.

108. *American Slavery As It Is*, 26, narrative of William Poe.

109. Thomas Jefferson, *Writings* (New York: Library of America, 1984), 288.

110. *American Slavery As It Is*, 46.

111. Olmsted, *A Journey in the Back Country*, 63.

112. Both items cited in Child, *The Patriarchal Institution*, 15.

113. Kelly Houston Jones, "'A Rough Saucy Set of Hands to Manage': Slave Resistance in Arkansas," *Arkansas Historical Quarterly* 71, no. 1 (Spring 2012): 17. This text is indebted to this source for the account here of this case.

114. Glenn McNair, "Slave Women, Capital Crime, and Criminal Justice in Georgia," *Georgia Historical Quarterly* 93, no. 2 (Summer 2009): 135–36.

115. Ibid., 146–47.

116. McLaurin, *Celia, a Slave*. See also Wilma King, "'Mad' Enough to Kill: Enslaved Women, Murder, and Southern Courts," *Journal of African American History* 92, no. 1 (Winter 2007). McLaurin's work is the principal source for the account in this text.

117. McLaurin, *Celia, a Slave*, 20.

118. Ibid., 31.

Chapter 6: Slave Revolt and State Nullification

1. Nat Turner, *The Confessions of Nat Turner, The Leader of the Late Insurrection in Southampton, VA*, edited by Thomas R. Gray (Baltimore: Lucas & Deaver, 1831), 8–9.

2. Ibid., 9.

3. Ibid.

4. Ibid., 9–10.

5. Ibid., 9.

6. Ibid., 10.

7. Ibid., 11.

8. Anthony Santoro, "The Prophet in His Own Words: Nat Turner's Biblical Construction," *Virginia Magazine of History and Biography* 116, no. 2 (2008): 120; "The planning continued until 13 August, when a solar phenomenon turned the sun bluish-green and caused the appearance on it of a prominent black spot."

9. For a chronology of events in Nat Turner's rebellion, see Henry Irving Tragle, *The Southampton Slave Revolt of 1831: A Compilation of Source Material* (New York: Vintage Books, 1971), xv–xviii.

10. Turner, *Confessions*, 11.

11. Santoro, "The Prophet in His Own Words," 123 and passim, as an excellent source to understanding Nat Turner's motives as rooted in Old Testament depictions of God's terrible wrath.

12. Turner, *Confessions*, 14.

13. Ibid.

14. Stephen B. Oates, *The Fires of Jubilee: Nat Turner's Fierce Rebellion* (New York: Harper Perennial, 2004 edition of 1975 original), 100, places the toll at "at least 120, probably more." Anthony Santoro, "The Prophet in His Own Words," 115, estimates that during and in the aftermath of the revolt, "perhaps two hundred blacks, both slave and free, were killed." The source for fifty-three jailed, which includes Turner, is John W. Cromwell, "The Aftermath of Nat Turner's Insurrection," *Journal of Negro History* 5, no. 2 (April 1920): 214.

15. Cromwell, "The Aftermath," 215.

16. As cited in Tragle, *The Southampton Slave Revolt*, 103.

17. Cromwell, "The Aftermath," 213.

18. Turner, *Confessions*, 11.

19. As cited in Alison Goodyear Freehling, *Drift toward Dissolution: The Virginia Slavery Debate of 1831–1832* (Baton Rouge: Louisiana State University Press, 1982), 84.

20. William W. Freehling, *The Road to Disunion: Secessionists at Bay, Volume I* (New York: Oxford University Press, 1990), 188.

21. *Ninth Census*, vol. 1 (Washington, DC: Government Printing Office, 1870), 7, for Virginia's slave population and ranking as the largest slave state in 1860. For figures for regional distribution of whites, slaves, and free Blacks, see William H. Brodnax, *The Speech of William H. Brodnax (of Dinwiddie) in the House of Delegates of Virginia, on the Policy of the State with Respect to Its Colored Population* (Richmond, VA: Thomas W. Wise, 1832), 27.

22. As cited in Freehling, *Drift toward Dissolution*, 86.

23. William B. Preston, *The Speech of William B. Preston (of Montgomery) in the House of Delegates of Virginia on the Policy of the State in Relation to Her Colored Population* (Richmond, VA: Thomas W. White, 1832), 4.

24. John Thompson Brown, *The Speech of John Thompson Brown, in the House of Delegates of Virginia, on the Abolition of Slavery* (Richmond, VA: Thomas W. White, 1832), 8.

25. William W. Freehling, *Prelude to Civil War: The Nullification Controversy in South Carolina, 1816–1836* (New York: Oxford University Press, 1992), 83.

26. John Chandler, *The Speech of John Chandler (of Norfolk County) in the House of Delegates of Virginia, on the Policy of the State with Respect to Her Slave Population* (Richmond, VA: Thomas W. White, 1832), 6.

27. Charles J. Faulkner, *The Speech of Charles Jas. Faulkner (of Berkeley) in the House of Delegates of Virginia, on the Policy of the State with Respect to Her Slave Population* (Richmond, VA: Thomas W. White, 1832), 15.

28. Preston, *The Speech of William B. Preston*, 4.

29. Brown, *The Speech of John Thompson Brown*, 5, 15, 31, 9.

30. Brodnax, *The Speech of William H. Brodnax*, 10, 29–30.

31. Thomas Marshall, *The Speech of Thomas Marshall, in the House of Delegates of Virginia, on the Abolition of Slavery* (Richmond, VA: Thomas W. White, 1832), 6.

32. Thomas J. Randolph, *Speech of Thomas J. Randolph in the House of Delegates of Virginia on the Abolition of Slavery* (Richmond, VA: Samuel Shepherd, 1832), 9, 7.

33. Cromwell, "The Aftermath," 231.

34. Charles Grier Sellers Jr., "Andrew Jackson versus the Historians," *Mississippi Valley Historical Review* 44, no. 4 (March 1958): 724.

35. *Annals of Congress*, House, 14th Congress, 2nd Session, 854.

36. Noble E. Cunningham Jr., "Nathaniel Macon and the Southern Protest against National Consolidation," *North Carolina Historical Review* 32, no. 3 (July 1955): 380.

37. *Annals of Congress*, Senate, 18th Congress, 1st session, 1308.

38. John Lauritz Larson, "'Bind the Republic Together': The National Union and the Struggle for a System of Internal Improvements," *Journal of American History* 74, no. 2 (September 1987): 385; and Daniel M. Mulcare, "Restricted Authority: Slavery Politics, Internal Improvements, and the Limitation of National Administrative Capacity," *Political Research Quarterly* 61, no. 4 (December 2008): 674 and passim.

39. Whitemarsh Seabrook, *A Concise View of the Critical Situation and Future Prospects of the Slave-Holding States, in Relation to Their Coloured Population* (Charleston, SC: E. E. Miller, 1825), 3, 15. Emphasis in original.

40. Brutus (Robert Turnbull), *The Crisis: or, Essays on the Usurpations of the Federal Government* (Charleston, SC: A. E. Miller, 1827), 9, 12, 14, 17, 43–44. Emphasis in original.

41. Robert V. Remini, *Andrew Jackson: The Course of American Empire, 1767–1821*, vol. 1 (Baltimore: Johns Hopkins University Press, 1998 edition of 1977 original), 21–25.

42. Bertram Wyatt-Brown, "Andrew Jackson's Honor," *Journal of the Early Republic* 17, no. 1 (Spring 1997): 12.

43. *Ninth Census*, vol. 1, as derived from statistics on 3–6.

44. *Register of Debates*, Senate, 19th Congress, 2nd Session, 329.

45. Freehling, *Prelude to Civil War*, 197.

46. Gaillard Hunt, "South Carolina during the Nullification Struggle," *Political Science Quarterly* 6, no. 2 (June 1891): 235.

47. Freehling, *Prelude to Civil War*, 174.

48. [John C. Calhoun], *Exposition and Protest, Reported by the Special Committee of the House of Representatives, on The Tariff* (Columbia, SC: D. W. Sims State Printer, 1829).

49. Freehling, *Prelude to Civil War*, 222.

50. John C. Calhoun, September 11, 1830, letter to Virgil Maxcy, 98–99, in William W. Freehling, ed., *The Nullification Era: A Documentary Record* (New York: Harper Torchbooks, 1967).

51. James Hamilton Jr., September 14, 1830, letter to John Taylor et al., *Freehling, The Nullification Era*, 100–101. Emphasis in original.

52. James Madison, August 28, 1830, to Edward Everett, *Founders Online*, National Archives, http://founders.archives.gov/documents/Madison/99-02-02-2138.

53. *Elliot's Debates*, vol. 4 (Washington, DC: Jonathan Elliot, 1836), Madison's Report on the Virginia Resolution, 548.

54. Kevin R. Gutzman, "A Troublesome Legacy: James Madison and 'The Principles of '98,'" *Journal of the Early Republic* 15, no. 4 (Winter 1995): 569. For a contrasting view, see Adrienne Koch and Harry Ammon, "The Virginia and Kentucky Resolutions: An Episode in Jefferson's and Madison's Defense of Civil Liberties," *William and Mary Quarterly* 5, no. 2 (April 1948).

55. Freehling, *Prelude to Civil War*, 248.

56. The Ordinance of Nullification, November 24, 1832, in Freehling, *The Nullification Era*, 151.

57. John C. Calhoun, July 8, 1832, to Waddy Thompson as cited in Freehling, *Prelude to Civil War*, 249.

58. Freehling, *Prelude to Civil War*, 255.

59. *Register of Debates*, Senate, 22nd Congress, 2nd Session, appendix, 2–8.

60. Andrew Jackson, December 10, 1832, proclamation, in Freehling, *The Nullification Era*, 155–56 and 163. Emphasis in original.

61. Richard E. Ellis, *The Union at Risk: Jacksonian Democracy, States' Rights and the Nullification Crisis* (New York: Oxford University Press, 1987), 93.

62. Freehling, *Prelude to Civil War*, 156.

63. *Register of Debates*, Senate, 22nd Congress, 2nd Session, 537–38.

64. Ibid., 102.

65. Ibid., 189.

66. Ibid., 537.

67. Ibid., 537.

68. Ibid., 537.

69. Calhoun's Fort Hill Address as cited in Freehling, *The Nullification Era*, 140.

70. *Elliot's Debates*, vol. 4, 548.

71. [John C. Calhoun], *Exposition and Protest*, 28.

72. *Register of Debates*, Senate, 22nd Congress, 2nd Session, 189–90.

73. Ibid., 188.

74. Ibid., 545.

75. Ibid., 190.

76. Ibid., 191–92.

77. [John C. Calhoun], *Exposition and Protest*, 25.

78. Freehling, *Prelude to Civil War*, 172

79. *Register of Debates*, Senate, 22nd Congress, 2nd Session, 544.

80. Ibid., 546.

81. Ibid., 548.

82. Ibid., 552.

83. Ibid., 547.

84. John C. Calhoun, edited by Ross M. Lence, ed., *Union and Liberty: The Political Philosophy of John C. Calhoun* (Indianapolis: Liberty Fund, 1992), 30–31; and Ralph Lerner, "Calhoun's New Science of Politics," *American Political Science Review* 57, no. 4 (December 1963): 927.

85. *Register of Debates*, Senate, 22nd Congress, 2nd Session, 190.

86. *Elliot's Debates*, vol. 4, 586.

87. Ibid., 590.

88. Ibid., 583.

89. Ibid., 586.

90. Ibid., 584.

91. Ibid., 587.

92. Ibid., 584.

93. Ibid., 588.

94. Ibid., 589.

95. Ibid., 590.

96. Ibid., 589.

97. Ibid., 590.

98. Kenneth M. Stampp, "The Concept of Perpetual Union," *Journal of American History* 65, no. 1 (June 1978): passim. This article is one of the most lucid examinations available of the central issues in the nullification debate.

99. Henry Steele Commager, ed., *Documents of American History* (New York: Appleton-Century-Crofts, 1958), Articles of Confederation, 111, 115.

100. *Elliot's Debates*, 585.

101. Ibid., 591.

102. *Register of Debates*, 22nd Congress, 2nd Session, appendix, 45.

103. Major L. Wilson, "'Liberty and Union': An Analysis of Three Concepts Involved in the Nullification Controversy," *Journal of Southern History* 33, no. 3 (August 1967): 344.

104. Richard P. McCormick, "The Jacksonian Strategy," *Journal of the Early Republic* 10, no. 1 (Spring 1990): 10.

105. John Quincy Adams, *An Oration Addressed to the Citizens of the Town of Quincy on the Fourth of July 1831* (Boston: Richardson, Lord and Holbrook, 1831), 7, 17–18, 23, 26, 34.

106. *Register of Debates*, House, 22nd Congress, 2nd Session, 1612.

107. Ibid., appendix, 43.

108. Ibid., 46, 43.

109. Ibid., 42.

110. Ibid., 53.

111. Ibid., 55.

112. Ibid., 60.

113. Ellis, *The Union at Risk*, 93. Emphasis in original.

114. Herman Belz, ed., *The Webster-Hayne Debate on the Nature of the Union* (Indianapolis, IN: Liberty Fund, 2000), 89, 91.

115. *Register of Debates*, Senate, 22nd Congress, 2nd Session, 556.

116. Ibid., 557.

117. Ibid., 563.

118. Ibid., 570.

119. Ibid., 567.

120. Ibid., 571.

121. Ibid., 572–73.

122. Ibid., 575–76.

123. Ibid., 570.

124. Ibid., 559.

125. Belz, *The Webster-Hayne Debate*, 128.

126. William H. Herndon and Jesse W. Weik, *Life of Lincoln* (New York: Da Capo Press, 1983 reprint), 386.

127. Roy P. Basler, ed., *The Collected Works of Abraham Lincoln*, 8 vols. (New Brunswick, NJ: Rutgers University Press, 1953), 4:264–65. Emphasis in original.

128. Belz, *The Webster-Hayne Debate*, 144. Emphasis in original.

129. Garry Wills, *Lincoln at Gettysburg: The Words That Remade America* (New York: Simon & Schuster, 1992), 145.

130. Basler, *The Collected Works of Abraham Lincoln*, 4:268.

131. *State Papers of Nullification: Including the Public Acts of the Convention of the People of South Carolina, Assembled at Columbia, November 19, 1832 and March 11, 1833; and the Proclamation of the President of the United States, and the Proceedings of the Several State Legislatures Which Have Acted on the Subject* (Boston: Dutton and Wentworth, 1834), 196–97.

132. Ibid., 229.

133. *Register of Debates*, Senate, 22nd Congress, 2nd Session, 302, 306.

Chapter 7: Abolitionists and Proslavery

1. Jennifer Rose Mercieca, "The Culture of Honor: How Slaveholders Responded to the Abolitionist Mail Crisis of 1835," *Rhetoric and Public Affairs* 10, no. 1 (Spring 2007): 57.

2. *Proceedings of the Citizens of Charleston on the Incendiary Machinations, Now in Progress against the Peace and Welfare of the Southern States* (Charleston, SC: A. E. Miller, 1835), 8.

3. William W. Freehling, *Prelude to Civil War: The Nullification Controversy in South Carolina, 1816–1836* (New York: Oxford University Press, 1992), 344.

4. Mercieca, "The Culture of Honor," 52, 55.

5. Ibid., 58. Emphasis in original.

6. *Niles' Weekly Register*, August 22, 1835, 448.

7. David Walker, *Walker's Appeal in Four Articles; Together with a Preamble to the Coloured Citizens of the World, but in Particular and Very Expressly, to Those of the United States of America*, 3rd ed. (Boston: published by the author, 1830), 73, 79.

8. Bertram Wyatt-Brown, "The Abolitionists' Postal Campaign of 1835," *Journal of Negro History* 50, no. 4 (October 1965): 237.

9. Lorenzo Dow Turner, "The First Period of Militant Abolitionism (1831–1850)," *Journal of Negro History* 14, no. 4 (October 1929): 417.

10. Anne C. Loveland, "Evangelicalism and 'Immediate Emancipation' in American Antislavery Thought," *Journal of Southern History* 32, no. 2 (May 1966): 183.

11. Parker Pillsbury, *Acts of the Anti-Slavery Apostles* (Concord, NH: published by the author, 1883), 12.

12. Loveland, "Evangelicalism and 'Immediate Emancipation,'" 187. Emphasis in original.

13. Wendell Phillips, "Garrison," *North American Review* 129, no. 273 (August 1879): 142.

14. John A. Duerk, "Elijah P. Lovejoy: Anti-Catholic Abolitionist," *Journal of the Illinois State Historical Society* 108, no. 2 (Summer 2015): 109.

15. Daniel Walker Howe, *What Hath God Wrought: The Transformation of America, 1815–1848* (New York: Oxford University Press, 2007), 479.

16. Catherine Clinton, *Harriet Tubman: The Road to Freedom* (New York: Back Bay Books, 2005), 126.

17. Williston H. Lofton, "Abolition and Labor: Reaction of Northern Labor to the Anti-Slavery Appeal: Part II," *Journal of Negro History* 33, no. 3 (July 1948): 274.

18. Manisha Sinha, *The Slave's Cause: A History of Abolition* (New Haven, CT: Yale University Press, 2016), 119.

19. Richard B. Kielbowicz, "The Law and Mob Law in Attacks on Antislavery Newspapers, 1833–1860," *Law and History Review* 24, no. 3 (Fall 2006): 570.

20. Joel Olson, "The Freshness of Fanaticism: The Abolitionist Defense of Zealotry," *Perspectives on Politics* 5, no. 4 (December 2007): 685.

21. David C. Frederick, "John Quincy Adams, Slavery, and the Disappearance of the Right of Petition," *Law and History Review* 9, no. 1 (Spring 1991): 132.

22. [Robert J. Turnbull], *The Crisis: Or, Essays on the Usurpations of the Federal Government* (Charleston, SC: A. E. Miller, 1827), 131.

23. *Congressional Globe*, 24th Congress, 1st Session, 27.

24. *Register of Debates*, Senate or House, 24th Congress, 1st Session, 2454, 2456.

25. Ibid., 2457, 2458, 2461, 2462.

26. Leonard L. Richards, *The Slave Power: The Free North and Southern Domination, 1780–1860* (Baton Rouge: Louisiana State University Press, 2009), 132.

27. Congressman Andrew Johnson of Tennessee, *Congressional Globe*, 28th Congress, 1st Session, 97.

28. *Register of Debates*, 24th Congress, 2nd Session, 1587.

29. Ibid., 1588, 1589, 1590, 1593.

30. Ibid., 1595.

31. Ibid., 1630.

32. Ibid., 1596.

33. Stanley Harrold, "On the Borders of Slavery and Race: Charles T. Torrey and the Underground Railroad," *Journal of the Early Republic* 20, no. 2 (Summer 2000): 283–84.

34. Corey Brooks, "Stoking the 'Abolition Fire in the Capital': Liberty Party Lobbying and Antislavery in Congress," *Journal of the Early Republic* 33, no. 3 (Fall 2013): 530.

35. Gilbert Hobbs Barnes, *The Anti-Slavery Impulse, 1830–1844* (New York: Harcourt, Brace & World Harbinger Book, 1964 edition of 1933 original), 90.

36. Sinha, *The Slave's Cause*, 249.

37. Brooks, "Stoking the 'Abolitionist Fire in the Capitol,'" 531.

38. *Congressional Globe*, 25th Congress, 2nd Session, 45.

39. Benjamin Lundy, *The War in Texas; A Review of Facts and Circumstances, Showing That This Contest Is the Result of a Long Premediated Crusade against the Government, Set on Foot by Slaveholders, Land Speculators, &c. with the View of Re-Establishing, Extending, and Perpetuating the System of Slavery and the Slave Trade in the Republic of Mexico* (Philadelphia: Merrihew and Gunn, 1836), 3. Emphasis in original.

40. John Quincy Adams, *Speech of John Quincy Adams, of Massachusetts, Upon the Right of the People, Men and Women, to Petition, on the Freedom of Speech and of Debate in the House of Representatives of the United States; on the Resolutions of Seven State Legislatures, and the Petitions of More Than One Hundred Thousand Petitioners, Relating to the Annexation of Texas to This Union* (Washington, DC: Gales and Seaton, 1838), 57. Emphasis in original.

41. Ibid., 29.

42. *Congressional Globe*, 25th Congress, 3rd Session, appendix, 175.

43. Ibid., 167–68, 169, 168.

44. *Congressional Globe*, 27th Congress, 2nd Session, 168.

45. Ibid., appendix, 975, 978.

46. Barnes, *The Anti-Slavery Impulse*, 134–35, 136.

47. Michael D. Pierson, "'Slavery Cannot Be Covered Up with Broadcloth or a Bandanna': The Evolution of White Abolitionist Attacks on the 'Patriarchal Institution,'" *Journal of the Early Republic* 25, no. 3 (Fall 2005): 399.

48. Michael D. Pierson, *Free Hearts and Free Homes: Gender and American Antislavery Politics* (Chapel Hill: University of North Carolina Press, 2003), 9–10.

49. Margaret Hope Bacon, "Lucretia Mott: Pioneer for Peace," *Quaker History* 82, no. 2 (Fall 1993): 65–66.

50. Ibid., 67.

51. Mary R. Beard, "Lucretia Mott," *American Scholar*, 2, no. 1 (January 1933): 10.

52. Jeanne Stevenson-Moessner, "Elizabeth Cady Stanton: Reformer to Revolutionary: A Theological Trajectory," *Journal of the American Academy of Religion* 62, no. 3 (Autumn 1994): 676.

53. Ida Husted Harper, *The Life and Work of Susan B. Anthony*, vol. 1 (Indianapolis, IN, and Kansas City, MO: Bowen-Merrill, 1899), 216.

54. Henry Bibb, *Narrative of the Life and Adventures of Henry Bibb, An American Slave, Written by Himself with and Introduction by Lucius C. Matlack* (New York: published by the author, 1849).

55. Dorothy B. Porter, "David Ruggles, an Apostle of Human Rights," *Journal of Negro History* 28, no. 1 (January 1943): 32.

56. David Ruggles, *The Abrogation of the Seventh Commandment, by the American Churches* (New York: David Ruggles, 1835), 8.

57. Eric Foner, *Gateway to Freedom: The Hidden History of the Underground Railroad* (New York: Norton, 2015), 65.

58. Porter, "David Ruggles," 36 fn.

59. Foner, *Gateway to Freedom*, 10.

60. Stephen G. Hall, "To Render the Private Public: William Still and the Selling of 'The Underground Rail Road,'" *Pennsylvania Magazine of History and Biography* 127, no. 1 (January 2003): 37.

61. William Still, *The Underground Rail Road* (Philadelphia: Porter & Coates, 1872), 124–28.

62. Kate Clifford Larson, *Bound for the Promised Land: Harriet Tubman, Portrait of an American Hero* (New York: Ballantine Books, 2003), xvii. The author is indebted to this work as a major source for the narrative of Harriet Tubman presented here.

63. Earl Conrad, *Harriet Tubman: Negro Soldier and Abolitionist* (New York: International Publishers, 1942), 14.

64. Still, *The Underground Rail Road*, 297.

65. Barnes, *The Anti-Slavery Impulse*, 98.

66. Stanley Harrold, *Reviews of American* History 39, no. 1 (March 2011): 96, citing Reinhard O. Johnson, *The Liberty Party, 1840–1848: Antislavery Third-Party Politics in the United States* (Baton Rouge: Louisiana State University Press, 2009); and Julie Roy Jeffrey, *The Great Silent Army of Abolitionism: Ordinary Women in the Antislavery Movement* (Chapel Hill: University of North Carolina Press, 1998), 135.

67. George Fitzhugh, *Slavery Justified*, as reprinted in his *Sociology for the South, or the Failure of Free Society* (Richmond, VA: A. Morris, 1854), 226.

68. Fitzhugh, *Sociology for the South*, 306.

69. Thomas R. Dew, *Review of the Debate in the Virginia Legislature of 1831 and 1832* (Richmond, VA: T. W. White, 1832), 8, 112, 9–10, 28. Emphasis in original.

70. Ibid., 28, 30, 36.

71. Ibid., 88, 111. Emphasis in original.

72. Ralph E. Morrow, "The Pro-slavery Argument Revisited," *Mississippi Valley Historical Review* 48, no. 1 (June 1961): 88.

73. *Congressional Globe*, 25th Congress, 3rd Session, appendix, 169. Emphasis in original.

74. William A. Smith, *Lectures on the Philosophy and Practice of Slavery* (Nashville, TN: Stevenson and Evans, 1856), 28–29.

75. Albert Taylor Bledsoe, *An Essay on Liberty and Slavery* (Philadelphia: Lippincott, 1860), 34, 32, 35–39.

76. *De Bow's Review* 21, no. 2 (August 1856): 135, 137.

77. Williston H. Lofton, "Abolition and Labor: Reaction of Northern Labor to the Anti-Slavery Appeal: Part II," *Journal of Negro History* 33, no. 3 (July 1948): 265, 267, citing articles published in 1844.

78. Fitzhugh, *Sociology for the South*, 81.

79. Arnaud B. Leavelle and Thomas I. Cook, "George Fitzhugh and the Theory of American Conservatism," *Journal of Politics* 7, no. 2 (May 1945): 149.

80. Jeremy J. Tewell, "A Difference of Complexion: George Fitzhugh and the Birth of the Republican Party," *The Historian* 73, no. 2 (Summer 2011): 238.

81. Fitzhugh, *Sociology for the South*, 38, 83–84.
82. Tewell, "A Difference of Complexion," 238.
83. Ibid., 243.
84. Fitzhugh, *Sociology for the South*, 246, 249.

Chapter 8: Texas

1. Joel H. Silbey, *Storm over Texas: The Annexation Controversy and the Road to Civil War* (New York: Oxford University Press, 2005), xvii.
2. Lyon Rathbun, "The Debate over Annexing Texas and the Emergence of Manifest Destiny," *Rhetoric and Public Affairs* 4, no. 3 (Fall 2001): 486, citing the *New York Morning News*, December 27, 1845.
3. *Congressional Globe*, 29th Congress, 2nd Session, 387.
4. Paul E. Sturdevant, "Robert J. Walker and Texas Annexation: A Lost Champion," *Southwestern Historical Quarterly* 109, no. 2 (October 2005): 190.
5. Robert J. Walker, *Letter of Mr. Walker of Mississippi Relative to the Reannexation of Texas* (Philadelphia: Mifflin and Parry, 1844), 9, 11, 12, 14.
6. Rathbun, "The Debate over Annexing Texas," 477.
7. David Zarefsky, "Henry Clay and the Election of 1844: The Letters of a Rhetoric of Compromise," *Rhetoric and Public Affairs* 6, no. 1 (Spring 2003): 88.
8. Silbey, *Storm over Texas*, 65.
9. Eric Foner, "The Wilmot Proviso Revisited," *Journal of American History* 56, no. 2 (September 1969): 266.
10. Richard K. Crallé, ed., *The Works of John C. Calhoun*, vol. 5 (New York: D. Appleton, 1857), 333–47.
11. *Congressional Globe*, 28th Congress, 2nd Session, 2, 7.
12. Foner, "The Wilmot Proviso Revisited," 270.
13. Leonard L. Richards, *The Slave Power: The Free North and Southern Domination, 1790–1860* (Baton Rouge: Louisiana State University Press, 2009), 149.
14. Amy S. Greenberg, *A Wicked War: Polk, Clay, Lincoln, and the 1846 U.S. Invasion of Mexico* (New York: Vintage, 2012), 101.
15. Henry Steele Commager, ed., *Documents of American History*, 6th ed. (New York: Appleton-Century-Crofts, 1958), 311.
16. *Congressional Globe*, 29th Congress, 2nd Session, 1214.
17. Ibid., 1217.
18. For the enslavement of Native Americans under Mexican rule in New Mexico, see Frank McNitt, *Navajo Wars: Military Campaigns Slave Raids and Reprisals* (Albuquerque: University of New Mexico Press, 1972), vii, 88–89, passim.
19. *Congressional Globe*, 29th Congress, 2nd Session, 353–54.
20. Ibid., appendix, 317.
21. *Congressional Globe*, 29th Congress, 2nd Session, 105.
22. Ibid., 333.
23. Ibid., 114.
24. Ibid., 601.
25. *Congressional Globe*, 30th Congress, 1st Session, 1023. Emphasis in original.

26. *Congressional Globe*, 29th Congress, 2nd Session, 378.

27. *Congressional Globe*, 30th Congress, 1st Session, appendix, 680.

28. *Congressional Globe*, 31st Congress, 1st Session, 29.

29. *Congressional Globe*, 29th Congress, 2nd Session, 453–54.

30. Ibid., appendix, 246.

31. Ibid., 455.

32. Ibid.

33. *Great Speech of the Hon. George Mifflin Dallas, Upon the Leading Topics of the Day* (Philadelphia: Times and Keystone, 1847), 15.

34. *Congressional Globe*, 30th Congress, 1st Session, appendix, 89.

35. *Congressional Globe*, 30th Congress, 2nd Session, appendix, 297.

36. Ibid., 275.

37. *Washington Union*, December 30, 1847.

38. Eric H. Walther, *William Lowndes Yancey and the Coming of the Civil War* (Chapel Hill: University of North Carolina Press, 2006), 11–12. This is the only modern biography of Yancey, and this text draws from it for many of the details of his life.

39. John Witherspoon DuBose, *The Life and Times of William Lowndes Yancey: A History of Political Parties in the United States, from 1834–1864; Especially as to the Origin of the Confederate State* (Birmingham, AL: Roberts & Son, 1892, reprint), 141–42.

40. *Journal of the Democratic Convention Held in the City of Montgomery on the 14th and 15th February, 1848* (Montgomery, AL: M'Cormick & Walshe, 1848), 12–13. Emphasis in original.

41. Greenburg, *A Wicked War*, 268.

42. *Congressional Globe*, 30th Congress, 1st Session, 394.

43. Corey M. Brooks, *Liberty Power: Antislavery Third Parties and the Transformation of American Politics* (Chicago: University of Chicago Press, 2016), 137. Emphasis in original.

44. Joseph G. Rayback, "Martin Van Buren's Desire for Revenge in the Campaign of 1848," *Mississippi Valley Historical Review* 40, no. 4 (March 1954): 710.

45. Jonathan H. Earle, *Jacksonian Antislavery & the Politics of Free Soil, 1824–1854* (Chapel Hill: University of North Carolina Press, 2004), 161.

46. Ibid., 162.

47. Brooks, *Liberty Power*, 149.

Chapter 9: The Last Great Compromise and Bleeding Kansas

1. George Ticknor Curtis, *Life of Daniel Webster*, vol. 2 (New York: D. Appleton, 1870), 397.

2. Ibid., 397

3. *Congressional Globe*, 31st Congress, 1st Session, 28, December 13, 1849.

4. Ibid., appendix, 224, February 15, 1850.

5. Herbert Darling Foster, "Webster's Seventh of March Speech and the Secession Movement, 1850," *American Historical Review* 27, no. 2 (January 1922): 250.

6. Figures derived from *Historical Statistics of the United States Colonial Times to 1970*, part 1 (Washington, DC: Bureau of the Census, 1975), 1085.

7. *Ninth Census—Volume I, The Statistics of the Population of the United States Embracing the Tables of Race, Nationality, Sex, Selected Ages and Occupations, Compiled from the Original Returns of the Ninth Census* (Washington, DC: Government Printing Office, 1872), 4–5.

8. David M. Potter, *The Impending Crisis: America before the Civil War, 1848–1861,* completed and edited by Don E. Fehrenbacher (New York: Harper Perennial, 2011 edition of 1976 original), 87. This text adopts in large measure the context presented in this seminal volume of America's pre-Civil War history.

9. *Congressional Globe*, 31st Congress, 1st Session, appendix, 116.

10. Ibid., 115.

11. Ibid., 119.

12. Ibid., 127.

13. Ibid., 149–50. Emphasis in original.

14. Ibid., 451–53, 455.

15. Ibid., appendix, 265, 266.

16. Ibid., 1024.

17. Foster, "Webster's Seventh of March Speech," 258.

18. Ibid., 249.

19. *Congressional Globe*, 31st Congress, 1st Session, appendix, 269, 271, 274.

20. Ibid., 274–75.

21. Ibid., 276.

22. Reverend Nathaniel Colver, *The Fugitive Slave Bill; or, God's Laws Paramount to the Laws of Men. A Sermon, Preached on Sunday, October 20, 1850* (Boston: J. M. Hewes, 1850), 4.

23. Robert R. Russel, "What Was the Compromise of 1850?," *Journal of Southern History* 22, no. 3 (August 1956). Russel points out that at least as of the publication date of his article, most histories of the Compromise of 1850 misstated or never quite got around to accurately describing what the compromise actually was, especially the terms organizing the New Mexico and Utah territories. The author's account of these provisions draws directly on Russel's work.

24. Joan D. Hedrick, *Harriet Beecher Stowe: A Life* (New York: Oxford University Press, 1994), 208.

25. Potter, *The Impending Crisis*, 140.

26. *De Bow's Review* 16, no. 1 (January 1854): 57, 50.

27. Harvey Wish, "George Frederick Holmes and the Southern Periodical Literature of the Mid-Nineteenth Century," *Journal of Southern History* 7, no. 3 (August 1941): 349.

28. *Historical Statistics of the United States Colonial Times to 1970*, Part 1, Bureau of the Census, 1074.

29. Robert W. Johannsen, *Stephen A. Douglas* (Champaign: University of Illinois Press, 1997 edition of 1973 original), 435–36.

30. Ibid., 434.

31. P. Orman Ray, *The Repeal of the Missouri Compromise: Its Origin and Authorship* (Cleveland, OH: Arthur H. Clark, 1909), 182–83, 272.

32. *Congressional Globe*, 33rd Congress, 1st Session, 222.

33. Ibid., 337.

34. Ibid., 353.

35. Robert R. Russel, "The Issues in the Congressional Struggle over the Kansas-Nebraska Bill, 1854," *Journal of Southern History* 29, no. 2 (May 1963): 198.

36. Yonatan Eyal, "With His Eyes Open: Stephen A. Douglas and the Kansas-Nebraska Disaster of 1854," *Journal of the Illinois State Historical Society* 91, no. 4 (Winter 1998): 193, 189.

37. *Congressional Globe*, 33rd Congress, 1st Session, 281–82.

38. Ibid., 337, 340.

39. Roy P. Basler, ed., *The Collected Works of Abraham Lincoln*, 8 vols. (New Brunswick, NJ: Rutgers University, 1953), 2:282.

40. *Congressional Globe*, 33rd Congress, 1st Session, appendix, 768, 770.

41. Ibid., 785.

42. Ibid., 787.

43. Ibid., 1321, for 35 to 13 Senate vote; and 1254 for 113 to 100 House vote.

44. Russel, "The Issues in the Congressional Struggle," 209, 208, counting in addition to the recorded vote in each house "all who were paired and all who were absent but later indicated how they would have voted had they been present."

45. Johannsen, *Stephen A. Douglas*, 451, 453–54.

46. Don E. Fehrenbacher, *The South and Three Sectional Crises* (Baton Rouge: Louisiana State University Press, 1980), 49.

47. Joanne B. Freeman, *The Field of Blood Violence in Congress and the Road to the Civil War* (New York: Farrar, Straus & Giroux, 2018), 216.

48. Fred Harvey Harrington, "'The First Northern Victory,'" *Journal of Southern History* 5, no. 2 (May 1939): 205.

49. Corey M. Brooks, *Liberty Power: Antislavery Third Parties and the Transformation of American Politics* (Chicago: University of Chicago Press, 2016), 211.

50. Ibid.

51. Harrington, "'The First Northern Victory,'" 204–5.

52. *Congressional Globe*, 33rd Congress, 1st Session, 340.

53. Howard Select Committee, *Report of the Select Committee to Investigate the Troubles in Kansas*, 34th Congress, 1st Session, House Report 200, serial 869, 9.

54. Potter, *The Impending Crisis*, 200.

55. James C. Malin, "The Proslavery Background of the Kansas Struggle," *Mississippi Valley Historical Review* 10, no. 3 (December 1923): 288.

56. Nicole Etcheson, *Bleeding Kansas Contested Liberty in the Civil War Era* (Lawrence: University Press of Kansas, 2004), 37; Eric H. Walther, *William Lowndes Yancey and the Coming of the Civil War* (Chapel Hill: University of North Carolina Press, 2006), 183.

57. Howard Select Committee, *Report*, 5–9.

58. Etcheson, *Bleeding Kansas*, 56.

59. Howard Select Committee, *Report*, 16.

60. Ibid., 16.

61. Ibid., 30, 34, 67.

62. Etcheson, *Bleeding Kansas*, 63.

63. Howard Select Committee, *Report*, 59, 1063, 1051.

64. Ibid., 65.

65. Ibid., 1095.

66. Ibid., 357.

67. Etcheson, *Bleeding Kansas*, 104.

68. Potter, *The Impending Crisis*, 220.

69. Bernard A. Weisberger, "The Newspaper Reporter and the Kansas Imbroglio," *Mississippi Valley Historical Review* 36, no. 4 (March 1950): 645.

70. Salmon Brown, "John Brown and Sons in Kansas Territory," *Indiana Magazine of History* 31, no. 2 (June 1935): 144–45.

71. Glenn M. Linden, *Voices from the Gathering Storm: The Coming of the American Civil War* (Wilmington, DE: Scholarly Resources, 2001), 91.

72. Charles Sumner, *The Crime against Kansas* (Boston: John P. Jewett, 1856), 5, 9.

73. *Richmond Enquirer*, June 2, 1856.

74. Loring Moody, *The Destruction of Republicanism: The Object of the Rebellion, The Testimony of Southern Witnesses* (Boston: Emancipation League, 1863), 11.

75. Freeman, *The Field of Blood*, 229.

76. Etcheson, *Bleeding Kansas*, 110.

77. Howard Select Committee, *Report*, 1194.

78. Ibid., 1097–98.

79. Ibid., 1196–97.

80. Weisberger, "The Newspaper Reporter and the Kansas Imbroglio," 640.

81. Stephen B. Oates, "John Brown's Bloody Pilgrimage," *Southwest Review* 53, no. 1 (Winter 1968): 1.

82. Dale E. Watts, "How Bloody Was Bleeding Kansas?," *Kansas History: A Journal of the Central Plains* 18, no. 2 (Summer 1995): 123.

83. Hampton Sides, *Blood and Thunder: The Epic Story of Kit Carson and the Conquest of the American West* (New York: Anchor Books, 2006), 152, 154.

84. Potter, *The Impending Crisis*, 287.

85. https://www.jamesbuchanan.org/p/james-buchanan-inaugural-address.html, accessed March 19, 2019.

86. Don E. Fehrenbacher, *The Dred Scott Case: Its Significance in American Law and Politics* (New York: Oxford University Press, 2001 edition of 1978 original), 322–34.

87. *Dred Scott v. Sandford*, 60 U.S., 404–5.

88. Ibid., 451.

89. Ibid., 425.

90. John M. Hay and John G. Nicolay, *Abraham Lincoln: A History*, 10 vols. (New York: Cosimo, 2009, reprint of 1917 original), 2:83.

91. Fehrenbacher, *The Dred Scott Case*, 418.

92. *Congressional Globe*, 35th Congress, 1st Session, 617.

93. Ibid., 547.

94. https://millercenter.org/the-presidency/presidential-speeches/december-19-1859-third-annual-message, accessed March 20, 2019.

95. Article VII, Section 1, https://www.kansasmemory.org/item/207409/text, accessed February 14, 2019.

96. Ibid., schedule, Section 7.

97. Etcheson, *Bleeding Kansas*, 160.

98. *Congressional Globe*, 35th Congress, 1st Session, appendix, 4–5.

99. Ibid., 35th Congress, 1st Session, 15, 17.

100. *House Reports*, 35th Congress, 1st Session, no. 377, serial 966, 93–94.

101. *Congressional Globe*, 35th Congress, 1st Session, 140.

102. Austin L. Venable, "The Conflict between the Douglas and Yancey Forces in the Charleston Convention," *Journal of Southern History* 8, no. 2 (May 1942): 229.

103. Potter, *The Impending Crisis*, 325.

104. *Congressional Globe*, 31st Congress, 1st Session, appendix, 69.

105. Ibid., 70.

106. Ibid., 71.

107. Drew Gilpin Faust, *James Henry Hammond and the Old South: A Design for Mastery* (Baton Rouge: Louisiana State University Press, 1982), 347.

108. *Congressional Globe*, 31st Congress, 1st Session, appendix, 371.

109. *De Bow's Review* 12, no. 2 (February 1852): 182.

110. *De Bow's Review* 13, no. 1 (July 1852): 18.

111. Charles W. Ramsdell, "The Natural Limits of Slavery Expansion," *Mississippi Valley Historical Review* 16, no. 2 (September 1929): 163.

112. *Ninth Census–Volume I, The Statistics of the Population of the United States Embracing the Tables of Race, Nationality, Sex, Selected Ages and Occupations, Compiled from the Original Returns of the Ninth Census* (Washington, DC: Government Printing Office, 1872), 7.

113. Potter, *The Impending Crisis*, 290.

114. See Robert E. May, *The Southern Dream of a Caribbean Empire, 1854–1861* (Gainesville: University Press of Florida, 2002 edition of 1973 original).

115. M. W. Cluskey, ed., *Speeches, Messages, and Other Writings of the Hon. Albert G. Brown, A Senator in Congress from the State of Mississippi* (Philadelphia: Jas. B. Smith, 1859), 595.

116. James Stirling, *Letters from the Slave States* (London: John W. Parker and Son, 1857), 75.

Chapter 10: Lincoln and Secession

1. Roy P. Basler, ed., *The Collected Works of Abraham Lincoln*, 8 vols. (New Brunswick, NJ: Rutgers University Press, 1953–1955), 4:240.

2. Douglas L. Wilson and Rodney O. Davis, eds., *Herndon's Informants: Letters, Interviews, and Statements about Abraham Lincoln* (Urbana: University of Illinois Press, 1997), 499.

3. Basler, *The Collected Works of Abraham Lincoln*, 3:27.

4. Ibid., 2:320. Emphasis in original.

5. Ibid., 2:404.

6. Eric Foner, *The Fiery Trial: Abraham Lincoln and American Slavery* (New York: Norton, 2010), 81.

7. Basler, *The Collected Works of Abraham Lincoln*, 2:461–62. Emphasis in original.

8. Abraham Lincoln, *Abraham Lincoln Papers: Series 1. General Correspondence. 1833 to 1916: John L. Scripps to Abraham Lincoln, Tuesday, June 22, 1858*. Library of Congress. Manuscript/Mixed Material. https://www.loc.gov/item/mal0090600/. Emphasis in original.

9. Basler, *The Collected Works of Abraham Lincoln*, 2:471.

10. Ibid., 2:467. Emphasis in original.

11. Ibid., 2:465–66. Emphasis in original.

12. *Congressional Globe*, 35th Congress, 1st Session, February 8, 1858, 617.

13. Basler, *The Collected Works of Abraham Lincoln*, 3:111.

14. David Zarefsky, "Lincoln and the House Divided: Launching a National Political Career," *Rhetoric and Public Affairs* 13, no. 3 (Fall 2010): 440.

15. William W. Freehling, *Becoming Lincoln* (Charlottesville: University of Virginia Press, 2018), 210.

16. Zarefsky, "Lincoln and the House Divided," 441.

17. Basler, *The Collected Works of Abraham Lincoln*, 2:548.

18. Ibid., 2:492.

19. Ibid., 2:500.

20. Ibid., 2:500–501.

21. Allen C. Guelzo, "Houses Divided: Lincoln, Douglas, and the Political Landscape of 1858," *Journal of American History* 94, no. 2 (September 2007): 407.

22. Kirk Jeffrey Jr., "Stephen Arnold Douglas in American Historical Writing," *Journal of the Illinois State Historical Society (1908–1984)* 61, no. 3 (Autumn 1968): 251–52.

23. William E. Dodd, *Jefferson Davis* (Philadelphia: George W. Jacobs, 1907), 190.

24. Matthew Norman, "The Other Lincoln-Debate: The Race Issue in a Comparative Context," *Journal of the Abraham Lincoln Association* 31, no. 1 (Winter 2010): 4.

25. Rodney O. Davis and Douglas L. Wilson, eds., *The Lincoln-Douglas Debates* (Chicago: Knox College Lincoln Studies Center, 2008), 36.

26. Basler, *The Collected Works of Abraham Lincoln*, 3:9–10.

27. Allen C. Guelzo, *Lincoln and Douglas: The Debates That Defined America* (New York: Simon & Schuster, 2008), 213, 246.

28. Basler, *The Collected Works of Abraham Lincoln*, 2:255.

29. Ibid., 3:16. Emphasis in original.

30. Ibid., 3:15.

31. Ibid., 2:411.

32. Ibid., 3:15.

33. Norman, "The Other Lincoln-Debate," 2, 10.

34. Basler, *The Collected Works of Abraham Lincoln*, 3:145–46.

35. Davis and Wilson, *The Lincoln-Douglas Debates*, 62.

36. Basler, *The Collected Works of Abraham Lincoln*, 3:179.

37. Ibid., 3:181.

38. Ibid., 2:403, 408.

39. A modern examination of this issue is found in Foner, *The Fiery Trial*

40. Basler, *The Collected Works of Abraham Lincoln*, 3:312.

41. Ibid., 3:311.

42. Ibid., 3:256.

43. Ibid., 3:304. Emphasis in original.

44. Ibid., 2:406. Emphasis in original.

45. Ibid., 3:51.

46. Edward McMahan, "Stephen A. Douglas: A Study of the Attempt to Settle the Question of Slavery in the Territories by the Application of Popular Sovereignty—1850–1860," *Washington Historical Quarterly* 2, (July 1, 1908), 322.

47. *Congressional Globe*, 35th Congress, 2nd Session, 1249.

48. Basler, *The Collected Works of Abraham Lincoln*, 3:207.

49. *Congressional Globe*, 35th Congress, 2nd Session, 1247.

50. Basler, *The Collected Works of Abraham Lincoln*, 2:262.

51. Kevin Waite, "Jefferson Davis and Proslavery Visions of Empire in the Far West," *Journal of the Civil War Era* 6, no. 4, The Civil War West: A Special Issue (December 2016): 539.

52. Ibid., 538.

53. Don E. Fehrenbacher, "Lincoln, Douglas, and the 'Freeport Question,'" *American Historical Review* 66, no. 3 (April 1961): 615.

54. John Witherspoon DuBose, *The Life and Times of William Lowndes Yancey: A History of Political Parties in the United States, from 1834–1864; Especially as to the Origin of the Confederate State* (Birmingham, AL: Roberts & Son, 1892, reprint of original), 388, 385, 376.

55. Ibid., 359; Eric H. Walther, *William Lowndes Yancey and the Coming of the Civil War* (Chapel Hill: University of North Carolina Press, 2006), 215.

56. DuBose, *The Life and Times of William Lowndes Yancey*, 358–59.

57. *Congressional Globe*, 36th Congress, 1st Session, 2154.

58. John M. Hay and John G. Nicolay, *Abraham Lincoln: A History*, 10 vols. (New York: Cosimo, 2009 reprint of 1917 original), 2:241.

59. Stephen B. Oates, "John Brown's Bloody Pilgrimage," *Southwest Review* 53, no. 1 (Winter 1968): 9. A significant portion of the account of John Brown's raid at Harpers Ferry in these pages is derived from this work.

60. http://law2.umkc.edu/faculty/projects/ftrials/johnbrown/brownconstitution.html, accessed December 21, 2019.

61. Oates, "John Brown's Bloody Pilgrimage," 17.

62. John B. Floyd, "Official Report of John Brown's Raid upon Harper's Ferry, Virginia, October 17–18, 1859," *Quarterly of the Oregon Historical Society* 10, no. 3 (September 1909): 323–24.

63. https://en.wikipedia.org/wiki/John_Brown%27s_raid_on_Harpers_Ferry, accessed April 18, 2019.

64. Charles J. G. Griffin, "John Brown's 'Madness,'" *Rhetoric and Public Affairs* 12, no. 3 (Fall 2009): 379.

65. Oates, "John Brown's Bloody Pilgrimage," 21, 22. Emphasis in original.

66. Griffin, "John Brown's 'Madness,'" 382.

67. Harold Holzer, *Lincoln at Cooper Union* (New York: Simon & Schuster Paperbacks, 2004), 9. Details in these pages surrounding Lincoln's speech at Cooper Union are derived from this work.

68. Ibid., 109.

69. Basler, *The Collected Works of Abraham Lincoln*, 3:522.

70. For a revealing account of Hamilton's direct involvement with slavery, see Jessie Serfilippi, *"As Odious and Immoral a Thing," Alexander Hamilton's Hidden History as an Enslaver*, Schuyler Mansion State Historical Site, Albany, NY, 2020.

71. Basler, *The Collected Works of Abraham* Lincoln, 3:535. Emphasis in original.

72. Ibid., 3:543–44.

73. Ibid., 3:545.

74. Ibid., 3:550. Emphasis in original.

75. Sutton S. Scott, *Recollections of the Alabama Democratic State Convention of 1860* (Montgomery, AL 1904), 318.

76. Dwight Lowell Dumond, *Southern Editorials on Secession* (New York: Century Co., 1931), appendix 1, 517–18.

77. Austin L. Venable, "The Conflict between the Douglas and Yancey Forces in the Charleston Convention," *Journal of Southern History* 8, no. 2 (May 1942): 234.

78. *Congressional Globe*, 36th Congress, 1st Session, 2322.

79. Venable, "The Conflict between the Douglas and Yancey Forces," 237.

80. Roy Franklin Nichols, *The Disruption of American Democracy* (New York: Free Press, 1967 edition of 1948 original), 295.

81. Allan Nevins, *The Emergence of Lincoln, Volume II* (New York: Scribner, 1950), 222–23, 227.

82. Nichols, *The Disruption of American Democracy*, 298.

83. *Speech of the Hon. William L. Yancey, of Alabama, Delivered in the National Democratic Convention, Charleston, April 28th, 1860, with the Protest of the Alabama Delegation*, Library of Congress, https://archive.org/details/speechofhonwilli00yanc/page/n4?q= speech+of+the+hon.+william+l.+yancey%2C+of+alabama%2C+delivered+to+the+ national+democratic, accessed April 24, 2019, 3, 4, 7, 13.

84. Paul Starobin, *Madness Rules the Hour: Charleston, 1860 and the Mania for War* (New York: Public Affairs, 2017), 58.

85. David M. Potter, *The Impending Crisis: America before the Civil War, 1848–1861*, completed and edited by Don E. Fehrenbacher (New York: Harper Perennial, 2011 edition of 1976 original), 422.

86. Don Green, "Constitutional Unionist: The Party That Tried to Stop Lincoln and Save the Union," *The Historian* 69, no. 2 (Summer 2007): 250. Slightly different but statistically insignificant numbers for the outcome of the 1860 presidential election are provided by this source, the Census Bureau's *Historical Statistics of the United States, Colonial Times to 1970, Part 1*, 1074; and Walter Dean Burnham, *Presidential Ballots, 1836–1892* (Baltimore: Johns Hopkins University Press, 1955), 247–57.

87. Freehling, *Becoming Lincoln*, 223–60. This text adopts the argument of Lincoln honing his message to being opposed to slavery's expansion and in favor of defending the union against secession directly from this work.

88. Basler, *The Collected Works of Abraham Lincoln*, 4:151–52, 4:151.

89. *Historical Statistics of the United States, Colonial Times to 1970, Part 1*, 1072.

90. Author's analysis from Burnham, *Presidential Ballots, 1836–1892*, 247–57.

91. Lillian A. Kibler, "Unionist Sentiment in South Carolina in 1860," *Journal of Southern History* 4, no. 3 (August 1938): 354.

92. *Southern Literary Messenger* 32, no. 2 (February 1861): 81, 88. Emphasis in original.

93. *Addresses Delivered before the Virginia State Convention* (Richmond, VA: Wyatt M. Elliott, 1861), 25.

94. Ulrich Bonnell Phillips, "The Course of the South to Secession. VI: The Fire-Eaters," *Georgia Historical Quarterly* 22, no. 1 (March 1938): 63.

95. *Congressional Quarterly*, 36th Congress, 2nd Session, appendix, 1, 3.

96. *The Address of the People of South Carolina Assembled in Convention to the People of the Slaveholding States of the United States* (Charleston, SC: Evans & Cogswell, 1860), 4, 16.

97. Ralph Wooster, "Membership of the South Carolina Secession Convention," *South Carolina Historical Magazine* 55, no. 4 (October 1954): 189.

98. For a summary of the of interpretations of why southern states seceded, see James Tice Moore, "Secession and the States: A Review Essay," *Virginia Magazine of History and Biography* 94, no. 1 (January 1986).

99. Nevins, *The Emergence of Lincoln, Volume II*, 370.

100. Timothy B. Smith, *The Mississippi Secession Convention* (Jackson: University Press of Mississippi, 2014), 15, 16, 27, 75.

101. Paul E. Herron, *Framing the Solid South: The State Constitutional Conventions of Secession, Reconstruction, and Redemption, 1860–1902* (Lawrence: University Press of Kansas, 2017), 82–83.

102. *An Address Setting Forth the Declaration of the Immediate Causes Which Induce and Justify the Secession of Mississippi from the Federal Union and the Ordinance of Secession* (Jackson: Mississippian Book and Job Printing, 1861), 3.

103. John F. Reiger, "Secession of Florida from the Union: A Minority Decision?," *Florida Historical Quarterly* 46, no. 4 (April 1968): 367.

104. William R. Smith, ed., *The History and Debates of the Convention of the People of Alabama Begun and Held in the City of Montgomery, on the Seventh Day of January, 1861: In Which Is Presented the Speeches of the Secret Sessions, and Many Valuable State Papers*, (Montgomery, AL: White Pfister, 1861), 69.

105. Ibid., 118.

106. *Address of Hon. W. L. Harris Commissioner from the State of Mississippi, Delivered Before the General Assembly of the State of Georgia on Monday, Dec. 17th, 1860* (Milledgeville: Houghton, Nisbet & Barnes, 1860), 5–6, 8.

107. Charles B. Dew, *Apostles of Disunion* (Charlottesville: University of Virginia Press, 2001).

108. *An Address to the Citizens of Alabama, on the Constitution and Laws of the Confederate States of America, by the Hon. Robert H. Smith, At Temperance Hall, on the 30th of March, 1861* (Mobile, AL: Mobile Daily Register, 1861), 19.

109. William W. Freehling and Craig M. Simpson, eds., *Secession Debated Georgia's Showdown in 1860* (New York: Oxford University Press, 1992), xi–xii.

110. Michael P. Johnson, "A New Look at the Popular Vote for Delegates to the Georgia Secession Convention," *Georgia Historical Quarterly* 56, no. 2 (Summer 1972): 260.

111. *Addresses Delivered before the Virginia State Convention*, 20.

112. Charles B. Dew, "Who Won the Secession Election in Louisiana?," *Journal of Southern History* 36, no. 1 (February 1970): 19.

113. Charles P. Roland, "Louisiana and Secession," *Louisiana History: The Journal of the Louisiana Historical Association* 19, no. 4 (Autumn 1978): 395.

114. Dew, "Who Won the Secession Election in Louisiana?," 29.

115. Charles B. Dew, "The Long Lost Returns: The Candidates and Their Totals in Louisiana's Secession Election," *Louisiana History: The Journal of the Louisiana Historical Association* 10, no. 4 (Autumn 1969): 358.

116. Edward R. Maher Jr., "Sam Houston and Secession," *Southwestern Historical Quarterly* 55, no. 4 (April 1952): 455.

117. *Journal of the Secession Convention of Texas 1861* (Austin: Austin Printing Co., 1912), 51.

118. Ibid., 122–23.

119. Matthew K. Hamilton, "'To Preserve African Slavery': The Secession Commissioners to Texas, 1861," *Southwestern Historical Quarterly* 114, no. 4 (April 2011): 372–73, 375.

120. *Journal of the Secession Convention of Texas 1861*, 63–64.

121. Donald E. Reynolds, *Texas Terror: The Slave Insurrection Panic of 1860 and the Secession of the Lower South* (Baton Rouge: Louisiana State University Press, 2007), 29–78.

122. Timothy Mulligan, "'I Love the Union . . . if': John M. Bright's Secessionist Speech December 1860," *Tennessee Historical Quarterly* 72, no. 1 (Spring 2013): 19.

123. Jack B. Scroggs, "Arkansas in the Secession Crisis," *Arkansas Historical Quarterly* 12, no. 3 (Autumn 1953): 208, 214.

124. William W. Freehling and Craig M. Simpson, eds., *Showdown in Virginia: The 1861 Convention and the Fate of the Union* (Charlottesville: University of Virginia Press, 2010), xiii.

125. Basler, *The Collected Works of Abraham Lincoln*, 4:271. Emphasis in original.

126. Potter, *The Impending Crisis*, 531–32.

127. Herron, *Framing the Solid South*, 103–4.

128. *Permanent Constitution of the Confederate States of America Adopted by the Confederate Congress, March 11, 1861* (Richmond, VA: James E. Goode, 1861), 3.

129. Edward H. Bonekemper III, *The Myth of the Lost Cause: Why the South Fought the Civil War and Why the North Won* (Washington, DC: Regnery History, 2015), 21.

130. Ibid., 16.

131. Ibid., 9.

132. Arthur Bestor, "State Sovereignty and Slavery: A Reinterpretation of Proslavery Constitutional Doctrine, 1846–1860," *Journal of the Illinois State Historical Society* 54, no. 2 (Summer 1961): 178.

133. Ibid., 178.

134. Henry Cleveland, ed., *Alexander H. Stephens, in Public and Private with Letters and Speeches, Before, During, and Since the War* (Philadelphia: S. A. George, 1866), 721.

135. Dew, *Apostles of Disunion*, 14–15.

136. Gary W. Gallagher, *The Confederate War* (Cambridge, MA: Harvard University Press, 1997), 93.

137. Basler, *The Collected Works of Abraham Lincoln*, 4:316–17.

138. Ibid., 4:323–24.

139. William K. Scarborough, "Propagandists for Secession: Edmund Ruffin of Virginia and Robert Barnwell Rhett of South Carolina," *South Carolina Historical Magazine* 112, nos. 3–4 (July–October 2011): 133.

140. J. David Hacker, "A Census-Based Count of the Civil War Dead," *Civil War History* 57, no. 4 (December 2011).

141. See, for example, Michael E. Woods, "What Twenty-First-Century Historians Have Said about the Causes of Disunion: A Civil War Sesquicentennial Review of the Recent Literature," *Journal of American History* 99, no. 2 (September 2012): 415–39; Jonathan Earle, "The Political Origins of the Civil War," *Organization of American Historians Magazine of History* 25, no. 2 (April 2011): 8–13; Frank Towers, "Partisans, New History, and Modernization: The Historiography of the Civil War's Causes, 1861–2011," *Journal of the Civil War Era* 1, no. 2 (June 2011): 237–64; James L. Huston, "Property Rights in Slavery and the Coming of the Civil War," *Journal of Southern History* 65, no. 2 (May 1999): 249–86; William J. Donnelly, "Conspiracy or Popular Movement: The Historiography of Southern Support for Secession," *North Carolina Historical Review* 42, no. 1 (January 1965): 70–84; Sean Wilentz, *No Property in Man: Slavery and Antislavery at the Nation's Founding* (Cambridge, MA: Harvard University Press, 2018); Kenneth M. Stampp, ed., *The Causes of the Civil War* (New York: Simon & Schuster, 1959); James Oakes, *The Scorpion's Sting: Antislavery and the Coming of the Civil War* (New York: Norton, 2014); Elizabeth R. Varon, *Disunion! The Coming of the American Civil War, 1789–1859* (Chapel Hill: University of North Carolina Press, 2008); Marc Egnal, *Clash of Extremes: The Economic Origins of the Civil War* (New York: Hill & Wang, 2009).

SELECTED BIBLIOGRAPHY

Having approached this work as a reporter rather than as a scholar, my thought is that a selected bibliography may be more useful to readers who want to pursue further reading. With some exceptions, this selection concentrates on works dealing with slavery, rather than volumes of biography or of general history.

Aptheker, Herbert. *American Negro Slave Revolts*. New York: Columbia University Press, 1943. Although Aptheker has his share of critics, this work remains a go-to source for the breadth of Black resistance to slavery.

Ashworth, John. *The Republic in Crisis, 1848–1861*. New York: Cambridge University Press, 2012; and *Slavery, Capitalism, and Politics in the Antebellum Republic, Volume 2: The Coming of the Civil War, 1850–1861*. New York: Cambridge University Press, 2007. Ashworth deploys extensive original research placing slavery as the pivot upon which the nation tilted to civil war.

Banning, Lance. *The Jefferson Persuasion: Evolution of a Party Ideology*. Ithaca, NY: Cornell University Press, 1978. Along with Peter S. Onuf, cited below, Banning has made a lasting contribution to understanding long-neglected or dismissed aspects of Thomas Jefferson's legacy and provided clarity to some of his political motivations.

Basler, Roy P., ed. *The Collected Works of Abraham Lincoln*, 8 vols. New Brunswick, NJ: Rutgers University Press, 1953. Lincoln in his own words. Available online at the Abraham Lincoln Association website, https://quod.lib.umich.edu/l/lincoln/.

Belz, Herman, ed. *The Webster-Hayne Debate on the Nature of the Union*. Carmel, IN: Liberty Fund, 2000. A compilation of the major speeches surrounding the historic face-off between Hayne and Webster that played into the nullification crisis.

Berlin, Ira. *Many Thousands Gone: The First Two Centuries of Slavery in North America*. Cambridge, MA: Belknap Press of Harvard University, 2003 edition of 1998 original. Although not a source for this book, Berlin's work is an indispensable and richly detailed account of the African American experience in North America prior to the Revolutionary War.

Blumenthal, Sidney. *All the Powers of Earth, 1856–1860: The Political Life of Abraham Lincoln*. New York: Simon & Schuster, 2019. This is the third of a projected five-volume project. At his best, Blumenthal places Lincoln's life and career within the context of his times.

Brooks, Corey M. *Liberty Power: Antislavery Third Parties and the Transformation of American Politics*. Chicago: University of Chicago Press, 2016. Brooks gives a vivid account of the long-neglected rise of the political wing of abolitionism and the creation of the Liberty Party, its successor the Free Soil Party, the precursor to Lincoln's Republican Party.

Clavin, Matthew J. *Toussaint Louverture and the American Civil War*. Philadelphia: University of Pennsylvania Press, 2010. Admirably fills a long-overlooked gap in scholarship in its account of the ramification in the United States of the Haitian Revolution and its leader, Toussaint Louverture.

Clinton, Catherine. *Harriet Tubman: The Road to Freedom*. New York: Back Bay Books, 2004. This narrative presents the full sweep of Tubman's remarkable life.

Davis, David Brion. *The Problem of Slavery in the Age of Revolution*. New York: Oxford University Press, 1999 edition of 1975 original; and *The Problem of Slavery in the Age of Emancipation*. New York: Knopf, 2014. These two volumes complete Davis's trilogy begun with the 1966 publication of *The Problem of Slavery in Western Culture*. Davis's work laid the foundation for decades of subsequent scholarship documenting the central role of slavery in American and Western culture.

Davis, Rodney, and Douglas L. Wilson, eds. *The Lincoln-Douglas Debates*. Chicago: Knox College Lincoln Studies Center and the University of Illinois Press, 2008. This volume includes many of the sharp edges from the debates that have been smoothed over in other studies. As close to a definitive text as is ever likely to be presented.

Dew, Charles B. *Apostles of Disunion: Southern Secession Commissioners and the Causes of the Civil War*. Charlottesville: University of Virginia Press, 2001. Indispensable to understanding the driving force protecting slavery had in the rush to secession in late 1860 and early 1861. Dew illuminates the role of white southern secession commissioners who formerly had been largely ignored.

Douglass, Frederick. *My Bondage and My Freedom*. New Haven, CT: Yale University Press, reprint edition 2016. Douglass's writing, lecturing, and political agitation made him the most influential Black man in America during the 1850s and beyond. This book is a testament to his eloquence.

Earle, Jonathan H. *Jacksonian Antislavery and the Politics of Free Soil, 1824–1854*. Chapel Hill: University of North Carolina Press, 2004. Insightful account of the political realignment that occurred as Free Soil ideology confronted the traditional northern Democratic norms.

Egerton, Douglas R. *Gabriel's Rebellion: The Virginia Slave Conspiracies of 1800 & 1802*. Chapel Hill: University of North Carolina Press, 1993. The most detailed account available of Gabriel's planned rebellion and the events that flowed from it.

———. *He Shall Go Out Free: The Lives of Denmark Vesey*, revised and updated edition. Madison, WI: Madison House, 2004. The reference work on the planned slave revolt in Charleston, updated to address the argument that Vesey's plan was little more than talk among some of the city's slaves used by authorities for a brutal crackdown under a false cover of legal prosecutions.

Ellis, Richard E. *The Union at Risk: Jacksonian Democracy, States' Rights and the Nullification Crisis*. New York: Oxford University Press, 1987. Ellis places particular attention on the constitutional ramifications of the nullification crisis.

Farrand, Max, ed. *The Records of the Federal Convention of 1787*, 3 vols. New Haven, CT: Yale University Press, 1937; and James H. Hutson, ed., *Supplement to Max Farrand's The Records of the Federal Convention of 1787*. New Haven, CT: Yale University Press, 1987. The standard reference and most comprehensive source for the proceedings of the Constitutional Convention.

Fehrenbacher, Don E. *The Dred Scott Case: Its Significance in American Law and Politics*. New York: Oxford University Press, 1978. The best modern account of the case and its meaning.

———. *The Slaveholding Republic: An Account of the United States Government's Relations to Slavery*, completed and edited by Ward M. McAfee. New York: Oxford University Press, 2001. A critical account of how proslavery sentiment was embedded into the Constitution and American politics up to the Civil War.

———. *The South and Three Sectional Crises*. Baton Rouge: Louisiana State University Press, 1980. This book is a gem, a short but superb work, a distillation of essence and insights concerning the Missouri Compromise, the Wilmot Proviso, and the fallout over the Kansas-Nebraska Act.

Finkelman, Paul. *Slavery and the Founders: Race and Liberty in the Age of Jefferson*, 2nd ed. Armonk, NY: M. E. Sharpe, 2001. Finkelman is a leading scholar in demanding a reevaluation of slavery's role in fashioning the Constitution and the early republic.

Foner, Eric. *Free Soil, Free Labor, Free Men: The Ideology of the Republican Party before the Civil War*. New York: Oxford University Press, 1995 edition of 1970 original. Foner is among the first rank of American historians. This work is the best reference for understanding northern Free Soil ideology as a cause of the Civil War and the foundation of the Republican Party.

———. *The Fiery Trial: Abraham Lincoln and American Slavery*. New York: Norton, 2010. This is the definitive work on this topic. Lincoln's greatness and his humanity emerge from a deeply researched work shorn of iconography.

———. *Gateway to Freedom: The Hidden History of the Underground Railroad*. New York: Norton, 2015. Recasts traditional understanding of the underground railroad by documenting the leading role Blacks played in the struggle for individual freedom.

Forbes, Robert Pierce. *The Missouri Compromise and Its Aftermath: Slavery and the Meaning of America*. Chapel Hill: University of North Carolina Press, 2007. Forbes does an outstanding job of placing the Missouri Compromise within the context of what it created and what flowed from it. I place this work among the essentials in a modern interpretation of slavery's role in American political life.

Freehling, William W. *Becoming Lincoln*. Charlottesville: University of Virginia Press, 2018. Freehling offers a fresh interpretation in recounting the process by which Lincoln narrowed his political stance onto the rally point of standing against slavery's expansion that proved to be key to his winning nomination and election to the presidency.

———. *Prelude to Civil War: The Nullification Controversy in South Carolina, 1816–1836*. New York: Oxford University Press, 1992 edition of 1965 original. Freehling places the nullification crisis squarely within the context of slavery while providing a portrait of South Carolina's planter elite on a path of paranoia that ultimately led to the apocalypse of civil war.

———. *The Road to Disunion, Volume I: Secessionists at Bay, 1776–1854*. New York: Oxford University Press, 1990; and *The Road to Disunion, Volume II: Secessionists Triumphant, 1854–1861*. New York: Oxford University Press, 2007. No historian has done more than Freehling to present a modern understanding of the currents that led to the Civil War, particularly the divergent strands of white southern thought and action. These two volumes are among the most influential on the topic ever published. Freehling's idiosyncratic style presents challenges, but the commitment needed for understanding is amply rewarded.

Freeman, Joanne B. *The Field of Blood Violence in Congress and the Road to Civil War.* New York: Farrar, Straus & Giroux, 2018. This works vividly explores the microcosm of conflict within Congress as a reflection of the nation's broader path to disunion and war.

Gordon-Reed, Annette. *The Hemingses of Monticello: An American Family.* New York: Norton, 2008. In recounting the story of the Hemings family, this work presents the fullest available account of the relationship between Sally Hemings and Thomas Jefferson.

Gudmestad, Robert H. *A Troublesome Commerce: The Transformation of the Interstate Slave Trade.* Baton Rouge: Louisiana State University Press, 2003. This work is the definitive modern account of the interstate slave trade and its influence on white southern ideology and politics.

Guelzo, Allen C. *Lincoln and Douglas: The Debates That Defined America.* New York: Simon & Schuster, 2008. Guelzo revels in the characters and politics of the moment in telling the story of the nation's greatest campaign debates.

Hammond, John Craig. *Slavery, Freedom, and Expansion in the Early American West.* Charlottesville: University of Virginia Press, 2007. A valuable contribution to the literature showing slavery's core influence in the early development of the nation's western frontier.

Hoffer, Peter Charles. *John Quincy Adams and the Gag Rule, 1835–1850.* Baltimore: Johns Hopkins University Press, 2017. A brisk study of the white South's demands to gag free speech in Congress and John Quincy Adams's fight to speak against slavery.

Holt, Michael F. *The Fate of Their Country: Politicians, Slavery Extension, and the Coming of the Civil War.* New York: Hill & Wang, 2004. An important contribution to understanding the causes of the Civil War, Holt emphasizes the role played by politicians whose ambitions blinded them to the consequences of their actions.

———. *The Political Crisis of the 1850s.* New York: Norton, 1983. This work focuses on the breakdown of the two-party system as an underlying dynamic that resulted in civil war.

Holzer, Harold. *Lincoln at Cooper Union: The Speech That Made Abraham Lincoln President.* New York: Simon & Schuster, 2004. Highly readable and well researched, this volume presents both a narrative of events surrounding Lincoln's Cooper Union address and an insightful interpretation of it.

———. *Lincoln President-Elect: Abraham Lincoln and the Great Secession Winter, 1860–1861.* New York: Simon & Schuster, 2008. Holzer presents an original interpretation of Lincoln between his election and inauguration as being far more politically astute and determined than he is seen in some earlier accounts.

Horne, Gerald. *Confronting Black Jacobins: The United States, the Haitian Revolution, and the Origins of the Dominican Republic.* New York: Monthly Review Press, 2015. Deeply researched and zealous rendering of the Haitian Revolution and its aftermath.

Jefferson, Thomas. *Notes on the State of Virginia.* New York: Harper Torchbooks, 1964. This volume presents the core of Jefferson's political thought as well as his views on slavery and African Americans.

Jeffrey, Julie Roy. *The Great Silent Army of Abolitionism: Ordinary Women in the Antislavery Movement.* Chapel Hill: University of North Carolina Press, 1998. A long-needed study of the critical role women played in the antislavery movement and how their involvement transformed American political life.

Klarman, Michael J. *The Framers' Coup: The Making of the United States Constitution.* New York: Oxford University Press, 2016. Klarman's chapter on slavery in the Constitution presents a modern view of balanced legal scholarship on the issue.

Mason, Matthew. *Slavery & Politics in the Early Republic.* Chapel Hill: University of North Carolina Press, 2006. Concentrating on the early 1800s, this study helps build the case for slavery's persistent, rather than episodic, role in American politics leading up to the Civil War.

McLaurin, Melton A. *Celia: A Slave.* Athens: University of Georgia Press, 1991. A gripping account of one female slave's ultimate resistance to the sexual predation of the man who owned her.

Mellon, James, ed. *Bullwhip Days: The Slaves Remember.* New York: Grove, 1988. A valuable source of narrations of the slave experience drawn from a 1930s oral history project by the Works Progress Administration.

Miller, John Chester. *The Wolf by the Ears: Thomas Jefferson and Slavery.* Charlottesville: University Press of Virginia, 1991. An essentially sympathetic and comprehensive view of Jefferson's complex relationship to slavery.

Moore, Glover. *The Missouri Controversy, 1819–1821.* Gloucester, MA: Peter Smith, 1967 edition of 1953 original. The most detailed account available of the congressional and regional politics surrounding the Missouri Compromise.

Nichols, Roy Franklin. *The Disruption of American Democracy.* New York: Free Press, 1948. This book remains among the most penetrating in recounting the rending of the Democratic Party and the coming of the Civil War.

Northup, Solomon. *Twelve Years a Slave.* Digireads.com, 2016. Since its publication in 1853, this book has ranked among the most vivid accounts of slavery and escape, in this case by a freeman kidnapped into bondage.

Oakes, James. *The Scorpion's Sting: Antislavery and the Coming of the Civil War.* New York: Norton, 2015. Oakes brings scholarship endowed by gifted writing to his studies of slavery and the Civil War. This volume offers fresh insights into the role political abolitionism played in leading up to the Civil War.

Oates, Stephen B. *The Fires of Jubilee: Nat Turner's Fierce Rebellion.* New York: Harper Perennial, 2016 edition of 1975 original. Oates recounts the context of Nat Turner's rebellion and its aftermath as well as providing a chilling rendition of the revolt itself.

Olmsted, Frederick Law. *The Cotton Kingdom: A Traveller's Observations on Cotton and Slavery in the American Slave States, 1853–1861.* Mason Brothers, 1861– . This work is a composite volume of Olmsted's accounts of his journeys in the slave states in the decade preceding the Civil War as a reporter for the *New York Times.*

His unmatched eye for detail ultimately presents a devastating picture of slavery in which white southerners are often oblivious to the obvious. Olmsted's work is among the essential sources for understanding the reality of slavery and the relationship of white southerners to it.

Onuf, Peter S. *Jefferson's Empire: The Language of American Nationhood.* Charlottesville: University Press of Virginia, 2000; and *The Mind of Thomas Jefferson.* Charlottesville: University of Virginia Press, 2007. Revelatory work. Insight into the man and his era that has redrawn the iconic portrait of Jefferson into a nuanced, complicated, and contradictory study of the man himself. This is scholarship at the highest level.

Ott, Thomas O. *The Haitian Revolution 1789–1804.* Knoxville: University of Tennessee Press, 1973. A concise history of the Haitian Revolution.

Potter, David M. *The Impending Crisis: America before the Civil War 1848–1861*, completed and edited by Don E. Fehrenbacher. New York: Harper Perennial, 2011 edition of 1976 original. Original, insightful, and written with clarity, this work may be considered among the few indispensable accounts of the American narrative in the years leading up to the Civil War. A pinnacle of scholarship.

Remini, Robert V. *At the Edge of the Precipice: Henry Clay and the Compromise That Saved the Union.* New York: Basic Books, 2010. A concise history of the Compromise of 1850.

Richards, Leonard L. *The Slave Power: The Free North and Southern Domination, 1780–1860.* Baton Rouge: Louisiana State University Press, 2000. Essential to understanding the northern experience of slavery's dominant role in American politics before the Civil War.

Robinson, Donald L. *Slavery in the Structure of American Politics, 1765–1820.* New York: Harcourt Brace Jovanovich, 1971. This is among those bedrock books of modern scholarship that initiated a reevaluation of slavery and its role in American politics. Although one could begin an inquiry into this subject at several points, this is certainly one of the most fruitful.

Sharp, James Roger. *American Politics in the Early Republic: The New Nation in Crisis.* New Haven, CT: Yale University Press, 1993. This works presents a central aspect of the overall reevaluation of Thomas Jefferson in modern scholarship, the fraught and nearly violent clashes in the early republic that produced the states' rights doctrine.

Silbey, Joel H. *Storm over Texas: The Annexation Controversy and the Road to Civil War.* New York: Oxford University Press, 2005. This story, deftly told by an eminent scholar of the period, explains why the road to the Civil War went through Texas.

Stampp, Kenneth M. *The Causes of the Civil War.* New York: Simon & Schuster, 1991. An excellent survey of the causes of the Civil War told largely in the words of contemporaries of the era but also of later leading scholars.

———. *The Peculiar Institution: Slavery in the Ante-Bellum South.* New York: Vintage Books, 1989 edition of 1956 original. The benchmark work in presenting a modern interpretation—shorn of Jim Crow and Lost Cause apologies—of slavery in the American South.

Tadman, Michael. *Speculators and Slaves: Masters, Traders, and Slaves in the Old South.* Madison: University of Wisconsin Press, 1996. A highly researched account of the human toll that the interstate slave trade extracted.

Tragle, Henry Irving. *The Southampton Slave Revolt of 1831: A Compilation of Source Material Including the Full Text of the "Confessions" of Nat Turner.* New York: Vintage Books, 1973. The most definitive compilation available of Nat Turner's revolt, including trial transcripts and newspaper accounts.

Van Cleve, George William. *A Slaveholders' Union: Slavery, Politics, and the Constitution in the Early American Republic.* Chicago: University of Chicago Press, 2010. Van Cleve makes the case for the Constitution as a proslavery document.

Varon, Elizabeth R. *Disunion! The Coming of the American Civil War, 1789–1859.* Chapel Hill: University of North Carolina Press, 2008. An original contribution to understanding the causes of the Civil War.

Walther, Eric H. *William Lowndes Yancey and the Coming of the Civil War.* Chapel Hill: University of North Carolina Press, 2006. The only modern account available of the famous "fire-eater's" life.

Wilentz, Sean. *No Property in Man: Slavery and Antislavery at the Nation's Founding.* Cambridge, MA: Harvard University Press, 2018. Presents a compelling case that for all their proslavery accommodations, the framers refused to concede that a right to property in man be written into the Constitution, creating a tension over that issue that led to civil war.

INDEX

Note: The photo insert images are indexed as *p1, p2, p3,* etc. Other page numbers in *italics* indicate other photos.

About the Author

Ben McNitt began his career as a political reporter at the *Arizona Daily Star* and later moved to the *Tucson Citizen* as Arizona's first environmental reporter. In the early 1980s, he worked as a freelance reporter for CBS News in the Middle East and then became CNN's Cairo Bureau Chief and Mid-East correspondent. In the late 1980s, he ghosted a syndicated column for United Features Syndicate and worked for the National Wildlife Federation as media director. He lives on a patch of the Sonoran Desert just north of Tucson, Arizona.